Integrating AI Into Pedagogical Education

Viktor Wang
California State University, San Bernardino, USA

IGI Global
Scientific Publishing
Publishing Tomorrow's Research Today

Vice President of Editorial	Melissa Wagner
Managing Editor of Acquisitions	Mikaela Felty
Managing Editor of Book Development	Jocelynn Hessler
Production Manager	Mike Brehm
Cover Design	Phillip Shickler

Published in the United States of America by
IGI Global Scientific Publishing
701 East Chocolate Avenue
Hershey, PA, 17033, USA
Tel: 717-533-8845
Fax: 717-533-8661
E-mail: cust@igi-global.com
Website: https://www.igi-global.com

Library of Congress Cataloging-in-Publication Data

Names: Wang, Viktor, editor.
Title: Integrating AI into pedagogical education / Edited by Viktor Wang.
Other titles: Integrating artificial intelligence into pedagogical education
Description: Hershey, PA : IGI Global, [2025] | Includes bibliographical references and index. | Summary: "By integrating AI technology into schools and classrooms, this book aims to address the current system's shortcomings and provide a more personalized learning experience for students"-- Provided by publisher.
Identifiers: LCCN 2024052847 (print) | LCCN 2024052848 (ebook) | ISBN 9798369361306 (hardcover) | ISBN 9798369361313 (paperback) | ISBN 9798369361320 (ebook)
Subjects: LCSH: Artificial intelligence--Educational applications. |
Critical pedagogy. | Individualized instruction.
Classification: LCC LB1028.43 .I5847 2025 (print) | LCC LB1028.43 (ebook) | DDC 371.33/4028563--dc23/eng/20241115
LC record available at https://lccn.loc.gov/2024052847
LC ebook record available at https://lccn.loc.gov/2024052848

British Cataloguing in Publication Data
A Cataloguing in Publication record for this book is available from the British Library.

Editorial Advisory Board

Table of Contents

Detailed Table of Contents

Artificial Intelligence (AI) is revolutionizing various sectors, and its integration into education is becoming increasingly pivotal. This chapter, "Integrating AI into Policy Making in Educational Leadership," examines the transformative potential of AI in shaping educational policies. The use of AI in educational leadership offers opportunities to enhance decision-making by making it more informed, efficient, and adaptive. Drawing on recent research, the chapter discusses how AI can impact key areas such as student motivation, engagement, anxiety reduction, and performance prediction. Additionally, it addresses the challenges and ethical considerations associated with implementing AI in policy-making processes. Through a comprehensive exploration of these themes, the chapter provides strategic insights for educational leaders seeking to leverage AI to improve outcomes and equity in education.

This chapter explores the transformative potential of AI in education, focusing on its ability to personalize learning experiences and enhance teaching effectiveness. Key strategies include the implementation of adaptive learning platforms and the integration of AI into pedagogical practices to establish international standards and best practices. The chapter emphasizes the importance of fostering innovation through the creation of dedicated hubs and partnerships. Addressing bias mitigation through regular audits and the use of inclusive datasets, as well as ensuring equitable access to AI technologies, are highlighted as essential steps towards inclusivity. Continuous professional development for educators and the incorporation of AI literacy into student curricula are identified as critical for effective and ethical AI integration. The chapter concludes with the necessity of conducting regular impact studies and establishing feedback mechanisms to facilitate continuous evaluation and improvement, ensuring that AI-driven initiatives in education are both effective and equitable.

The chapter delves into the transformative potential of Artificial Intelligence (AI) in enhancing personalized learning experiences within K-12 education. It discusses the learner-centered nature of personalized learning systems and the requisite skills and competencies for both teachers and students. The integration of AI in education is highlighted to achieve improved learning outcomes and teaching methods by reshaping the educational landscape. This chapter emphasizes the role of self-regulated learning (SRL) and adaptive learning technologies (ALTs) in maximizing student achievement. A theoretical framework is proposed to guide educators and researchers in integrating these personalized learning systems into their pedagogical practices effectively. The chapter also explores the implications of AI-powered learning tools without bias, thus fostering inclusivity and equity. Additionally, it addresses the ethical challenges and the necessity for policies to ensure fairness in AI applications.

Although AI will undoubtedly have a prominent role in the cultivation of language learning, its application in modern-day English as a Foreign Language (EFL) classrooms remains limited. The failure to adapt theory to practice may be the result of assumptions about technology, which posit that all learners will benefit equally from unilateral adoption of new techniques. In reality, the benefits of specific AI technologies may differ significantly based on characteristics of an educational environment. In Confucian countries, for example, traditional cultural values for group action may adversely impact autonomous learning styles that value LLM "tutors" like ChatGPT. It is essential that cultural and contextual factors of an educational environment be considered before AI technologies are utilized. Therefore, the present book chapter examines educational variables associated with Confucian contexts, yielding insights for the improvement of EFL instruction.

This chapter explores the ethical implications of integrating Artificial Intelligence (AI) into educational practices, focusing on the balance between technological advancement and moral responsibility. It examines the transformative potential of AI in personalized learning, administrative efficiency, and student engagement while addressing critical ethical concerns such as bias, transparency, privacy, and data security. The chapter also discusses the theoretical frameworks of Utilitarianism, Deontology, and Virtue Ethics as they apply to AI in education, providing a comprehensive guide for responsible AI deployment. Through case studies and analysis, the chapter offers insights into successful and problematic implementations of AI, emphasizing the need for robust ethical guidelines to ensure that AI enhances educational outcomes while safeguarding the rights and well-being of students.

The chapter delves into the transformative potential of Artificial Intelligence (AI) in education, particularly through a qualitative case study at Deakin University. It explores how AI can enhance pedagogical and andragogical approaches by improving student learning outcomes and integrating seamlessly into educational frameworks. The anthology highlights various AI applications, such as intelligent tutoring systems and virtual reality in anatomy education, emphasizing the positive impact on teaching methods, assessments, and student support. Methodologically, the chapter employs rigorous research designs, including case studies, interviews, and document reviews, to showcase the innovative use of AI tools in education. It also addresses potential biases and offers methodological suggestions for future research. The case study underscores the need for cautious yet optimistic adoption of AI in education, advocating for ongoing research to responsibly harness AI's capabilities while mitigating its limitations and biases.

Foreword

Integrating AI into Pedagogical and Andragogical Education, edited by Viktor Wang, is a groundbreaking anthology that delves into one of the most transformative developments in modern education: the integration of Artificial Intelligence (AI) into teaching and learning practices. The contributors of this book have masterfully compiled a comprehensive exploration that spans the breadth of education, from K-12 to higher education and adult learning, offering a nuanced understanding of how AI is reshaping educational philosophies, practices, and policies.

Each chapter in this anthology is a testament to the critical role AI plays in the evolution of education. Viktor Wang and Linda Ellington's examination of AI's influence on teaching philosophies in higher education sets a profound tone, emphasizing the alignment of AI with lifelong learning principles and the continuous evolution of educators. Geraldine Torrisi-Steele's focus on the transformative role of AI for students highlights the revolutionary impact of AI-driven tools on learning experiences and student outcomes.

The anthology's strength lies in its balanced perspective, addressing both the opportunities and challenges that come with AI integration. Seema Yadav's exploration of AI's potential to transform education for diverse learners, coupled with insights into the necessity of addressing bias and ensuring equity, is particularly timely and crucial. Similarly, Praveen K. Dubey's discussion on personalized learning provides a theoretical framework that is invaluable for educators and researchers striving to maximize student engagement and achievement in AI-enabled classrooms.

As the book progresses into the realm of adult education, Valerie A. Storey and Amiee Wagner's analysis of AI's alignment with andragogical principles offers a forward-looking perspective that is both insightful and practical. The cultural considerations presented by Andrew Schenck, particularly in Confucian contexts, add a critical layer of understanding, reminding us that AI integration is not a one-size-fits-all approach.

The concluding chapters, particularly the comprehensive reflections by Greg Kaiser and Sue Kaiser, bring the anthology full circle by synthesizing the collective insights into a cohesive vision for the future of education. The inclusion of case studies and success stories serves not only as an inspiration but also as a practical guide for educators, policymakers, and researchers.

This anthology is an essential resource for anyone committed to advancing education through the thoughtful integration of AI. The contributors have offered a diverse and thorough examination of the opportunities and challenges that accompany this technological revolution, emphasizing the need for ethical and culturally responsive approaches. As we navigate the complexities of AI in education, *Integrating AI into Pedagogical and Andragogical Education* stands out as a critical guide for enhancing educational practices in the 21st century.

Viktor Wang and the Editorial Advisory Board deserve commendation for their dedication to this important work. This book is not just a collection of essays; it is a beacon of insight and innovation, guiding us towards a future where AI and education intersect to create more effective, inclusive, and dynamic learning environments.

William Rothwell
Penn State University, USA

Foreword

In the Call for Chapters for this latest collaboration with educationists and researchers in the field of education, *Integrating AI into Pedagogical and Andragogical Education*, Dr. Wang echoes the enthusiasm of many about Artificial Intelligence (AI). AI is described as a revolutionary field of computer science that focuses on creating machines and systems that can mimic human-like thinking, learning, and problem-solving. AI is, indeed, breaking ground in the field of Adult Education in which we toil. AI is sure to have an impact on our praxis as we now seek to enrich the foundations of our profession by planting these AI seedlings into our education terrain. AI certainly has the potential to revolutionize our traditional teaching and learning methods. Equally certain is a solemn concern about what a transformation of our teaching and learning approaches should look like. AI's function in the education landscape is generally understood as a technology that allows machines to execute tasks that have traditionally required human cognition. Hence, it is a matter of great concern that ought to be seriously vetted *by and with* the very human stakeholders who will nurture and harvest what exactly will grow from this new AI plant in our midst, given its promise to improve our praxis. Will we purposefully cultivate this AI plant *or* allow it to become an invasive species in our field? The collection of chapters in this book brings us myriad thoughts to analyze; and it gives us a robust opportunity to clarify our assumptions, hopes, and fears about this new plant taking root in our field.

In the words of Kenneth Gergen (2009), "As we confront the future of our professional endeavors, we tend to rely with confidence on longstanding and widely honored assumptions about the world and ourselves" (p. x). Yet, in the 19 chapters, patterns of themes emerge from the presented perspectives, which nudge us rather serendipitously to also find intersections among the authors' standpoints. Within the context of values and principles of instructional approaches, applied by the authors to the utilization of AI, we can uncover and question the prevailing fundamental *paradigmatic assumptions* (Brookfield, 1995, 2017) about *andragogy v. pedagogy* --- perhaps our own as much as those of our author colleagues here. Consequently, in addition to providing us solid insights into instructional practices to enhance our repertoire of learning activities, we may clarify the essential differences and intended purposes of these two *...gogies*. Typically, we simply drew the line at teaching adults versus teaching children to define the two theories. Yet, within the chapters of this collection, we also uncover that, by clarifying the appropriate use of instructional methods and that of tools like AI, we can more succinctly tailor the teaching to the learning tasks at hand. With that I mean, we can select and apply instructional methods that align to the readiness level of learners by moving back and forth along a metagogical spectrum of pedagogic *and* andragogic approaches (Strohschen 2011; 2014; Strohschen & Elazier, 2019; 2020). This refocuses our practices from an *either-or* approach toward (perhaps a truly) transforming praxis suitable for a 21st Century paradigm of lifelong and life wide learning (Römer, 2021).

Integrating AI into Pedagogical and Andragogical Education offers more than useful considerations about AI-based strategies, methods, and techniques. Showing us how to embrace AI in our teaching, the chapter themes center on principles of the *...gogies*, specific tools, students' skillset needs and personalized learning, contemporary socio-environmental changes and their influences on teaching methods, competence in curriculum design, and teacher training and development needs. And, remarkably, critical questions about the impact of AI on our education mission are included. Given this era of The Fourth Industrial Revolution (Wigmore, 2020), as educationists we *are* called upon to examine and spearhead appropriate changes for educating adults. We need to be prepared with the requisite knowledge, skills, and attitude to achieve our vision of improving the quality of life *for and with* students by means of education. *Integrating AI into Pedagogical and Andragogical Education* aids us in "...stretching our imaginations and dreams of possibility" (Gergen, 2009, p. x). This book is an essential resource for critical reflection on and development of our profession.

Gabriele Strohschen
DePaul University, USA

REFERENCES

Brookfield, S. (2017). *Becoming a critically reflective teacher*. John Wiley & Sons. (original publication 1995)

Gergen, K. (2009). Foreword. In *The handbook of Blended Shore education*. Adult Education Program Development and Delivery. Springer Verlag International.

Römer, K. (2021, February 9). *It's time to embrace not just the lifelong but the life-wide dimension of learning* [Blog]. https://thelifelonglearningblog.uil.unesco.org/2021/02/09/its-time-to-embrace-not-just-the-lifelong-but-the-life-wide-dimension-of-learning/

Strohschen, G. (2011). Teaching Adults across Cultures, Distance, and Learning Preferences: Universal Tools for the 21st Century. In Wang, V. X. (Ed.), *Encyclopedia of Information Communication and Adult Education Integration* (pp. 469–484). IGI Global.

Strohschen, G. (2014). Education Collaboration Development: A Blended Shore Education Approach to Sustainable Development. In Wang, V. X. (Ed.), *Handbook of Research on Transnational Higher Education* (pp. 512–525). IGI Global.

Strohschen, G., & Elazier, K. (2019, November 25-26). The Metagogy Theorem: A Framework for Educating Adults. *International Forum of Teaching and Studies, 15*(1), 3-15.

Strohschen, G., & Elazier, K. (2020). Metagogy: Toward a Contemporary Adult Education Praxis. In Pushpanadham, K. (Ed.), *Teacher Education in the Global Era, Perspectives and Practices* (pp. C1–C2). Springer.

Wigmore, I. (2020). *Fourth Industrial Revolution. TechTarget.* https://www.techtarget.com/whatis/definition/fourth-industrial-revolution

Preface

The rapid integration of Artificial Intelligence (AI) into education signifies a transformative moment in teaching and learning, marking a pivotal step toward the future of education. **Integrating AI Into Pedagogical Education** provides an in-depth exploration of this critical shift, focusing on how AI is reshaping educational philosophies, pedagogical practices, policy-making, and ethical considerations. This comprehensive guide is intended to support educators, administrators, and policymakers as they navigate the challenges and opportunities brought about by AI's evolving role in K-12 education.

SETTING THE STAGE FOR TRANSFORMATION

The advent of AI technologies presents a dual-edged sword, offering unprecedented opportunities for enhancing educational outcomes while also posing significant challenges. As we stand at this crossroads, educators need to embrace this change, recognizing that the integration of AI can foster a more equitable and personalized learning environment. This anthology invites readers to reflect on the evolving nature of teaching and learning and to consider how AI can be harnessed as a powerful ally in the quest for educational excellence.

Chapter 1, "Integrating AI into One's Teaching Philosophies and Dispositions in Pedagogical Education," sets the tone for the book by examining the ways AI is influencing teaching philosophies in K-12 settings. AI is transforming how educators approach instruction, moving beyond traditional teaching models to embrace data-driven decision-making, adaptive teaching strategies, and personalized learning experiences. This chapter emphasizes the need for educators to align their teaching dispositions with the principles of lifelong learning, adaptability, and innovation. As AI empowers educators to make more informed instructional choices, the chapter explores how technology can foster environments that are more responsive to student needs, enhancing the overall learning experience.

Policy and Leadership in the Age of AI

Moving from the individual educator to the institutional level, Chapter 2, "Integrating AI into Policy Making in Educational Leadership," shifts focus to the role of educational leaders in utilizing AI-driven data analytics. These tools can inform policymaking, curriculum development, and resource allocation, leading to more effective and equitable educational practices. The chapter highlights how AI can be harnessed to create policies that improve educational outcomes across diverse populations. Moreover, it emphasizes the critical role of leadership in fostering a culture of continuous improvement, ensuring that AI's potential is fully realized in addressing the challenges and opportunities facing modern education systems.

Addressing Diversity Through AI

The transformative power of AI in addressing the needs of diverse learners is further emphasized in Chapter 3, "Advancing Education with AI-Driven Education for Diverse Learners: Integrating AI into Pedagogical Practices." This chapter discusses how adaptive learning platforms and AI-driven pedagogical strategies are vital in creating inclusive educational environments that cater to various learning abilities and preferences. The chapter not only examines the practical applications of AI in promoting inclusivity but also discusses the importance of incorporating AI literacy into the curriculum for both educators and students. As AI becomes central to teaching and learning processes, fostering AI literacy becomes crucial for both teachers and learners.

Personalized Learning Reimagined

A deeper exploration of personalized learning is found in Chapter 4, "Personalized Learning and Pedagogy: Harnessing AI for Tailored Education." The integration of AI into personalized learning systems allows educators to create individualized learning paths, ensuring that instruction aligns with each learner's unique needs and abilities. This chapter outlines theoretical frameworks necessary for effectively utilizing adaptive learning technologies (ALTs) and self-regulated learning (SRL) strategies in the classroom. By providing concrete examples of how AI can enhance student engagement and achievement, the chapter offers educators practical insights into implementing personalized learning at scale.

Cultural Contexts in AI Adoption

The cultural dimensions of AI adoption are explored in Chapter 5, "What Would Confucius Do? A Study of Cultural Factors Impacting the Use of AI in Confucian EFL Contexts." This chapter provides a critical analysis of how traditional cultural values influence the integration and success of AI technologies in educational settings. It argues that understanding cultural factors is essential for the successful implementation of AI. While educational technology is globally accessible, it must be adapted to fit specific cultural contexts to maximize its effectiveness. This chapter serves as a reminder that successful technology integration goes beyond technical considerations; it requires cultural sensitivity and contextual awareness.

Redefining Learning in the Digital Age

Broadening the discussion, Chapter 6, "Redefining Learning in the Digital Age," examines the profound shifts in education resulting from the digital age. The chapter discusses how AI, in conjunction with other digital tools, is reshaping traditional learning models. Educators must adapt their pedagogical methods to harness the full potential of these innovations. It explores how digital tools enhance critical thinking, creativity, and problem-solving skills, emphasizing the need for teachers to adopt an agile mindset to stay ahead of the curve in a rapidly evolving educational landscape.

Personalized Language Learning

In Chapter 7, "Personalized Language Learning with AI for Pedagogical and Andragogical Approaches," the role of AI in tailoring language instruction is highlighted. This chapter discusses how AI-enhanced tools can create more engaging and effective language learning experiences, personalized to meet the diverse linguistic and cognitive needs of both young students and adult learners. By ensuring that learners of all ages benefit from AI, this chapter underscores the importance of integrating AI into both pedagogical (youth-oriented) and andragogical (adult-oriented) approaches.

Ethical Considerations in AI Integration

As AI becomes more prevalent in classrooms, ethical considerations take center stage in Chapter 8, "The Ethical Use of AI in Education." This chapter provides a thoughtful reflection on the challenges and responsibilities associated with AI integration. Topics such as data privacy, algorithmic bias, and the ethical use of AI in student assessment are critically examined. The chapter offers guidelines for making informed, ethical decisions about AI use, ensuring that technology serves as a tool for enhancement rather than exploitation. Educators and institutions are called upon to navigate these complex ethical dilemmas with care and foresight.

Real-World Applications of AI in Education

Real-world examples of AI integration in education are presented in Chapter 9, "AI-Driven Innovations in Pedagogical and Andragogical Approaches: A Case Study Analysis." This chapter analyzes successful implementations of AI in various educational contexts, providing insights into the practical applications of AI-driven teaching methods. These case studies showcase the potential of AI to revolutionize both pedagogical and andragogical practices, leading to improved educational outcomes for learners across different settings and disciplines.

Future Directions for AI in Education

The book concludes with Chapter 10, "AI in Education: Reflections and Future Directions for Pedagogical and Andragogical Integration." This final chapter synthesizes key themes discussed throughout the book and explores future possibilities for AI's role in education. As AI continues to advance, ongoing research, collaboration, and ethical reflection are emphasized as vital components in ensuring that AI serves as a tool for equity, innovation, and positive transformation in education.

A Comprehensive Examination of AI in Education

Together, these chapters offer a comprehensive and diverse examination of AI's impact on education. Each chapter provides unique insights into the opportunities and challenges that accompany this technological revolution, emphasizing the importance of thoughtful, ethical, and culturally responsive approaches to AI adoption. As AI continues to shape the future of teaching and learning, **Integrating AI Into Pedagogical Education** serves as a vital resource for educators, administrators, and policymakers committed to enhancing educational practices through innovative, ethical, and informed AI integration.

CONCLUSION

We hope this anthology will become an invaluable guide for those dedicated to advancing education in this new era of AI. By fostering a deeper understanding of how AI can be responsibly and effectively integrated into education, this book aims to inspire meaningful progress toward more personalized, inclusive, and dynamic learning environments for all. As we embark on this journey together, let us embrace the potential of AI to enrich the educational landscape, transform the learning experience, and ultimately improve outcomes for all learners.

Viktor Wang
California State University, San Bernardino, USA

Acknowledgment

I extend my deepest gratitude to the contributors for their invaluable insights and to the Editorial Advisory Board for their unwavering support. Together, we hope this book will serve as a critical resource for those committed to advancing education through the thoughtful integration of AI.

Chapter 1
Integrating AI Into One's Teaching Philosophies and Dispositions in Higher Education

Viktor Wang
https://orcid.org/0000-0001-9557-0054
California State University, San Bernardino, USA

Linda Ellington
https://orcid.org/0000-0002-7697-056X
Southern New Hampshire University, USA

ABSTRACT

AI's role in higher education is multifaceted, influencing how teachers perceive and implement their teaching philosophies. Teachers who embrace AI tools may develop dispositions that value data-driven decision-making, continuous assessment, and the customization of instruction to meet diverse student needs. Furthermore, AI can reinforce a philosophy of lifelong learning among educators as they continually adapt to new technologies and methodologies. This ongoing professional development shapes teaching dispositions open to innovation, reflective practice, and a collaborative learning community. The authors assert that as AI becomes more embedded in educational practices, it transforms teaching philosophies and reshapes educators' fundamental dispositions, aligning them more closely with modern, technology-enhanced teaching philosophies.

DOI: 10.4018/979-8-3693-6130-6.ch001

INTRODUCTION

As the integration of AI in higher education continues to evolve, andragogical approaches are fundamentally altering. Educators face the challenge of learning to use AI technologies and effectively incorporating AI into their curricula. Understanding the advantages of AI is pivotal for teachers to fully embrace and utilize AI tools in their instructional strategies (Kim & Kim, 2022). Shared values of personalization, adaptability, ethical responsibility, enhancement of human capabilities, and a commitment to innovative educational practices characterize the intersection of AI philosophy and teaching philosophy. Educators can integrate AI philosophies into the teaching philosophies by finding common ground in these areas, leading to more effective and enriching student educational experiences.

Within higher education, the integration of AI in learning is circumscribed by adult learning and the frame of andragogical approaches. Adults bring a store of prior experiences to the learning situation and hold expectations and motivations different from those of young learners. Adult learners have developed a mature view of self-responsibility for their learning; they expect meaningful, practical, and rewarding learning in their life situations. They bring with them 'habitual' ways of thinking developed through their interactions with others and social norms (Mezirow, 1991). Subsequently, transformative and emancipatory learning is at the heart of adult education. Andragogy and transformative learning principles are synergistic, guiding adult learners to solve problems with applicable learning resources and supporting self-directedness and problem-solving (Torrisi-Steele & Carim, 2019). Hence, to effectively implement transformative learning, adult educators require more than knowledge of the principles of adult learning and transformative learning. Embedded in context, education practice results from the interplay of situational factors intrinsic to learners and teachers. Factors intrinsic to learners include learner needs, preferences, and expectations. Factors intrinsic to the teacher include teacher philosophy, beliefs, expectations, and preferences. Situational factors may include the nature of the discipline and even the attributes of the physical environment (e.g., availability of resources, institutional factors). In this chapter, the authors argue that it is important for educators to be consciously aware of the factors that shape their practice. The authors also say these factors necessitate a contextual philosophy upon which practice is realized. Notably, the contextual philosophy must be dynamic and should change in consonance with variations as learning situations change. The changes now include the integration of AI into adult educators' teaching philosophy, which is a complex process that requires careful consideration of its potential benefits and challenges. The discussion begins with considering adult learners, adult education, teaching philosophies, and the connection to artificial intelligence ideology.

LEARNING THEORIES AND AI

Efficiently and effectively using artificial intelligence tools within the educational process will create a favorable AI intelligence-based learning landscape at higher education institutions characterized by efficiency, interactivity, inclusivity, innovation, and accessibility (Zadorina et al., 2024). A study by Zadorina et al. (2024) showed that artificial intelligence integrated into the educational process is used to design simulation-based activities, organize personalized learning, form specific skills among students, and automate the administrative process. AI enhances learning outcomes among students, increases efficiency, and provides greater accessibility to education during world chaos, such as the global pandemic, when the educational process can be disrupted. Some theories may seem quite ancient, yet we can connect them to AI during times of change.

Transformative Learning Theory

Adult education practice is framed by the principles of Mezirow's transformative learning (2000). However, adult educators must also incorporate two other dimensions into their practice: recognition of the complexity and dynamism of adult learning and the role of education philosophy, all at the intersection of AI.

Transformational learning theory becomes especially pertinent during world chaos, such as the global pandemic, when traditional educational processes are disrupted. Transformational learning is a profound process where individuals change their frames of reference by critically reflecting on their experiences, leading to new perspectives and behaviors. AI can play a significant role in this type of learning by providing personalized, adaptive, and interactive experiences that foster deep reflection and change. There are several ways AI can be integrated into transformational learning:

Intelligent Tutoring Systems: AI-powered tutors can provide personalized feedback, answer questions, and offer support anytime, helping learners explore concepts more deeply and from different perspectives.

Example: Virtual tutors that use natural language processing to converse with learners, guiding them through complex problem-solving processes.

Simulations and Virtual Reality: AI cameras enhance simulations and VR environments to create immersive learning experiences that allow learners to experiment with new behaviors and perspectives in a safe and controlled setting.

Example: VR simulations that use AI to adapt scenarios based on the learner's actions, providing real-time feedback and opportunities for reflection.

Collaborative Learning Platforms: AI can facilitate collaborative learning by connecting learners with peers and mentors, suggesting collaborative projects, and monitoring group dynamics to ensure productive interactions.

Example: AI-drive platforms that match learners with similar interests and goals, facilitating meaningful discussions and joint projects.

Content Curation and Recommendation: AI can curate and recommend content tailored to individual learning needs, interests, and goals. This helps learners discover new perspectives and resources they might not have found independently.

Example: AI-powered recommendation systems that suggest articles, videos, and courses based on the learner's current knowledge and learning objectives.

Emotional and Cognitive Support: AI can monitor learners' emotional and cognitive states, providing support and interventions when needed. This helps maintain motivation and engagement, which are crucial for transformational learning.

Example: AI-based systems that detect frustration or confusion and offer encouragement, additional resources, or breaks to help learners stay on track.

Facilitating Critical Thinking: AI can present scenarios and questions that challenge learners' beliefs and assumptions, encouraging them to think critically and consider alternative viewpoints.

Example: AI-driven debate platforms that simulate discussions with diverse perspectives, prompting learners to evaluate and defend their positions critically.

Lifelong Learning Companions: AI can act as lifelong learning companions, helping individuals continuously reflect on their experiences, set new learning goals, and stay updated with relevant knowledge.

Example: Personal AI assistants that track learning progress over time, suggest new learning opportunities, and help set and achieve long-term learning goals.

AI benefits a teaching philosophy about transformative learning theory by providing tools that enhance the core principles of this educational approach.

Adult education practice is framed by the principles of Mezirow's transformative learning and Knowles' adult learning theory (1975). However, adult educators must also incorporate two other dimensions into their practice: recognition of the complexity and dynamism of adult learning and the role of education philosophy, all at the intersection of AI. The AI competencies that learners should possess, mainly those without a computer science background (non-experts), are solving problems, reasoning, making decisions, perceiving, and acting. They can achieve this learning in association with teachers who deliver the content to students using AI-based technologies, such as cloud computing to students in a format and form suitable for various student needs (Kabudi et al., 2021). In other words, the AI and teachers can work together to create the best delivery method for students with maximum positive outcomes. The benefits of using AI or delivering educational content include providing individualized and customized learning and universal access for all students who speak different languages or have some disability, such as visual or hearing impairment. Thus, it can be argued that AI-based education delivery is more learner-centric than the traditional educational delivery method.

Complexity and Dynamism of Adult Learning

Human learning at any age is a complex process. However, because of life experiences and often demanding personal situations and responsibilities, learning as an adult is much more complicated than learning at a young age. Many more social and economic factors come into play when teaching adults than children. There is much greater variability among adult learners than there is among child learners. Furthermore, adult educators must be agile, constantly anticipating, and responsive to changing circumstances, including AI-based teaching in all aspects of educating learners. The adult learner is caught up in *liquid modernity*, "the complex sociocultural-economic-political-technological change in a global environment, and is "the center of new societal demands" (Nicolaides & Marsick, 2016, pp. 9-11). Understanding and considering this complexity is foundational to successful adult education practices (Nicolaides & Marsick, 2016). Adult educators' understanding of the complexity of the adult learner's profile is as important as their knowledge of the subject matter they teach (Wang, 2003).

Equipped with an understanding of andragogy and sensitivity to the complexity and dynamism of adult learning, andragogical educators will have a solid basis for reflecting on and designing learning practices suited to adult education. However, as is well documented, teaching practices acquire much of their form because of the teacher's beliefs or philosophy about learners, the purpose of education, and the role of the teacher. Although a teacher's philosophy is personal, it likely embodies recognizable elements of the established philosophical perspectives in education and adult education frameworks. In addition to an understanding of andragogy and sensitivity and awareness of the complexity of adult learning, it is equally important for adult educators to be aware of the philosophical perspectives in their practice.

Philosophical Perspectives in Adult Education

Despite some variation in adult education frameworks, the philosophical perspectives guiding adult education (see, for example, Elias & Merriam, 1995; Tisdell & Taylor, 2000) can be categorized as liberalism, progressivism, behaviorism, humanism, and critical philosophy. Different aims of adult education are implicit in each philosophical perspective, including AI ideology.

From a liberal perspective, adult education aims to acquire knowledge but from a rational perspective. Critical thinking and the development of moral citizens are goals of education. *Liberalism* has its roots in the Greek philosophers and the Enlightenment philosophers such as Locke and Kant. The product of a liberal education is a well-rounded person. Until recently, liberalism informed higher education, and it still does in countries where universities are not seen as job-training institutions. In the U.S., when people refer to a "liberal arts college," they talk about the institution where students receive a broad humanities, social sciences, and arts background.

While a broad background in humanities, social sciences, and the arts is essential in a liberal education, the demand for education that prepares people for work in an industrial society spawned *progressivism.* Progressivism is founded on pragmatism, which values practical experience over abstract and theoretical concepts. Dewey (1938) popularized this philosophical perspective, and his influence remains strong today. When Dewey proposed that students (children and adults) learn best by doing things, this was a radical notion in a world where educational methods favored rote recall. Progressivism is the philosophical framework for adult vocational education, apprenticeship programs, skills-based training, and technical education, among other fields. Progressivism incorporates problem-solving and experiential learning; the teacher becomes a facilitator and mentor rather than an authority figure. Lindeman, who wrote *The Meaning of Adult Education* (1926), was strongly influenced by Dewey, and he applied the concepts to adult education. Much later, Knowles (1980) also drew on progressivism as he developed his andragogy model.

In an attempt to understand learning more objectively, an approach to understanding learning as stimulus-response was articulated in the *behaviorist* perspective. Skinner (1974) popularized and made a lasting contribution to behaviorism with his conceptualization of operant conditioning. Reinforced responses persist, even though the reinforcement may not be continuous. Responses that are ignored tend to fade away. Stimulus-response chains can be created to explain complicated learning sets (Kidd, 1973). Thorndike was one of the earliest behaviorists and co-author of Adult Learning (Thorndike et al., 1928). Skinner's work provided the foundation for programmed instruction, computer-assisted instruction, modularized instruction, competency-based education, and many strategies still used today in training and acquiring technical knowledge. However, as work evolves from skill-based routine tasks to AI-based jobs, practical behaviorism cannot be considered adequate in adult education and training (Torrisi-Steele & Carim, 2019). Kidd (1973) points out that the simplistic, mechanical nature of behaviorist learning theories was a "rebellion against sophisticated explanations of learning based on religious or philosophical interpretations and upon an assumption that an individual was possessed of certain properties and faculties" (p. 160).

Behaviorist learning theories are significantly influenced by the advancements in AI, such as:

Enhanced Data Collection and Analysis: AI technologies enable collecting and analyzing vast amounts of behavioral data. This aligns with behaviorist principles by providing detailed insights into how individuals respond to various stimuli, allowing for more precise shaping of desired behaviors.

Simulation and Gamification: AI-driven simulations and gamified learning environments provide immersive and interactive experiences that engage learners. These environments use behaviorist principles by offering rewards, challenges, and immediate feedback to reinforce learning behaviors.

Behavioral Analytics: AI provides sophisticated tools for behavioral analytics, allowing for the detailed examination of learning patterns. These analytics can identify which stimuli are most effective in promoting learning, helping to refine behaviorist strategies.

Scalable Behavior Modification: AI enables scaling behavior modification techniques to large groups of learners. This scalability ensures that behaviorist strategies can be applied consistently and effectively across diverse educational settings.

Continuous Improvement: AI systems can learn and improve over time by analyzing the effectiveness of different instructional strategies. This constant improvement aligns with behaviorist principles by refining reinforcement techniques based on empirical evidence of what works best.

Humanism, in stark contrast to the simplistic stimulus-response mechanism of behaviorism, is founded on the assumption that people can control their destiny, are inherently good, and have the potential for growth and development. The individual learner and the value of that person's experiences are central to humanism. This focus on the self does not mean that humanism highlights self-centeredness; individual development contributes to the good of all humanity. Maslow (1970) is generally considered the first to use humanistic psychology to understand learning. Maslow's widely recognized hierarchy of human needs posits that basic physical needs and the need for safety must precede further learning. Self-actualization—becoming all that an individual can become—is the goal of learning. Rogers (1969), a humanist psychologist who developed client-centered therapy as a model for working with clients, also influenced how adult learning is understood. Knowles (1975) applied Rogers' humanist philosophy to his conceptualization of self-directed learning and, more generally, andragogy. Humanist philosophy, centered on human values, dignity, and the potential for individual growth, is increasingly influenced by advancements in AI, such as:

Augmented Human Capabilities: AI enhances human potential by providing tools that improve decision-making, creativity, and productivity. This augmentation aligns with the humanist emphasis on personal development and achievement.

Redefining Human Identity: AI challenges traditional notions of what it means to be human. With machines performing tasks that once required human intelligence, humanists re-examine humans' unique societal qualities and roles.
Education and Learning: AI-powered tools personalize learning experiences, catering to individual needs and fostering lifelong learning, a core humanist principle. This technology democratizes access to knowledge and promotes intellectual growth.
Social Justice and Equality: AI has the potential to address social inequalities by providing solutions in healthcare, education, and economic opportunities. Humanist philosophy now includes advocating for the equitable distribution of AI benefits.
Future of Work: The rise of AI automation affects employment and the nature of work. Humanists are concerned with ensuring that technological progress benefits all, supporting policies that protect workers and promote meaningful employment.
Human-AI Collaboration: The interaction between humans and AI systems promotes a collaborative approach to problem-solving. This partnership underscores humanist values of cooperation, mutual respect, and collective progress.

By including various aspects of society and individual lives, AI is prompting a re-evaluation of humanist principles to ensure that technological advancements contribute positively to human flourishing.

Critical philosophy's tenets extend beyond the individual's confines to bring change to the broader social and political domains. Social change has long been a goal of adult education, from the founding of the Antigonish movement in Canada in the late 1920s to the founding of the Highland Folk School in the United States in 1932. Selman (1989) takes this back much further to the Corresponding Societies in Britain in the late 1700s, which were interested in political change, and the Adult Schools, which were dedicated to promoting literacy. At that time, adult educators interested in social reform were seen by many as agitators (promoting literacy empowered people in a time when the empowerment of the "masses" was seen as a threat). Freire's (1970) educational philosophy is based on the belief that the oppressed are unaware of their oppression and are, therefore, unable to overcome it. Freire's work has had a significant impact on adult education, one that continues to this day. Brookfield (2005) applied some of the central tenets of critical philosophy to adult education. He identified seven adult learning tasks drawn from critical theory. Critical theory is based on three core assumptions1) that Western democracies are unequal societies, 2) the inequities are reproduced in such a way as to seem normal and inevitable, and 3) the state of affairs can be understood and changed (Brookfield, 2005, p. viii). The latter is the goal of education from the critical philosophy perspective.

Critical philosophy, which involves the rigorous examination of assumptions, power, and structures in society, is impacted in several ways:

Epistemological Questions: AI challenges traditional notions of knowledge and truth. Critical philosophers explore how AI systems generate and validate knowledge, questioning the reliability and biases inherent in algorithmic decision-making processes.

Ethical and Moral Issues: AI raises significant ethical questions about autonomy, responsibility, and potential harm. Critical philosophers engage with these issues, debating the moral implications of AI deployment in various contexts and advocating for ethical frameworks that prioritize human well-being and justice.

Ideological Influence: AI shapes the cultural and ideological landscape through algorithms that influence what content people see and engage with. Critical philosophy examines how these algorithms reinforce dominant ideologies, manipulate public opinion, and potentially undermine democratic processes.

Resistance and Empowerment: While AI can be a tool of oppression, it also has the potential to empower individuals. Critical philosophy argues that AI can resist domination, promote social justice, and elevate marginalized voices while critically examining the implications and risks of such technologies.

Achieving understanding and change of the 'state of affairs' is achieved by seven learning tasks. Firstly, *challenging ideologies*—the ideologies embedded in language, social habits, and cultural forms. By "ideology," we mean those values and beliefs that are seen to be self-evident and true. Ideologies are hard to articulate or detect; they are deeply embedded and assumed to be beyond questioning. The second learning task is *contesting hegemony* (Brookfield, 2005). Hegemony occurs when people embrace conditions (and see them as usual) that serve those in power but work against their own best interests. For example, we value "hard work" to the point where individuals experience considerable stress, but we believe we are doing the right thing. Alternatively, people genuinely believe that possessing the products and using the services provided by corporations leads them to a happy and fulfilled life. The third learning task is *unmasking power*, which is how power plays a role in the relationships between teacher and learner or among learners. Power structures are often seen as a given; unmasking power involves recognizing how power is exercised in our own lives in everyday actions.

AI's connection to challenging ideologies in critical thinking theory is multifaceted. Mickunas (2023) emphasized the need for a critical understanding of AI, particularly its impact on vulnerable populations. This is echoed by Zhou (2022), who discussed the integration of AI into ideological and political education. However, Leung (2019) critiqued AI's reductionist approach to human thinking and highlighted the debate between human-centered and machine-centered approaches. It is necessary to strengthen mainstream ideology and to find effective ways to study the integration of information technology into the new age of philosophy of education, which can significantly improve the quality of teaching. This can potentially create new ideas confronting specific problems of thought (Zhou, 2022). Ideological teachers and policymakers must keep up with the all-around trend of the times, make full use of the benefits of intelligent new technologies and platforms, and further increase the attractiveness, attraction, persuasion, and contagion of ideological education (Zhou, 2022, p.1).

In the AI age, characterized by technology's pervasive influence, the intersection of critical thinking and artificial intelligence has become a topic of paramount importance (Moustaghfir & Brigui, 2024). In education, the pivotal question of our time is how to transform artificial intelligence from a perceived adversary to a valued ally, harnessing its strengths rather than viewing it as a threat to human thought. It is essential to navigate this into teaching philosophy. Instead of fearing the unknown, we invite students to become AI evaluators, decision-makers, and contributors. This aligns with the requirements of our digitally driven future and positions students as active participants in shaping the narrative of human-AI collaboration (Moustaghfir & Brigui, 2024).

Overcoming alienation is the fourth learning task of critical theory. We are alienated when we cannot be ourselves or be authentic in our lives and work. For example, a work context that is repetitive, structured, and bound tightly by policies and procedures that go against our values is alienating. A relationship (including a relationship between teacher and learner) in which we must hide our beliefs and assumptions to maintain the relationship is alienating. The adult learning task is to develop a sense of free agency and realize how social contexts shape our lives.

The impact of AI on students' feelings of alienation is complex and multifaceted. Li et al. (2023) found that while AI has increased learning opportunities and enthusiasm, it has also led to anxiety and a conflict between natural and intelligent feelings. This is consistent with Holian (1971), who found a close correspondence between alienation from university and society. Mahoney (2000) further identified neuroticism and low conscientiousness as corrections of alienation. Xu (2024) suggested that AI can positively impact academic achievement, potentially mitigating alienation. The authors collectively suggested that various individual and social factors influence AI's impact on alienation.

Learning liberation is the fifth adult learning task. One-dimensional thought focuses on improving current social systems rather than breaking away from them or replacing them with new ways of thinking. To do this, individuals need to separate themselves from the current social systems, such as the norms about what education can and should do, and see that system in a new way.

Reclaiming reason is the sixth task in a critical theory approach to adult learning. We consider reason appropriate for making technical decisions and working with instrumental knowledge but not for moral issues, values, and interpersonal relations. Our values and beliefs have become reified; they are not open to questioning. For example, we may believe that a person with more gadgets, a bigger house, or a higher income is happier than someone without those things. "Quality of life" indices are based on the possession of dishwashers and microwaves. Alternatively, we may assume that working-class people want to "improve themselves" by moving into a middle-class lifestyle. Reclaiming reason involves applying reason to examining how our lives have been shaped. AI can enhance reasoning skills in adult learning, particularly in the context of critical theory. Susanto, et al. (2023) highlighted the role of AI in improving critical thinking and reasoning skills. Mickunas (2023) emphasized the importance of critically understanding AI and developing a reasoning framework. Using AI in learning environments can improve problem-solving and information analysis skills. According to Susanto et al. (2023), AI has a significant influence on the level of student's ability to argue, i.e., reason, which includes tools to gain knowledge, increase curiosity, own attention, own observation, and apply what is learned.

Finally, *practicing democracy* is the seventh learning task that Brookfield (2005) lists. Brookfield argues that the ideal of democracy is taken for granted. The word "democracy" is used in many ways and with so many agendas that it has no real meaning. What we need to do is to practice democracy through rational discourse, paying attention to ideal speech conditions, increasing our awareness of the contradictions inherent in the ideal of democracy, and paying attention to power structures related to diversity (for example, race, class, gender, ethnicity, and sexual orientation).

The use of AI in higher education can potentially enhance the practice of democracy in learning and teaching at the college level. Democratic principles in teaching can be supported by AI tools that provide personalized learning experiences (Bulathwela et al., 2021). AI systems can promote an open, transparent, and collaborative learning environment. Conversations are going on about how AI can empower access to education beyond political, cultural, language, geographical, and learning ability barriers. If correctly designed and deployed, AI tools could deliver in the long run on their potential of providing access to education beyond the political, cultural, geographical, and learning ability barriers and help create equitable lifelong learning schools of the future. The challenge is to design them to be a driver of equity and inclusion rather than a source of greater inequality of opportunity (Bulathwela et al., 2021, p. 6). Designing AI systems must provide equal opportunities for all, avoiding biases that could disadvantage certain groups. By focusing on fairness and inclusivity, AI can be a tool for positive social change instead of reinforcing disparities.

Depending on their beliefs and perspectives, adult educators may adopt different conceptions of adult learners. Educators prefer a humanistic approach to view adult learners as highly motivated and self-directed. From a humanistic perspective, adult learners assume responsibility for learning and self-development. In contrast, from a progressive philosophical perspective, educators may view adult learners as having unlimited potential for development through education. These progressive educators consider learner needs, interests, and experiences as key learning elements. On the other hand, educators who have adopted a behaviorist philosophy seek to provide an intense learning environment where learners take an active role in learning, practicing new behavior, and receiving feedback. Educators influenced by liberal philosophies of education may maintain that adult learners seek knowledge rather than information. In contrast, those with a radical perspective emphasize students' equality with their teacher in learning. In contemporary adult education, understanding the diversity and variability of adult learners may help adult educators identify the philosophies they need to adopt and adapt. An inappropriate philosophy, without question, will fail to serve the needs of tr. Ultimately, teachers can create a more supportive and effective learning environment that fosters personal and professional growth for all students by understanding and embracing the variability among adult learners.

Contextual Philosophy

For any teacher, "acquiring a philosophy is powerful, in that it directs and influences a teacher's teaching practices in the classroom as well as how they perceive teaching and learning and the students around them" (Soccorsi, 2013, p. 21). Acquiring a philosophy is a reflective process in which the teacher considers their practices and the impact of those practices to become explicitly aware of their beliefs and values about learners, learning, the role of the teacher, and the purpose of education. Forming a philosophy is complicated as teachers reflect on their practices, ideally through their experiences and understanding of theoretical frameworks. While literature is rife with discussion of the importance of teaching philosophy and guidance on developing a teaching philosophy, the importance of contextual philosophy is neglected. It is acknowledged that philosophy should evolve (Soccorsi, 2013) but the importance of aligning philosophy to context is understated. Teachers are encouraged to develop a philosophy, and though it may incrementally evolve, they may cling to it, like a 'personal brand' or mantra, often partly decontextualized, and only requires refinement over time. The interaction of their philosophy with context is only 'hinted at' as part of any reflection on practices.

Teaching philosophy must fully embody the relationship between theory and practice if it is to be valid; philosophy must be inseparable from practice (Papadima, 2021). In adult education, where the learners are caught up in 'fluid modernity' (Nicolaides & Marsick, 2016) and highly diverse, the link between theory and practice means that a contextually adaptive, agile philosophy is imperative.

A contextually adapted philosophy means that adult educators must adjust their underlying belief systems in response to different contexts to assume the most appropriate roles for helping adult learners achieve transformation and emancipation. A contextually adapted philosophy will influence curriculum content, delivery methods, and communication with adult learners with different learning styles and personalities (for example, see Cranton, 2006). A contextually adapted philosophy may guide decisions and policy-setting (Merriam & Brockett, 1997). Above all, a contextually adapted philosophy helps define the role of adult educators by providing a conceptual framework for incorporation into their teaching methodologies. Understanding this complex, interactive process, educators often consistently embrace one philosophy or belief system without regard for the context of their practice or the characteristics of their learners. This is encouraged by leading adult educators (Knowles et al., 1998, 2011; Rogers, 1969), who argue that adult learning professionals should be humanistic and progressive. To conform to this approach, adult educators must assume the role of learning facilitators. However, what adult educators do in practice or what they must do in a specific context may conflict with these ideologies. Conflict between what adult educators do or must do in practice and the ideologies of humanism and progressivism arises because adult educators may fail to understand the relationship between a teacher's contextually adapted philosophy and a student's transformation and emancipation. Learning does not take place in isolation. Instead, it relates to adult educators' contextually adapted philosophy, situational roles, learners' preferences, and other factors. A contextual philosophy aligns adult educators' practice with the contemporary societal demands experienced by adult learners and enables practices adaptive to adult learners' diverse characteristics and needs. If it is now considered that transformative and emancipatory learning is possible only in context, then it is evident that education practice must be appropriate to the context. Philosophies must, therefore, also be contextual. Contextualized philosophies connect to teacher dispositions (the values, beliefs, attitudes, and other habits of mind). Dispositions translate into action, i.e., the teaching methods and teacher roles in education practice (Figure 1.0). As also depicted in Figure 1.0, the teaching method used by the adult educator is the result of the interaction between learner and teacher, which occurs within a situational context. The nature of the interactions is determined by how the learner's experiences, needs, motivations, and learning styles (influenced by the situational context, which is dynamic) interact with the teacher's philosophies. Aligning philosophies with the learner and situational contexts, teaching methods that effectively facilitate critical reflection will support transformative learning.

Figure 1. Disposition connected to philosophies and contextually adapted

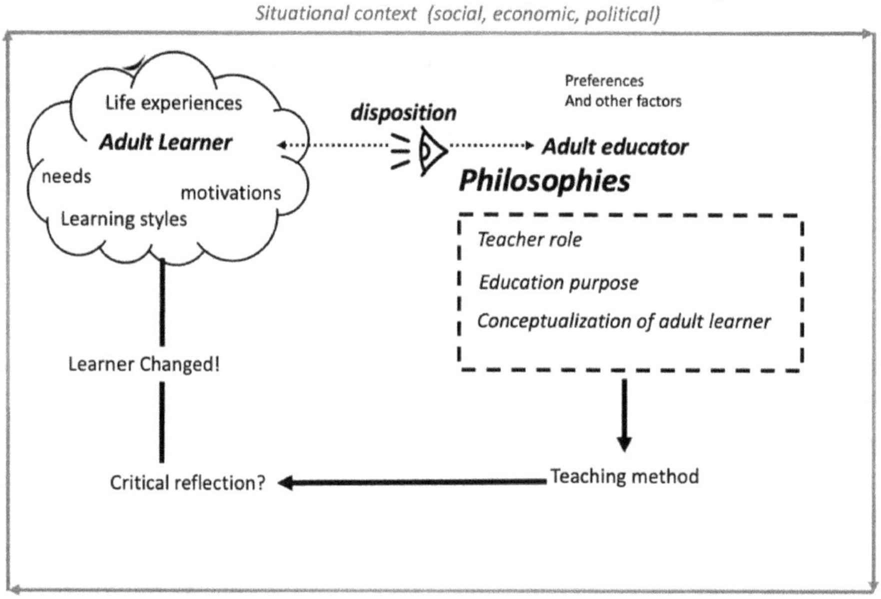

Philosophies the teacher holds influence how the teacher sees their role and what they see as the purpose of education. The beliefs or philosophies held by the teacher (along with preferences and other factors) shape understanding the learner's experiences, needs, motivations, and learning styles within the situational context (that includes broader society, institutional factors, etc.), and together with other factors, contribute to disposition, which in turn dictates action. Note the cyclic arrows around the model. The intent here is to show the dynamic nature of situational context (which influences learner, teacher, interactions, and what is required to create critical reflection appropriate for transformative learning.

The intersection of AI and contextualized educational philosophies offers transformative potential for creating more responsive, adaptive, and inclusive educational practices. When combined with AI, these philosophies can be operationalized in innovative ways to meet diverse educational needs:

Responsiveness: AI Systems can analyze vast amounts of data to identify individual learning patterns and needs. Educators can respond more effectively to students' circumstances by integrating this analysis with contextualized philosophies. For instance, AI can help detect early signs of academic struggle or disengagement, allowing teachers to intervene promptly with tailored support strategies that consider the student's background and personal challenges.

Adaptiveness: AI-powered educational tools can offer adaptive learning experiences that adjust to students' performance and learning pace in real-time. This adaptiveness is enhanced when infused with contextual understanding. For example, an AI system that understands a student's cultural context can provide more relevant and relatable examples and scenarios, making learning more meaningful and effective. This dynamic adjustment ensures that each student receives a personalized learning journey that evolves with their progress and needs.

Inclusivity: Inclusion in education ensures that all students have equal access to learning opportunities regardless of their backgrounds or abilities. AI can play a critical role by providing differentiated instruction and resources. When AI tools are designed with contextualized philosophies, they can offer multilingual support, culturally sensitive content, and accessible formats for students with disabilities. This ensures that educational practices are not just universally designed but also tailored to meet the diverse needs of all students, promoting a more inclusive learning environment.

The synergy between AI and contextualized philosophies paves the way for educational practices that are more attuned to students' varied and dynamic needs. This approach enables teachers to create learning environments that are more effective, engaging, equitable, and inclusive.

The question arises as to what philosophies are congruent with transformative learning. Humanistic, progressive, and critical philosophies usually apply to transformative learning. Because transformative learning is concerned with individual growth and perspective change, it is humanistic. It is also progressive because it involves learning through experience. It is critical because it draws from Freire's interpretation of Marxist socialism based on the critique of power structures and its emphasis on transformation and emancipation.

The *purpose of education* as defined by the teacher is influenced by the theoretical perspectives held by the teacher, whether that is to build students' intellectual powers of the mind (liberal education), develop behaviors for the preservation of the human species (behaviorist perspectives), promote social change (progressive perspective), or achieve self-actualization (humanist perspective).

Together with the contextually adapted philosophy adult educators may hold, these situational roles affect the teaching methods adult educators may use to help adult learners promote individual transformation and emancipation.

Adult Educators as Facilitators

Adult educators' roles in fostering transformative learning vary depending on the educators' philosophical perspectives and their conceptions of adult learners. For example, humanistic adult education teachers see themselves as facilitators, helpers, and partners in the learning process. They establish a context for learning and serve as a flexible resource for adult learners.

Humanistic teachers trust students to assume responsibility for their learning (Elias & Merriam, 1995, 2004). Progressive adult educators tend to regard themselves as organizers. They guide learning through educative experiences, present stimuli, and instigate and evaluate learning. In doing so, progressive teachers also become learners because the relationships between teachers and learners are reciprocal. Both should plan and learn from each other (Elias & Merriam, 1995, 2004).

Humanistic philosophy, which emphasizes the development of the whole person and values personal growth, individuality, and human potential, connects to AI in several meaningful ways:

Connection: AI can tailor educational experiences to individual learning styles and needs, aligning with the humanistic focus on personalizing education to foster each student's unique growth.

Example: AI-driven platforms like Coursera or Khan Academy adapt course recommendations based on learners' progress and interests.

Connection: Humanistic philosophy aims for self-actualization, where individuals realize their full potential. AI can support this by providing tools and resources that help individuals explore their interests deeply and develop talents.

Example: AI-based career guidance systems like Pymetrics use neuroscience-based assessment and AI to help individuals find career paths that align with their strengths and interests.

Connection: Humanistic education values inclusivity and equal opportunities for all learners. AI can democratize access to high-quality education by providing resources and support to students regardless of their geographical or socio-economic background.

Example: AI-powered language translation tools, such as Google Translate, help non-native speakers access educational content in their preferred language.

Connection: Humanistic philosophy emphasizes the importance of the emotional and social aspects of learning. AI can help monitor and support students' emotional well-being.

Example: AI-driven applications like Woebot offer mental health support and can help students manage stress and anxiety through conversational AI.

Connection: Humanistic teaching values deep, meaningful interactions between teachers and students. AI can handle administrative and repetitive tasks, giving teachers more time to focus on these interactions.

Example: AI tools like TeacherAssist automate grading and administrative work, allowing teachers to spend more time on personalized instruction and mentoring.

Connection: Humanistic philosophy encourages active participation and engagement in learning. AI can create immersive and interactive educational experiences that engage students more profoundly.

Example: Virtual and augmented reality tools, such as those developed by companies like zSpace and Nearpod, use AI To create interactive learning environments that make subjects like science and history come alive.

Behaviorist teachers predict, direct learning outcomes, and design a learning environment that elicits desired behavior. According to Elias and Merriam (1995, 2004), teachers influenced by a behavioral philosophy become contingency managers, environmental controllers, or behavioral engineers who plan in detail the conditions necessary to bring about desired behavior. Liberal teachers of adults consider themselves experts, transmitters of knowledge, and authoritative, and they direct the learning process. Liberal teachers develop intellect through reading, reflection, and production (Elias & Merriam, 1995, 2004).

AI's influence on behavioral philosophy lies in its ability to provide deeper insights, create personalized experiences, and raise new ethical challenges that must be addressed to ensure the responsible use of technology. New tools and methods exist to understand, predict, and modify behavior. Several ways AI contributes to this field are:

Behavior Analysis: AI can analyze vast amounts of data to identify patterns in human behavior. Machine learning algorithms can process information from various sources, such as social media, wearable devices, and online activities, to offer insight into behavioral trends and individual habits.

Predictive Modeling: AI systems can create models forecasting future behaviors based on historical data. These models are used in diverse fields, including psychology, marketing, and healthcare, to anticipate actions and outcomes, allowing for proactive interventions.

Ethical Considerations: Integrating AI into behavioral philosophy raised critical ethical questions about autonomy, privacy, and behavior manipulation. Philosophers and ethicists must address these concerns to ensure that AI applications respect individual rights and promote well-being.

Adaptive Learning Systems: AI creates adaptive learning environments that respond to students' needs and learning styles in education. These systems adjust the content and pace of instruction, enhancing engagement and effectiveness.

Both preferences and philosophical perspectives influence teaching methods. Preferences influence strategies to promote and evaluate learning (Cranton & Hoggan, 2012). For those who espouse a liberal philosophy of adult education, dialectic lectures and critical reading may be the preferred approaches for teaching adult learners. Under a liberal philosophy of education, learning is most often evaluated through essays, research papers, book reviews, etc. Educators working within a behaviorist framework will subscribe to teaching methods that are structured and linear, emphasizing student response rather than the process of learning. Programmed instruction, modularized instruction, and online teaching are often preferred by those who have adopted a behaviorist philosophy of adult education. Learning is evaluated primarily through objectively scored measurements (multiple choice, short answer) or performance observation.

Proponents of a progressive philosophy practice problem-solving and the scientific method when teaching adult learners; they use group work, case studies, problem-based learning, and experiential learning activities in settings appropriate to the discipline (shops, hospitals, schools, farms, and the like). Learning is evaluated through observing performance in a field setting or examining products students produced while engaging in experiential activities.

For those educators who base their practice on a critical philosophy, methods are created to present the learners with perspectives that are at odds with their current perspectives. This may include using movies and videos that portray an alternative perspective on an issue, reading fiction, holding critical debates, and using role plays in which participants take on different roles in different contexts. Learning is best evaluated through learner self-evaluation, as it is usually only the learner who can say whether their perspectives have changed.

Kinney (1953), who defined six teacher roles, suggested that adapting one's methods in teaching adult learners is necessary. They define six roles of the teacher: a director of learning, a counselor and guidance worker, a mediator of the culture, an influential member of the school community, a liaison between school and community, and a member of the profession. (p. 8) In his description of andragogy, Knowles strongly emphasized the helping role of adult educators based on his humanistic philosophy of adult education. Knowles, in *The Adult Learner* (Knowles et al., 1998, 2011), expressed the following view:

Finally, I found myself performing a different set of functions that required a different set of skills. Instead of performing the function of content planner and transmitter, which required primarily presentation skills, I was performing the function of process designer and manager, which required relationship building, needs assessment, involvement of students in planning, linking students to learning resources, and encouraging student initiative. (p. 201)

Because Knowles is considered one of the most influential figures in adult education, his humanistic philosophy has generated a wide following in the field. Inherently, followers of Knowles view themselves as learning facilitators instead of information disseminators to show that their practice is driven by their deeply held humanistic philosophy.

Knowles would likely see AI as a powerful enabler of personalized, self-directed, and practical learning experiences for adults, enhancing the overall effectiveness of adult education. Here are a few ways he might interpret AI's role:

Just-in-Time Learning: AI could provide immediate access to information and resources, aligning with Knowles' principle that adult learners learn best when they perceive the need to know something. This on-demand access to knowledge would support professionals needing quick solutions to specific problems.

Learner Autonomy: AI tools could enhance self-directed learning, a core concept in Knowles' andragogy. Intelligent tutoring systems, virtual assistants, and AI-driven feedback mechanisms would empower learners to take control of their education, offering guidance and support tailored to their pace and learning style.

Collaborative Learning: Knowles valued the social aspects of learning. AI could support this through virtual collaboration platforms, where learners can interact, share experiences, and solve problems collectively, regardless of geographical boundaries.

Lifelong Learning and Skill Development: AI could facilitate continuous learning opportunities, providing adults with ongoing access to skill development programs. This aligns with Knowles' belief that adult education should be lifelong.

CONCLUSION

Liberalism, progressivism, humanism, behaviorism, and critical philosophy are philosophies identified within the various frameworks of adult education. Implicit in each of these philosophies are beliefs about the nature of adult learners, the role of education, and the teacher. Teacher dispositions manifest as actions or, more specifically, as teaching practice. The authors believe connecting teacher dispositions to philosophies is essential to facilitate a more holistic and contextualized exploration of teaching practices. Discussing the teacher roles, educational purpose, and methods from the viewpoint of each of the philosophies provides a valuable framework for understanding dispositions and elements of teaching practices characteristic of those dispositions. More than multidisciplinary, students need to be transdisciplinary – to be proficient in various intellectual frameworks beyond the disciplinary perspectives. AI is not a pure STEM discipline. It requires a spectrum of capabilities not covered by current teaching dispositions and philosophies across academic fields.

Dignum (2021) identified skills needed for building the AI ecosystem that is central in education curricula across the world:

Collaborate: The AI ecosystem makes collaboration possible and assumes collaboration across distance, time, cultures, and contexts.
Question: AI systems are great at finding answers and will do this increasingly well; however, it is up to us to ask the right questions, critically evaluate results, and contribute to responsible implementations within the educational ecosystem.
Imagine Skills: For creative problem-solving, using empathy, logic, and novel thinking are needed. Nurturing humanities education and including humanities subjects in all technology curricula is imperative.
Learn to Learn: Quickly adapting and picking up new skills is vital for success. It requires us to learn, grow, and adapt to change continuously. Understanding what is necessary to know, knowing when to apply a particular concept, and knowing how to do it are keys to continuous success.

From this perspective, adult educators must skillfully contextually adapt both their philosophies and dispositions such that their practices are appropriate to the complex, variable needs of adult learners. Notwithstanding AI's tremendous promise to improve educational systems, full integration of AI into education requires strong leadership support. Leadership in education needs moral and financial support to concentrate on creating learners who can thrive in the AI society. Governments are finding it challenging to keep up with the rapid advancements in AI for education by private organizations such as LightSide, Coursera, McGraw-Hill, Pearson, and IBM (Nagar, 2024). Addressing issues through state legislation can help set standards, provide solutions, and foster the growth of innovative ecosystems that can integrate AI into educational settings involving several vital strategies, such as allocating funding and resources toward R&D to explore cutting-edge AI applications in education. Encouraging innovative research can lead to discovering new methods to enhance learning and teaching processes, establishing partnerships among educational institutions, technology companies, and government agencies to create a robust support network, and developing scalable and flexible AI infrastructure that educational institutions of all sizes can quickly adapt. This includes cloud-based platforms and tools that support various educational applications.

REFERENCES

Brookfield, S. D. (2005). *The power of critical theory*. Jossey-Bass.

Bulathwela, S., Perez-Ortiz, M., Holloway, C., & Shawe-Taylor, J. (2021). Could AI democratize education? *Socio-Technical Imaginaries of an EdTech Revolution.*

Cranton, P. (2006). *Understanding and promoting transformative learning: A guide for educators of adults*. Jossey-Bass.

Cranton, P., & Hoggan, C. (2012). We are evaluating transformative learning. In Taylor, E. W., & Cranton, P. (Eds.), *Handbook of transformative learning: Theory, research, and practice*. Jossey-Bass.

Dewey, J. (1938). *Education and experience*. Collier Books.

Dignum, V. (2021). The role and challenges of education for responsible AI. *London Review of Education*, 19(1), 1–11. DOI: 10.14324/LRE.19.1.01

Elias, J. L., & Merriam, S. B. (1995). *Philosophical foundations of adult education*. Krieger Publishing Company.

Elias, J. L., & Merriam, S. B. (2004). *Philosophical foundations of adult education* (3rded.). Krieger Publishing Company.

Freire, P. (1970). *Pedagogy of the oppressed*. Seabury Press.

Habermas, J. (1971). *Knowledge and human interests*. Beacon Press.

Holian, J. (1971). Alienation and social awareness among college students. *The Sociological Quarterly*, 13(1), 114–125. DOI: 10.1111/j.1533-8525.1971.tb01835.x

Kabudi, T., Pappas, I., & Olsen, D. H. (2021). AI-enabled adaptive learning systems: A systematic mapping of the literature. *Computers and Education: Artificial Intelligence, 2*.

Kidd, J. R. (1973). *How adults learn* (revised). Association Press.

Kim, N. J., & Kim, M. K. (2022). Teacher's perceptions of using an artificial intelligence-based educational tool for scientific writing. *Frontiers in Education*, 7, 7. DOI: 10.3389/feduc.2022.755914

Kinney, L. B. (1953). *The measure of a good teacher*. Teachers Association.

Knowles, M. S. (1975). *Self-directed learning*. Association Press.

Knowles, M. S. (1980). *The modern practice of adult education: From pedagogy to andragogy*. Association Press.

Knowles, M. S., Holton, E., & Swanson, A. (1998). *The adult learner: The definitive classic in adult education and human resource development*. Gulf Publishing Company.

Knowles, M. S., Holton, E., & Swanson, A. (2011). *The adult learner: The definitive classic in adult education and human resource development* (7th ed.). Taylor & Francis.

Leung, K.-H. (2019). *The picture of artificial intelligence and the secularization of thought*. Political Theology. DOI: 10.1080/1462317X.2019.1605725

Li, J., Peng, Y., & Su, J. (2023). Analysis of the impact of artificial intelligence on college students and countermeasures based on the perspective of comprehensive development. The *Frontiers of Society. Science, and Technology*, 5(9), 24–33.

Lindeman, E. C. (1926). *The meaning of adult education*. Research Center for Continuing Professional and Higher Education.

Mahoney, J. M., & Quick, B. G. (2000). Personality correlates of alienation in a university sample. *Psychological Reports*, 87(3_suppl), 1094–1100. DOI: 10.2466/pr0.2000.87.3f.1094 PMID: 11272749

Maslow, A. H. (1970). *Motivation and personality* (2nd ed.). Harper Collins.

Merriam, S. B., & Brockett, R. G. (1997). *The profession and practice of adult education: An introduction*. Jossey-Bass.

Mezirow, J. (1975). *Education for perspective transformation: Women's reentry programs in community colleges*. Center for Adult Education, Teachers College, Columbia University.

Mezirow, J. (1991). *Transformative dimension of adult learning*. Jossey-Bass.

Mezirow, J. (2000). Learning to think like an adult. In Mezirow, J. (Eds.), *Learning as transformation: Critical perspectives on a theory in progress* (pp. 3–31). Jossey-Bass.

Mickunas, A., & Pilotta, J. (2023). *A critical understanding of artificial intelligence: A phenomenological foundation*. Bentham Books. DOI: 10.2174/97898151234011230101

Moustaghfir, S., & Brigui, H. (2023). Exploring Moroccan English teacher's perception towards the use of interactive tools in teaching English as a foreign language on the development of critical thinking skills in young students. *International Journal of Linguistics, Literature, and Translation*, 6(8), 236–249. DOI: 10.32996/ijllt.2023.6.8.24

Nagar, N. (2024). Importance of artificial intelligence in education. [IJSREM]. *International Journal of Scientific Research in Engineering and Management*, 8(4).

Nicolaides, A., & Marsick, V. (2016). Understanding adult learning in the midst of complex social "liquid modernity.". *New Directions for Adult and Continuing Education*, 149(Spring), 9–20. DOI: 10.1002/ace.20172

Papadima, G. (2021, July). Is there a split between adult educator's educational philosophy in learning and teaching process? *International Journal of Instruction*, 14(3), 583–596. DOI: 10.29333/iji.2021.14334a

Rogers, C. R. (1969). *Freedom to learn*. Merrill.

Selman, G. (1989). The enemies of adult education. *Canadian Journal of University Continuing Education*, 15, 68–81.

Skinner, B. F. (1974). *About behaviorism*. Knopf.

Soccorsi, L. (2013). Instilling a personal teaching philosophy in preservice teachers: Vitally important but not always easy to achieve. *Journal of Student Engagement: Education Matters*, 3(1), 21–28.

Susanto, S., Andrianingsih, A., Sutawan, K., Marwintaria, V. A., & Astika, R. (2023). Transformation of learner learning: Improving reasoning skills through artificial intelligence (AI). [JoERI]. *Journal of Education, Religious, and Instructions*, 1(2), 37–46. DOI: 10.60046/joeri.v1i2.74

Thorndike, E. L., Bregman, E. O., Tilton, J. W., & Woodyard, E. (1928). *Adult learning*. Macmillan.

Tisdell, E. J., & Taylor, E. W. (2000). Adult education philosophy informs practice. *Adult Learning*, 11(2), 6–10. DOI: 10.1177/104515959901100203

Torrisi-Steele, G., & Carim, G.Jr. (2019). An adult-learner approach to the learning design of safety management system training in aviation. *International Journal of Adult Vocational Education and Technology*, 10(3), 39–53. DOI: 10.4018/IJAVET.2019070103

Wang, V. (2003). *Principles of adult education*. Pearson.

Xu, W. (2024). The correction strategy of artificial intelligence embedding into the negative social mentality of the marginal group of college students in the new era. *Journal of Electrical Systems*, 20(2). https://journal.esrgroups.org/jes/article/view/1222

Zadorina, O., Kurskaya, V., Sobolyeva, S., Grekova, L., & Vasylyuk-Zaitseva, S. (2024). The role of artificial intelligence in the creation of future education: Possibilities and challenges. *Futurity Education*, 4(2), 163–185.

Zhou, Y. (2022). Beliefs and practice evaluation based on artificial intelligence models under the IP environment. *Journal of Environmental and Public Health*, 2022(1), 1415142. DOI: 10.1155/2022/1415142 PMID: 36203503

Chapter 2
Integrating AI Into Policy Making in Educational Leadership

Dayna Lynn Mitchell
California State Polytechnic University, Pomona, USA

ABSTRACT

Artificial Intelligence (AI) is revolutionizing various sectors, and its integration into education is becoming increasingly pivotal. This chapter, "Integrating AI into Policy Making in Educational Leadership," examines the transformative potential of AI in shaping educational policies. The use of AI in educational leadership offers opportunities to enhance decision-making by making it more informed, efficient, and adaptive. Drawing on recent research, the chapter discusses how AI can impact key areas such as student motivation, engagement, anxiety reduction, and performance prediction. Additionally, it addresses the challenges and ethical considerations associated with implementing AI in policy-making processes. Through a comprehensive exploration of these themes, the chapter provides strategic insights for educational leaders seeking to leverage AI to improve outcomes and equity in education.

INTRODUCTION

Artificial Intelligence (AI) is transforming various sectors, including education. Research has found that AI can impact student motivation, engagement, and participation; reduce student anxiety; and predict future outcomes and academic performance (Celik, 2023; Elhussein et al., 2024; Khan, 2023; Owan et al., 2023; Pratama et al., 2023). In educational leadership, the integration of AI into policymaking holds the promise of more informed, efficient, and adaptive decision-making processes. This

DOI: 10.4018/979-8-3693-6130-6.ch002

chapter explores the potential benefits, challenges, and strategies for incorporating AI into educational policymaking.

THE ROLE OF AI IN EDUCATIONAL LEADERSHIP

AI technologies can analyze data, identify patterns, and provide insights humans might overlook. For educational leaders, this means accessing real-time data on student performance, resource allocation, and operational efficiencies. AI can support predictive analytics, helping leaders anticipate future trends and challenges, thereby facilitating proactive rather than reactive policymaking.

Benefits of Integrating AI into Policymaking

Data-Driven Decision Making

AI enables the collection and analysis of large datasets, providing evidence-based insights to inform policy decisions. This reduces reliance on intuition and anecdotal evidence, leading to more effective and objective policies. The potential of this data to inform pedagogy, decision-making, and policy is widely recognized. One example of AI in educational decision-making and policy is data dashboards. Used widely to track federal, state, and local accountability metrics, a data dashboard provides analytics to transform how educational institutions monitor, analyze, and improve student performance outcomes by providing actionable insights into improvement. By tracking metrics aligned to outcome indicators, educators receive a comprehensive view of individual students and institutional performance and progress through AI-generated data visualizations and prediction models (Owen et al., 2023).

AI can support decision-making by providing data-driven insights and recommendations to university leaders and administrators. Saaida (2023) found that AI has the potential to significantly influence resource allocation, budgeting, and decision-making processes within universities. By analyzing data and generating predictive models, AI can optimize the allocation of resources such as faculty assignments, classroom scheduling, and course offerings. This optimization allows universities to utilize their resources more efficiently, ensuring effective budget allocation and maximizing the use of facilities and personnel. Leaders can use AI insights to facilitate informed decisions regarding strategic initiatives, resource distribution, and policy formulation, enhancing higher education institutions' operational efficiency and effectiveness.

Personalized Education

AI-driven tools and systems hold the potential to revolutionize education by personalizing learning experiences, enhancing teacher productivity, and increasing student engagement. Personalized learning systems are powerful AI tools that customize educational experiences for individual students. Adjusting content based on individual learning needs, these systems enhance student and teacher learning outcomes (Akgun & Greenhow, 2022). AI recommends tailored interventions and resources by analyzing individual learning styles and progress, promoting inclusivity, and addressing diverse educational needs. Traditional, one-size-fits-all teaching methods can be replaced by personalized learning experiences enabled by AI technology. AI transforms education by customizing the learning experience to meet individual students' needs, enhancing engagement, and improving overall learning outcomes (Pratama et al., 2023). Compared to traditional teacher-led instruction, personalized learning systems can significantly boost student performance on standardized tests. A recent Microsoft study involving over 2,000 students and teachers from four countries found that AI-powered platforms effectively support student learning progress. AI systems can identify knowledge gaps and modify educational resources to individual needs, fostering growth and development (Akgun & Greenhow, 2022). When aligned with the neuroscientific principles of Universal Design for Learning (UDL), AI-supported learning environments can empower students to become expert learners by offering tools that enhance accessibility and adapt the educational experience to their needs. Further, personalizing content by connecting it to students' lives supports culturally responsive pedagogy. AI tools can aid educators and students in customizing these learning experiences, ensuring that instruction is responsive to the diverse needs of all learners (CDE, 2024).

AI facilitates personalized learning by utilizing learner profiling techniques that analyze learning data generated by students. This data-driven approach continuously updates and refines individualized profiles for each student, allowing for a customized educational experience that adapts to their unique learning needs and progress (Montebello, 2021). By analyzing student data from various sources such as assessments, homework, and quizzes, AI can identify students' learning needs and provide targeted feedback, helping to create personalized learning plans that align with each student's progress, strengths, and growth areas. AI can facilitate individualized instruction, allowing students to learn independently and focus on areas needing additional support. AI-powered adaptive learning platforms exemplify this approach by using data analytics to develop personalized learning paths. These platforms often start with a pre-assessment that generates specific goals and recommendations aligned with each student's unique learning profile (Owan et al., 2023).

Further, AI has elevated the accessibility and efficiency of personalized educational experiences through interactive mobile phone technology. AI-driven virtual reality extends learning beyond traditional boundaries, creating a global classroom where students can engage in immersive educational environments. Additionally, AI-based chatbots enhance online learning by providing personalized interactions that can simulate instructor-led dialogues. These chatbots can assess students' comprehension levels, facilitating a tailored learning experience that adapts to individual needs (Chen et al., 2020). While AI in personalized learning offers significant advantages, it also presents critical challenges (Kaswan et al., 2024). Concerns about privacy, ethical implications, and the potential for bias in AI algorithms necessitate careful policymaking to ensure these technologies are used responsibly and equitably. Successful implementation requires robust infrastructure, access to high-quality data, and comprehensive teacher training to effectively utilize AI tools and maximize their benefits in the educational context.

Efficiency and Cost Savings

Recent advancements in AI research have highlighted its potential to automate administrative processes across industry sectors, offering benefits such as streamlining workflows, reducing manual errors, and reallocating resources to more critical tasks, which can save cost. This efficiency allows educational leaders to focus on strategic planning and policy development rather than routine administrative duties. AI-driven text generation algorithms like GPT-3 can replicate various writing styles, enabling the automated creation of emails, reports, and other forms of written communication. This automation not only enhances efficiency but also saves time for end users by reducing the need for repetitive tasks and allowing them to focus on more complex and value-added activities (Parycek et al., 2023; Willis et al., 2020).

Integrating AI in education has enhanced the efficiency and quality of administrative functions performed by instructors. AI technologies enable automated processes for tasks such as reviewing and grading student assignments, which traditionally require considerable time and effort. By utilizing AI-driven web-based platforms and intelligent tutoring systems, instructors can streamline these administrative responsibilities, resulting in more effective and timely student feedback. This automation reduces the manual burden on educators and enhances their overall teaching effectiveness by allowing them to focus more on instructional activities and student engagement. The application of AI in administrative tasks thus contributes to improved education through greater efficiency and precision in managing and assessing student work (Chen et al., 2020).

Enhanced Monitoring and Evaluation

Integrating advanced AI tools in education is a relatively recent development that requires careful oversight and continuous monitoring to ensure effective outcomes (Elhussein et al., 2024). Integrating AI requires consideration of student safety in educational settings, focusing on policy adherence regarding terms of use, data privacy, and ethical guidelines. Educators must engage in targeted professional development to understand AI's capabilities and limitations, enabling them to guide students responsibly as AI becomes pervasive in personal and professional contexts. Policy-driven professional learning should emphasize creating safe, AI-enhanced learning environments that uphold ethical standards and academic integrity. Additionally, collaborative development of AI use policies between educators and students is essential for fostering responsible AI usage, ensuring students are equipped to navigate AI technologies effectively while maintaining ethical standards (CDE, 2024). Integrating AI technologies into educational assessments allows educators to gain real-time, data-driven insights into student learning trends, effectively identifying strengths and growth areas. This approach enhances the evaluation of non-standard assessments, informs instructional decision-making, and supports curriculum development, ultimately improving the overall quality of education (Elhussein et al., 2024).

Challenges in Integrating AI

Data Privacy and Security

The use of AI in education requires access to sensitive student data. Ensuring the privacy and security of this data will protect students and comply with legal requirements. Protecting sensitive information within the technological infrastructure supporting teachers, students, and staff is a core ethical imperative. Realizing AI's potential in education necessitates acquiring granular data beyond traditional student records to detailed interactions between learners and technology, educators, and instructional tools. Stemming from federal and state student outcome data, a heightened reliance on data underscores the critical need for robust privacy, security, and governance frameworks. Given that AI models are primarily developed without explicit consideration for educational applications or student privacy, their integration into educational environments may pose significant challenges to compliance with federal regulations such as the Family Educational Rights and Privacy Act (FERPA) and corresponding state statutes (Cardona et al., 2023). Although FERPA, enacted in 1974, does not explicitly mention AI, its principles of protecting student education records directly apply to the use of AI in education in both TK-

12 and higher education regarding privacy, data security, sharing, ownership, and control. FERPA requires educational institutions to protect student records (U.S. Department of Education, 2021). When AI systems process student data, this data must be handled by FERPA's strict privacy regulations. FERPA mandates robust security measures to safeguard student information. This includes protecting data from unauthorized access, use, disclosure, or destruction, which is equally vital in AI. FERPA places limitations on the disclosure of student records to third parties. When AI systems involve external parties, institutions must ensure compliance with these restrictions. Students and parents have the right to access and control their education records. These rights must be upheld even when AI systems are processing data. While FERPA does not provide specific guidelines for AI, it sets a strong foundation for protecting student data privacy and security. Educational institutions must carefully consider FERPA's requirements when developing and deploying AI systems. Complexities can arise at the intersection of FERPA and AI, such as student profiling, third-party data sharing, student work and copyright, and student surveillance.

AI-Powered Student Profiling: AI systems can analyze student data to predict academic performance or behavior (Huang et al., 2020). This analysis could potentially reveal sensitive information about students, such as learning disabilities, emotional struggles, or family background. How can schools ensure the AI system does not generate or store information considered a protected educational record under FERPA? What safeguards are necessary to prevent unauthorized access to or use of this information? To mitigate this issue, schools should collect only the data necessary for the AI system to function, avoid collecting sensitive information unless essential, and incorporate privacy considerations into the AI system's development from the outset. This includes conducting privacy impact assessments and removing personally identifiable information from data used for AI modeling whenever possible. Schools should conduct periodic audits of the AI system to ensure compliance with FERPA and other privacy regulations.

AI and Third-Party Data Sharing: Third-party vendors can pose risks to an institution, its data, and its constituents. A third-party servicer may be an individual, a state, or a private profit or non-profit organization that enters a contract with an educational organization to administer data processing. Many schools and educational organizations use third-party vendors to provide students with personalized learning platforms. To provide these services, these vendors must access and process student data. It is incumbent upon the educational organization to ensure that these vendors comply with FERPA regulations. One of the ways to ensure compliance is through contractual provisions protecting student data. Educational organizations must establish precise data use agreements with third-party vendors, outlining the permitted uses of student data, data security measures, and data return or destruction policies; ensure that all employees involved in data sharing with third parties receive comprehensive FERPA training; and monitor the third-party vendor's compliance with FERPA through regular audits and reviews.

AI-Generated Student Work and Copyright: AI systems can generate text, images, and other creative content. If students use AI to assist with assignments, questions about ownership, plagiarism, and the potential for AI-generated content to contain personally identifiable information can arise. Schools can address the use of AI in student work while maintaining student privacy by developing clear policies for students regarding the use of AI tools in their coursework; educating students about the ethical implications of AI use and the importance of originality; utilizing plagiarism detection tools that can identify AI-generated content; and establishing clear ownership guidelines for AI-generated content, emphasizing that the student retains ownership of their original ideas and contributions (Chan, 2023).

AI and Student Surveillance: AI-powered surveillance systems are used in schools to monitor, detect, and classify objects and activities, alerting staff to out-of-the-ordinary situations that use algorithms to identify threats. However, these systems may collect and analyze data that is considered personally identifiable. Schools can balance security concerns with student privacy by clearly defining the purpose of the surveillance system and limiting data collection to what is necessary to achieve that purpose; implement policies for data retention, ensuring that data is deleted after a specified period unless there is a legitimate educational need to retain it; inform students and parents about the surveillance system, its purpose, and how data is collected and used; and establish clear accountability measures for the use of surveillance data, including regular reviews and oversight.

Bias and Fairness

AI systems can inadvertently perpetuate existing biases in the data on which they are trained, reflecting historical and societal inequalities. Educational leaders must ensure that AI applications promote fairness and equity in policymaking. In educational contexts, biased algorithms can lead to unequal treatment of students, particularly those from marginalized groups (Baker & Hawn, 2021; Binns, 2018; CDE, 2024; Khan, 2023). Baker & Hawn (2021) explain, "Algorithms often encode the biases of their developers or the surrounding society, producing predictions or inferences that are clearly discriminatory towards specific groups" (p. 2) related to race, nationality, gender, native language, and parent education, military background, and socio-economic status. Further, AI-driven assessment tools might inaccurately evaluate students' abilities based on biased training data, leading to unfair grading or placement decisions. Research has identified biases identified in algorithms to predict student drop-out, analyze engagement, evaluate behavior, and personalize learning (Baker & Hawn, 2021; Idowu et al., 2024). The use of AI in personalized learning platforms may perpetuate existing disparities by recommending educational resources based on biased assumptions about students' capabilities. Ensuring fairness in AI systems requires rigorous testing for bias, transparency in algorithmic decision-making, and the inclusion of diverse perspectives in the development process to create more equitable educational technologies (Baker & Hawn, 2021; Binns, 2018).

Through a mixed-methods analysis of literature reviews and stakeholder interviews, Khan's (2023) research identified specific biases in AI educational tools, such as gender and cultural insensitivities and inaccuracies in performance predictions. The analysis uncovered instances where AI-driven educational tools exhibited biases, revealing the complex interplay between technology, data, and societal influences. One finding was the tendency of specific AI algorithms to predict academic performance based on gender stereotypes. For example, female students in mathematics and science-related modules were often recommended for foundational or introductory courses, while male students were directed toward advanced or challenging modules. These gendered recommendations not only reinforce existing stereotypes but also limit students' potential by restricting their exposure to diverse learning opportunities. Another finding was the presence of cultural and linguistic biases in AI-driven content recommendations. Algorithms trained predominantly on Western-centric datasets frequently overlooked or misinterpreted cultural nuances, leading to a skewed representation of history, literature, or societal norms. This lack of cultural sensitivity can alienate students from diverse backgrounds, perpetuating feelings of exclusion and marginalization. Further, many educators also expressed concerns about AI's "black box" nature, where algorithms generate recommendations or predictions without providing clear rationales. This lack of transparency hinders educators' ability to critically evaluate and adapt AI-driven tools, leading to distrust and apprehension. Students, particularly those from marginalized communities, reported emotional and psychological impacts from encountering biased AI-driven content. Feelings of inadequacy, frustration, and disengagement were common, highlighting the profound effect of AI biases on students' well-being and academic experiences. The findings underscore the need for robust ethical frameworks and practices in AI-driven education. Addressing these biases requires a multifaceted approach that prioritizes diversity in dataset collection, fosters algorithmic transparency, promotes stakeholder collaboration, and emphasizes continuous monitoring and evaluation. The findings stress that addressing bias in AI education is not just a technical issue but a moral responsibility. It calls for collaborative efforts from academia, industry, and policymakers to ensure a more inclusive and equitable future in education (Khan, 2023).

Technical Expertise and Infrastructure

Integrating AI requires significant technical expertise and infrastructure. Educational institutions should invest in training and technology to implement AI-driven policies effectively. AI has significantly transformed instructional pedagogy. However, a challenge of using AI-powered instructional tools is that educators may need a greater understanding of how the technology functions and possess the technical expertise required to grasp the algorithms fully and their impact on student outcomes (Owan et al., 2023). For teachers to fully leverage the potential of AI in education, they need to understand the instructional benefits and knowledge to implement AI-based tools effectively. The more teachers recognize the advantages of AI-based tools, the more likely they will use them to enhance learner motivation and engagement. Teachers with a deeper understanding of AI can make better choices when selecting appropriate AI tools for their teaching needs. Knowledge of AI enables educators to utilize AI-based tools for personalized learning and timely feedback. Therefore, assessing teachers' understanding of integrating AI-based tools into education is crucial. Possessing technological and pedagogical knowledge is essential for successfully integrating technology in educational settings (Celik, 2023).

Interdisciplinary research in the learning sciences has enhanced our understanding of learning processes and effective teaching practices; this knowledge should inform the design of AI technologies used in education and training. Insights can come from both researchers in the learning sciences and practicing educators. Partnerships supporting inter-stakeholder co-design can bridge the gap between learning sciences research and AI development in education. The increasing prevalence of AI in education underscores the need for collaboration, ensuring that educators help AI developers understand teaching and learning. In contrast, AI developers equip educators with insights about AI and its applications (Luckin & Cukurova, 2019).

Ethical Considerations

The use of AI raises ethical questions, particularly concerning the transparency of AI decision-making processes and the accountability of those decisions. Clear ethical guidelines and governance frameworks are necessary to address these concerns. Memarian & Doleck's (2023) systematic literature review found that Fairness, Accountability, Transparency, and Ethics (FATE) must be integrated into AI systems. Given the rapid pace at which AI can analyze datasets and generate new models for educational programming, teaching, and learning, AI is at risk of being misused due to flawed logic or data. While AI can surpass human decision-making in computational and mathematical terms, educators must question whether these advancements align with ethical standards and consider human and environmental needs. Memarian & Doleck (2023) found that the challenge in addressing ethics within AI in education is not about identifying what needs attention—areas where ethical considerations are lacking are well-known, as AI is deeply embedded in society, culture, ideologies, politics, economy, and industry (Ungerer & Slade, 2022). Instead, the difficulty lies in developing the capacity to implement ethical changes or integrations at the appropriate times.

The U.S. Department of Education's Office of Educational Technology identified an urgent need for safeguards to ensure AI's safe and ethical use in education (Cardona et al., 2023). Given the accelerating pace of AI integration, policymakers and educators must proactively establish requirements, disclosures, and regulations to shape a positive future for all stakeholders. These policies should prioritize the following:

1. **Human-Centered AI:** Leverage automation to enhance learning while preserving human judgment and decision-making.
2. **Data Quality:** Ensure AI models are trained on accurate, unbiased data to prevent unfair or inaccurate outcomes.
3. **Equity:** Assess how AI technologies may impact equity in education and take steps to mitigate any negative consequences.
4. **Safeguards:** Implement human oversight and safeguards to prevent AI systems from undermining equity. (Cardona et al., 2023)

Strategies for Successful Integration

Building Capacity and Skills

To build capacity and skills, leaders must invest in training programs for educational leaders and staff to develop the necessary skills to work with AI technologies. This includes understanding AI fundamentals, data literacy, and ethical considerations. Bowers et al. (2019) identify key competency and skill domains essential for professional development and training for practitioners and researchers in education:

1. **Leadership in Schools and Communities**: This includes competencies in school and system leadership, community building, shared instructional leadership, leadership for learning, and culturally responsive leadership. It also emphasizes data-driven decision-making and program evaluation.
2. **Training in "e-Administration" and Database Management**: With educational datasets growing in size and complexity, expertise is needed in managing these systems. As schools incorporate more data streams—such as recommender systems, personalized learning platforms, and educational apps—the ability to

track long-term student outcomes and organizational interactions through tools like academic analytics and intelligent tutors becomes increasingly essential.

3. **Proficiency in Multiple Programming Languages**: Practitioners must be competent in various statistical and data science languages, such as R, Python, STATA, and SPSS.
4. **Statistical and Machine Learning Methods**: These skills are vital for analyzing educational data, predicting outcomes, and developing early warning systems. Mastery in data mining, learning analytics, and inferential statistics is necessary for making informed policy decisions and enhancing classroom instruction.
5. **Data Dashboards and User Interface Design**: The ability to design intuitive and interactive data visualizations is crucial for translating analytics into actionable insights for stakeholders.
6. **Ethical Management and Use of Data:** Ethical data practices are crucial for safeguarding privacy and ensuring that decision-making algorithms in education are transparent. This transparency allows for a better understanding of machine-driven decisions and helps identify potential biases.

Collaborative Approach

While the potential for data-driven decision-making is significant, challenges related to data quality, accessibility, and interpretation can create a disconnect between policymakers and educators. AI advancements can empower educators by providing them with tools for data-driven decision-making. This shift can redefine the relationship between policymakers and practitioners, fostering a more collaborative and data-informed approach to education (Howard et al., 2022). Research supports collaborations among educational institutions, technology providers, and researchers to develop AI applications tailored to the educational context. Luckin and Cukurova's (2019) framework can guide a collaborative approach. To ensure teachers and learners understand and feel confident using AI, a promising approach is through a co-designed, interdisciplinary process involving educators, learners, and AI developers that can enhance developers' understanding of teaching and learning while providing educators with insights into the technology development process. Luckin and Cukurova (2019) propose a framework for effective AI integration in education, emphasizing that all stakeholders must have a foundational understanding of AI to use it effectively and safely. This framework addresses the essential role of educators in providing education and training while also considering how they can gain the necessary understanding of AI. The framework aims to ensure that AI in education is pedagogically and technically sound. It involves creating an ecosystem that promotes the co-design of AI applications. The model consists of two interconnected elements: one centered around data, which powers AI and informs evidence of learner progress, and three key activities:

- Train educators to understand AI, enabling them to use it effectively and teach learners to work alongside it.
- Train AI developers to deepen their understanding of teaching and learning to create relevant educational applications.
- Foster collaboration between educators, AI developers, and researchers to develop AI applications, enhancing mutual understanding and generating robust evidence of educational effectiveness.

The second element of the framework outlines activities necessary within education and training systems to maximize the benefits of AI:

- Prioritize human intelligence aspects that cannot be automated, such as social and emotional intelligence, metacognition, and self-efficacy.
- Provide training on AI to ensure safe and effective use.
- Develop AI solutions to address significant educational challenges, including teacher shortages and achievement gaps.

Robust Data Governance

Educational organizations must establish strong data governance policies to ensure data privacy, security, and ethical use of AI. This includes creating protocols for data access, storage, and sharing. The U.S. Department of Education cites a critical safety concern in the need for robust data privacy and security in educational AI systems. The development and deployment of AI require extensive data collection, often beyond traditional student records. This data includes detailed information about student learning activities and teacher instructional practices. Given AI's reliance on data, renewed attention to data privacy, security, and governance is essential. Since AI models are not constantly developed with educational use or student privacy in mind, their application in education may not align with institutions' efforts to comply with federal and state privacy laws (Cardona et al., 2023). School districts can use federal and state guidance when developing data governance policies. The California Department of Education (CDE, n.d.) provides recommendations for creating AI protocols and policies to ensure privacy, security, transparency, data retention, accessibility and inclusion, stakeholder involvement, and monitoring:

- Ensure legal compliance with FERPA, Children's Online Privacy Protection Act (COPPA), and other relevant data privacy laws

- Review data collection, storage, and management practices
- Clarify data ownership, access, and sharing rights
- Assess encryption, authentication, and authorization protocols
- Verify robust access controls to restrict data access
- Understand how AI algorithms make decisions and whether vendors can provide insights
- Determine data retention policies and alignment with district standards
- Ensure the AI system is accessible to all students, including those with disabilities
- Engage parents, students, educators, and administrators in the evaluation process
- Establish procedures for ongoing monitoring and evaluation of AI system compliance

Other states also offer similar recommendations. For example, the Kentucky Department of Education (KDE, 2024) offers guidelines for developing ethical and responsible AI governance models within the education sector. These recommendations also emphasize compliance with state and federal privacy laws to ensure AI's safe and ethical use by prioritizing transparency, data protection, fairness, non-discrimination, ethical practices, and ongoing monitoring in their daily operations.

Almaraz-Menéndez et al. (2022) applied Drachsler & Greller's (2016) academics analytics checklist to university AI applications, which can be used in the development of data governance policies:

- Justifying the data use and value of analysis
- Transparently explaining the purpose and including what data is used and when accessed
- Explaining the legitimacy of the application and data use
- Involving stakeholders in the implementation and design process and providing an opportunity for stakeholders to communicate concerns
- Gathering informed consent for data analysis, which can be withdrawn
- Ensuring anonymized data
- Establishing protocols to ensure the responsible use of personal data
- Guaranteeing that outside agencies implement security protocols and comply with data protection laws

Although Almaraz-Menéndez et al.'s (2022) governance application was designed for the university context, it can also be applied to the K-12 context to ensure data privacy, security, and ethical use of AI.

Pilot Programs and Iterative Development

People's attitudes toward technology can influence their willingness to adopt it. Adopting new technology, including AI, often presents challenges. To successfully navigate AI implementation, organizations can utilize various strategies. One practical approach is to start with pilot programs to test AI applications on a smaller scale and use the insights gained from these pilots to refine and scale AI integration in policymaking. Organizations can begin by identifying a specific problem or opportunity where AI can add value, then conduct small-scale pilots or prototypes to test different approaches and assess their effectiveness. This iterative learning process can help to minimize risks associated with large-scale deployments.

Holstein et al.'s (2019) research utilized prototyping to learn about the benefits of an iterative co-design in educational technology. The researchers used Replay Enactments (REs) as a prototyping method to address the challenges of designing data-driven algorithmic systems for learning analytics. REs involved replaying recorded classroom sessions with participants and having them think aloud as they analyzed the data. The researchers found critical benefits in this prototype, such as the use of real-world data and scenarios, a focus on specific aspects of a system's design, such as explanations, biases, or data scenarios, and insights into social nuances and potential issues before deploying a system in the real world. The researchers found this process to be a promising approach for designing learning analytics systems that are usable, useful, fair, and trustworthy.

Using AI and user-centered design principles, Charles' (2023) research aimed to develop a personalized mobile education system for New Zealand students with tailored learning content and recommendations based on individual preferences. The study demonstrated the potential of AI-powered personalization to improve the learning experience for students and contribute to the increasing use of AI algorithms and systems in education. Participants were involved in several phases of research to ensure that user-centered design principles were effectively implemented. The research findings identified several user challenges, including difficulty managing time, stress, work-life balance, feeling overwhelmed by workload, and struggling with financial management. A prototype of a task management app was created and tested with participants, and the feedback received was used to make improvements before moving on to the final testing stage. The app includes task prioritization, integration with productivity tools, custom categories, and social features. Research findings show that the app was well-received by participants and addressed many of their needs.

Ethical Frameworks

Ethical principles should inform and guide educational stakeholders in developing and deploying AI in education. Developing and implementing ethical frameworks that guide the use of AI in educational policymaking should address issues of transparency, accountability, and bias. Both technical and policy transparency are essential considerations for policymakers. Higher education institutions using AI algorithms in admissions may need help explaining decisions to applicants. Similarly, parents may need more clear explanations for pedagogical or remediation decisions made by school districts. Teachers might also resist the use of vague tools to evaluate their performance and impact compensation or employment. Transparent AI policies in educational institutions should require publicly accessible explanations for any decisions made, documentation of these decisions, and established channels for contesting problematic results or processes (Schiff, 2022).

Nguyen et al. (2023) found that sustainable development of AI in education requires addressing several critical challenges. At the systemic level, these include comprehensive public policy, equitable AI integration, teacher preparation, AI understanding of education, quality data systems, and ethical data practices. At the individual level, concerns range from systemic bias and discrimination to ethical issues related to privacy and data bias. The widespread implications of AI in education have also raised concerns about widening inequalities, commercialization, and the home-school divide. As AI becomes more prevalent, individuals may face risks without realizing it. These challenges necessitate urgent efforts to educate teachers and students about the ethical implications of AI in education and how to navigate them. Further, Nguyen et al. (2023) suggest, embedding the principles of AI ethics in education, and also ethics issues such as responsibility, inclusion, fairness, security, and explainability in conducting educational research will not only mitigate emerging societal abuses rooted in algorithmic injustice but also bear instrumental implications to the landscape of AI governance and policymaking for the long-term development of significant industries.

Adams et al. (2023) analyzed existing AI ethics guidelines for children and K-12 education and identified core principles such as transparency, justice, nonmaleficence, responsibility, privacy, beneficence, freedom, and autonomy. Four new ethical principles specific to K-12 education were also identified: pedagogical appropriateness, children's rights, AI literacy, and teacher well-being. The analysis highlighted the need for a decolonized, human-centered approach to AI ethics in education. Such an approach should address the growing human-AI collaboration in classrooms and consider the complex ethical implications for children's cognitive, social-emotional, physical, and cultural development.

Case Studies

The following case studies demonstrate how AI has optimized resource allocation in schools, leading to improved student outcomes and operational efficiencies; personalized learning to impact student engagement and achievement; and used predictive analytics to inform policy decisions and effectively anticipate and address future challenges.

AI in Resource Allocation

Accessible Digital Textbooks for All Initiative. UNICEF's initiative, *Accessible Digital Textbooks for All* (ADT), aligns with its global agenda for inclusive education, emphasizing the appreciation of learners' diversity, respect for their dignity and autonomy, and promoting their well-being. This initiative recognizes individuals' unique needs and capacity to participate meaningfully in society. Article 24 of the Convention on the Rights of Persons with Disabilities (UN, 2006) asserts the right of persons with disabilities to inclusive education at all levels, free from discrimination and with equal opportunities. With over 240 million children worldwide living with disabilities, many lack access to inclusive technologies, accessible learning materials, and essential educational support, which limits their ability to engage in learning thoroughly. Approximately half of these children are out of school, and one billion individuals with disabilities need assistive technology but lack access.

Accessible digital textbooks can help address the issue of accessible learning materials, which is one component necessary to create an inclusive learning environment for students with disabilities. Traditional printed textbooks cannot offer the flexibility and accessibility features needed to ensure that all students can engage fully with the curriculum. This initiative aimed to enhance educational outcomes by providing students access to the curriculum through multiple media. Accessible digital textbooks are tools designed to provide all learners, including those with disabilities, access to information in alternative formats. AI has played a crucial role in scaling the initiative cost-effectively, enabling widespread implementation and ensuring accessibility even in areas without internet connectivity.

ADT applies the principles of Universal Design for Learning (UDL) and accessible technology to create digital tools that accommodate a wide range of learners, particularly those with disabilities. The traditional "one-size-fits-all" approach to education fails to acknowledge the diverse learning needs of students, including those with disabilities, often resulting in frustration, disengagement, and lower motivation. A Universal Design for Learning (UDL) approach ensures that educational resources are more effective for a broader range of students. This approach allows students to leverage their unique learning preferences, reducing unnecessary barriers traditional learning materials pose. These digital resources can be customized to meet the needs of students who are blind or have low vision, are deaf or hard of hearing, have intellectual or developmental disabilities, or prefer accessing information without visual input.

The ADT initiative, operational in collaboration with Ministries of Education across three countries in Eastern and Southern Africa and six in Latin America and the Caribbean, aimed to reach 500,000 children by mid-2024. The initiative emphasized a co-creation approach with local stakeholders, enhancing the ADT ecosystem and fostering better learning outcomes. Educational outcomes can be significantly improved by offering differentiated learning opportunities and materials that cater to various learning styles. Research and development efforts by UNICEF and its partners suggest that ADTs can significantly boost students' motivation, classroom participation, and peer interaction, ultimately contributing to a more inclusive and accessible educational environment (Elhussein et al., 2024). User testing results indicated that ADTs can effectively support teachers in delivering lessons to all students, regardless of disabilities. Students of both genders, with and without disabilities, expressed enthusiasm and engagement while using ADTs. Teachers reported that the ADTs were beneficial for fostering an inclusive environment and provided feedback on better integrating these tools into their daily teaching practices. Observations showed that students utilized various accessibility features, such as audio voice-over and sign language videos, according to their needs and learning preferences. Those who interacted directly with the prototypes demonstrated focused engagement with the content and could navigate it at their own pace. Teachers also supported students with additional needs, such as novice signers, to ensure they comprehended the material and actively participated throughout the sessions (UNICEF, n.d.; UNICEF, 2023).

Personalized Learning Initiatives

The Programme for International Student Assessment (PISA) is an international study evaluating education systems in participating countries, measuring 15-year-old students' reading, mathematics, and science literacy. In recent years, PISA scores in Brazil and Latin America fell below average, highlighting significant literacy challenges among 28 million public school students, particularly those from economically disadvantaged families, unprepared for university and the workforce. Nearly one-third of Brazilians aged 15 to 64 are functionally illiterate, lacking essential reading, writing, and math skills for daily life. To tackle this literacy gap at scale, Letrus developed an AI-powered educational program that engages students in the classroom while supporting teachers with specific, prompt feedback on writing submissions. Letrus goes beyond basic spelling and grammar, fostering students' skills in diction, organization, flow, reading comprehension, and other areas critical for functional literacy. Letrus has been implemented in middle and high schools across Brazil, benefiting 170,000 students in 670 schools, with the primary goal to bridge the literacy gap between low- and high-income students. Utilizing proprietary natural language processing technology to provide real-time constructive feedback in reading and writing, the program focuses on personalized learning, offering immediate feedback to students, real-time data for educators, and monitoring tools for school managers. Teachers receive tailored recommendations for content and methodologies, allowing for integration into the curriculum to enhance specific skills. This iterative process and approach to literacy development adapts to the evolving needs of individual students and the entire class. School leaders can track progress, gain immediate insights into areas needing improvement, and identify emerging learning gaps that may benefit from targeted interventions, such as teacher training initiatives or strategic curriculum adjustments.

In 2022, Letrus achieved success in public schools in Espírito Santo. A randomized controlled trial demonstrated that using Letrus in the final year of high school improved students' essay scores on Brazil's college entrance exam by 0.1 standard deviations (equivalent to 17 points out of a possible 1,000) compared to the control group, potentially reducing inequalities between public and private schools. Within five months of implementation, participating students ranked second in national writing exams, an improvement from the eighth position attained by the control group. As a result, Letrus was designated the official literacy development program for high school students in the state, contributing to Espírito Santo's status as the top-performing state in the writing component of the National Exam, with a performance delta five times the national average from 2021 to 2022. If Letrus proves to have a positive impact on educational and labor market outcomes, it could contribute to the global dialogue on the importance of functional literacy and bolster the case for the cost-effectiveness and scalability of AI-based educational models in classrooms worldwide (Elhussein et al., 2024; USAID, 2023).

Predictive Analytics for Policy Planning

The National Institute for Student Success (NISS, n.d.) uses holistic data analysis and predictive analytics to assist universities in identifying and addressing equity gaps and institutionally created completion barriers to impact policies, practices, and structures to support student success. Partnering with NISS, Georgia State University (GSU) used predictive analytics to significantly impact student success by implementing the GPS Student Advising system in 2012. The university tracks 800 risk factors for over 40,000 students daily, leading to over 90,000 interventions in the 2023-24 school year. The system enables timely advisement, corrects course registrations before the semester begins, and supports students at risk of underperforming in prerequisite courses. Since the implementation of the GPS Advising system, freshman fall-to-spring retention rates at Georgia State University have increased, and graduating seniors are completing their degrees with fewer excess courses. The use of predictive analytics has also led to a notable increase in the graduation of underserved students, with a 103% rise in bachelor's degrees awarded to African American students and Georgia State ranking first nationally among non-profit institutions for conferring degrees to this demographic. As a result of a shift in student advisement policy, GSU has eliminated achievement gaps, with black, Hispanic, first-generation, and low-income students graduating at rates equal to or above the overall student body. The findings demonstrate that predictive analytics can help all students graduate at comparable rates and level the playing field for diverse backgrounds (Georgia State, 2017; NISS, n.d.).

CONCLUSION

The integration of AI into policymaking in educational leadership holds transformative potential. By leveraging AI technologies, educational leaders can make more informed, efficient, and equitable decisions. However, realizing this potential requires addressing challenges related to data privacy, bias, technical expertise, and ethical considerations. Through strategic planning, collaboration, and a commitment to ethical practices, AI can become a powerful tool in shaping the future of education. AI policy serves as a framework for ethical decision-making in the educational context, ensuring the responsible and equitable use of AI technologies. By establishing clear guidelines, AI policy mitigates potential risks associated with AI, including bias, privacy breaches, and data misuse. Moreover, a clear and transparent AI policy safeguards student privacy by outlining data collection, storage, and utilization rules. To promote equity and inclusion for all students, AI policy ensures that AI technologies are employed to foster these values. Furthermore, AI policy enhances transparency and accountability in using AI in education, enabling stakeholders to comprehend how decisions are made. As AI becomes increasingly prevalent, educational leaders must be prepared to navigate its challenges and opportunities. AI policy offers a roadmap for effectively integrating AI into educational settings. By developing and implementing robust AI policies, educational leaders can ensure that AI technologies are harnessed to enhance learning and improve outcomes for all students.

REFERENCES

Adams, C., Pente, P., Lemermeyer, G., & Rockwell, G. (2023). Ethical principles for artificial intelligence in K-12 education. *Computers and Education: Artificial Intelligence*, 4, 100131.

Akgun, S., & Greenhow, C. (2022). Artificial intelligence in education: Addressing ethical challenges in K-12 settings. *AI and Ethics*, 2(3), 431–440. https://doi.org/10.1007/s43681-021-00096-7

Almaraz-Menéndez, F., Maz-Machado, A., López-Esteban, C., & Almaraz-López, C. (Eds.). (2022). *Strategy, policy, practice, and governance for AI in higher education institutions*. IGI Global.

Baker, R. S., & Hawn, A. (2021). Algorithmic bias in education. *Journal of Educational Data Mining*, 13(2), 1–22.

Binns, R. (2018). Fairness in machine learning: Lessons from political philosophy. In *Proceedings of the 2018 Conference on Fairness, Accountability, and Transparency* (pp. 149–159).

Bowers, A. J., Bang, A., Pan, Y., & Graves, K. E. (2019). Education Leadership Data Analytics (ELDA): A White Paper Report on the 2018 ELDA Summit. *Online Submission*.

California Department of Education. (n.d.). Learning With AI, Learning About AI - Professional Learning (CA Dept of Education). Retrieved from https://www.cde.ca.gov/ci/pl/aiincalifornia.asp

California Department of Education. (2024). Artificial intelligence in California schools. California Department of Education. https://www.cde.ca.gov/ci/pl/aiincalifornia.asp

Cardona, M. A., Rodríguez, R. J., & Ishmael, K. (2023). Artificial intelligence and the future of teaching and learning: Insights and recommendations. U.S. Department of Education, Office of Educational Technology. https://tech.ed.gov/files/2023/05/ai-future-of-teaching-and-learning-report.pdf

Celik, I. (2023). Towards Intelligent-TPACK: An empirical study on teachers' professional knowledge to ethically integrate artificial intelligence (AI)-based tools into education. *Computers in Human Behavior*, p. *138*, 107468.

Chan, C. K. Y. (2023). A comprehensive AI policy education framework for university teaching and learning. *International Journal of Educational Technology in Higher Education*, 20(1), 38.

Charles, F. (2023). AI-powered personalized mobile education for New Zealand students. [IJSECS]. *International Journal Software Engineering and Computer Science*, 3(1), 33–39.

Chen, L., Chen, P., & Lin, Z. (2020). Artificial intelligence in education: A review. *IEEE Access : Practical Innovations, Open Solutions*, 8, 75264–75278.

Drachsler, H., & Greller, W. (2016). Privacy and analytics — It's a DELICATE issue. A Checklist for trusted learning analytics. Proceedings of the 6th International Conference on Learning Analytics and Knowledge (LAK '16), 25–29 April 2016, Edinburgh, UK (pp. 89–98). New York, NY: ACM. https://doi.org/10.1145/2883851.2883893

Elhussein, G., Hasselaar, E., Lutsyshyn, O., Milberg, T., & Zahidi, S. (2024, April). Shaping the future of learning: the role of AI in Education 4.0. World Economic Forum

Georgia State University, Office of Institutional Research. (2017). GPS Advising. https://success.gsu.edu/initiatives/gps-advising/

Holstein, K., McLaren, B. M., & Aleven, V. (2019). Co-designing a real-time classroom orchestration tool to support teacher–AI complementarity. *Journal of Learning Analytics*, 6(2), 27–52. DOI: 10.18608/jla.2019.62.3

Howard, S. K., Swist, T., Gasevic, D., Bartimote, K., Knight, S., Gulson, K., & Selwyn, N. (2022). Educational data journeys: Where are we going, what are we taking and making for AI? *Computers and Education: Artificial Intelligence*, (p. 3), 100073.

Huang, A. Y., Lu, O. H., Huang, J. C., Yin, C. J., & Yang, S. J. (2020). Predicting students' academic performance by using educational big data and learning analytics: Evaluation of classification methods and learning logs. *Interactive Learning Environments*, 28(2), 206–230.

Idowu, J. A., Koshiyama, A. S., & Treleaven, P. (2024). Investigating Algorithmic Bias in Student Progress Monitoring. *Computers and Education: Artificial Intelligence*, 100267. Kshetri, N. (2013). Privacy and security issues in cloud computing: The role of institutions and institutional evolution. *Telecommunications Policy*, 37(4-5), 372–386.

Kaswan, K. S., Dhatterwal, J. S., & Ojha, R. P. (2024). AI in personalized learning. In *Advances in Technological Innovations in Higher Education* (pp. 103–117). CRC Press.

Kentucky Department of Education. (2024). Artificial Intelligence Guidance Brief. www.education.ky.gov/districts/tech/Documents/AI%20Guidance%20Brief.pdf

Khan, S. (2023). The Ethical Imperative: Addressing Bias and Discrimination in AI-Driven Education. *Social Sciences Spectrum*, 2(1), 89–96.

Luckin, R., & Cukurova, M. (2019). Designing educational technologies in the age of AI: A learning sciences-driven approach. *British Journal of Educational Technology*, 50(6), 2824–2838.

Memarian, B., & Doleck, T. (2023). Fairness, Accountability, Transparency, and Ethics (FATE) in Artificial Intelligence (AI), and higher education: A systematic review. *Computers and Education: Artificial Intelligence*, 100152.

Montebello, M. (2021). Personalized Learning Environments. *International Symposium on Educational Technology (ISET)* (pp. 134-138).

National Institute for Student Success. (n.d.). *Elevating Student Success at a Scale*. https://niss.gsu.edu/

Nguyen, A., Ngo, H. N., Hong, Y., Dang, B., & Nguyen, B. P. T. (2023). Ethical principles for artificial intelligence in education. *Education and Information Technologies*, 28(4), 4221–4241.

Owan, V. J., Abang, K. B., Idika, D. O., Etta, E. O., & Bassey, B. A. (2023). Exploring the potential of artificial intelligence tools in educational measurement and assessment. *Eurasia Journal of Mathematics, Science and Technology Education*, 19(8), em2307.

Parycek, P., Schmid, V., & Novak, A. S. (2023). Artificial Intelligence (AI) and automation in administrative procedures: Potentials, limitations, and framework conditions. *Journal of the Knowledge Economy*, 1–26.

Pratama, M. P., Sampelolo, R., & Lura, H. (2023). Revolutionizing education: harnessing the power of artificial intelligence for personalized learning. *Klasikal: Journal of Education. Language Teaching and Science*, 5(2), 350–357.

Saaida, M. B. (2023). AI-Driven transformations in higher education: Opportunities and challenges. *International Journal of Educational Research and Studies*, 5(1), 29–36.

Schiff, D. (2022). Education for AI, not AI for education: The role of education and ethics in national AI policy strategies. *International Journal of Artificial Intelligence in Education*, 32(3), 527–563.

Ungerer, L., & Slade, S. (2022). Ethical considerations of artificial intelligence in learning analytics in distance education contexts. In *Learning analytics in open and distributed learning: Potential and challenges* (pp. 105–120). Springer Nature Singapore.

UNICEF. (n.d.). Accessible digital textbooks for learners with and without disabilities. https://www.unicef.org/reports/accessible-digital-textbooks-all

UNICEF. (2013). Accessible Digital Textbooks: Creating Digital Tools to Enable Inclusive Education, Jamaica. https://www.unicef.org/innocenti/media/2641/file/UNICEF-Accessible-Digital-Textbooks-Jamaica-2023.pdf

United Nations, Department of Economic and Social Affairs, Disability. (2006). *Conventions on the Rights of Persons with Disabilities (CRPD)*, Article 24. https://www.un.org/development/desa/disabilities/convention-on-the-rights-of-persons-%20%20%20with-%20%20disabilities/article-24-education.html#:~:text=States%20Parties%20shall%20ensure%20that%20persons%20with%20disabilities%20are%20able,an%20equal%20basis%20with%20others

United States Agency for International Development. (2023). Testing and Scaling an Artificial Intelligence-Based Functional Literacy Program. https://divportal.usaid.gov/s/project/a0g3d000000cbEmAAI/testing-and-scaling-an-artificial-intelligence-based-functional-literacy-program

U.S. Department of Education. (2021). *Family Educational Rights and Privacy Act (FERPA)*. https://www2.ed.gov/policy/gen/guid/fpco/ferpa/index.html

Willis, M., Duckworth, P., Coulter, A., Meyer, E. T., & Osborne, M. (2020). Qualitative and quantitative approach to assess the potential for automating administrative tasks in general practice. *BMJ Open*, 10(6), e032412.

Chapter 3
Advancing Education With AI-Driven Education for Diverse Learners:
Integrating AI Into Pedagogical Practices

Seema Yadav
https://orcid.org/0000-0002-8477-5895
Bhopal School of Social Sciences, India

ABSTRACT

This chapter explores the transformative potential of AI in education, focusing on its ability to personalize learning experiences and enhance teaching effectiveness. Key strategies include the implementation of adaptive learning platforms and the integration of AI into pedagogical practices to establish international standards and best practices. The chapter emphasizes the importance of fostering innovation through the creation of dedicated hubs and partnerships. Addressing bias mitigation through regular audits and the use of inclusive datasets, as well as ensuring equitable access to AI technologies, are highlighted as essential steps towards inclusivity. Continuous professional development for educators and the incorporation of AI literacy into student curricula are identified as critical for effective and ethical AI integration. The chapter concludes with the necessity of conducting regular impact studies and establishing feedback mechanisms to facilitate continuous evaluation and improvement, ensuring that AI-driven initiatives in education are both effective and equitable.

DOI: 10.4018/979-8-3693-6130-6.ch003

INTRODUCTION

The world has changed dramatically because of generative language models. We think that this new AI application has a lot of potential in clinical care and medical education, even in its current technological state (Wong et al., 2023). The potential for understanding learning and enhancing education through data is enormous. However, researchers in AI and machine learning won't just be able to fulfill fulfil their promise by creating novel models that can predict labelled data more precisely (Rosé et al., 2019). The field of artificial intelligence (AI) has advanced significantly in the last several years and has potential uses in many fields, including education. The basis for a child's future learning and development is laid throughout the crucial early childhood education (ECE) period (Mohammed, 2023). The application of artificial intelligence (AI) in educational settings could have an impact on instructors' use of formative assessment in the classroom in both positive and negative ways (Hopfenbeck et al., 2023). In this new AI-driven digital era, they contend that formative assessment can be used more successfully by reiterating the value of critical thinking and self-regulated learning (Hopfenbeck et al., 2023). A new age in teaching and learning methodologies is heralded by the incorporation of Artificial Intelligence (AI), which represents a dramatic shift in the educational landscape (Walter, 2024). Artificial intelligence (AI) technologies are being integrated into schooling as well as other aspects of human life daily. However, teachers' awareness, preparedness, and actual use of the whole AI toolkit in their professional activities determine how much of these tools are integrated into the educational process (Sysoyev, 2023). Integrating AI into pedagogical practices transforms education by leveraging technologies to personalize learning experiences and optimize teaching processes. AI enables personalized learning through adaptive platforms and tutoring systems that cater to individual student needs and learning styles. Data-driven insights from AI analytics enhance educators' ability to track student progress, identify areas of improvement, and personalize instruction effectively. AI also automates administrative tasks, freeing teachers to focus more on interactive and immersive learning experiences facilitated by technologies like VR, AR, and gamification. Continuous professional development ensures educators are adept at using AI tools ethically and effectively while addressing ethical considerations such as data privacy and algorithm fairness. Collaborative learning is fostered through AI-enabled peer interactions and group activities, enhancing engagement and collaboration among students. By integrating AI responsibly, education can become more adaptive, inclusive, and responsive to the needs of diverse learners in a rapidly evolving digital landscape.

OVERVIEW OF AI-DRIVEN PERSONALIZATION IN EDUCATION

AI-driven personalization in education is revolutionizing learning experiences by leveraging artificial intelligence to cater to individual student needs and preferences. Adaptive learning platforms use real-time data analysis to adjust the pace and difficulty of content, ensuring students learn at their own speed. Personalized learning paths are created based on performance data, interests, and goals, offering customized instruction aligned with specific learning requirements. AI-driven content recommendation systems suggest supplementary resources tailored to each student's progress. Virtual tutors and chatbots provide personalized assistance and feedback outside of traditional classroom hours, enhancing learning support. Additionally, AI analyses behavioural data to offer emotional and behavioural support, while predictive analytics identify at-risk students early for timely interventions. These technologies not only streamline administrative tasks but also foster collaborative learning and continuous improvement through data-driven insights. However, ethical considerations such as data privacy and algorithm transparency remain crucial as AI transforms educational practices globally. In regular educational discussions and exchanges, students' voices must be given due consideration. This mindset can be rooted in the well-known practice of asking students for feedback, but it can be expanded upon and reframed to view students as conversation partners rather than as customers or assessors (Cook-Sather & Matthews, 2023). There are often difficulties and disagreements when using AI in medicine, especially when using generative language models (Wong et al., 2023). The aspects that impact their attitudes towards artificial intelligence are examined, encompassing their acquaintance with the technology, educational convictions, cultural background, and access to training programs. The first results show that educators have a wide range of opinions about the use of AI in ECE settings. AI is seen by some educators as having great potential to improve early childhood development, offer individualized education, and enhance teaching and learning experiences. They acknowledge the potential advantages of AI in fostering young learners' cognitive, social, and emotional development (Mohammed, 2023). The effects of AI on human connection, children's privacy, and the responsibility of educators in promoting holistic development are among the concerns raised. and guided the development and application of AI technologies in a way that matched the requirements and goals of the Ghanaian ECE community by providing information on educators' views and concerns to politicians, educational institutions, and AI innovators (Mohammed, 2023). A comprehensive and effective learning experience that meets each student's individual needs may be provided by combining chatbots, AI technologies, and human education. Learners can construct a language-learning environment that is engaging and encouraging by combining human interaction with chatbot and AI functions. This will ultimately lead to learner success. This rigorous and fair methodology acknowledges the significant benefits of chatbots and AI, such as their ability to give a wealth of linguistic resources, customize learning paths to meet the needs of each user, and provide instant feedback (AbuSahyon et al., 2023). Adaptive content recommendation and customization through AI algorithms is a rapidly advancing field. Here are some key innovations and techniques in this area:

1. **Collaborative Filtering**

Collaborative Filtering is a popular technique in recommendation systems that leverages user feedback or interactions to predict preferences and make personalized recommendations. There are two main types:

1. *User-Based Collaborative Filtering:* This approach recommends items based on the preferences and behaviors of similar users. It identifies users with similar tastes and recommends items that similar users have liked or interacted with.
2. *Item-Based Collaborative Filtering:* Instead of focusing on users, this method recommends items that are similar to those that a user has liked or interacted with in the past. It identifies patterns in item preferences across users and suggests items that are most similar to the ones a user has shown interest in.

Collaborative Filtering does not require explicit knowledge about the items themselves but relies on user interactions or preferences. It's effective for discovering patterns and making recommendations in domains like e-commerce, streaming services, and social media platforms, where user preferences play a crucial role in content engagement and satisfaction.

2. **Content-Based Filtering**

Content-based filtering is a recommendation technique that suggests items to users based on the features or attributes of the items themselves. Unlike Collaborative Filtering, which relies on user interactions and preferences, Content-Based Filtering focuses on the characteristics of the items and the user's past interactions with similar items. Here's how it works:

1. *Profile Creation:* First, a user profile is created based on their preferences, interests, and past interactions with items. This profile is built using features extracted from the content of items, such as keywords, genres, or metadata.

2. *Similarity Calculation:* The system then identifies items that are similar to those the user has interacted with or liked in the past. Similarity is calculated based on how closely the features of other items match the features of items the user has shown interest in.
3. *Recommendation Generation:* Using the similarity scores, the system generates recommendations by suggesting items that have the highest similarity to those the user has already enjoyed.

Content-based filtering is particularly useful in domains where item attributes are informative and stable over time, such as recommending movies based on genres, books based on topics, or news articles based on content themes. It does not require a large user base or historical data on user interactions, making it suitable for scenarios with sparse or cold-start data. However, it may struggle with recommending items outside the user's established preferences unless combined with other techniques like Collaborative Filtering for a more comprehensive recommendation system.

3. **Hybrid Methods**

Hybrid Methods in recommendation systems combine different techniques, such as Collaborative Filtering, Content-Based Filtering, and sometimes other approaches like knowledge-based or demographic-based methods, to overcome the limitations of individual methods and provide more accurate and personalized recommendations. Here's how hybrid methods typically work and their advantages:

1. *Integration of Multiple Techniques:* Hybrid methods leverage the strengths of different recommendation approaches. For example, combining Collaborative Filtering with Content-Based Filtering allows the system to benefit from both user preferences and item attributes in generating recommendations.
2. *Improved Recommendation Accuracy:* By using multiple sources of information, hybrid methods can provide more accurate and diverse recommendations. They can mitigate the weaknesses of individual techniques, such as the cold-start problem in Collaborative Filtering or the inability of Content-Based Filtering to capture evolving user preferences.
3. *Flexibility and Adaptability:* Hybrid methods can be customized and adapted based on specific application requirements and the nature of the data available. They are versatile in handling different types of recommendation scenarios, from e-commerce and entertainment platforms to educational and content streaming services.

4. *Enhanced User Experience:* By offering more relevant and personalized recommendations, hybrid methods can enhance user satisfaction and engagement. They can cater to a broader range of user preferences and adapt to changes in user behavior over time.
5. *Challenges and Considerations:* Implementing hybrid methods requires careful integration and management of different algorithms and data sources. It also necessitates addressing scalability issues and ensuring that the combined recommendations are coherent and effective.

Overall, hybrid methods represent a sophisticated approach to recommendation systems, leveraging the complementary strengths of multiple techniques to deliver enhanced user experiences and maximize recommendation accuracy across various domains.

4. **Deep Learning**

Deep Learning is a subset of machine learning that involves training artificial neural networks with multiple layers (hence "deep") to learn hierarchical representations of data. Here are key aspects and applications of Deep Learning:

1. *Neural Networks:* Deep Learning uses neural networks with many layers (deep architectures) to process data. Each layer extracts increasingly abstract features from the input data, allowing the network to learn complex patterns.
2. *Training Process:* Training involves feeding large amounts of labeled data into the network. Through forward propagation and backpropagation algorithms, the network adjusts its weights to minimize prediction errors and improve accuracy.
3. *Applications:*
   - Image and Speech Recognition: Deep Learning powers advancements in image classification, object detection, and speech recognition tasks.
   - Natural Language Processing (NLP): Techniques like recurrent neural networks (RNNs) and transformers enable language modelling, sentiment analysis, and machine translation.
   - Healthcare: Deep Learning aids in medical image analysis, disease diagnosis, and personalized treatment planning.
   - Autonomous Vehicles: Enables perception tasks such as object detection and path planning.
   - Finance and Marketing: Used for fraud detection, market analysis, and personalized recommendation systems.

4. *Challenges:* Deep Learning requires large datasets and significant computational resources for training complex models. Overfitting, interpretability, and ethical considerations regarding bias and fairness are also critical challenges.
5. *Future Directions:* Ongoing research aims to improve the efficiency, interpretability, and generalization capabilities of deep neural networks. Innovations include transfer learning, reinforcement learning for sequential decision-making, and advancements in unsupervised learning techniques like generative adversarial networks (GANs).

Deep Learning continues to drive breakthroughs across various industries, pushing the boundaries of what is possible in artificial intelligence by leveraging its ability to automatically learn intricate patterns and representations from data.

5. Natural Language Processing (NLP)

Natural Language Processing (NLP) is a branch of artificial intelligence that focuses on enabling computers to understand, interpret, and generate human language in a way that is both meaningful and contextually relevant. Here are key aspects and applications of NLP:

1. *Language Understanding:*
    - o Text Classification: Assigning categories or labels to text based on its content (e.g., sentiment analysis, spam detection).
    - o Named Entity Recognition (NER): Identifying and classifying named entities such as names of people, organizations, locations, etc., in text.
    - o Syntax and Parsing: Analysing the grammatical structure of sentences to understand relationships between words.
2. *Language Generation:*
    - o Text Generation: Creating coherent and contextually relevant text, such as in chatbots, automatic summarization, and content generation.
    - o Machine Translation: Translating text from one language to another, leveraging techniques like neural machine translation (NMT).
3. *Applications:*
    - o Virtual Assistants: NLP powers voice assistants like Siri, Alexa, and Google Assistant, enabling natural language interaction and task completion.
    - o Information Retrieval: Facilitating search engines to deliver relevant results based on user queries.
    - o Sentiment Analysis: Analysing opinions and sentiments expressed in text, useful for social media monitoring and customer feedback analysis.

- o Question Answering Systems: Building systems that can understand and respond to questions posed in natural language, such as in FAQ bots or search engines.

4. *Techniques and Models:*
   - o Statistical Methods: Initially, NLP relied heavily on statistical approaches like n-grams and probabilistic models.
   - o Deep Learning: Recent advancements in deep learning, particularly with recurrent neural networks (RNNs), transformers, and pre-trained language models like BERT and GPT, have significantly improved NLP tasks.
5. *Challenges and Future Directions:*
   - o Ambiguity and Context: Handling ambiguity and understanding context in language remains a challenge.
   - o Ethical Considerations: Addressing biases in language models and ensuring fairness in NLP applications.
   - o Multilingual and Cross-Lingual Understanding: Improving NLP systems to handle multiple languages and dialects effectively.
   - o Continual Learning: Developing systems that can adapt and learn from new data over time, enhancing performance and relevance.

NLP continues to evolve rapidly, driven by advancements in machine learning and computational linguistics, and it holds immense potential for transforming how humans interact with technology through natural language interfaces and intelligent systems.

6. *Personalization Algorithms*
   - User Segmentation: Divides users into segments to provide more targeted recommendations.
   - Dynamic Personalization: Adapts to changing user preferences in real-time.
7. *Explainable AI (XAI)*
   - Transparency: Provides users with understandable explanations for recommendations.
   - Trust Building: Enhances user trust and engagement by clarifying why certain items are suggested.

RELATIONSHIP BETWEEN PERSONALIZED LEARNING AND STUDENT-CENTERED PEDAGOGIES

Personalized learning and student-cantered pedagogies share a fundamental focus on tailoring educational experiences to the individual needs, preferences, and strengths of students. (Lewis & Stoyanovich, 2022) examined the pedagogical ramifications of responsible data science, drawing clear connections between state-of-the-art research in data science and cutting-edge scholarship in education. They look at how artificial intelligence (AI) is changing education and emphasize the need for improved critical thinking abilities, AI literacy, and quick engineering expertise. AI in education represents a dramatic shift from traditional teaching approaches by providing personalized learning and support for a wide range of educational needs, including special needs pupils. Notwithstanding, the integration poses certain obstacles, such as the requirement for extensive training for educators and modifications to the curriculum to conform to societal frameworks. It is determined that AI literacy is essential, including knowledge of AI technology and its wider social implications (Walter, 2024).

While they are closely related, they emphasize slightly different aspects of the learning process:

1. **Customization of Learning Experience:** Personalized learning employs technology and data analytics to customize the pace, content, and style of learning for each student. It adapts to the learner's proficiency level and learning preferences, ensuring that instruction meets individual needs effectively. In contrast, student-cantered pedagogies prioritize student agency and autonomy in the learning process, encouraging learners to take ownership of their learning goals, methods, and outcomes.
2. **Emphasis on Student Engagement:** Both approaches emphasize the importance of engaging students actively in their learning. Personalized learning achieves this through adaptive technologies that maintain student interest by matching content to their abilities and interests. Student-centered pedagogies achieve engagement by empowering students to make decisions about what and how they learn, fostering intrinsic motivation and curiosity.
3. **Role of the Educator:** In personalized learning, educators act as facilitators who guide students through personalized learning paths and leverage data to inform instructional decisions. They monitor student progress closely and intervene when necessary to provide support or adjust learning strategies. In student-centered pedagogies, educators act as mentors or coaches who support students in setting goals, exploring topics of interest, and reflecting on their learning experiences. They prioritize building relationships and creating a supportive

learning environment where students feel empowered to take risks and explore ideas.

4. **Learning Outcomes:** Both approaches aim to improve learning outcomes by catering to individual student needs and fostering deeper understanding and mastery of concepts. Personalized learning focuses on using data to optimize learning efficiency and effectiveness, while student-cantered pedagogies prioritize holistic development, critical thinking, and lifelong learning skills.

In practice, personalized learning often incorporates elements of student-cantered pedagogies, such as collaborative learning, project-based learning, and inquiry-based approaches, to enhance the overall educational experience. Together, they represent a shift towards more learner-centric educational practices that recognize and respect the unique abilities and potential of each student.

TECHNOLOGICAL INNOVATIONS: AI ALGORITHMS FOR ADAPTIVE CONTENT RECOMMENDATION AND CUSTOMIZATION

AI algorithms for adaptive content recommendation and customization are revolutionizing education by personalizing learning experiences and optimizing teaching outcomes. These innovations include adaptive learning platforms that create customized learning paths and dynamically adjust content based on real-time assessments, and intelligent tutoring systems (ITS) that provide personalized feedback and adaptive questioning. AI-driven content recommendation engines suggest tailored supplementary materials and adapt to different learning styles, while natural language processing (NLP) automates summarization and translation. Predictive analytics enable early intervention and performance forecasting, and gamification maintains student engagement through adaptive games and interactive simulations. Collaborative learning tools use AI to form effective study groups and moderate discussions, while personalized professional development resources and lesson planning support enhance educator effectiveness. Ensuring ethical use, AI systems detect and mitigate biases, and robust data privacy measures protect student information, leading to better educational experiences and success for students. Generative AI can be a very useful teaching tool or virtual tutor, offering flexible, real-time examples of the creative process. Higher education instructors may also use generative AI to develop highly customized and interesting teaching materials that have the potential to improve the teaching and learning process (Creely & Blannin, 2023). AI algorithms for adaptive content recommendation and customization are transforming education and teaching by personalizing learning experiences, improving engagement, and optimizing educational outcomes. It is critical to recognize that human educators are essential for giving emotional support, cultural context, and advanced language instruction. There is little question that the cooperation of chatbots, AI, and human teachers can successfully achieve language-learning goals, enabling students to successfully acquire language skills and thrive in an international setting. By combining chatbots, artificial intelligence (AI), and human teachers, English language learning can be improved to include a more thorough and balanced method. With the ability to offer personalized learning approaches and timely feedback, chatbots and AI can help students progress according to their own skill levels (AbuSahyon et al., 2023). It is crucial to recognize the indispensable role that human educators play in language education. They provide priceless insights, emotional support, cultural awareness, contextual understanding, and the ability to customize instruction to meet the unique needs of students. In a modern world where social media and connectivity are the norm, the combination of chatbots, artificial intelligence, and human teachers could elevate English language instruction to a new level (AbuSahyon et al., 2023).

The use of AI writing tools like ChatGPT and Claude 2.0 has signaled a significant shift in pedagogical practices in the quickly changing field of English composition education. These tools have demonstrated the nuanced integration of AI in iterative and recursive tasks like developing ideas at the paragraph level and refining arguments. This highlights the need for updated instructional strategies that combine traditional writing techniques with advice on the appropriate and moral use of AI tools (Hutson et al., 2024). It also points to a trend towards a hybrid model of writing instruction, where traditional methods are supplemented by the strategic use of emerging technologies. provide insightful information to educators and organizations trying to create a well-rounded and successful hybrid writing education strategy that meets the demands of modern English composition classes without sacrificing academic integrity (Hutson et al., 2024).

Here are some key innovations and their applications:

1. **Adaptive Learning Platforms**
    - Personalized Learning Paths: AI algorithms analyse student performance, learning styles, and preferences to create customized learning paths, ensuring that each student progresses at their own pace.
    - Dynamic Content Delivery: Content is dynamically adjusted based on real-time assessments, providing students with materials that are neither too easy nor too challenging.
2. **Intelligent Tutoring Systems (ITS)**

- Personalized Feedback: ITS provide immediate, personalized feedback and hints to students, helping them understand concepts and correct mistakes.
- Adaptive Questioning: These systems can adjust the difficulty and type of questions based on the student's performance, promoting mastery of subjects.

3. **Content Recommendation Engines**
   - Customized Resource Suggestions: AI-driven recommendation systems suggest supplementary materials, such as videos, articles, and exercises, tailored to individual student needs and interests.
   - Learning Style Adaptation: Recommendations consider different learning styles (visual, auditory, kinesthetic) to provide the most effective resources for each student.
4. **Natural Language Processing (NLP)**
   - Automated Summarization: NLP algorithms can summarize lengthy texts, making it easier for students to grasp key points and essential information.
   - Language Translation: AI provides real-time translation and language support, helping non-native speakers access educational content in their preferred language.
5. **Predictive Analytics**
   - Early Intervention: Predictive models analyse data to identify students at risk of falling behind, enabling timely interventions by educators.
   - Performance Forecasting: AI predicts future performance based on historical data, helping educators tailor their teaching strategies to meet student needs.
6. **Gamification and Engagement**
   - Adaptive Games: Educational games use AI to adjust difficulty levels and challenges based on student performance, maintaining engagement and motivation.
   - Interactive Simulations: AI-powered simulations provide interactive and immersive learning experiences, adapting scenarios in real-time to match student inputs.
7. **Collaborative Learning Tools**
   - Group Formation: AI algorithms can form study groups based on complementary skills and knowledge levels, fostering collaborative learning.
   - Discussion Moderation: AI moderates online discussions, highlighting key points and ensuring productive and respectful interactions.
8. **Professional Development for Educators**

- Personalized Training: AI recommends professional development resources and courses tailored to individual educators' needs and teaching styles.
- Lesson Planning Support: AI tools assist in creating and customizing lesson plans, integrating adaptive content that aligns with curriculum standards and student needs.

9. **Ethical and Bias Considerations**
    - Bias Detection: AI systems are designed to detect and mitigate biases in content recommendations, ensuring fair and equitable treatment of all students.
    - Privacy Protection: Implementing robust data privacy measures to protect student information and maintain trust.

The integration of AI algorithms for adaptive content recommendation and customization in education enhances personalized learning, improves engagement, and optimizes teaching outcomes. By leveraging advanced technologies, educators can provide more effective, individualized instruction, ultimately leading to better educational experiences and success for students.

STRATEGIES FOR INTEGRATING AI-DRIVEN PERSONALIZATION INTO PEDAGOGICAL PRACTICES

Integrating AI-driven personalization into pedagogical practices involves utilizing adaptive learning platforms, learning analytics, intelligent tutoring systems, and content recommendation systems to tailor educational experiences to individual students. Techniques like NLP for automated assessment, gamification, VR/AR for immersive learning, and AI-powered collaborative tools enhance engagement and interactivity. Teachers benefit from AI-assisted planning and professional development while ensuring ethical use by protecting student data and mitigating biases. Implementation steps include assessing needs, selecting appropriate tools, providing training, integrating and testing tools, and continuously improving based on feedback. This approach aims to create effective, engaging, and individualized learning experiences. Artificial intelligence (AI) education necessitates an engagement with representational politics that enables users to grasp knowledge politically in order to be employed in ways that align with principles for justice and democracy. In order to effectively use AI education, it is necessary to reject the quasi-scientific mode of description that hides the values, politics, interests, and ideologies guiding the framing of data and the use of the technology, as well as to be explicit about the ethical and political norms guiding its use and purpose. Technology can be used to support social interpretation in democratic education initiatives, which allows for collective agency to address societal issues, oppose repressive power structures, and promote democratic social interactions (Saltman, 2020). Integrating AI-driven personalization into pedagogical practices involves leveraging technology to tailor learning experiences to individual students' needs, preferences, and progress. Here are some key strategies:

1. **Adaptive Learning Platforms**
    - Personalized Content Delivery: Utilize AI to adjust the difficulty and type of content based on each student's learning pace and understanding.
    - Real-Time Feedback: Provide instant feedback on assignments and quizzes to help students understand mistakes and learn effectively.
2. **Learning Analytics**
    - Data-Driven Insights: Analyse student performance data to identify strengths, weaknesses, and learning patterns.
    - Predictive Analytics: Use AI to predict student outcomes and intervene early to support at-risk students.
3. **Intelligent Tutoring Systems**
    - Personalized Tutoring: Implement AI-driven tutors that adapt to each student's learning style and provide customized instruction and support.
    - Interactive Learning: Use AI to create engaging and interactive learning experiences that adjust based on student responses.
4. **Content Recommendation Systems**
    - Resource Suggestions: Recommend additional learning materials, such as videos, articles, and exercises, tailored to students' interests and needs.
    - Customized Learning Paths: Develop personalized learning pathways that guide students through the curriculum based on their progress and goals.
5. **Natural Language Processing (NLP)**
    - Automated Assessment: Use NLP to grade essays and provide feedback on writing assignments, focusing on content, grammar, and style.
    - Language Learning: Implement AI tools for language learning that offer real-time pronunciation, grammar corrections, and vocabulary building.
6. **Gamification and Engagement**
    - Adaptive Gamification: Integrate gamified elements that adapt to student performance, ensuring challenges remain appropriate and engaging.
    - Motivational AI: Use AI to provide personalized motivational messages and rewards to keep students engaged and motivated.
7. **Virtual and Augmented Reality (VR/AR)**

- Immersive Learning: Create immersive VR/AR experiences that adapt to individual learning needs, offering hands-on practice and exploration.
- Simulated Environments: Use AI-driven simulations to provide real-world problem-solving scenarios that adjust based on student input.

8. **Collaborative Learning Tools**
   - AI-Powered Collaboration: Facilitate group projects and discussions by using AI to form balanced teams and suggest relevant discussion topics.
   - Peer Learning: Encourage peer feedback and collaboration through AI tools that match students based on their learning needs and expertise.
9. **Teacher Support Tools**
   - AI-Assisted Planning: Help teachers create personalized lesson plans and adapt their teaching strategies based on student data.
   - Professional Development: Use AI to recommend professional development resources tailored to teachers' strengths and areas for improvement.
10. **Ethical and Responsible Use**
    - Privacy Protection: Ensure student data privacy and security when implementing AI tools.
    - Bias Mitigation: Continuously monitor and address biases in AI algorithms to promote fairness and equity in education.

Implementation Steps for AI-Driven Pedagogies

1. **Assessment of Needs:** Identify the specific needs and goals of students and educators.
2. **Selection of Tools:** Choose AI tools and platforms that align with educational objectives.
3. **Training and Support:** Provide training for teachers and students on how to use AI tools effectively.
4. **Integration and Testing:** Integrate AI tools into the existing educational framework and conduct pilot tests to gather feedback.
5. **Continuous Improvement:** Regularly evaluate the impact of AI tools and make necessary adjustments based on feedback and performance data.

By strategically integrating AI-driven personalization, educators can create more engaging, effective, and individualized learning experiences that cater to the diverse needs of their students.

PROFESSIONAL DEVELOPMENT FOR EDUCATORS TO SUPPORT PERSONALIZED LEARNING INITIATIVES

Professional development for educators to support personalized learning initiatives involves comprehensive training on personalized learning concepts, AI-driven tools, and educational technologies. Key strategies include hands-on workshops, ongoing mentorship and coaching, collaborative learning communities, and data literacy training. Educators learn to design personalized curricula, implement differentiated instruction, and use technology effectively in blended learning environments. Emphasis is also placed on student engagement, ethical practices, and continuous professional development through regular updates and feedback. This approach ensures that teachers are well-equipped to create inclusive, effective, and engaging personalized learning experiences for their students. As with any AI program, ChatGPT's effectiveness is largely dependent on the caliber of the training set. Generative language models are still in need of refinement because they can produce false or nonexistent information (Wong et al., 2023).

Professional development for educators is crucial to effectively support personalized learning initiatives. Here are key strategies and components for such professional development:

1. **Foundational Training**
    - Understanding Personalized Learning: Provide educators with a solid understanding of personalized learning concepts, benefits, and strategies.
    - Introduction to AI and EdTech Tools: Familiarize teachers with AI-driven tools and technologies that support personalized learning.
2. **Practical Workshops**
    - Hands-On Training: Offer workshops where educators can practice using personalized learning tools and technologies in a controlled environment.
    - Scenario-Based Learning: Use real-life classroom scenarios to help teachers apply personalized learning strategies effectively.
3. **Ongoing Support and Coaching**
    - Mentorship Programs: Pair teachers with mentors who have experience in personalized learning to provide guidance and support.
    - Instructional Coaches: Utilize instructional coaches to offer continuous, on-the-job support as teachers implement personalized learning.
4. **Collaborative Learning Communities**

- Professional Learning Communities (PLCs): Create PLCs where educators can share experiences, challenges, and best practices related to personalized learning.
- Peer Collaboration: Encourage peer observation and feedback sessions to foster a collaborative learning environment.

5. **Data Literacy**
    - Understanding Data: Train teachers to analyse and interpret student data to inform personalized learning strategies.
    - Using Analytics Tools: Provide training on using learning analytics tools to track student progress and adjust instruction accordingly.
6. **Technology Integration**
    - EdTech Tools Training: Offer comprehensive training on various educational technology tools that support personalized learning.
    - Blended Learning Models: Teach educators how to effectively integrate technology into blended learning environments.
7. **Curriculum Design and Differentiation**
    - Personalized Curriculum Development: Guide teachers in designing and adapting curriculum to meet individual student needs.
    - Differentiated Instruction: Train educators on techniques for differentiating instruction based on students' varying abilities and learning styles.
8. **Student Engagement Strategies**
    - Motivational Techniques: Teach strategies to keep students motivated and engaged in a personalized learning environment.
    - Interactive and Gamified Learning: Provide tools and methods for incorporating interactive and gamified elements into lessons.
9. **Ethics and Equity**
    - Bias Mitigation: Educate teachers on recognizing and addressing biases in personalized learning tools and strategies.
    - Inclusive Practices: Ensure professional development includes training on creating inclusive learning environments that cater to all students.
10. **Continuous Professional Development**
    - Regular Updates and Refreshers: Offer periodic training sessions to keep educators updated on the latest personalized learning strategies and technologies.
    - Professional Development Credits: Provide opportunities for teachers to earn credits or certifications through personalized learning professional development programs.

Implementation Steps for Professional Development of Teachers

1. **Needs Assessment:** Conduct a thorough assessment to identify the specific professional development needs of educators in the context of personalized learning.
2. **Program Design:** Develop a comprehensive professional development program tailored to the identified needs, including both foundational and advanced training components.
3. **Pilot Programs:** Implement pilot professional development programs to test and refine the training approach before a full-scale rollout.
4. **Feedback and Evaluation:** Collect feedback from participants to continuously improve the professional development offerings.
5. **Scalability and Sustainability:** Plan for scaling the professional development program across the institution and ensuring its long-term sustainability.

By providing comprehensive and ongoing professional development, educators can be better equipped to implement personalized learning initiatives, ultimately leading to improved student outcomes and engagement.

OPPORTUNITIES FOR FURTHER RESEARCH AND INNOVATION IN AI-DRIVEN PERSONALIZATION

Further research and innovation in AI-driven personalization in education can significantly enhance learning experiences. Key areas include developing advanced algorithms, integrating multi-modal data for real-time analytics, and creating highly personalized learning pathways and adaptive assessments. Research into ethics and fairness is essential to mitigate biases and protect privacy. Engaging students through advanced gamification and emotional AI, facilitating AI-enhanced peer learning, and adapting to diverse cultural contexts are also critical. Supporting teachers with AI-driven professional development tools, ensuring scalable solutions, and studying long-term impacts are crucial for the successful implementation and sustainability of personalized learning initiatives. Personalised learning, interaction, data-driven decision-making, more resource accessibility, and enhanced efficiency are among the advantages of integrating AI in ECE settings that are thought to be beneficial. By boosting learning outcomes, fostering personalized and dynamic learning settings, and elevating young children's overall educational experiences, these advantages have the potential to revolutionize early childhood education (Mohammed, 2023). AI tools are just now beginning to be incorporated into teaching. Teaching, learning, and organisational potential of AI tools is generally not well understood by university faculty. In order to paint a whole picture of the potential applications of AI in education, many educators are limited by their segmented expertise, which is primarily tied to their work as teachers of particular disciplines. In addition, the majority of academics at universities claim to be impartial or open to incorporating AI technologies into their lesson plans. Only a few instances of employing particular technologies to teach particular disciplinary components have been observed when AI tools have been used in the pedagogical process (Sysoyev, 2023). The quick development of generative artificial intelligence (AI) may open up new avenues for creative expression in higher education. Although technologies have always played a big role in creative output, including student assignments, it can be argued that generative AI is elevating this support by producing original and meaningful content. Given this, educators and decision-makers in higher education must reconsider generative AI from a fresh angle in order to improve student learning and assessment (Creely & Blannin, 2023). Numerous advantages come with AI-driven technologies and chatbots, including personalized feedback, flexible learning paths, and real-world language exchanges. They also encourage learners' motivation, involvement, and self-directed learning. However difficulties with these tools' conception, application, and evaluation also surface (AbuSahyon et al., 2023).

AI-driven personalization in education offers numerous opportunities for further research and innovation. Here are some key areas to explore:

1. **Advanced Algorithms and Models**
    - Deep Learning: Develop more sophisticated deep learning models to better understand and predict student behavior and learning needs.
    - Reinforcement Learning: Explore reinforcement learning techniques for more dynamic and adaptive personalized learning experiences.
2. **Multi-Modal Learning Analytics**
    - Data Integration: Research methods to integrate various data sources (e.g., text, video, audio, and sensor data) for a comprehensive understanding of student learning.
    - Real-Time Analytics: Innovate real-time analytics systems that provide immediate feedback and insights to educators and learners.
3. **Personalized Learning Pathways**
    - Customized Curricula: Investigate algorithms for creating highly personalized learning pathways tailored to individual student goals, strengths, and weaknesses.
    - Adaptive Assessments: Develop adaptive assessment tools that adjust in real-time to accurately measure student progress and understanding.
4. **Ethics and Fairness**

- Bias Mitigation: Research methods to detect and mitigate biases in AI algorithms to ensure fairness and equity in personalized learning.
- Privacy Protection: Innovate privacy-preserving techniques that protect student data while enabling effective personalization.

5. **Engagement and Motivation**
    - Gamification: Explore advanced gamification strategies that use AI to adapt games to individual learning styles and preferences.
    - Emotional AI: Develop AI systems that can recognize and respond to students' emotional states to keep them engaged and motivated.
6. **Collaboration and Social Learning**
    - AI-Enhanced Peer Learning: Research AI tools that facilitate effective peer-to-peer learning and collaboration.
    - Group Dynamics: Study AI's role in understanding and optimizing group dynamics in collaborative learning environments.
7. **Cross-Cultural Personalization**
    - Cultural Adaptation: Investigate how AI can personalize learning content and strategies to fit diverse cultural contexts and backgrounds.
    - Language Support: Develop AI tools that provide multilingual support to enhance accessibility for non-native speakers.
8. **Teacher Support and Professional Development**
    - AI for Teacher Training: Research AI-driven tools that support ongoing professional development and personalized training for educators.
    - Instructional Design: Innovate AI systems that assist teachers in designing and delivering personalized instruction effectively.
9. **Scalability and Implementation**
    - Scalable Solutions: Develop scalable AI-driven personalization solutions that can be implemented in diverse educational settings, from small classrooms to large institutions.
    - Implementation Strategies: Study effective strategies for integrating AI personalization tools into existing educational systems and practices.
10. **Longitudinal Studies**
    - Impact Assessment: Conduct longitudinal studies to assess the long-term impact of AI-driven personalization on student outcomes.
    - Best Practices: Identify and disseminate best practices for implementing and sustaining AI-driven personalization initiatives.

Further research and innovation in AI-driven personalization have the potential to significantly enhance educational experiences by making them more adaptive, inclusive, and effective. By addressing challenges such as bias, privacy, and scalability, and by exploring new technologies and methodologies, researchers and practitioners can develop powerful tools to support personalized learning for all students.

POLICY RECOMMENDATIONS FOR PROMOTING RESPONSIBLE USE OF AI IN EDUCATION

Promoting the responsible use of AI in education requires policies that prioritize ethics, transparency, fairness, and effectiveness. Key recommendations include establishing clear ethical guidelines, enforcing robust data privacy and security measures, and conducting regular bias audits to ensure fairness. Equitable access to AI technologies and continuous professional development for educators is essential, along with integrating AI literacy into the student curriculum. Continuous evaluation and stakeholder involvement in policy-making processes are crucial, as are regulatory frameworks and standards for AI tools. Funding research and fostering innovation through partnerships can drive ethical AI development, while global collaboration can establish international standards and promote knowledge sharing. These measures can ensure AI enhances learning experiences while safeguarding ethical standards and equity. Therefore, when using ChatGPT, physicians and medical students must always verify the information with reliable and evidence-based sources such as practice guidelines, peer-reviewed literature, and trusted medical databases (Wong et al., 2023). Promoting the responsible use of AI in education requires thoughtful policy recommendations that prioritize ethics, transparency, fairness, and effectiveness. Here are key policy recommendations:

1. **Establish Clear Ethical Guidelines**

Establishing clear ethical guidelines for AI use in education is crucial to ensure that these technologies are implemented responsibly and effectively. Developing and implementing ethical frameworks specifically tailored to AI in education can provide a foundation for responsible practices. These guidelines should address key issues such as fairness, accountability, and data privacy, ensuring that AI applications do not perpetuate biases or infringe on student rights. Ethical frameworks can help educators and developers navigate the complexities of AI integration, promoting practices that prioritize student welfare and educational integrity. Transparency is a fundamental component of these ethical guidelines. Mandating transparency in AI algorithms and decision-making processes allows stakeholders, including educators, students, parents, and policymakers, to understand how AI systems operate and make decisions. This openness can help build trust in AI technologies, as stakeholders can see that these systems are designed and implemented with their best interests in mind. Transparency also enables stakeholders to identify and address potential issues, such as biases or errors in AI algorithms, fostering a culture of continuous improvement and accountability. By establishing clear ethical guidelines and ensuring transparency, educational institutions can create an environment where AI technologies are used responsibly, enhancing learning outcomes while protecting student rights and promoting fairness.

2. **Data Privacy and Security**

Ensuring data privacy and security is paramount when integrating AI into educational practices. Robust data protection laws must be enforced to safeguard student information and prevent misuse. These laws should mandate stringent security measures, such as encryption, secure storage, and access controls, to protect sensitive data from breaches and unauthorized access. Educational institutions and AI developers must comply with these regulations to maintain the confidentiality and integrity of student data. In addition to legal protections, it is crucial to empower students and parents with control over their data. Clear and comprehensive consent protocols should be established for data collection and use, ensuring that individuals are fully informed about what data is being collected, how it will be used, and who will have access to it. Consent should be obtained in a transparent and straightforward manner, allowing students and parents to make informed decisions about their data. Furthermore, mechanisms should be in place for students and parents to easily access, review, and manage their data, including options to opt out of data collection or request data deletion. By enforcing strict data protection laws and ensuring consent and control over data, educational institutions can create a secure and trustworthy environment for AI integration. This approach not only protects student privacy but also fosters confidence among students, parents, and educators in the use of AI technologies in education.

3. **Bias Mitigation and Fairness**

Bias mitigation and fairness are critical components of integrating AI into educational practices, ensuring that all students receive equitable treatment. Regular bias audits should be mandated for AI systems used in education to identify and address any biases that may exist. These audits should systematically evaluate the AI algorithms and their outcomes to detect any patterns of unfair treatment or discrimination. By regularly conducting these audits, educational institutions can take proactive measures to rectify biases, ensuring that AI systems promote fairness and inclusivity. Using inclusive datasets is another essential strategy to reduce the risk of bias in AI models. AI systems should be trained on diverse and representative datasets that reflect the varied backgrounds, experiences, and characteristics of the student population. This diversity helps ensure that the AI models do not favor any particular group and can generalize well across different demographics. Promoting the use of such datasets requires collaboration between educational institutions, AI developers, and policymakers to gather and curate data that accurately represents the diversity within the student body. By requiring regular bias audits and promoting the use of inclusive datasets, educational institutions can enhance the fairness and reliability of AI systems in education. These measures help to build AI tools that are more equitable and capable of supporting all students effectively, thereby fostering a more inclusive and just educational environment.

4. **Equitable Access**

Equitable access to AI-driven personalized learning is crucial to ensure that all students, regardless of their background or socioeconomic status, have the opportunity to benefit from these technologies. Educational institutions must prioritize providing access to the necessary technology and resources for every student to participate fully in AI-driven educational initiatives. This includes ensuring that students have access to devices such as computers, tablets, or smartphones, as well as reliable internet connectivity, which are essential for engaging with AI-powered learning platforms and tools effectively. To address disparities in access to AI technologies, especially in underserved communities, policies should be implemented that specifically target these disparities. This may involve initiatives such as providing financial support or subsidies for technology purchases, partnering with community organizations to distribute devices, or establishing technology centres in schools or community centers. Educational institutions should also collaborate with government agencies, non-profit organizations, and private sector partners to develop comprehensive strategies that address the unique challenges faced by underserved communities in accessing AI technologies. By ensuring equitable access to technology and supporting underserved communities, educational institutions can create a more inclusive learning environment where all students have the opportunity to benefit from AI-driven personalized learning experiences. These efforts not only promote educational equity but also contribute to narrowing the digital divide and preparing students for success in a technology-driven world.

5. **Teacher and Student Training**

To effectively integrate AI into education, comprehensive training programs are essential for both educators and students. Professional development opportunities should be continuously offered to teachers, focusing on the ethical and effective implementation of AI in teaching practices. This includes training on how to integrate AI tools into lesson planning, personalize learning experiences, and leverage AI for assessment and feedback. Educators should also receive guidance on privacy protection, data security, and addressing biases in AI systems to ensure responsible use. Simultaneously, integrating AI literacy into the curriculum is crucial to equip students with essential knowledge about AI technologies and their societal implications. AI literacy education should cover fundamental concepts such as machine learning algorithms, data ethics, and the impact of AI on various industries and everyday life. Students should engage in activities that promote critical thinking, ethical decision-making, and hands-on experience with AI applications. By understanding AI, students can better navigate its benefits and challenges, preparing them for future academic and career pathways in a technology-driven world. Overall, providing continuous professional development for educators and integrating AI literacy into the curriculum for students ensures that both groups are equipped with the skills and knowledge needed to responsibly harness the potential of AI in education. These efforts not only enhance teaching effectiveness and student engagement but also promote ethical awareness and readiness for the evolving digital landscape.

6. **Continuous Evaluation and Improvement**

Continuous evaluation and improvement are essential to harness the benefits of AI in education while addressing challenges and ensuring effectiveness. Conducting regular impact studies is crucial to assess how AI technologies influence educational outcomes. These studies should analyse metrics such as student performance, engagement levels, and teacher satisfaction to understand the effects of AI integration. Data-driven insights from these studies can inform policy adjustments and strategic decisions, ensuring that AI initiatives align with educational goals and benefit all stakeholders. Establishing feedback mechanisms is equally important to gather input from students, teachers, and parents regarding AI tools used in educational settings. These mechanisms should be designed to encourage open communication and provide a platform for stakeholders to voice concerns, provide suggestions for improvement, and report issues related to AI technologies. Feedback can be collected through surveys, focus groups, or dedicated channels where stakeholders can share their experiences and perspectives. This continuous feedback loop enables educational institutions to address challenges promptly, refine AI implementations, and enhance user satisfaction. By conducting impact studies and establishing robust feedback mechanisms, educational institutions can continuously evaluate the effectiveness of AI initiatives and make informed decisions to improve educational practices. These efforts support evidence-based policymaking, promote transparency and accountability, and ultimately contribute to maximizing the benefits of AI in enhancing teaching and learning experiences.

7. **Stakeholder Involvement**

Involving a diverse range of stakeholders in the policy-making process is essential for developing effective and inclusive AI-related educational policies. Inclusive policy-making should engage educators, students, parents, and AI experts, ensuring that the perspectives and needs of all parties impacted by AI in education are considered. Educators can provide insights into practical classroom applications and potential challenges, while students and parents can share their experiences and expectations regarding AI technologies in learning environments. AI experts can contribute their technical knowledge, ensuring that policies are grounded in current scientific and technological understanding. This collaborative approach helps create policies that are comprehensive, balanced, and tailored to the real-world contexts in which they will be implemented. Public consultations further enhance the policy-making process by gathering broader input and building consensus on AI-related educational policies. These consultations can take the form of public forums, surveys, and community meetings, allowing stakeholders from various backgrounds to voice their opinions, concerns, and suggestions. Engaging the public fosters transparency and trust, as stakeholders see that their views are valued and considered in decision-making processes. Additionally, public consultations can reveal potential issues and areas of concern that policymakers might not have initially identified, leading to more robust and effective policies. By integrating stakeholder involvement through inclusive policy-making and public consultations, educational institutions can develop AI policies that are well-informed, widely supported, and capable of enhancing the educational experience for all students.

8. **Regulation and Standards**

Establishing regulation and standards for AI in education is critical to ensure that these technologies are developed, deployed, and used in ways that are safe, ethical, and effective. Developing comprehensive regulatory frameworks involves creating guidelines and policies that govern every aspect of AI integration in educational settings. These frameworks should address data privacy, security, and ethical considerations, ensuring that AI applications do not compromise student information or perpetuate biases. Additionally, they should provide clear protocols for the development and implementation of AI tools, emphasizing transparency and accountability from developers and institutions. Creating standards and certification processes for AI tools is equally important to maintain high quality and ethical standards across the board. Standards should outline the technical and ethical benchmarks that AI tools must meet before they can be used in educational environments. Certification processes can validate that AI applications comply with these standards, providing educators and administrators with a reliable means to assess the suitability and safety of AI tools. This ensures that only vetted, high-quality AI technologies are integrated into educational systems, protecting students and enhancing learning outcomes. By establishing rigorous regulatory frameworks and certification processes, stakeholders can foster trust in AI applications and support their responsible and beneficial use in education.

9. **Promote Research and Innovation**

Promoting research and innovation in AI for education requires strategic investment and collaboration to drive ethical, effective, and equitable advancements. Allocating funding for research is essential to explore the vast potential of AI in educational contexts, ensuring that the applications developed are not only innovative but also align with ethical standards and promote fairness. By prioritizing research funding, governments and organizations can support studies that delve into the implications of AI on learning, teaching methodologies, and educational outcomes, while addressing issues such as bias, data privacy, and access disparities. Furthermore, establishing innovation hubs and fostering partnerships between educational institutions and tech companies can catalyze responsible AI development. These hubs serve as collaborative spaces where researchers, educators, and technologists can work together to create and test new AI tools and solutions, sharing insights and expertise. Partnerships with tech companies can provide educational institutions with access to cutting-edge technology and resources, while academic contributions ensure that these innovations are pedagogically sound and aligned with educational goals. This synergy can lead to the development of AI applications that are both technologically advanced and educationally effective, ultimately enhancing learning experiences and outcomes for students. Supporting research and innovation through funding and collaborative initiatives ensures a forward-looking approach to integrating AI in education, fostering an environment where technological advancements can be responsibly and effectively leveraged to benefit learners across diverse contexts.

10. **Global Collaboration**

Global collaboration in AI for education involves working with international bodies to establish global standards and best practices, ensuring that the deployment and use of AI in educational settings are ethical, effective, and equitable. By setting universal guidelines, countries can align their efforts to harness AI's potential while mitigating risks such as bias, data privacy concerns, and unequal access to technology. Additionally, promoting knowledge sharing and collaboration across countries is crucial for addressing common challenges in AI integration and leveraging collective expertise. This collaborative approach facilitates the exchange of innovative solutions, research findings, and successful implementations, helping countries learn from each other's experiences and avoid common pitfalls. Joint initiatives can focus on developing AI tools that are culturally adaptable, accessible to diverse populations, and capable of supporting various educational systems. By fostering a global community of practice, stakeholders can ensure that AI advancements benefit learners worldwide, leading to more inclusive and effective educational experiences. This global effort also encourages the continuous improvement of AI technologies through shared research and development, ultimately enhancing the quality of education across different contexts and regions. Implementing these policy recommendations can help promote the responsible use of AI in education, ensuring it enhances learning experiences while safeguarding ethical standards, fairness, and equity. By prioritizing transparency, privacy, and continuous improvement, policymakers can create an educational environment where AI contributes positively to student outcomes and societal well-being.

CONCLUSION

Integrating AI into education holds immense potential for transforming teaching and learning experiences, but it requires a comprehensive and responsible approach. Key strategies include developing adaptive content recommendation systems, integrating AI into pedagogical practices, and fostering global collaboration to establish international standards and promote knowledge sharing. Research and innovation must be prioritized through funding and the creation of innovation hubs, while robust regulatory frameworks and ethical guidelines ensure responsible AI use. To address data privacy and security, strict data protection laws and clear consent protocols are essential. Bias mitigation and fairness can be achieved through regular audits and the use of diverse datasets. Ensuring equitable access to AI technologies and supporting underserved communities is crucial for inclusive education. Professional development for educators and AI literacy for students prepare both groups to effectively and ethically engage with AI tools. Continuous evaluation through impact studies and feedback mechanisms allows for ongoing improvement and data-driven policy adjustments. In conclusion, a multi-faceted approach encompassing regulation, ethical guidelines, equity, education, and continuous evaluation is essential for harnessing the transformative power of AI in education. By prioritizing these strategies, educational institutions can create a responsible, inclusive, and effective

AI-driven learning environment that prepares students for the challenges and opportunities of the future.

REFERENCES

AbuSahyon, A. S. E., Alzyoud, A., Alshorman, O., & Al-Absi, B. (2023). AI-driven technology and thatbots as tools for enhancing English language learning in the context of second language acquisition: A review study. *International Journal of Membrane Science and Technology*, 10(1), 1209–1223. DOI: 10.15379/ijmst.v10i1.2829

Cook-Sather, A., & Matthews, K. (2023). Practising student voice in university teaching and learning: Three anchoring principles. *Journal of University Teaching & Learning Practice*, 20(6), 1–13. DOI: 10.53761/1.20.6.2

Creely, E., & Blannin, J. (2023). The implications of generative AI for creative composition in higher education and initial teacher education. In Cochrane, T., Narayan, V., Brown, C., MacCallum, K., Bone, E., Deneen, C., & Vanderburg, R. (Eds.), *ASCILITE publications* (pp. 357–361)., DOI: 10.14742/apubs.2023.618

Hopfenbeck, T. N., Zhang, Z., Sun, S. Z., Robertson, P., & McGrane, J. A. (2023). Challenges and opportunities for classroom-based formative assessment and AI: A perspective article. *Frontiers in Education*, 8, 1–9. DOI: 10.3389/feduc.2023.1270700

Hutson, J., Plate, D., & Berry, K. (2024). Embracing AI in English composition: Insights and innovations in hybrid pedagogical practices. *International Journal of Changes in Education*, 19–31. DOI: 10.47852/bonviewIJCE42022290

Lewis, A., & Stoyanovich, J. (2022). Teaching responsible data science: Charting new pedagogical territory. *International Journal of Artificial Intelligence in Education*, 32(3), 783–807. DOI: 10.1007/s40593-021-00241-7 PMID: 33880114

Mohammed, A. S. (2023). Examining the implementation of artificial intelligence in early childhood education settings in Ghana: Educators' attitudes and perceptions towards its long-term viability. *American Journal of Education and Technology*, 2(4), 36–49. DOI: 10.54536/ajet.v2i4.2201

Rosé, C. P., McLaughlin, E. A., Liu, R., & Koedinger, K. R. (2019). Explanatory learner models: Why machine learning (alone) is not the answer. *British Journal of Educational Technology*, 50(6), 2943–2958. DOI: 10.1111/bjet.12858

Saltman, K. J. (2020). Artificial intelligence and the technological turn of public education privatization: In defence of democratic education. *London Review of Education*, 18(2). Advance online publication. DOI: 10.14324/LRE.18.2.04

Sysoyev, P. V. (2023). Artificial intelligence in education: Awareness, readiness and practice of using artificial intelligence technologies in professional activities by university faculty. *Vysshee Obrazovanie v Rossii = Higher Education in Russia, 32*(10), 9–33. DOI: 10.31992/0869-3617-2023-32-10-9-33

Walter, Y. (2024). Embracing the future of artificial intelligence in the classroom: The relevance of AI literacy, prompt engineering, and critical thinking in modern education. *International Journal of Educational Technology in Higher Education*, 21(15), 1–29. DOI: 10.1186/s41239-024-00448-3

Wong, R. S. Y., Ming, L. C., & Ali, R. A. R. (2023). The intersection of ChatGPT, clinical medicine, and medical education. In *JMIR Medical Education* (Vol. 9, Issue 1). DOI: 10.2196/47274

KEY TERMS AND DEFINITIONS

Adaptive Learning Platforms: These are AI-driven educational systems that personalize the learning experience for each student by analyzing their performance, learning style, and preferences to tailor content and pacing, ensuring optimal engagement and knowledge retention.

Ethical Guidelines: These are established principles and standards designed to govern the development and use of AI in education, ensuring that AI applications are implemented responsibly, transparently, and equitably while protecting the privacy and rights of students.

Data Privacy and Security: This involves the implementation of robust laws and protocols to protect student information from unauthorized access, misuse, or breaches, ensuring that data collection and usage are conducted with informed consent and strict security measures.

Bias Mitigation: This refers to the systematic efforts to identify, reduce, and eliminate biases in AI algorithms and datasets, ensuring fair and equitable treatment for all students regardless of their background, and promoting inclusivity in educational outcomes.

Equitable Access: This concept emphasizes the necessity of providing all students, including those from underserved communities, with the necessary technology and resources to benefit from AI-driven personalized learning, thereby bridging the digital divide.

Professional Development: Continuous training and development programs for educators aimed at equipping them with the knowledge and skills to effectively and ethically integrate AI tools into their teaching practices, enhancing their ability to deliver personalized and engaging learning experiences.

AI Literacy: The inclusion of education about AI technologies within the curriculum, enabling students to understand the fundamentals of AI, its applications, and its implications, thus preparing them for future academic and career opportunities in a technology-driven world.

Impact Studies: Regularly conducted research that evaluates the effectiveness and outcomes of AI technologies in education, using data-driven insights to inform policy decisions and strategic adjustments, ensuring that AI integration continues to meet educational goals and benefit stakeholders.

Chapter 4
Personalized Learning and Pedagogy:
Harnessing AI for Tailored Education

Praveen Kumar Dubey
Montana State University Northern, USA

ABSTRACT

The chapter delves into the transformative potential of Artificial Intelligence (AI) in enhancing personalized learning experiences within K-12 education. It discusses the learner-centered nature of personalized learning systems and the requisite skills and competencies for both teachers and students. The integration of AI in education is highlighted to achieve improved learning outcomes and teaching methods by reshaping the educational landscape. This chapter emphasizes the role of self-regulated learning (SRL) and adaptive learning technologies (ALTs) in maximizing student achievement. A theoretical framework is proposed to guide educators and researchers in integrating these personalized learning systems into their pedagogical practices effectively. The chapter also explores the implications of AI-powered learning tools without bias, thus fostering inclusivity and equity. Additionally, it addresses the ethical challenges and the necessity for policies to ensure fairness in AI applications.

INTRODUCTION

A personalized learning system is considered as learner-centered and requires new skills and competencies for teachers and students to use as a newer way of learning. Artificial Intelligence (AI) has been used to improve students' personalized learning

DOI: 10.4018/979-8-3693-6130-6.ch004

experiences. AI offers engaging opportunities to enhance personalized learning experiences for students which reshapes the educational landscape through better learning outcomes and improved teaching methods (Jin et al., 2023). Educators, researchers, and policymakers are navigating this new evolving landscape of the K12 education system and trying to comprehend the symbolic relationship between Artificial Intelligence (AI) and pedagogy which has become an essential element for fostering inclusive, equitable, justice, and effective learning environment for all learners. While the educational landscape is evolving with new developments in AI-powered learning tools, new policies and procedures must be in place to establish ethics and fairness.

Self-regulated learning (SRL) is an approach to helping students achieve higher academic performances and their learning objectives through AI-driven tools (Jin et al., 2023). Lin & Chang (2023) in their study proposed that generative Artificial Intelligence (AI) tools such as Personalized Chatbots, Self-Regulated Learning, and Active Learning hold the central role in maximizing enhanced learner experiences and outcomes for students. The aim of these self-regulated learning (SRL) regarding adaptive learning technologies (ALTs) is to develop learners' self-regulated learning skills (Molenaar, 2022). Therefore, a theoretical framework is needed that addresses practical guidance to educators and researchers on how to integrate personalized learning systems into their pedagogical practices (Lin & Chang, 2023).

As the students have different learning requirements, teachers are constantly searching for new learning methods through the inclusion of AI technology to enhance students' learning experiences and alleviate teacher workload which will benefit overall learning opportunities for students (Kerr, 2020). Additionally, research suggests that when AI-Powered personalized learning systems were applied to students' learning, the learning gains were not affected based on student's prior knowledge, gender, age, or parental education which suggests that AI learning tools adapt to students' learning needs (Wang et al., 2020). Thus, it is paramount to include AI learning tools in education to enhance overall personalized learning experiences and the most productive way to support such digital learning would be to include a sense of inquiry, reflective action, and experimental ways to know what students and teachers do and seek to understand (Bruce & Casey, 2012).

Applying pedagogical knowledge in AI-tailored education, this chapter examines the convergence of Artificial Intelligence (AI) in personalized learning and how teachers play a role in adaptive learning for the most effective learning outcomes. The intersection between pedagogy and AI-powered adaptive learning embodies a unique combination of factors that provides a framework for personalized learning and reveals insights about ethical challenges educators are facing to achieve 21st-century learning goals for students' learning while exploring newer educational landscapes. Additionally, this work aims to untangle the layers of personalized learning, adaptive learning, and teacher effectiveness in an AI-enabled classroom. As educators, researchers, and policymakers navigate this evolving landscape, it becomes essential to foster a more inclusive, equitable, and effective educational environment for all students.

This chapter examines how personalized-adaptive learning plays a role in AI-powered classrooms in creating a new educational landscape. While exploring AI-powered adaptive learning, teachers' perception and effectiveness provide a deeper understanding of the realities of the K12 classroom. As AI holds considerable promise in improving educational context, the ethical considerations are hard to miss. However, it is important to place AI and adaptive learning in the broader context as an analytical approach in the K12 educational system.

Pedagogy in K12 Education

Pedagogy is defined as a science that studies the methods and activities involved in teaching. The idea of pedagogy was first introduced by Shulman in 1986 to connect the roles of teachers in teaching with their acquired content knowledge and structure to the instruction and described it as the "missing paradigm" (Shulman, 1986). Bruce & Casey (2012) described three stages of learning in a traditional pedagogy appropriate to their domains 1) development of basic skills; 2) acquiring relevant content knowledge; and 3) skills to integrate acquired knowledge, be creative, and apply to practical usage. Thus, considering the given information, teaching represents a special technical information that is key to how educators approach the process of teaching-learning to meet the goals of learning. It involves teachers using teaching strategies, different learning activities, and a learner-based approach with suitable assessments to enhance student achievement. The art of teaching accounts for students' learning interests, likes and dislikes, and their cognitive as well as emotional development.

Educational philosopher John Dewey once said, "Learning cannot happen without personal meaning. The best learning occurs when the act of learning itself is intrinsically rewarding". Now the question is- how can an educator achieve such an important goal without careful consideration of methods of teaching. Thus, the importance lies in understanding the foundations of teaching with the use of strategies and available technological tools to empower students so that they are meeting the goals of democratic citizens. Ball et al. (2008) proposed that pedagogical content knowledge should be divided into two subdomains: (a) knowledge of content and students, and (b) knowledge of content and teaching. The importance of curricular knowledge is so evident that teachers need to explore two levels: a) lateral curriculum - crosswalk through different subjects within the grades, and b) vertical curriculum - familiarity through different grade levels (Shulman, 1986).

To meet the goals of teaching-learning, intersection of the pedagogical and content knowledge is demanded as it bridges the gap. Several content areas such as mathematics, science, history, English, engineering and others have hypothesized the theoretical frameworks of pedagogical knowledge into content knowledge to gain the mastery of the specific contents. The researchers have introduced the Domains of Mathematics Knowledge (DMK) for teaching (Ball et al., 2008). DMK claims that it is the extension of Shulman's proposed pedagogical model and could expand teachers' knowledge not only in mathematics but in other subject areas. Thus, it is evident that pedagogical knowledge plays an extremely important role for educators to attain content knowledge with specialized focus on subject matter and curriculum designs.

ROLE OF TECHNOLOGY IN EDUCATION

Technology creates an opportunity for the teaching-learning process through collaboration and participation (Heflin et al., 2017). It motivates teachers to refine their teaching practices while implementing personal beliefs and attitudes to bring a student-centered learning in the classroom which is considered as Self-regulated learning (SRL) in AI-Powered personalized learning systems. To support the vision of implementing technology in schools, teachers are at the forefront by setting an example in creating the role of technology, how to use it, and opportunities for peer-collaboration. While using AI, educators should focus on students' gender, and differences in public and private schools when exploring how AI can help overall development, well-being, data, privacy, and safety of students (Sanusi et al., 2022).

Surprisingly, technology was never considered as a part in the intersection of content knowledge and pedagogical knowledge. In fact, these two fields got combined and emerged as pedagogical content knowledge. Schools were focused on enhancing teaching-learning through well-versed techniques and thorough implementation of pedagogy as a part of content knowledge or vice versa. Mishra & Koehler (2006) extended the idea of pedagogical content knowledge and introduced it into Technological Pedagogical Content Knowledge Framework (TPACK). The claim was that this framework presents a deeper understanding to provide instruction to activate higher student participation for learning.

The TPACK framework opened the door to focus the connection among technology, content, and specific pedagogy; and integrated the content and pedagogical strategies with technology to enhance student learning (Harris et al., 2009). Creating such a framework helped to explore different technological tools such as Artificial Intelligence (AI), Chatbots, Intelligent Tutoring (IT), Adaptive learning, AI-Powered Assessment, Feedback, etc. to improve teacher pedagogical knowledge for teaching-learning. AI-powered learning tools opened new doors for educators. However, while considering AI technology in student-centered learning, educators should create an enabling environment for student-centered learning so that students can practice teamwork, cognitive and learning skills, and collaboration when using AI for learning (Sanusi et al., 2022).

Artificial Intelligence in Education

The purpose of Artificial Intelligence (AI) in education is to teach students content knowledge, pedagogical knowledge, and relevant skills while empowering educators to enhance teaching-learning experiences (Jin et al., 2023). Artificial intelligence (AI) has widely become available in every aspect of education through AI-powered tools such as ChaptGPT, intelligent tutoring systems, real-time analysis of students' learning process, and AI assisted instructors for English as a foreign language. AI applications are useful for supporting metacognitive, cognitive, and across different Self-regulated learning areas (Jin et al., 2023). However, the student's cognitive skills and self-learning competence play a role and affect their understanding of AI intelligence in the course content (Sanusi et al., 2022).

Intelligent personal assistants (IPAs) such as Amazon Alexa, Google Assistant, Siri, etc. are the aspect of AI that relies on automatic speech recognition and natural language processing (NLP); and are being used in education for learning a second language (Godwin-Jones, 2019; Dizon et al., 2022). In recent years, learners have been using IPA to learn different foreign languages such as Spanish, Japanese, German, English, and more. The learning of foreign languages using IPA outside school varies depending on the participation of students; and learners may benefit from strategic training or professional development (Dizon et al., 2022). In their study, Dizon et al. (2022) found that while learning foreign languages using IPA, learners abandon the misunderstood language and rephrase and repeat as the most frequently used communication strategy. Thus, the suggestion would be to add more vocabulary in AI-powered search tools so that learners have more word choices to search for learning.

The recent adoption of AI in education has opened new doors for innovation and implementation of best practices strategies. The success of AI education depends on how abstract concepts are introduced considering students' development stages and learning theories, and it enhances AI literacy while empowering students (Lee & Kwon, 2024). The increase in the use of AI technology in education promises the potential for customized learning, well-versed assessments, and meaningful online learning experiences (Zhang & Aslan, 2021). Several studies suggest that students' motivation and attitude toward AI have a positive impact on their engagement and interest in learning AI (Lee & Kwon, 2024).

As the traditional role of the teacher is changing with the influx of AI-powered learning systems, project-based learning stood out as one of the best strategies and is vital in AI education as it enables students to apply real-world problem-solving concepts and enhances their skills to solve problems (Lee & Kwon, 2024). To meet the demands of AI-powered classrooms, schools need to play a proactive role in acquiring adaptive curriculums, technological resources, and properly trained teachers in the classroom to avoid learning gaps and meet the learning needs of diverse student populations. While designing the lesson, student teamwork in AI literacy courses to keep up with the pace of emerging technologies is important for achieving desired learning goals (Sanusi et al., 2022).

UNDERSTANDING PERSONALIZED LEARNING

In recent years, personalized learning has surfaced as a dynamic solution to meet the learning needs of diverse student populations in K12 educational settings. Lots of definitions have been tossed by researchers, policymakers, public officials, etc. to define personalized learning (Bernacki et al., 2021). It is interesting to know that researchers, policymakers, and practitioners all have used different terminology to describe personalized learning with no consensus. The most common definition of personalized learning used for this study is provided by the U.S. Department of Education as "instruction in which the pace of learning and the instructional approach are optimized for the needs of each learner. Learning objectives, instructional approaches, and instructional content (and its sequencing) may vary based on learner needs. In addition, learning activities are meaningful and relevant to learners, driven by their interests, and often self-initiated" (U.S. Department of Education, 2016, p. 7).

Personalized learning (PL) has existed for centuries in our educational systems in the form of apprenticeship and mentoring but it became popular in the early 2000s with the invention and adoption of different technologies in education (Shemshack & Spector, 2020). In recent educational history, personalized learning has been mainly used in areas of teaching mathematics, but some work is also conducted in other humanities subjects (Bernacki et al., 2021). Bray and McClaskey (2013) described three stages to create a personalized learning environment- 1) Teacher-Centered with Learner Voice and Choice, 2) Learner-Centered with Teacher and Learners as Co-Designers, and 3) Learner-Driven with Teacher as Partner in Learning. The idea is to create a learning environment where the teacher switches from the traditional role as a sole source of knowledge to as a facilitator for a learner-driven learning environment. In other words, personalized learning switches the focus from teacher-centered learning to a student-centered learning environment.

In recent years, personalized learning has become so popular that the Department of Education throughout the United States adopted a framework as a pathway to provide authentic learning experiences for diverse learners and the review of educational policy confirms such claims (Zhang et al., 2020). For example, the Ohio Department of Education has implemented 'The Ohio Personalized Learning Framework' that has components and indicators to lay down the foundational process for schools to adopt. In the framework, the components of personalized learning are: 1) learner-driven, 2) Flexible Learning Environment, 3) Authentic Learning, 4) Optimal Path and Pace, and 5) Evidence of Learning and Feedback (Ohio Department of Education, 2024).

The potential of personalized learning and how it impacts students is discussed and identified by researchers, policymakers, and educators. Personalized learning (PL) has been used to push for reforms, but its definition varied widely in terms of interpretation and implementation over time and for different contexts (Zhang et al., 2020). In the United States, the Every Student Succeeds Act 2015 encourages school districts to increase rigor, improve the use of technology for teaching-learning, adopt diverse instructional practices, and use Universal Design for Learning (UDL) in their teaching (ESSA, 2015). Due to the increase in the diversity of learners, the evolving needs of the education system, and the integration of technology in K12 education, the implementation of PL at a large scale is vital (Zhang et al., 2020).

In 2008, the National Academy of Engineering (NAE) identified 14 game-changing goals for improving human life in the 21st century, and advancing personalized learning is one of fourteen grand challenges. NAE reported that today's classrooms have a variety of student learning needs. The first group of learners are highly self-motivated and self-driven and need little to no support. While the second group of learners needs more structure, one-on-one step-by-step instructional support with external rewards. Additionally, the third group of learners resist learning altogether and have little or no motivation to achieve any learning goals. These findings not only create unique classroom dynamics but also provide unseen challenges for classroom teachers. However, these challenges could be resolved and changed into learning opportunities for students learning with the intervention of a newly AI-powered learning tool. New neuroscience research is providing insights into how the human brain works which would help to refine and optimize learning opportunities for teaching and learning (NAE, n.a).

Over time, to meet the goals of future learning using personalized learning as recommended by the National Academy of Engineering (NAE, 2008), researchers have proposed several frameworks to fully prepare students. Gudivada (2017) suggested attributes of personalized learning to help provide students equitable learning opportunities and those attributes are: 1) no predefined order in which students need to learn the topics, 2) the availability of pre-and post-test so that students can earn credits for completing, 3) auto-generated testing, 4) timely and conceptual feedback, and 5) reuse and repurposes of main contents. To apply these attributes to everyday learning, educators should integrate hands-on activities and project-based learning with the use of real-world data to provide enhanced learning for students (Lee & Kwon, 2024). The recommendations of Lee & Kwon (2024) highlighted that educators should adopt various age and grade-appropriate AI tools to offer interactive and deeper learning in their curriculum.

Teachers' Perception of Personalized Learning

The foundation of personalized learning rests on the idea that students learn through experience by creating constructive knowledge and are influenced and accomplished by their prior experiences (Shemshack, & Spector, 2020). Teachers' perception of personalized learning is to customize learning opportunities to meet students' individual learning needs, strengths, and passions (Gunawardena et al., 2024). Educators and policymakers adopt personalized learning to improve student achievement or motivation which improves student engagement in learning but often lack resources to determine the right program design to meet the desired learning goals (Bernacki et al., 2021). Teachers have some differences in their scope; and how and when to use personalized learning in class. The stark differences of opinion among teachers about personalized learning appear when translating complex concepts from a theoretical perspective to implementation and highlighting how straightforward theories are practically complex to practice (Gunawardena et al., 2024).

Personalized learning is about giving students control over their learning and the goals they want to achieve with the appropriate structure for feedback (Shemshack, & Spector, 2020). In personalized learning, student engagement and motivation are the main factors affecting the implementation of strategies for school-adopted curriculum in addressing students' needs and interests (Gunawardena et al., 2024). Even though educators are the main catalyst for pedagogical change, the definitions of personalized learning are challenged because its interpretation and implementation vary throughout the content and context (Zhang et al., 2020). The teachers experienced the same level of complexity with strategies when they used it for the entire class, but it increased when they had to address students' individual learning needs and curriculum demands imposed in the personalized learning class (Gunawardena et al., 2024).

The research suggests that the schools lack resources for personalized learning which might be the result of no formal training to understand the characteristics of learners or the absence of transparency about how to design the delivery elements of lessons or could be a combination of both (Bernacki et al., 2021). Additionally, the definitions and models to implement personalized learning vary widely among researchers and practitioners that provide schools an opportunity to address the needs of their increasingly diverse student population for higher achievements based on their specific learning requirements (Zhang et al., 2020). These definitions are so varied throughout the subject and grade level, that the challenges of implementing personalized learning include limited time to help individual students, limitations with curriculum, class sizes, and teaching multiple subjects (Gunawardena et al., 2024).

Teachers have a positive attitude towards personalized learning and are inclined to adopt it for primary students but struggle with ideas of how to implement it (Gunawardena et al., 2024). Interestingly, teachers know that AI has the right tools to reduce the learning struggles at the elementary level. However, teachers' struggles take a different turn at the secondary level, and they face more complexities in implementing personalized learning compared to lower grades (Gunawardena et al., 2024). To fully utilize the intricacies of AI, it is evident that interactive AI learning tools and project-based learning are better ways of teaching as it has a higher impact on student learning experiences (Lee & Kwon, 2024). Overall, it is safe to say that teachers are excited about the prospect of using AI learning tools for teaching-learning and showing a positive attitude to implement appropriate professional development and training.

Role of AI in Personalized Learning

The introduction of the applications of Artificial Intelligence such as AI chatbots and virtual instructors has offered substantial opportunities for students to enhance their educational practices and improve their learning outcomes (Bahroun et al., 2023). Artificial Intelligence (AI) is playing a prominent role in the field of teaching and learning. Research suggests that elementary teachers recognize the importance of AI tools in student evaluation and management, while secondary teachers use them for students' self-reflection and career guidance (Seo et al., 2024).

Bahroun et al. (2023) in their research found that generative artificial intelligence in education has emerged as a transformative force to revolutionize education through improved student learning outcomes, enhanced student engagement, and the possibility for improved personalized learning experiences. In their research, Childress & Benson (2024) described Artificial Intelligence as the best hope to accelerate student achievement by using a range of pedagogical and technological innovations that are best suitable to deliver individual education through personalized learning systems.

The integration of AI in education has made a paradigm shift and paved for personalized learning experiences so that it helps to meet the individual learning needs, styles, and preferences of students (Ayeni et al., 2024). Bahroun, et al., (2023) described the intersection of Artificial Intelligence (AI) and education as a transformative force to reshape traditional pedagogical paradigms and redefine the possibilities of personalized learning. The role of Artificial Intelligence in education not only provides better learning opportunities but the concept of personalized learning models lies in the idea that it gives students control over their learning, differentiating instruction, and instructional strategies, content, and activities that fit their learning needs (Shemshack, & Spector, 2020). Additionally, the limitations of resources in schools make AI the only viable and logical way to bring learning goals into reality.

The use of AI chatbots, such as ChatGPT, has shown better performance in subject content exams and the potential of natural language to provide enhanced student feedback with concerns about authenticity, credibility, systematic errors, and the risk of plagiarism (Bahroun et al., 2023). Ayeni et al. (2024) added that AI in education has a promise to revitalize the entire education sector with opportunities such as how knowledge is imparted and acquired for learning, and ways to make education more adaptive, inclusive, and effective. Personalized learning is challenging traditional school settings by moving focus from whole-class instruction to individual instruction as a leading way to improve student achievement (Childress & Benson, 2024). The success of AI education depends on how abstract concepts are introduced considering students' development stages and learning theories, and how it enhances AI literacy while empowering students (Lee & Kwon, 2024).

ADAPTIVE LEARNING TECHNOLOGIES IN EDUCATION

The adaptivity of a learning system is defined as its capacity to modify lessons by using specific parameters to meet the learning needs of a student. Adaptive learning systems use a similar approach (as traditional learning) that involves the development and implementation of educational interventions through accommodation to meet students' learning differences (Lee & Park, 2008). Achieving such learning goals can be more effective if pedagogical procedures are aligned to meet the student's individual learning needs. Lee & Park (2008) stated that the use of this approach accommodates students' learning differences in the development and implementation of interventions. Such learning opportunities are most relevant and resource abundant with AI-powered adaptive learning systems. To provide such a learning experience, adaptive learning technology uses data-driven instruction to create personalized learning experiences for students which is adjusted and tailored to meet the individual learning needs. It tracks student progress data, engagement, and their performance to provide the best learning plan. Therefore, to create a rigorous adaptive educational technology that reflects evidence-based practices, it is recommended that collaboration should be practiced while developing such technological tools (Akbulut & Cardak, 2012).

White (2020) found that adaptive learning technology is as effective as any other study methods and positive perception about it may be due to flexibility and personalized opportunity. He suggested that the reason for the mixed result could be a lack of consideration of student characteristics such as initiative, satisfaction, and convenience (White, 2020). In other words, to provide encouraging learning outcomes, students' opinions should be considered. The use of information and communication technology (ICT) is strongly related to students' belief that technology is useful in learning and highly related to their self-reported digital skills which implies that the use of digital technology has a higher effect on student skills and disbelief (Schmida & Petkob, 2019). In other words, the use of digital technologies in school helps improve students' digital skills and self-efficacy. It is safe to say that adapting learning technology enhances students' digital skills and provides them with better learning opportunities. Additionally, while implementing personalized learning, adaptive learning subject materials are effective in helping students improve achievement and self-efficacy when students' online learning behaviors are considered (Tseng et al., 2008).

The study has found that personal trait attributes are responsible for students' learning behavior and how they use their skills to initiate the learning processes; and the most sought-after personal trait required for students in personalized learning for adaptive learning technology is cognition learning domain (Normadhia et al., 2019). In other words, personal traits of the cognition learning domain including learning style, cognitive style, and personality type are the most desirable characteristics needed for personalized learning in an adaptive learning setting. The limitations that exist in techniques required to identify personal traits in adaptive learning environments are the shortcomings we face in fully implementing personalized learning strategies in classrooms (Normadhia et al., 2019). Thus, the success in implementing personalized learning using adaptive learning technology depends on how effective personal traits finding techniques are so that educators can find students' personal traits promptly and proper accommodation would be provided to help students achieve intended learning goals.

Individual instruction provides individual students with effective personalized learning support for content, tutoring, tools, and environment (Bloom, 1984). Additionally, research suggests that students have individual differences (gender, prior knowledge, cognitive styles, etc.) which may lead to different learning outcomes (Cassidy, 2012; Chen, 2010). Thus, the student's progress lies in what, how, and when students are getting individual learning opportunities. Adaptability offers students possibilities for improved learning by giving them responsibility for their own learning and control through self-regulation or monitoring of their own understanding of content (Griffin et al., 2013).

Teacher Effectiveness in AI Adaptive Classroom

Teachers are at the forefront of student learning, but they lack knowledge and face difficulties using technology in the classroom (Mishra et al., 2019). Research suggests that teachers know their use of technology and would like to improve their ICT knowledge based on their own wishes and needs (Top et al., 2021). Top et al. (2021) suggest that teachers are interested in learning new technology programs or new features about already learned technology as they are already using it for various teaching-learning purposes. Additionally, research suggests that "educators are increasingly under pressure to use technology to prepare students to live in a technologically interconnected, globalized world" (Chun et al., 2016, p. 65). Teacher mentoring could be the answer to reduce the stress and pressure for pre-and in-service teachers. Thus, pre-service and in-service teachers mentoring becomes one of the extremely important professional development strategies to support teachers' professional growth (Wang, 2002).

Technology is considered as a new way to enhance teachers' creativity and intellectual capability (Chun et al., 2016) which forces teachers to gain such opportunities to provide the best learning experiences to their students. However, literature lacks such opportunities that enable teachers to freely and flexibly experience such training in ICT (Top et al., 2021). Teachers need technology to enhance their classroom learning, however; "technology should not be seen as a panacea, or a goal in and of itself, but rather as one means to support specific learning" (Chun et al., 2016, p. 77). Teachers need to transform their deeper understanding of subject knowledge into the purposes of their teaching (Shulman, 1986). Such strategies have been followed through by the educators. To make the process reliable and accessible for teachers, they need to be able to use technology effectively in their lives and empower them to integrate technology into their environment (Top et al., 2021). The goals of higher teacher effectiveness can be achieved through mentoring as it helps to build their influence, confidence, self-esteem, attitude, and ability to teach (Mathur et al., 2012).

Research suggests that in AI science learning activities, students showed higher performance, better work quality, and better problem-solving and cognitive skills with teacher support than otherwise (Wu & Yang 2022). In other words, teacher support of learning with AI is an indicator of learning effectiveness. In the K12 school, teacher support has a higher influence on students' intrinsic motivation and their competence to learn with AI chatbot (Chiu et al., 2023) and motivates students to perform better at school. In other words, science activities helped students to enhance their learning with proper curriculum design. Students felt self-regulated, had higher digital literacy, and were better satisfied with relatedness when they were supported by their teachers (Chiu et al., 2023). The results of the two studies pointed out that the AI learning system cannot be assigned to reduce class size alone, but its use helped students outperform in both whole-class and small-group instruction (Wang et al., 2020). In other words, teachers who are skilled at using AI in their classrooms are preparing students better and their academic performances are higher than the classrooms where teachers are not using it as a learning tool.

Ethical Consideration in K12 Education

The use of AI chatbots, such as ChatGPT has shown the potential of providing enhanced peer feedback and intelligent tutoring systems (Bahroun et al., 2023). The results are so promising that educators and policymakers are inclined to create AI-inclusive classrooms. However, the use of generative AI in education concerns the importance of ethical considerations and responsible usage, and its limitations prompted the discussions on ethics, and academic integrity with its potential effect on teaching and learning methods (Bahroun et al., 2023). In their research, Bahroun et al. (2023) shared concerns regarding AI use in education which are authenticity, credibility, systematic errors, and the risk of plagiarism, and recommended for caution and the responsible integration of AI tools.

AI experts and research scientists around the globe understand the risks and harm that AI could cause to learners. They have shared the ethical concerns that are the driving factors for AI principles for the responsible use of AI in education. Several organizations have created ethical guidelines and frameworks which include the Asimolar AI Principles, the Responsible Machine Learning Principles, the Montreal Declaration for Responsible Development of Artificial Intelligence, and the "five overarching principles for an AI Code" put forward by the House of Lords Select Committee on Artificial Intelligence. A group created by The European Commission named, "The Ethics Guidelines for Trustworthy AI" puts seven requirements of Trustworthy AI such as- 1) Human Agency and Oversight, 2) Accountability, 3) Technical Robustness and Safety, 4) Diversity, Non-discrimination and Fairness, 5) Privacy and Data Governance, 6) Transparency, and 7) Societal and Environmental Wellbeing (The Institute for Ethical AI in Education, 2020).

The applications of AI tools in education are evident but "despite the benefits of AI applications for education, they pose societal and ethical drawbacks" (Akgun & Greenhow, 2022, p. 432). For example, schools are using mobile apps to enhance students' learning experiences; and while using AI-driven mobile apps for educational purposes educators should observe four ethical principles such as beneficence, nonmaleficence, autonomy, and justice (Klimova et al., 2023). Because of the ethical concerns in K12 education, students and teachers urgently need to introduce the ethical challenges involving AI applications and how to navigate such situations (Akgun & Greenhow, 2022). Considering the current situation of ethical issues of AI in education "it is imperative that forthcoming efforts concentrate on interdisciplinary investigations to confront ethical difficulties, integrate conscientious AI education into academic curricula, and promote collaborative endeavors aimed at formulating comprehensive regulations and principled directives" (Bahroun et al., 2023, p. 18).

The effect of AI in education is profound with major positive contributions towards learning both in and out of school but with any technology some experiences will not be as positive as planned (Reiss, 2021). While providing student learning experiences in personalized learning systems, educators need to include ethical considerations, privacy concerns, and potential algorithmic biases (Bahroun et al., 2023). The use of AI in personalized learning will improve students' opportunities for learning but students will still be grouped in groups of 10, 20, 30, or more (Reiss, 2021). In the K12 settings, based on bias and ethical challenges in using AI applications, schools should focus on the problems of privacy, surveillance, autonomy, bias, and discrimination. While considering these issues, it is important to acknowledge that educators face different ethical concerns and challenges depending on their student's grades and age (Akgun & Greenhow, 2022).

Due to the potential for algorithmic biases, scrutiny needs to be considered regarding ethics and privacy concerns because doing it will offer an opportunity for inclusive learning and practices in an organization (Miller et al., 2018). While considering the strategies and recommendations regarding AI ethical uses, it is recommended that student-specific age and grade level should be targeted (Akgun & Greenhow, 2022). It is recommended that AI program developers find a way to incorporate student and teacher awareness regarding potential bias and value for inclusion while guiding machine learning processes (Miller et al., 2018). Students' perception about the role of AI in society has an ethical implication which provides valuable insight for preparing responsible AI citizens (Lee & Kwon, 2024). In machine learning, computers are designed to process the data that they receive which might be restricted as these data including language are virtually rooted in human perception and interpretation which makes it inevitable for machine learning to be unbiased (Miller et al., 2018). Additionally, schools are in critical need of developing AI curricula to integrate various subjects which leads to a full adoption of AI in schools by teachers considering all the ethics, biases, and prejudices (Lee & Kwon, 2024).

SUMMARY

A general definition of personalized learning is an educational approach that focuses on customizing skills, interests, and strengths to create new learning opportunities for students. Generative artificial intelligence has several applications which include assessment, personalized learning, and intelligent tutoring (Bahroun et al., 2023). In studies, students showed outstanding performance in classes taught by AI-Powered personalized learning tools compared to expert teachers (Wang et al., 2020). Thus, the purpose of the use of Artificial Intelligence (AI) in education is to teach concepts, pedagogical knowledge, and skills needed which enhance the learning experiences of students, alongside empowering educators that fulfill their learning goals.

A consensus among teachers, administrators, and policymakers is to include AI-power learning tools for student learning. When AI-Powered personalized learning systems were applied to students' learning, the learning gains were not affected based on student's prior knowledge, gender, age, or parental education which suggests that AI learning tools adapt to students' learning needs (Wang et al., 2020). Also, the study suggests that teachers understand the effectiveness of AI and recognize that it provides valuable tools for creating instructional materials that align with students' learning needs (Seo et al., 2024). Thus, to utilize AI technology to its fullest potential, teachers should be provided training on the intersection of pedagogy and AI tools (Sanusi et al., 2022).

Adaptive learning systems can provide a one-on-one tutoring experience to achieve higher student learning outcomes (Wang et al., 2020). The introduction of AI promises to challenge older work practices and paths of inclusion and exponentially increase disruption in organizations, society, government, and our everyday lives through adaptive learning tools (Miller et al., 2018). As adaptive learning systems accommodate individual students' needs and level of knowledge way better than highly skilled teachers do not in classroom settings (Wang et al., 2020). Thus, the recommendation is that AI-powered personalized learning systems are the best way to move forward which include intelligent tutoring, adaptive learning, and AI-powered assessments and feedback.

The review of educational policy suggests that the majority of the US states have adopted personalized learning for K-12 students to improve their learning opportunities (Zhang et al., 2020). Ethical considerations are extremely important for AI-powered learning tools as "prejudices produce actions that, in turn, produce data" (Miller et al., 2018, p. 8). Since there is potential for algorithmic biases; educators, researchers, and policymakers should carefully scrutinize ethical considerations and privacy concerns as it affects the learning opportunity for inclusive learning and practices in any organization (Miller et al., 2018). Additionally, it is recommended that strategies and recommendations regarding AI ethical usage should consider students' age, grade-level, and their background to avoid violation of student right for inclusive educational experiences (Akgun & Greenhow, 2022).

REFERENCES

Afini Normadhi, N. B., Shuib, L., Md Nasir, H. N., Bimba, A., Idris, N., & Balakrishnan, V. (2019). Identification of personal traits in adaptive learning environment: Systematic literature review. *Computers & Education*, 130, 168–190. https://doi.org/10.1016/j.compedu.2018.11.005

Akbulut, Y., & Cardak, C. S. (2012). Adaptive educational hypermedia accommodating learning styles: A content analysis of publications from 2000 to 2011. *Computers & Education*, 58(2), 835–842. https://doi.org/10.1016/j.compedu.2011.10.008

Akgun, S., & Greenhow, C. (2022). Artificial intelligence in education: Addressing ethical challenges in K-12 settings. *AI and Ethics*, 2(3), 431–440. https://doi.org/10.1007/s43681-021-00096-7

Ayeni, O. O., Al Hamad, N. M., Chisom, O. N., Osawaru, B., & Adewusi, O. E. (2024). AI in education: A review of personalized learning and educational technology. *GSC Advanced Research and Reviews*, 18(2), 261–271. https://doi.org/10.30574/gscarr.2024.18.2.0062

Bahroun, Z., Anane, C., Ahmed, V., & Zacca, A. (2023). Transforming education: A comprehensive review of generative artificial intelligence in educational settings through bibliometric and content analysis. *Sustainability*, 15(17), 12983. https://doi.org/10.3390/su151712983

Bernacki, M. L., Greene, M. J., & Lobczowski, N. G. (2021). A systematic review of research on personalized learning: Personalized by whom, to what, how, and for what Purpose(s)? *Educational Psychology Review*, 33(4), 1675–1715. https://doi.org/10.1007/s10648-021-09615-8

Bernacki, M. L., Greene, M. J., & Lobczowski, N. G. (2021). A systematic review of research on personalized learning: Personalized by whom, to what, how, and for what Purpose(s)? *Educational Psychology Review*, 33(4), 1675–1715. https://doi.org/10.1007/s10648-021-09615-8

Bloom, B. S. (1984). The 2 sigma problem: The search for methods of group instruction as effective as one-to-one tutoring. *Educational Researcher*, 13(6), 4. https://doi.org/10.2307/1175554

Bruce, B. C., & Casey, L. (2012). The practice of inquiry: A pedagogical 'Sweet spot' for digital literacy? *Computers in the Schools*, 29(1-2), 191–206. DOI: 10.1080/07380569.2012.657994

Cassidy, S. (2012). Exploring individual differences as determining factors in student academic achievement in higher education. *Studies in Higher Education*, 37(7), 793–810. https://doi.org/10.1080/03075079.2010.545948

Chen, L. (2010). Web-based learning programs: Use by learners with various cognitive styles. *Computers & Education*, 54(4), 1028–1035. https://doi.org/10.1016/j.compedu.2009.10.008

Childress, S., & Benson, S. (2014). Personalized learning for every student every day. *Phi Delta Kappan*, 95(8), 33–38. https://doi.org/10.1177/003172171409500808

Chiu, T. K., Moorhouse, B. L., Chai, C. S., & Ismailov, M. (2023). Teacher support and student motivation to learn with artificial intelligence (AI) based chatbot. *Interactive Learning Environments*, 1–17. https://doi.org/10.1080/10494820.2023.2172044

Chun, D., Kern, R., & Smith, B. (2016). Technology in language use, language teaching, and language learning. *Modern Language Journal*, 100(S1), 64–80. https://doi.org/10.1111/modl.12302

Dizon, G., Tang, D., & Yamamoto, Y. (2022). A case study of using Alexa for out-of-class, self-directed Japanese language learning. *Computers and Education: Artificial Intelligence*, 3, 100088. https://doi.org/10.1016/j.caeai.2022.100088

Every Student Succeeds Act, Pub. L. No. 114-95 (2015), https://www.govinfo.gov/app/details/PLAW-114publ95

Godwin-Jones, R. (2019). In a World of SMART Technology, Why Learn Another Language? *Journal of Educational Technology & Society*, 22(2), 4–13. https://www.jstor.org/stable/26819613

Griffin, T. D., Wiley, J., & Salas, C. R. (2013). Supporting effective self-regulated learning: The critical role of monitoring. *International Handbook of Metacognition and Learning Technologies*, 19-34. https://doi.org/10.1007/978-1-4419-5546-3_2

Gudivada, V. N. (2017). Cognitive Analytics Driven Personalized Learning. *Educational Technology*, 57(1), 23–31. http://www.jstor.org/stable/44430537

Gunawardena, M., Bishop, P., & Aviruppola, K. (2024). Personalized learning: The simple, the complicated, the complex and the chaotic. *Teaching and Teacher Education*, 139, 104429. https://doi.org/10.1016/j.tate.2023.104429

Harris, J., Mishra, P., & Koehler, M. (2009). Teachers' technological pedagogical content knowledge and learning activity types. *Journal of Research on Technology in Education*, 41(4), 393–416. https://doi.org/10.1080/15391523.2009.10782536

Heflin, H., Shewmaker, J., & Nguyen, J. (2017). Impact of mobile technology on student attitudes, engagement, and learning. *Computers & Education*, 107, 91–99. https://doi.org/10.1016/j.compedu.2017.01.006

Jin, S., Im, K., Yoo, M., Roll, I., & Seo, K. (2023). Supporting students' self-regulated learning in online learning using artificial intelligence applications. *International Journal of Educational Technology in Higher Education*, 20(1). https://doi.org/10.1186/s41239-023-00406-5

Kerr, K. (2020). Ethical Considerations When Using Artificial Intelligence-Based Assistive Technologies in Education. In B. Brown, V. Roberts, M. Jacobsen, C. Hurrell, K. Kerr, H. van Streun, N. J. Neutzling, J. Lowry, S. Zarkovic, J. Ansorger, T. Marles, E. Lockyer, & D. Parthenis (Eds.), *Ethical use of technology in digital learning environments: Graduate student perspectives – Simple book publishing*. Library Publishing for Open Textbooks. https://pressbooks.openeducationalberta.ca/educationaltechnologyethics/

Klimova, B., Pikhart, M., & Kacetl, J. (2023). Ethical issues of the use of AI-driven mobile apps for education. *Frontiers in Public Health*, 10. https://doi.org/10.3389/fpubh.2022.1118116

Lee, J., & Park, O. (2008). Adaptive instructional systems. In Spector, J. M., Merrill, M. D., Merriënboer, J. v., & Driscoll, M. P. (Eds.), *Handbook of research on educational communications and technology* (3rd ed., pp. 469–484). Taylor Francis.

Lee, S. J., & Kwon, K. (2024). A systematic review of AI education in K-12 classrooms from 2018 to 2023: Topics, strategies, and learning outcomes. *Computers and Education: Artificial Intelligence*, 6, 100211. https://doi.org/10.1016/j.caeai.2024.100211

Lin, M. P., & Chang, D. (2023). CHAT-ACTS: A pedagogical framework for personalized chatbot to enhance active learning and self-regulated learning. *Computers and Education: Artificial Intelligence*, 5, 100167. https://doi.org/10.1016/j.caeai.2023.100167

Loewenberg Ball, D., Thames, M. H., & Phelps, G. (2008). Content knowledge for teaching. *Journal of Teacher Education*, 59(5), 389–407. https://doi.org/10.1177/0022487108324554

Mathur, S. R., Gehrke, R., & Kim, S. H. (2012). Impact of a teacher mentorship program on mentors' and Mentees' perceptions of classroom practices and the mentoring experience. *Assessment for Effective Intervention*, 38(3), 154–162. https://doi.org/10.1177/1534508412457873

Miller, F. A., Katz, J. H., & Gans, R. (2018). The OD imperative to add inclusion to the algorithms of artificial intelligence. *OD Practitioner*, 5(1), 6–12.

Mishra, C., Ha, S. J., Parker, L. C., & Clase, L., K. (2019). Describing teacher conceptions of technology in authentic science inquiry using technological pedagogical content knowledge as a lens. *Biochemistry and Molecular Biology Education*, 47(4), 380–387. https://doi.org/10.1002/bmb.21242

Mishra, P., & Koehler, M. J. (2006). Technological pedagogical content knowledge: A framework for teacher knowledge. *Teachers College Record*, 108(6), 1017–1054. DOI: 10.1111/j.1467-9620.2006.00684.x

Molenaar, I. (2022). The concept of hybrid human-AI regulation: Exemplifying how to support young learners' self-regulated learning. *Computers and Education: Artificial Intelligence*, 3, 100070. https://doi.org/10.1016/j.caeai.2022.100070

Personalized learning. (2024, April 22). Ohio Department of Education and Workforce. https://education.ohio.gov/Topics/Teaching/Personalized-Learning

Reiss, M. J. (2021). The use of AI in education: Practicalities and ethical considerations. *London Review of Education*, 19(1). https://doi.org/10.14324/lre.19.1.05

Sanusi, I. T., Olaleye, S. A., Agbo, F. J., & Chiu, T. K. (2022). The role of learners' competencies in artificial intelligence education. *Computers and Education: Artificial Intelligence*, 3, 100098. https://doi.org/10.1016/j.caeai.2022.100098

Schmid, R., & Petko, D. (2019). Does the use of educational technology in personalized learning environments correlate with self-reported digital skills and beliefs of secondary-school students? *Computers & Education*, 136, 75–86. https://doi.org/10.1016/j.compedu.2019.03.006

Seo, K., Yoo, M., Dodson, S., & Jin, S. H. (2024). Augmented teachers: K–12 teachers' needs for artificial intelligence's complementary role in personalized learning. *Journal of Research on Technology in Education*, 1–18. DOI: 10.1080/15391523.2024.2330525

Shemshack, A., & Spector, J. M. (2020). A systematic literature review of personalized learning terms. *Smart Learning Environments, 7*(1). https://doi.org/10.1186/s40561-020-00140-9

Shulman, L. S. (1986). Those who understand: Knowledge growth in teaching. *Educational Researcher*, 15(2), 4. https://doi.org/10.2307/1175860

The Institute for Ethical AI in Education. (2020). Interim report: towards a shared vision of ethical AI in Education. https://www.buckingham.ac.uk/wp-content/uploads/2021/03/The-Institute-for-Ethical-AI-in-Education-The-Ethical-Framework-for-AI-in-Education.pdf

Top, E., Baser, D., Akkus, R., Akayoglu, S., & Gurer, M. D. (2021). Secondary school teachers' preferences in the process of individual technology mentoring. *Computers & Education*, 160, 104030. https://doi.org/10.1016/j.compedu.2020.104030

Tseng, J. C., Chu, H., Hwang, G., & Tsai, C. (2008). Development of an adaptive learning system with two sources of personalization information. *Computers & Education*, 51(2), 776–786. https://doi.org/10.1016/j.compedu.2007.08.002

U. S. Department U.S. Department of Education. (2016). *Future ready learning: Reimagining the role of technology in education*. Createspace Independent Publishing Platform.

Wang, J. (2001). Contexts of mentoring and opportunities for learning to teach: A comparative study of mentoring practice. *Teaching and Teacher Education*, 17(1), 51–73. https://doi.org/10.1016/s0742-051x(00)00038-x

Wang, S., Christensen, C., Cui, W., Tong, R., Yarnall, L., Shear, L., & Feng, M. (2020). When adaptive learning is effective learning: Comparison of an adaptive learning system to teacher-led instruction. *Interactive Learning Environments*, 31(2), 793–803. https://doi.org/10.1080/10494820.2020.1808794

White, G. (2020). Adaptive learning technology relationship with student learning outcomes. *Journal of Information Technology Education*, 19, 113–130. https://doi.org/10.28945/4526

Wu, S., & Yang, K. (2022). The effectiveness of teacher support for students' learning of artificial intelligence popular science activities. *Frontiers in Psychology*, •••, 13.https://doi.org/10.3389/fpsyg.2022.868623

Zhang, K., & Aslan, A. B. (2021). AI technologies for education: Recent research & future directions. *Computers and Education: Artificial Intelligence*, 2, 100025. https://doi.org/10.1016/j.caeai.2021.100025

Zhang, L., Basham, J. D., & Yang, S. (2020). Understanding the implementation of Personalized learning: A research synthesis. *Educational Research Review*, 31, 100339. DOI: 10.1016/j.edurev.2020.100339

Chapter 5
What Would Confucius Do?
A Study of Cultural Factors Impacting the Use of AI in Confucian EFL Contexts

Andrew Schenck
https://orcid.org/0000-0002-3864-6267
Fort Hays State University, USA

ABSTRACT

Although AI will undoubtedly have a prominent role in the cultivation of language learning, its application in modern-day English as a Foreign Language (EFL) classrooms remains limited. The failure to adapt theory to practice may be the result of assumptions about technology, which posit that all learners will benefit equally from unilateral adoption of new techniques. In reality, the benefits of specific AI technologies may differ significantly based on characteristics of an educational environment. In Confucian countries, for example, traditional cultural values for group action may adversely impact autonomous learning styles that value LLM "tutors" like ChatGPT. It is essential that cultural and contextual factors of an educational environment be considered before AI technologies are utilized. Therefore, the present book chapter examines educational variables associated with Confucian contexts, yielding insights for the improvement of EFL instruction.

DOI: 10.4018/979-8-3693-6130-6.ch005

INTRODUCTION

Following the introduction of ChatGPT, I gave my English learners a writing project. They were asked to brainstorm potential problems with AI and were then given time to conduct research and develop an outline, which was followed by in-class writing. What problems did they describe? If you would like to know, just use the following prompt in ChatGPT "Tell me about some problems with AI." The structure of each outline reflected variations of the following points:

1. Bias and Fairness
2. Lack of Transparency and Explainability
3. Privacy Concerns
4. Job Displacement and Economic Impact
5. Security Risks
6. Ethical Considerations

Although learners often added research or personal experiences to supplement the points, similarities illustrate a fundamental change in the way students think. Rather than constructing an outline based on background knowledge or research, learners can now readily adopt propositions put forth by chatbots like ChatGPT.

Changes in student behavior reveal a need to investigate the impact of AI, as well as a need for educational reform. While the need for educational improvement is clear, the best means of enacting positive change is not. Concerning this issue, Zawacki-Richter et al. (2019) write that AI has been around for 30 years, yet "it is still unclear for educators how to make pedagogical advantage of it on a broader scale, and how it can actually impact meaningfully on teaching and learning in higher education." (p. 1). We do not adequately understand how AI should be adapted to diverse educational contexts to facilitate concrete educational gains. Despite this failure, research has identified the potential of AI to transform a learner's experience, providing personalized and adaptive instruction, as well as intelligent tutoring systems (Zawacki-Richter et al., 2019, p. 1). In the field of English as a Foreign Language (EFL) instruction, the development of AI also has tremendous potential. Learners may interact with chatbots like ChatGPT to learn new ideas about a research topic. In addition, machine translation may promote understanding of English texts through translation into the L1 (Sharadgah & Sa'di, 2022). Such powerful AI tools can provide valuable individual feedback, leading to self-discovery and learner autonomy. As in the case of other educational fields, the potential of AI in EFL is enormous, yet successful utilization of AI tools remains a future dream rather than a present-day reality (Renandya et al., 2023).

Despite the potential to stimulate student development and improve EFL instruction, adaptation of AI to practice remains limited, primarily because researchers and educators lack information about how technology should be changed to accommodate diverse learners and educational contexts. Currently, educational research tends to investigate AI technology using a one-size-fits-all approach, which examines the overall effectiveness of one treatment. While an important first step, this study does not provide enough information to differentiate techniques based upon learner needs. Diverse learners may react very differently to AI. Some learners may use translation devices as a scaffold, which gradually leads to better communication in English. Other learners may use it to avoid thinking in the L2, thereby reducing the time required to interpret or construct complex discourse in a foreign language. As in the case of translation, learners may react to chatbots very differently. Whereas some learners may use the technology for autonomous practice and personal growth, others may use it to complete assignments and avoid studying altogether. There is a great deal of potential for AI, yet there is also a great deal of potential variability. Therefore, we must understand this variability before AI can be effectively utilized.

As the diversity of learner backgrounds can influence efficacy, it is no wonder that systematic, widespread adoption of technology often yields lackluster results. In addition to individual learner characteristics, research suggests that various cultural factors may be impacting the efficacy of AI technology in Confucian EFL classrooms. Traditional learning methods rely heavily on virtues that stress group action and teacher authority. This perspective is exemplified by the predominance of standardized testing in countries like China, Korea, and Japan, where national curricula are designed to inculcate a common body of knowledge and core social values (Ozturgut, 2011). Such memorization has strengthened perceptions of cultural homogeneity. Consequently, learners from Confucian settings may not be willing to adopt more individualistic or autonomous learning practices, which are commonly found within Western contexts (Egitim, 2022a; Schenck, 2023; Wang & Torrisi-Steele, 2015). Because traditional cultural values encourage adherence to group norms and collective action, self-directed learning styles that value LLM "tutors" like ChatGPT may be difficult to implement. In addition to issues related to learner autonomy, implicit cultural biases embedded in AI technology like ChatGPT further complicate education in Confucian countries (Schenck, 2024a).

Although AI will undoubtedly have a prominent role in the cultivation of language learning, our knowledge of just how to use it remains limited. We are currently restricted to a one-size-fits-all approach, lacking the detailed knowledge needed to adapt technology to diverse language contexts. The present book chapter will further examine the variables impacting learners in Confucian contexts such as China, South Korea, Vietnam, and Japan. Through this examination, the importance of cultural and contextual factors on the efficacy of AI techniques will be explained, along with recommendations for the improvement of instruction in Confucian EFL contexts.

THE IMPACT OF CONFUCIAN VALUES ON EFL EDUCATION

In countries such as South Korea, China, Japan, Singapore, and Vietnam, the influence of cultural beliefs on education may be especially prevalent, due primarily to well-established Confucian norms that regulate all aspects of society (Marginson, 2011). Confucianism is a philosophical worldview, which strives to cultivate a harmonious and productive social order through the promulgation of key moral virtues. Via this worldview, individuals are compelled to strive for *Junzi*, a representation of human excellence, by cultivating two virtues called *Ren* and *Li* (Snell et al., 2022). *Ren* refers to an internal sense of benevolence that reveals one's commitment to society. After the cultivation of *Ren*, one is expected to outwardly express this virtue by using a discreet system of etiquette, which is referred to as *Li* (Li & Hayhoe, 2012). Because values like *Junzi*, *Ren*, and *Li* all appear to promote collectivist thought and action, cognitive skills development has often been regarded as problematic in a Confucian context. The belief in moral absolutes appears to suggest that old traditions should be honored at the expense of new, innovative means of solving tasks (Shin & Koh, 2005). As a result, learners may avoid trying new things or thinking in ways that do not adhere to accepted cultural norms.

The virtue of *Li*, which promotes a hierarchical social order and obedience to authority, may also be problematic for critical thinking skills development (Kim, 2013; Park & Chesla, 2007). *Li* establishes order, strictly regulating social behavior and etiquette according to hierarchical relationships (e.g., father and son; husband and wife; older brother and younger brother; and friends). As a result, teachers have held a dominant position in the classroom as content experts, whereas students have been traditionally regarded as recipients of knowledge (Kim, 2013). In the role of passive recipient, learners in Confucian countries have often been characterized as lacking in critical thinking ability. Concerning this issue, questionnaire data from Japanese EFL learners in an academic writing course "suggested that teacher-centered educational approaches in high school English classes significantly hindered the development of learner autonomy and critical thinking skills among the students" (Egitim, 2017; p. 163). In a study by McGuire (2007), teacher-centered approaches in South Korea were also found to promote rote memorization in the language learning classroom, thereby clashing with communicative approaches that promoted interaction and critical thinking. More recent research continues to suggest that Korean EFL learners follow traditional norms for behavior in the classroom, showing a reluctance to speak or express opinions (DeWalsche, 2015; Niederhauser, 2012). A great deal of research suggests that cultural beliefs dominate educational institutions in Confucian countries, thereby perpetuating teacher-centered approaches to learning.

Although *Li*, *Ren*, and *Junzi* appear to promote homogeneity that negatively impacts critical thinking in the classroom (Li & Hayhoe, 2012; Xu et al., 2018), researchers such as Tan (2017) contend that education in Confucian contexts should be viewed as an "open tradition," thereby allowing for innovation and change. Some researchers even posit that the dynamic relationship between *Ren* and *Li* represents an educational opportunity to promote constructivist inquiry (Wei, 2019). From this perspective, people with Confucian values can use personal experience to justify or modify how *Ren* is expressed, as did Confucius. In this way, social behaviors and etiquette associated with *Li* represent an individual's critical evaluation of core Confucian values. Rather than being static, Confucian values can be dynamic forces that regulate the roles, responsibilities, and harmony of a group. If education and technology are developed within this philosophical framework, constructivist inquiry may be possible. Although often considered to be moral absolutes, whereby old traditions are honored at the expense of innovative solutions, Confucian values may indeed change.

Due to the potential influences of Confucianism on education, students' cultural values must be examined along with attitudes about education in countries such as South Korea, China, Japan, Singapore, and Vietnam. Thus far, some EFL research has been conducted to investigate learner attitudes in China and Japan (Akatsuka, 2019; Du & Zhang, 2022; Manalo et al., 2013; McKinley, 2013; Zhang, 2022). A study by Zhang (2022), for example, examined attitudes about critical thinking among 104 English learners at a Chinese university. Results revealed that students lacked a clear knowledge of critical thinking yet held high expectations for receiving training from teachers. This finding appears to mirror the Confucian values of *Li* and *Ren*, whereby skills are to be acquired from a content expert, rather than cultivated in an individualistic way. Education in Confucian contexts was further investigated by Manalo et al. (2013), who used a questionnaire to investigate the beliefs of 363 undergraduate students from both Japan and New Zealand. The study found that cultural context influenced preferences for the use of various educational strategies needed for critical thinking. Overall, research suggests that there is indeed a cultural influence on education in Confucian contexts.

THE IMPACT OF CONFUCIAN VALUES ON AI IN EFL CONTEXTS

Cultural values appear to impact education in Asian EFL contexts, yet little research has examined this issue along with new technologies for language learning. Modern educational research in Asian countries tends to use a standard experimental method, whereby one treatment with new technological tools is evaluated (Daud & Husin, 2004; Ding, 2016; Yang et al., 2012; Yang et al., 2014). Although studies do not often investigate links between cultural factors and technology, some research does indeed explore these relationships. In a recent study of 40 Vietnamese university students, Pham et al. (2020) examined learner attitudes as well as performance; the study concluded that electronic writing feedback can improve reflective thinking and writing, helping learners to "overcome the Confucian cultural barriers to get engaged in giving and receiving critique from their peers" (p. 1). As suggested by the article, digital writing feedback can help learners avoid confrontation about writing issues, promoting group harmony (*Ren*). Although the impact of technology on traditional Confucian norms is exemplified through such study, the influence of cultural values on the utilization of technology is not adequately explored. Cultural values may also influence how technology is used. In fact, modern research of Confucian EFL contexts suggests that aspects of *Ren* and *Li* have a significant impact on how AI technology is used to learn a foreign language.

The Confucian virtue of *Ren*, which values group harmony and adherence to accepted norms, appears to influence how learners utilize AI for cognitively demanding tasks. In a recent study of South Korean university learners, overreliance on ChatGPT as a replacement for critical thinking was a prevalent theme in narratives (Schenck, 2024c). Students often reported that other learners were using ChatGPT instead of carefully constructing persuasive essays. Having the power to use AI without restriction appears to have reduced the cognitive effort of some learners, who use ChatGPT for brainstorming, organizing ideas, and/or writing entire essays (See Table 1).

Table 1. Student concerns about ChatGPT (Schenck, 2024c)

Student Number	Concerns about ChatGPT
Student 1	I think because of ChatGPT, our school life got a bit easier, but it made us think less. I think it has both positive and negative changes. It made us do things very easily and by reading what ChatGPT says, we can also improve our knowledge and also think critically if it is correct or not. However, some students rely on ChatGPT and don't even think about the things. For these students, ChatGPT made them think less critically.
Student 2	It disrupts our critical thinking. Many students use it when organizing their essay outline, and I think the most critical process of an essay is outlining because it requires critical thinking and organizing skills.
Student 3	To be honest, ChatGPT is useful in many academic ways. It provides useful information. However, in English, it interrupts students' critical thinking by finishing their work for them.
Student 4	GPT can provide an idea of essay topics or help writers narrow the given topics. However, some students are abusing AI to write their papers. It's not only effective in improving students' critical thinking skills but also not helpful in improving their English skills.
Student 5	I would say it has helped and prevented me from critical thinking. I can ask a question to ChatGPT that just not directly answer my question but helps me to brainstorm. For example, if I have no domain knowledge about treatment and need to write an essay about it, I can ask ChatGPT, "What are some common problems treatments have?". However, since I am not restricted to asking any type of questions to ChatGPT, I can ask a question that directly answers my question.
Student 6	The effect that occurred on critical thinking by CharGPT will differ from how we use it. If we use ChatGPT to actualize our critical thinking or make us think will bring positive effects to us. However, if we use ChatGPT to substitute our thinking will bring negative effects.
Student 7	Chat GPT helped both ways. Since people usually think based on what they have preserved in their experiences, asking questions to Chat GPT helps people to see the view they haven't thought of. However, problems come when people rely on ChatGPT for everything.
Student 8	I think it is bad for critical thinking because it limits creativity if students become overly dependent on the AI for answers.
Student 9	Both, on the side of positive, GPT is a good data bank. When we write about some topics, chat GPT can help us to gather information. It saves time. But, on the side of the negative, some students could abuse the Chat GPT to write easily the essay.
Student 10	I think the change is positive, but it depends on how you use ChatGPT. Unlike the Internet, which presents only a specific perspective, AI helps us think from our perspective. However, the more you use AI, the more likely it is to hurt critical thinking. In other words, the more results from AI, the more they will interfere with our subjective thinking. Therefore, I think it has a positive effect on critical thinking if we use it appropriately.

If technology is used too much, it may serve as a substitute for critical thinking, thereby limiting creativity and innovation in writing. Learners who are accustomed to receiving knowledge from a content expert (the teacher) may also accept content from ChatGPT without careful consideration. This would explain several remarks in Table 1, which cite abuse of ChatGPT and avoidance of cognitively demanding writing tasks. Although academic dishonesty is by no means isolated to Confucian contexts, such a prevalence may reflect collectivist pressures associated with *Ren*, as has been reported in some Chinese EFL contexts (Ma et al., 2013; Tsui & Ngo, 2016). Such a group tendency may need to be reformed through the renegotiation of *Ren* and *Li*. As with some prestigious regional universities in China, collectivist values may need to be transformed to create new cultural norms concerning the use of AI, which support academic integrity and higher individualism (Zhang & Yin, 2019).

In addition to group pressures, passive student roles mandated by *Li* seem to have impacted how AI technology is used to comprehend English subject matter. Many Confucian learners may accept output generated by LLMs like ChatGPT, without careful consideration of the content. For example, South Korean university students who preferred to use technology for learning subject matter did not think critical thinking was important and were more likely to skip classes if online materials were provided (Schenck, 2024c). The finding suggests a growing passivity among students who extensively rely on AI technology. It is important to note that learners in the study with clear goals and a desire for engagement appear to use technology in more productive ways. These learners also placed a larger value on the importance of critical thinking, suggesting a potential to learn more autonomously (Schenck, 2024c). Overall, research suggests that Confucian EFL contexts such as South Korea have learners who rely on traditional autocratic control and learners who are willing and able to accept more educational autonomy. A clear assessment of individual differences will be needed before instruction can be tailored to a student's needs.

Finally, a predilection for autocratic classroom management, which is also closely linked to the value of *Li* (Schenck, 2024b), appears to impact how technology is used for the transmission or creation of knowledge. South Korean university students who desired a more teacher-centric class preferred using technology for knowledge transmission, rather than creative inquiry or knowledge discovery (Schenck, 2023). Findings suggest that Confucian learners traditionally use technology, avoiding tasks that may violate educational norms. Because creativity, innovation, and critical thinking may not adhere to group standards for behavior or propriety, these students may prefer learning behaviors that emphasize knowledge transmission. At the same time, not all students of the study exemplified traditional Confucian values. Many of the learners with experiences in Western contexts supported more democratic classroom leadership practices, as well as a desire to use technology for knowledge creation and discovery (Schenck, 2023, Schenck, 2024b). Research results reveal a need to understand traditional Confucian values, as well as a need to consider cultural differences that impact the use of technology when designing EFL tasks.

Helping Traditional Confucian Learners Use AI for Language Learning

Confucian educational contexts present unique opportunities and challenges, which should be considered when designing EFL lessons. For traditional learners, who prefer more autocratic classroom control, strict regulation of technological resources may be needed. Firm control of technology will also be necessary in educational contexts where brainstorming, outlining, and even writing entire papers with AI has become the norm. To ensure the cultivation of cognitive skills associated with tasks like brainstorming or creating an essay outline, learners may first need to complete classroom tasks without any technological support. Students can then generate AI samples for comparison. Through regimented control of technological resources in this way, teachers can ensure that cognitive skills needed for language learning are acquired.

To further promote creativity and innovation, teachers may need to make changes to how students collaborate with technology. In traditional Confucian classrooms, students may be reluctant to speak or express opinions as a class, fearing that they may violate a teacher's authority or accepted group norms. Due to potential obstacles to collaboration and critical thinking, teachers may need to separate learners into peer groups when technology is used. Whether virtual or face-to-face, peer groups can prompt more democratic participation in Confucian contexts, since all learners have the same egalitarian role in accordance with *Li*. Via such groups, students can take risks and utilize AI in more innovative ways, without challenging a teacher's authority. At the same time, teachers may monitor performance, ensuring that students utilize technology for academic development, innovation, and critical thinking.

Another means to promote positive utilization of AI is through crafting smaller and more manageable learning tasks. Critical thinking is often challenging for traditional Confucian learners. In addition, students who lack time for thoughtful consideration of class content may turn to AI for task completion. Research confirms this notion, suggesting that time constraints are one cause of overreliance on AI (Schenck, 2024c). Due to challenges with critical thinking and time constraints, Confucian learners may need additional help or scaffolding. For example, rather than crafting an outline for an entire essay, learners may be prompted to craft a creative and innovative hook for an essay introduction. Other aspects of outline creation may be completed in smaller, discrete units. By keeping tasks small and manageable, students may have the time to effectively utilize critical thinking skills. In addition, students may gain confidence, thereby cultivating strategies needed for lifelong learning.

A final pedagogical reform to help Confucian learners deal with AI may be the utilization of ipsative assessment. Ipsative assessment is the process of providing formative feedback for learning rather than simply using criterion-based assessments for evaluation (Hughes, 2011). Comparison of grades and performance often brings about anxiety among Confucian learners, who feel pressure to adhere to group standards. Heightened pressures, in turn, may increase temptation to cheat using AI technologies. To address issues associated with group pressure and anxiety, educators may need an individualistic approach to student assessment, which reduces competition and ensures that each learner develops to their full potential. By giving all learners an equal opportunity to be successful, group harmony may be maintained following the virtue of *Ren*. Furthermore, ipsative assessment can reduce the pressure to perform like peers, thereby reducing the temptation to cheat using AI technologies.

Helping All Learners Develop More Autonomy

Educators in Confucian contexts may promote learning through strict control and assessment methods that adhere to traditional norms, yet students should also be encouraged to develop more learning autonomy with the use of technology. Such a proposition may not be an easy task. This perspective is illustrated by a recent study, which suggested that students in Chinese educational contexts lack the behavioral or technical skills necessary for independent learning (Lin & Reinders, 2019). Other studies also suggest that traditional teacher-centric approaches (e.g., the grammar-translation approach) have led to challenges concerning the development of student autonomy and critical thinking skills (Egitim, 2022b). Despite potential challenges, students may develop more autonomous learning skills through cultivating an awareness of critical thinking, which is filtered through a technological lens.

To effectively utilize AI for language learning, modern techniques for critical thinking must prompt reflection of technological influences. Rather than being discreet constructs, critical thinking, and technology are intricately intertwined. This perspective is illustrated when metacognitive and cognitive strategies are examined through a technological lens. Metacognitive strategies are executive functions used to monitor one's own learning process. Via such strategies, students can plan for learning, think about the learning process, and monitor progress. Cognitive strategies, in contrast, are limited to specific learning tasks, involving direct manipulation of the material itself (Brown, 2007, p. 134-135). AI technologies may hinder the development of metacognitive and cognitive skills needed for language learning. Consider the following potential problems associated with essay construction:

1. AI technologies can generate outlines, essays, and written points without giving the student a good understanding of a topic.
2. AI technologies like ChatGPT often fail to provide specific contextual and pragmatic information needed to understand the importance of rhetoric.
3. AI technologies do not require reflection about the language learning process.
4. AI technologies do not require planning or rehearsal to obtain results.
5. Research can be automatically retrieved and linked to essay content without direct oversight from the user.
6. AI may translate without cognitive effort on the part of the learner.
7. The grouping of ideas and outlining can be done solely by AI.
8. Deductive reasoning to construct support for a topic can be performed by AI.
9. Recombination of essay points may be done through user prompts rather than direct manipulation of content by the writer.
10. Existing knowledge is not necessarily required to construct an essay with AI.

As revealed from the examples above, AI technologies can be used to compose essays and research papers, limiting an individual's ability to process language through critical inquiry. Learners do not need to conduct research, nor do they require a comprehensive understanding of a topic to produce a paper. In addition, the papers produced by AI technologies often lack significant pragmatic information needed to make discourse clear and persuasive. This view is supported by research of essays generated by ChatGPT, which did not effectively utilize persuasive rhetoric related to cultural values like power distance (Schenck, 2024a). As a result of potential negative influences from AI technologies on metacognition, it will be important to provide additional instruction concerning the impact of technology and its limits on a student's own cognitive development. For example, learners may be taken through think-aloud protocols as they conduct brainstorming and outlining activities with and without AI. Students may also be asked to write more reflective essays or paragraphs, which describe the process they used to construct a paper. This will help promote an awareness of technology's impact on cognition and language learning.

Although EFL curricula often stimulate cognitive reflection, they usually lack opportunities to ponder the impact of technology on language learning. As a result, learners may not acquire metacognitive and cognitive strategies that can be applied in today's digital world. To cultivate an awareness of technological influences that affect cognition, learners may need to complete language tasks with and without AI. Learners may then be compelled to examine the cognitive strategies needed to complete these tasks, thereby heightening awareness of technological influences. Through the application of more modern pedagogical designs, cognitive and metacognitive strategies may be cultivated and applied, ensuring that language development and student growth is sustainable. Learners will also gain a crucial awareness of how to use technology responsibly.

CONCLUSION

According to Hartse and Morphett (2024), writing is a form of technology that restructures thought. Regarding this viewpoint, the authors go on to explain that "writing itself is arguably the most important tool for thinking that university students need to master" (para. 4). By removing the need to think from writing or other language learning tasks, AI can prevent learners from gaining valuable cognitive skills. While a need for more student engagement and critical thinking with technology is clear, the best means to enact reforms is not. Diversity of learner background makes different educational strategies necessary.

In Confucian cultural contexts, values for *Ren* and *Li* should be considered when promoting critical thinking and innovation with technology. Traditional learners may benefit from strict oversight of technological resources in a more teacher-centric classroom. In contrast, learners who are willing and able to use technology more autonomously may benefit from classroom tasks that use democratic and empowered peer groups. Furthermore, educators in Confucian contexts may need to reconsider assessment. The widespread availability of AI often makes existing standardized measures of proficiency seem superfluous. A change in mindset, which focuses on individual growth and development, may be needed. Ipsative measures of student achievement should be developed to help each student focus on personal development. This may be especially important in Confucian contexts, where group pressures to conform result in extreme measures (e.g., cheating) to ensure that an academic standard is achieved.

Although educational reforms may differ based on context, heightened student autonomy will always be an ideal to strive for. Preferably, learners will need to gain an awareness of how technology impacts learning and cognition, which aids in the development of self-monitoring strategies needed for lifelong learning. Whereas careful training will help learners gain the skills needed to utilize technology for growth and development, how this autonomy is implemented may differ based on context. A teacher will need to carefully assess learner needs, developing educational strategies that are culturally appropriate, while promulgating autonomous practices that support lifelong learning and development.

REFERENCES

Akatsuka, Y. (2019). Awareness of critical thinking attitudes and English speaking skills: The effects of questions involving higher-order thinking. *Journal of Pan-Pacific Association of Applied Linguistics*, 23(2), 59–84. DOI: 10.25256/PAAL.23.2.4

Brown, H. D. (2007). *Principles of language learning and teaching: A course in second language acquisition* (5th ed.). Pearson.

Daud, N. M., & Husin, Z. (2004). Developing critical thinking skills in computer-aided extended reading classes. *British Journal of Educational Technology*, 35(4), 477–487. DOI: 10.1111/j.0007-1013.2004.00405.x

DeWaelsche, S. A. (2015). Critical thinking, questioning and student engagement in Korean university English courses. *Linguistics and Education*, 32, 131–147. DOI: 10.1016/j.linged.2015.10.003

Ding, X. (2016). The effect of WeChat-assisted problem-based learning on the critical thinking disposition of EFL learners. [iJET]. *International Journal of Emerging Technologies in Learning*, 11(12), 23–29. DOI: 10.3991/ijet.v11i12.5927

Du, X., & Zhang, L. (2022). Investigating EFL learners' perceptions of critical thinking learning affordances: Voices from Chinese university English majors. *SAGE Open*, 12(2), 1–12. DOI: 10.1177/21582440221094584

Egitim, S. (2017). The role of autonomy in critical thinking. *Global Japanese Review, 9*(1), 155-164. http://hdl.handle.net/10291/20647

Egitim, S. (2022a). Do Japanese students lack critical thinking? Addressing the misconception. *Power and Education*, 14(3), 304–309. DOI: 10.1177/17577438221107203

Egitim, S. (2022b). Voices on language teacher stereotypes: Critical cultural competence building as a pedagogical strategy. *Journal of Language, Identity, and Education*, •••, 1–15. DOI: 10.1080/15348458.2022.2070847

Hartse, J. H., & Morphett, T. (2024, March 26). Writing is a technology that restructures thought - and in an AI age, universities need to teach it more. *The Conversation*. https://theconversation.com/writing-is-a-technology-that-restructures-thought-and-in-an-ai-age-universities-need-to-teach-it-more-219482

Hughes, G. (2011). Towards a personal best: A case for introducing ipsative assessment in higher education. *Studies in Higher Education*, 36(3), 353–367. DOI: 10.1080/03075079.2010.486859

Kim, S. (2013). Confucianism and acceptable inequalities. *Philosophy and Social Criticism*, 39(10), 983–1004. DOI: 10.1177/0191453713507015

Li, J., & Hayhoe, R. (2012). Confucianism and higher education. In Banks, J. A. (Ed.), *SAGE encyclopedia of diversity in education* (Vol. 1, pp. 443–446). Sage.

Lin, L., & Reinders, H. (2019). Students' and teachers' readiness for autonomy: Beliefs and practices in developing autonomy in the Chinese context. *Asia Pacific Education Review*, 20(1), 69–89. DOI: 10.1007/s12564-018-9564-3

Ma, Y., McCabe, D. L., & Liu, R. (2013). Students' academic cheating in Chinese universities: Prevalence, influencing factors, and proposed action. *Journal of Academic Ethics*, 11(3), 169–184. DOI: 10.1007/s10805-013-9186-7

Manalo, E., Kusumi, T., Koyasu, M., Michita, Y., & Tanaka, Y. (2013). To what extent do culture-related factors influence university students' critical thinking use? *Thinking Skills and Creativity*, 10, 121–132. DOI: 10.1016/j.tsc.2013.08.003

Marginson, S. (2011). Higher education in East Asia and Singapore: Rise of the Confucian model. *Higher Education*, 61(5), 587–611. DOI: 10.1007/s10734-010-9384-9

McGuire, J. M. (2007). Why has the critical thinking movement not come to Korea? *Asia Pacific Education Review*, 8(2), 224–232. DOI: 10.1007/BF03029258

McKinley, J. (2013). Displaying critical thinking in EFL academic writing: A discussion of Japanese to English contrastive rhetoric. *RELC Journal*, 44(2), 195–208. DOI: 10.1177/0033688213488386

Niederhauser, J. S. (2012). Motivating learners at South Korean universities. *English Teaching Forum, 50*(3), 28-31. https://files.eric.ed.gov/fulltext/EJ997526.pdf

Ozturgut, O., null, , null, , & null, . (2011). Learning by example: Standardized testing in the cases of China, Korea, Japan, and Taiwan. *Academic Leadership: The Online Journal*, 9(3), 1–10. DOI: 10.58809/DPYD4742

Park, M., & Chesla, C. (2007). Revisiting Confucianism as a conceptual framework for Asian family study. *Journal of Family Nursing*, 13(3), 293–311. DOI: 10.1177/1074840707304400 PMID: 17641110

Pham, T. N., Lin, M., Trinh, V. Q., & Bui, L. T. P. (2020). Electronic peer feedback, EFL academic writing and reflective thinking: Evidence from a Confucian context. *SAGE Open*, 10(1), 1–20. DOI: 10.1177/2158244020914554

Renandya, W. A., Ivone, F. M., & Hidayati, M. (2023). Harnessing the power of technology in ELT. *Journal of Studies in the English Language*, 18(2), 143–160. https://so04.tci-thaijo.org/index.php/jsel/article/view/268591

Schenck, A. (2023). Investigating the influence of classroom leadership preferences on the use of technology: A survey of Korean university learners. *Journal of Higher Education Policy and Leadership Studies*, 4(3), 118–130. DOI: 10.61186/johepal.4.3.118

Schenck, A. (2024a). ChatGPT is powerful, but does it have power distance? A study of culturally imbued discourse in AI-generated essays. [IJAET]. *International Journal of Adult Education and Technology*, 15(1), 1–17. DOI: 10.4018/IJAET.338219

Schenck, A. (2024b). Examining relationships between classroom leadership styles and Confucian values: A study of Korean EFL learner preferences. *The Asia-Pacific Education Researcher*, 33(3), 659–670. DOI: 10.1007/s40299-023-00762-w

Schenck, A. (2024c). Examining relationships between technology and critical thinking: A Study of South Korean EFL Learners. *Education Sciences*, 14(6), 1–14. DOI: 10.3390/educsci14060652

Sharadgah, T. A., & Sa'di, R. A. (2022). A systematic review of research on the use of artificial intelligence in English language teaching and learning (2015-2021): What are the current effects? *Journal of Information Technology Education*, 21, 337–377. DOI: 10.28945/4999

Shin, S., & Koh, M. S. (2005). Korean education in cultural context. *Essays in Education*, 14(1), 1–10. https://openriver.winona.edu/eie/vol14/iss1/10

Snell, R. S., Wu, C. X., & Lei, H. W. (2022). Junzi virtues: A Confucian foundation for harmony within organizations. *Asian Journal of Business Ethics*, 11(1), 183–226. DOI: 10.1007/s13520-022-00146-1

Tan, C. (2017). Confucianism and education. In Noblit, G. (Ed.), *Oxford research encyclopedia of education* (pp. 1–18). Oxford University Press. DOI: 10.1093/acrefore/9780190264093.013.226

Tsui, A. P. Y., & Ngo, H. Y. (2016). Social-motivational factors affecting business students' cheating behavior in Hong Kong and China. *Journal of Education for Business*, 91(7), 365–373. DOI: 10.1080/08832323.2016.1231108

Wang, V., & Torrisi-Steele, G. (2015). Confucian and Western teaching and learning. [IJAVET]. *International Journal of Adult Vocational Education and Technology*, 6(1), 52–64. DOI: 10.4018/ijavet.2015010104

Wei, Z. (2019). *Constructivism and teachers in Chinese culture: Enriching Confucianism with constructivism*. Springer., DOI: 10.1007/978-981-13-2691-2

Xu, G., Chen, Y., & Xu, L. (Eds.). (2018). *Understanding Chinese culture: Philosophy, religion, science and technology*. Palgrave Macmillan. DOI: 10.1007/978-981-10-8162-0

Yang, Y. T. C., Gamble, J. H., Hung, Y. W., & Lin, T. Y. (2014). An online adaptive learning environment for critical-thinking-infused English literacy instruction. *British Journal of Educational Technology*, 45(4), 723–747. DOI: 10.1111/bjet.12080

Yang, Y. T. C., & Wu, W. C. I. (2012). Digital storytelling for enhancing student academic achievement, critical thinking, and learning motivation: A year-long experimental study. *Computers & Education*, 59(2), 339–352. DOI: 10.1016/j.compedu.2011.12.012

Zawacki-Richter, O., Marín, V. I., Bond, M., & Gouverneur, F. (2019). Systematic review of research on artificial intelligence applications in higher education–where are the educators? *International Journal of Educational Technology in Higher Education*, 16(39), 1–27. DOI: 10.1186/s41239-019-0171-0

Zhang, M. (2022). A survey of English majors' attitudes towards critical thinking. *Athens Journal of Humanities & Arts*, 9(1), 27–48. DOI: 10.30958/ajha.8-1-2

Zhang, Y., & Yin, H. (2019). Collaborative cheating among Chinese college students: The effects of peer influence and individualism-collectivism orientations. *Assessment & Evaluation in Higher Education*, 45(1), 54–69. DOI: 10.1080/02602938.2019.1608504

Chapter 6
Redefining Learning in the Digital Age

Eun-Ok Baek
https://orcid.org/0000-0002-0697-6763
California State University, San Bernardino, USA

Romina Wilson
https://orcid.org/0009-0005-7502-5135
California State University, San Bernardino, USA

Chang Liu
California State University, San Bernardino, USA

ABSTRACT

This chapter explores the potential alignment and challenges between generative AI tools and constructivist principles in the context of education. Despite the significant advancements in generative AI technology, there is still a need for further investigation and research when integrating AI into education. The integration of generative AI technologies into the educational setting holds immense potential for enhancing constructivist learning approaches. By leveraging the natural language processing capabilities of AI models, interactive, learner-centered learning environments can be created, promoting active knowledge construction, meaning-making, and authentic learning experiences. However, the effective integration of generative AI in education requires a deep understanding of its affordances, potential challenges, and ethical considerations. This chapter delves into the fundamental principles of constructivism and generative AI, examining their interplay within the educational sphere. It includes case studies and addresses ethical considerations.

DOI: 10.4018/979-8-3693-6130-6.ch006

INTRODUCTION

Since ancient times, humanity has continually refined the techniques and sciences behind toolmaking and craftsmanship. We have long envisioned a future where technology significantly enhances our lives. We created tools to help us learn and live better. Contemporary advancements in technology now offer numerous study and learning opportunities, especially in the field of education. The rise of new technologies has led to the emergence of Generative Artificial Intelligence. Generative AI tools, such as language models and neural networks, play a crucial role in this advancement with its impact on various fields, such as education, healthcare, and communication (Stretton et al., 2023). These tools can generate human-like conversation, provide instant feedback on text, and create realistic study cases and scenarios. These capabilities unveil new possibilities for teaching and learning, enhancing the educational experience for students and educators.

While chatbots in general have given users a glimpse of AI through natural-sounding language abilities, ChatGPT made a significant record with a million user sign ups in the five days succeeding its launch on November 30, 2022 (Baek & Wilson, 2024) and continues to generate great enthusiasm in all sectors including the education field. On the other hand, it also raises concerns about its potential for misuse. For instance, soon after ChatGPT's introduction to the world, New York City public schools banned its use in classrooms (Elsen-Rooney, 2023) and "Panic over AI" (O'Brien, 2023) made schools from Seattle to Paris blocked ChatGPT use. After much reflection, attitudes and emotions toward ChatGPT have evolved in the months following, with New York City public schools eventually reversing their original decision (Rosenblatt, 2023; Siegel, 2023).

This breakthrough has shifted the idea of "knowing" through rote memorization to placing a high value on discovering, evaluating, and utilizing information effectively through higher-order thinking. This skill set includes self-regulation, critical thinking, and problem-solving abilities in multiple contexts (Liu et al., 2022). Constructivism, a learning theory emphasizing the importance of learner initiation and hands-on experience, stresses the cultivation of these higher-order thinking skills. This process of learners' actively searching for knowledge corresponds well with the characteristics of generative AI, such as ChatGPT. These tools prioritize self-centered studying, allowing learners to customize educational experiences to each of their unique needs and interests. ChatGPT provides instant responses, which enhances motivation through immediate feedback and support (McGuire, et al., 2024). Its ability to provide unlimited access to information enables learners to independently explore a wide range of topics. This benefits both instructors and students with teachers leveraging this advanced technology through access to more sophisticated learning materials, while students can take control and ownership of their own learning processes, as studies have shown that ChatGPT can generate complex teaching content with proper prompts (Stretton et al., 2024). ChatGPT supports metacognition by helping learners become aware of their learning processes (Exintaris, et al., 2024), fostering a cycle of continuous learning and improvement, and encouraging more interactive and enjoyable educational experiences. While more schools have adopted generative AI for use in classrooms, concerns about its misuse and unethical use remain unresolved. Now, more than ever, it is crucial to discuss how to effectively use generative AI to facilitate teaching and learning. Thus, this paper aims to explore how generative AIs can be incorporated into classroom teaching through a literature review.

Constructivism is a well-established pedagogical learning theory emphasizing the active role of learners in their own learning process. Its foundations can be traced back to philosophical and psychological concepts from the early 20th century. Constructivism posits that instead of passively receiving information, learners actively construct their understanding of the world based on their experiences, interactions, and reflections (Duffy & Cunningham, 1996). Learners utilize their previous knowledge as a foundation and build upon it with newly acquired knowledge (Narayan et al., 2013).

The rapid advancement of artificial intelligence (AI) technologies, particularly generative AI, has created new opportunities for teaching and learning, naturally forming an intersection between generative AI and constructivism as a result. Integrating generative AI technologies into educational settings is especially relevant and timely, as institutions at all levels grapple with the use of cutting-edge technology while maintaining pedagogical effectiveness. Integration holds immense potential for enhancing constructivist learning by leveraging AI's natural language processing capabilities to create interactive, learner-centered environments, promoting active knowledge construction, meaning-making, and authentic learning experiences. The alignment of generative AI and constructivist principles presents a unique opportunity to explore innovative pedagogical strategies that enhance and support constructivist approaches to teaching and learning.

This chapter aims to investigate this intersection, contributing to the ongoing discourse on the responsible and effective use of AI in education while promoting learner agencies, meaningful knowledge acquisition, and transformative learning experiences. Despite significant advancements in generative AI technology, there is meager information available to aid with its integration into education, underscoring the need for further investigation and research. With this chapter we explore the potential alignment and challenges between generative AI tools and constructivist principles in the context of education. We analyze the potential of generative AI models in facilitating key principles of constructivism—namely, that learning is an active process of knowledge construction, knowledge being socially constructed, learners being motivated by their own interests and experiences, and problem-solving approaches being used to facilitate higher-order thinking skills.

By addressing these areas, we seek to deepen our understanding of the potential of generative AI in enhancing constructivist educational practice and contribute to the broader discussion on the effective use of technology in education.

BACKGROUND

This section is to provide a brief overview of generative AI, its mechanisms, and applications, and discuss the key principles of constructivism, focusing on knowledge construction through social interaction and real-world experience.

1. Generative AI Overview

Artificial Intelligence (AI) encompasses software systems programmed to carry out specific tasks, broadly covering a system's capacity to learn, adapt, reason, and solve problems–functions usually associated with human intelligence. Woods (2023) describes AI as "the ability of a computer to perform tasks that typically require human intelligence" (p. 1). Within this broad categorization, generative AI represents a significant advancement, capable of autonomously producing new content based on its training data using neural networks and sophisticated algorithms (Wu & Chang, 2023). AI models are software trained on specific datasets to perform particular tasks (Woods, 2023). Generative AI models like ChatGPT (Generative Pre-trained Transformer) can create original content through pattern recognition in existing data. These models can generate various outputs including text (e.g., poems, plays, essays), images, code, music, and videos (Woods, 2023).

Prominent text-generating AI models include OpenAI's ChatGPT, Google Gemini (formerly Bard), Anthropic's Claude, and Perplexity. Image generation is another key application, with models like MidJourney and DALL-E producing digital artworks, deep fake photos, and photorealistic images of non-existent people. This technology also extends to creating audio (Google AI Test Kitchen), 3D models, and videos (e.g., SORA) (Woods, 2023). These natural language processing systems are trained on data extracted from the internet, enabling them to respond to text or voice prompts in a human-like manner, with significant potential for enhancing educational quality and efficiency (Kim & Adloff, 2023).

ChatGPT stands out as one of the most popular generative AI models. Its ability to generate clear and relevant content makes it suitable for applications such as chat-bots, writing materials, and language translation. The model has evolved through versions GPT-3, GPT-3.5, to GPT-4, attracting interest from educators and subject matter experts for various educational applications (Marr, 2024).

Specialized generative AI tools have emerged in specific fields. In medicine, ChatGPT's Doctor GPT (Strickland, 2023) and ChatLabs (writingmate.ai), are widely used. These platforms integrate various large language models (LLMS) and offer capabilities like AI image generation and GPT-4 version. While valuable for medical students, these tools are limited by their inability to interpret specialized medical scans, among others. Other specialized tools include ResearchRabbit (Bello, 2024), which assists researchers through visual mapping of citation connections between articles.

2. Constructivism Principles

Constructivism is a learning theory that underscores the importance of learners actively engaging in their learning process. Constructivism, as influenced by the works of notable learning theorists such as Dewey, Bruner, Vygotsky, and Piaget, defines learning as a "dynamic process of knowledge construction shaped by students' needs, learning materials, tools, and the overall learning environment" (Taber, 2011, p. 43). Founded on philosophical and psychological theories from the early 1900s, it suggests that learning involves more than the passive reception of information. Instead, learners construct their understanding actively through experiences, interactions, and reflections, as detailed by Duffy and Cunningham (1996) and Driscoll (2018). They also build upon their prior knowledge by incorporating new information, a process described by Narayan et al. (2013).

According to constructivist scholars Duffy and Cunningham, learning is an active process in which learners build new knowledge based on their prior experiences. They emphasized the concept of the "mind as rhizome," likening the mind to a network of interconnected roots. This perspective suggests that learning is not a linear process but rather one that progresses through various pathways and connections, with all ideas interlinked (Duffy & Cunningham, 1996, p. 8). In education, constructivist philosophy emphasizes the "active role of learners in building understanding by integrating new information with prior knowledge and firsthand experiences." (Grubaugh et al., 2023, p. 81). With the increasing accessibility of learning resources, there is a growing interest in self-directed learning, allowing learners to explore ways of furthering their knowledge acquisition without the constraints of time and geographical location (Firaina & Sulisworo, 2023).

The theory of constructivism in learning emphasizes that learners construct knowledge through active thinking, exploration, and practice, which is crucial in developing self-learning competencies. Constructing knowledge is inherently related to metacognition, which involves learners' awareness of their cognitive processes, enabling them to monitor, evaluate, and adjust their learning strategies (Vu & Nguyen, 2024). This is closely linked to self-regulated learning (SRL), in which Zimmerman and Schunk (2011) noted that self-regulated learning is key in goal-setting, progress tracking, and the adoption of effective strategies. Motivation plays a vital role in this process, driving engagement and persistence in SRL behaviors. It nurtures a sense of control, mastery, autonomy, and competence in learners, which boosts their intrinsic motivation (Ng et al., 2024). Intrinsic motivation and self-regulation are critical in developing students' scientific knowledge, as they help maintain engagement and perseverance in learning tasks. Together, these elements form a synergistic relationship where motivation enhances learning performance and sustains students' drive to achieve their educational goals (Ng et al., 2024).

3. Social Interaction and Collaboration

As a learning theory, constructivism is rooted in the idea that the construction of knowledge happens when learners build new knowledge through their interactions with surroundings, and through activities and experiences which they can then apply to novel contexts through collaborative work and problem-solving scenarios (active learning). Collaboration is vital in a constructivist learning environment as it enables the development of core skill sets such as communication, problem-solving, and leadership opportunities to prepare learners for careers in the future (Zhou & Schofield, 2024). This learner-centered approach encourages critical thinking and productivity, acknowledging that effective learning occurs through meaningful interactions between teachers and students (Schuh, 2003 as cited in Rasul, 2023), and among learners themselves.

Scaffolding and the Zone of Proximal Development (ZPD) play crucial roles in facilitating cognitive development and learning processes within a constructivist learning environment. Developed by Lev Vygotsky (1978), ZPD outlines the zone within which a learner can independently acquire knowledge and skills, the areas for progress through guidance from mentors or experienced peers (Alghamdy, 2024), and through interactions with others having more knowledge than them (Sazali et al., 2022). Scaffolding complements ZPD and represents the support provided by mentors, peers, parents, caregivers, or teachers to help learners advance toward their ZPD goals (Alghamdy, 2024).

Scaffolding is a fundamental educational strategy aimed at nurturing independent learning and skill development. Through tailored support, educators can assist learners in understanding unfamiliar concepts and acquiring new skills. This support is gradually reduced as students become more proficient, ultimately enabling them to perform tasks autonomously (Alghamdy, 2024). Furthermore, scaffolding serves as a valuable feedback mechanism in education, fostering deeper understanding, reducing learner stress, and enhancing overall satisfaction levels (Chien et al., 2024). For generative AI to effectively be integrated as a scaffolding tool, assessment strategies need to be reviewed and updated (Bobula, 2024). Mollick & Mollick (2023) suggest that generative AI combined with instructional design strategies can be an efficient way to improve teaching practices and implement quality instruction, alleviating the issue of teacher burnout and overwork (Liang et al., 2023), freeing time to identify and evaluate their students' learning needs.

Moreover, these two concepts emphasize the importance of considering individual learners' prior knowledge and experiences. Building on these foundational ideas, Narayan et al. (2013) state that learners rely on their prior knowledge as a foundation when actively searching for new information. This closely aligns with active learning, the first principle of constructivism introduced here. In doing so, learners construct new knowledge and reflect on their understanding. Learners take the initiative to construct the information themselves, as opposed to passively receiving and consuming content. This approach highlights the active role of learners in their learning process and demonstrates the importance of engagement and interaction in the learning process.

To guarantee effectiveness, instruction should be tailored to the specific needs and backgrounds of each student, thereby promoting a deep and meaningful understanding of the subject matter. The role of the instructor transforms into that of a facilitator or guide, rather than as an authority figure. This approach makes learners more autonomous and self-directed in the learning process and in taking ownership of their education by actively engaging with the learning material in a way that is personally relevant and meaningful to them. Thus, students not only gain a deeper understanding of the subject matter but also develop critical thinking skills and creativity needed to become successful in both academic and real-world settings.

4. The Use of a Problem-Solving Approach Enhances Higher-Order Thinking Skills

Constructivism aims to guide learners in developing critical thinking skills and constructing their own understanding. This empowers learners in applying knowledge to different contexts, instead of merely memorizing facts (Duffy & Jonassen, 2013). Cognitive engagement in constructivism is students' investment in their learning through the practical application of principles (Liang et al., 2023). This manifests in exercises involving solving problems and making decisions (Liang et al., 2023) and correlates with improved academic performance (Wang & Eccles, 2011).

Problem-Based Learning (PBL) exemplifies constructivist principles with its emphasis on active learning through real-world problem-solving. This methodology promotes self-managed learning, collaboration, critical thinking, and reflection

(Ali, 2019). In the domains of Analysis, Evaluation, and Creation, PBL effectively enhances critical thinking skills and facilitates meaningful learning (Lapuz & Fulgencio, 2020).

5. Scope and Methodology of Literature Review

Through an extensive literature review, this study explores constructivist educational principles and the alignment and potential challenges between generative AI tools and constructivism. In addition, the research seeks to identify pertinent case studies and develop pedagogical strategies for incorporating generative AI into constructivist learning environments, while also addressing associated challenges and ethical issues. Keywords for the study included constructivism, AI in education, the integration of constructivism and AI, and problem-based learning with AI. The study focused on answering specific guiding questions, and any unrelated studies were excluded from the analysis.

INTERSECTION OF GENERATIVE AI AND CONSTRUCTIVISM

Generative AI models such as ChatGPT have the potential to significantly enhance constructivist learning approaches. This section explores how the integration of generative AI in education can embody and support constructivist principles.

1. How Can Generative AI Simulate or Enhance Constructivist Learning Environments?

The potential for generative AI advancements seems limitless with its applications in almost all fields of endeavor, and it has caused so much excitement and consternation at the same time for technology forecasters and stakeholders. When applied to constructivist learning environments, it can elevate the learning experience by personalizing and adapting individualized learning experiences, and at the same time generate engaging and captivating content that can provide real-time feedback, fine-tuning knowledge acquisition. Iterative in nature, Generative AI aligns well with the principles of personal and social constructivism (Robertson et al., 2024). According to Merrill (1991), knowledge has a universal structure that learners interact with in various ways. Generative AI can facilitate these interactions by helping learners construct mental models and providing contextualized and new knowledge. It can create complete learning experiences by assembling knowledge components from abstractions. Merrill noted that constructivism breaks down broad knowledge into specific, transferable scenarios. Generative AI can identify essential concepts and adapt them to related contexts. It can also tailor instructional strategies to different learning preferences, such as visual aids for visual learners or interactive activities for experiential learners. Overall, generative AI can foster a balanced learning ecosystem where students learn independently and collaboratively, with the teacher as a facilitator.

Through the lens of constructivist learning environments, generative AI is a prime example of support for constructivist learning through active exploration, scaffolding prior knowledge, and providing personalized feedback as a thinking partner (Rasul et al., 2023) or a "More Knowledgeable Other" (MKO) (Stojanov, 2023, p. 2), enhancing and offering simulated constructivist learning environments as form of social constructivism, (Robertson et al., 2024) with its ability to provide personalized evaluations (Rasul et al., 2023); allowing active exploration by using stored, previous knowledge as scaffolds (Rasul et al., 2023). Generative AI enables iterative refinement through prompting, leading to more comprehensive results (Short & Short, 2023). The bi-directional and dynamic feedback (Kasneci et al., 2023) motivates active student engagement, since it is easy for generative AI to provide visualization and additional resources, deepening cognitive engagement (Liang et al., 2023).

As a scaffolding tool, generative AI replicates real-life interactions, delivering human-like responses to user queries. Educators can enrich learning experiences with generative AI through a variety of interaction modes, including personalized assistance, easy access to knowledge, and interactive dialogues, enhancing and encouraging a conducive learning environment (Chien et al., 2024). Studies show that students engaged in collaborative and interactive learning achieve better results and have greater educational satisfaction (Sazali et al., 2022). These features align with Vygotsky's (1978) emphasis on active knowledge construction by learners.

Generative AI models, with their natural language processing capabilities, can engage learners in interactive dialogues, provide feedback, and encourage learners to articulate and explore their understanding. This aligns with the constructivist principle of active knowledge construction through problem-based learning and social interactions. These AI models serve as cognitive tools, offering personalized guidance and support by tailoring responses to individual learner's needs, acting as scaffolding tools to help learners build upon their existing knowledge and address misconceptions. Generative AI models can be integrated into collaborative learning activities, facilitating knowledge co-construction through discussions and shared perspectives. This aligns with the constructivist emphasis on social negotiation of meaning. By presenting learners with authentic, real-world scenarios or problems, generative AI encourages the application of knowledge, critical thinking, and problem-solving skills in meaningful contexts, in line with constructivist pedagogy. The adaptive capabilities of generative AI align well with constructivist principles, effectively catering to different learning needs and providing enriching and dynamic learning opportunities (Grubaugh et al., 2023). With generative AI, educators can enhance constructivist pedagogy, leading to increased student engagement, metacognitive self-reflection, shifts in conceptualizations, and the creation of a more immersive learning environment (Grubaugh et al., 2023). This approach is deemed more effective than the traditional objectivist philosophy as it is better at developing essential problem-solving abilities (Tam, 2000).

Incorporating generative AI into constructivist pedagogy can result in dynamic and adaptable curriculums, metacognitive development, and transformative experiences in education (Grubaugh et al., 2023). Generative AI tools, when used as intelligent tutors, work well in a learner-centered environment as they can actively adjust their responses to students' learning needs. By integrating this into constructivist pedagogy, teachers can enhance and promote higher-order thinking, student engagement, and metacognition without compromising educational integrity (Grubaugh et al., 2023). The interactive and built-in immediate feedback system of generative AI results in higher levels of cognitive engagement in students, also resulting in higher levels of learning achievement (Liang et al., 2023).

According to the principles of Interactive Theory–the interplay among individuals, between humans and technology, and between humans and their surroundings (Zhou & Wei, 2010; Freeman & Ambady, 2011) --real-time feedback gathered from the human-machine interaction is of the essence, and must be interactive and fluid (Freeman & Ambady, 2011). Generative AI models this scenario perfectly with its ability to provide instant feedback, allowing the unconstrained application of targeted interventions and the adjustment of learning materials and strategies consistent with learner needs (Liang et al., 2023). AI-powered virtual environments can facilitate collaborative problem-solving and knowledge sharing. Allowing generative AI into learning activities can enhance collaborative learning by improving student-teacher interaction through timely feedback and assistance, as well as encouraging community-building in digital environments (Zhou & Schofield, 2024).

A study conducted by Liang et al. (2023) illustrates the intersection of Constructivism and generative AI by exploring students' experiences with generative AI and its relationship with high academic performance. The study took into account cognitive engagement and students' feeling of personal competence, showing new perspectives on students' regulating their own abilities and about their cognitive engagement while interacting with new technology in education. Liang et al. (2023), also states that as a regulator, cognitive engagement combined with self-efficacy, has a positive impact on academic achievement levels of the student participants.

2. How can AI Facilitate Personalized Learning Experiences, Peer Interactions, and Reflective Thinking?

Robertson et al. (2024), identified the three overarching constructivist dimensions of AI prompting that foster human-AI collaborative dialogue, which is as follows:

1. Context-centered knowledge co-construction - optimal conditions of learning are possible when students are exposed to real-world contexts where they can connect and apply stored knowledge and experiences (Piaget, 1995).
2. Context in human-AI collaboration is important, as various (raw, organized, processed, and system-generated) data forms (Paschen et al., 2019) enable the creation of environments specific to the needs of students (Robertson et al., 2024).
3. Prompters can create prompts that link users' existing knowledge with new AI-driven content, enhancing learning experiences effectively (Jarrahi et al., 2023), which can help learners connect what they already know with what generative AI can provide (Robertson et al., 2024).

Constructivist learning promotes the creation of mental cognitive visualizations and meaningful associations with information, prioritizing understanding over rote memorization to enhance learning effectiveness (Vygotsky, 1978). Well-structured prompts in AI facilitate collaborative knowledge construction between users and AI models, enhancing learning outcomes and fostering beneficial human-AI relationships (Robertson et al., 2024; Jarrahi, 2018).

Assessing contextual and structural components plays an important role in knowledge organization and construction (Kim & Adloff, 2023) aiding the refinement of learners' mental processes (Dwivedi et al., 2023) and combating misinformation (Berente, 2021, as cited in Robertson et al., 2024). Incorporating generative AI into foundational activities is in alignment with Bloom's Taxonomy, as it allows learners to grasp core concepts before advancing to higher-order thinking skills like information synthesis and critical evaluation (Zhou & Schofield, 2024). Zhou & Schofield (2024), provide examples of this:

1. Speed-reading to get the essential information, main themes, and concepts needed from the assigned reading material.
2. Employing generative AI to condense and efficiently capture key insights from reading assignments enhances the review process, aiding in comprehensive understanding.

3. Subsequently, students can engage in collaborative discussions to exchange perspectives and insights gleaned from their readings, enabling them to broaden their understanding and uncover nuances they might have missed.

3. Exploring the Role of AI in Supporting the Creation of Dynamic Learning Content That Adapts to Learner Interactions

Generative AI makes personalized learning opportunities possible through:

- Developing customizable educational materials that match students' learning needs, preferences, and abilities
- Providing instant feedback for error correction and guidance
- Offer individualized strategies by analyzing past performance to address weaknesses and enhance strengths (Yu & Guo, 2023; Javaid et al., 2023)
- Introducing the PAIGE (Promoting Assignment Integrity using generative AI in Education) Framework by Shanto et al., 2023, for ethical integration. The framework focuses on teaching ethical usage, promoting creativity and critical thinking in assignments, utilizing AI as personalized support, and encouraging honesty and integrity in academic settings, including the deployment of AI detection tools.

Grubaugh et al. (2023), also propose a combination of constructivist theory and generative AI tools to transform teaching methods:

- **Personalized Learning Pathways:** Custom-made education for each student by integrating their existing knowledge and experiences with new information to generate fresh insights.
- **Dynamic Curriculum Adjustments:** Leveraging the adaptability of generative AI alongside learning theories enables real-time curriculum modifications, ensuring an optimal learning environment for students.
- **Metacognitive Growth:** Generative AI applications facilitate active knowledge construction by promoting self-awareness, reflective thinking, self-regulation skills, and a disposition towards continuous learning.
- **Empowering Conceptual Change:** Teaching with generative AI aids in addressing and correcting students' misunderstandings, encouraging a deeper understanding beyond simple memorization.
- **Upholding Humanistic Values:** The essence of teaching remains centered on human development, albeit the advancements in technology, fostering empathy, strong relationships, and a sense of community among students.

Constructivism views learning as a subjective, step-by-step process where learners actively build their understanding, recognizing the inherent differences between teacher and student knowledge. Meaningful experiences with generative AI can empower active knowledge construction (Guo et al., 2024). Learning involves integrating new information with existing knowledge, a process complicated by individual differences. Generative AI serves as a bridge, adapting to each learner's unique learning preferences and needs, and facilitating easier learning (Guo et al., 2024). Learning requires active engagement and is influenced by what motivates the teaching strategies. This engagement influenced by teaching strategies shifts traditional passive methods into dynamic approaches through involvement in higher-order thinking activities such as analysis, synthesis, and evaluation (Bonwell & Eison, 1991), recognizing that learners are active participants in building their own knowledge. Constructivism and generative AI share the potential to foster personalized, dynamic learning experiences that enhance engagement, advocate for higher-order thinking, and catalyze transformative changes in learning perspectives (Grubaugh et al., 2023). The human-like interactions offered by generative AI tools make them ideal partners for collaborative knowledge construction and dissemination (Suh et al., 2021, as cited in Robertson et al., 2024). More importantly, generative AI falls in alignment with the core principles of constructivist learning which are active learning, adaptability/personalized scaffolding, metacognitive reflection, and facilitating conceptual change (Grubaugh et al., 2023).

Given the recent emergence of this technological breakthrough, further research is essential to offer educators adequate examples and use cases for utilizing generative AI tools in their specific contexts (Bobula, 2024). The following table summarizes key constructivist principles or themes and their connections to generative AI.

Table 1. Summarizes key constructivist principles or themes and their connections to generative AI.

Common Constructivist-related Themes	Key Concepts	How it Relates to Generative AI	Key Authors
Active Learning	● Knowledge Construction ● Self-directed learning ● Metacognition ● Mind as a Rhizome ● Transferrability of knowledge by breaking down generalized and broad information for application into other concepts or settings	● ChatGPT supports independent exploration ● Generative AI tools provide instant feedback ● Enhances self-regulated learning ● Emphasize learners integrating new information with prior knowledge. ● Align with AI's ability to provide interconnected, non-linear learning. ● Use AI to share, co-create, and transfer knowledge for diverse applications.	Duffy & Cunningham (1996) Narayan et al. (2013) Grubaugh et al. (2023) Vu & Nguyen (2024) Zimmerman & Schunk (2011) Ng et al. (2024) Guo et al. (2024) Merrill (1991)
Social Interaction and Collaboration	● Zone of Proximal Development (ZPD) ● Scaffolding/More Knowledgeble Other (MKO) ● Peer Interaction	● AI can simulate social interactions ● Provides personalized scaffolding ● Supports collaborative problem-solving ● Generative AI as an MKO enhancing and offering simulated constructivist learning environments	Vygotsky (1978) Alghamdy (2024) Chien et al. (2024) Sazali et al. (2022) Zhou & Schofield (2024) Stojanov (2023)
Learner-Centered Approach	● Individual interests & experiences ● Integrating new information with prior knowledge ● Personalized Learning ● Bi-directional and dynamic feedback/iterative refinement ● Emphasis on student empowerment and agency, dignity, and developing healthy relationships between learners and teachers.	● AI adapts to individual learner needs ● Allows exploration of diverse topics ● Customizes educational experiences ● Enhances generative AI-human conversations by refining outputs and aiming for more comprehensive results ● Uphold human-centered principles and incorporate student feedback to ensure a balanced and effective human-AI relationship within a constructivist pedagogy.	Narayan et al. (2013) Taber (2011), Rasul et al. (2023), Kasneci (2023), Short & Short (2023) Herman (1995) Grubaugh et al. (2023) Makridakis (2017) Roll et al. (2011)

continued on following page

Table 1. Continued

Common Constructivist-related Themes	Key Concepts	How it Relates to Generative AI	Key Authors
Problem-based learning-	● Real-world problem-solving ● Critical thinking enhancement ● Shift from rote memorization to higher-order thinking skills ● Need for development of self-regulation and critical thinking ● Importance of metacognition in AI-enhanced learning/ metacognitive reflection	● AI generates complex scenarios ● Supports inquiry-based learning ● Facilitates analysis and evaluation ● Expansion of knowledge from knowing to discovering, evaluating and utilizing information effectively through higher order thinking. ● Generative AI can assist learners as they navigate through processes of understanding new information to replace old ideas and misconceptions. ● Generative AI supports this shift as a tool in discovering information and providing feedback and evaluation	Ali (2019) Lapuz & Fulgencio (2020) Wu & Chang (2023) Liu et al. (2022) Grubaugh et al. (2023) Vu & Nguyen (2024)
Role of Instructor	● Facilitator rather than authority ● Guide for student exploration ● AI enhanced teaching	● AI assists in creating teaching materials ● Frees instructors to focus on facilitation ● Enhancing educational quality and efficiency	Schuh (2003, as cited in Rasul et al.2023) Kim & Adloff (2023)
Motivation and Engagement	● Intrinsic motivation ● Self-regulation ● Active participation ● Cognitive engagement	● AI provides immediate feedback ● Supports goal-setting and progress tracking ● Encourages interactive learning experiences ● Students' investment in their own learning	Zimmerman & Schunk (2011) Ng et al. (2024) Firaina & Sulisworo (2023) Liang et al. (2023) Wang & Eccles (2012)
Personalized Learning	● Potential for customized educational experiences ● Support for metacognition through AI tools ● Overcoming time and geographical constraints ● Dynamic learning	● Generative AI tools can significantly enhance and personalize learning through immediate feedback, awareness of their learning processes, and self-paced learning	McGuire et al. (2024) Exintaris et al. (2024) Firaina & Sulisworo (2023) Grubaugh et al. (2023)

CASE STUDIES

In this section, we delve into various case studies that highlight the application of generative AI within higher education environments. These examples are analyzed through the lens of constructivist principles, as identified through a comprehensive literature review. By examining these case studies, we aim to demonstrate how generative AI can enhance learning experiences and support educational practices grounded in constructivist theory.

Case 1: PBL Meets Generative AI in a College Chemistry Course

Problem-solving is a crucial skill during the learning process, especially in Chemistry subjects. The process often involves multiple different steps and methods. Different kinds of teaching and learning approaches, such as a worked example, which shows students the whole process including necessary steps and answers, have been used in chemistry/science education. Scaffolding, which includes metacognitive and instructional scaffolding, is another approach. These methods guide students through the problem-solving and encourage reflection throughout the process.

PBL, when combined with generative AI, offers a potent approach to addressing real-world challenges while developing critical thinking skills. Integration of these can help educational institutions adapt to technological advancements and evolving workforce demands (Wu & Chang, 2023). This also equips students with tools and opportunities to practice self-directed learning, benefits teachers with efficiency, and, as a conduit for seamless communication and effective delivery of feedback, foster healthy student-teacher interactions in the process (Wang, 2023).

Background

At Australia's Monash University, 213 chemical engineering and pharmaceutical science students participated in the 'SMARTCHEMPer' (Strategic Metacognitive Approaches to Solving Chemistry Problems) activity, to develop their metacognitive and critical thinking skills (Exintaris, et al., 2023). The 'SMARTCHEMPer' activity included practice activities, such as metacognitive scaffolding, problem-solving practices, and critiquing of ChatGPT-generated solutions. The methodology consisted of four (4) two-hour problem-solving workshops. In the first small group session, students discussed their perspectives on problem-solving. They shared their thoughts and experiences in advance, setting the pace for the latter workshop. Next, students were introduced to the metacognitive approach to problem-solving. This includes checking for understanding of the problem, analysis, solution planning, implementation, and evaluation. This helped improve students' metacognition by understanding how to reflect and be aware of their thinking processes while solving problems. Students were also introduced to the 'Goldilocks Help scaffold,' a metacognitive scaffold that helps students and teachers with structured problem-solving in chemistry (White et al., 2022), and the problem-solving assessment rubric. During the third session of the workshop, students were given four chemistry problems varying in difficulty with specific instructions on the process. The last session of the workshop required students to critique the provided solutions [to the four chemistry problems from the previous session] offered in the workshop. Two of these solutions were generated by ChatGPT. Students were not informed whether or not the solution was correct, as this final task aimed at encouraging critical thinking and reinforcing chemistry concepts and problem-solving methods they have learned.

Outcomes, Benefits, and Challenges Observed

During the workshop's critique session, 187 students shared their experiences and perspectives on the solutions generated by ChatGPT. Some students reported figuring out the main steps and key terms a lot easier than before, leading to a better understanding of the concepts, and better analysis of the questions. Other students found ChatGPT a useful starting point for problem-solving, with short generation times, user-friendly interface, and an easy-to-follow content structure.

While there were some concerns identified such as accuracy, academic integrity, and over-reliance, feedback from SMARTCHEMPer participants was mostly positive. Students found that interacting with ChatGPT improved their critical thinking, analysis skills, problem-solving confidence, ability to differentiate reliable information, awareness of AI limitations, and critical perspective on generative AI.

The SMARTCHEMPer activity illustrated active learning principles, showcasing students' engagement in building knowledge rather than passively receiving information (Duffy & Cunningham, 1996). It highlighted the contextual nature of learning processes, emphasizing the importance of educators thoughtfully designing learning environments (Duffy & Cunningham, 1996). The activity's setting affected decision-making and judgment, shaping students' understanding of both the subject matter and AI's role in problem-solving.

From an educator's perspective, using generative AI content can be a time-saving tool. It offers expedient access to diverse educational materials catering to varying student needs However, ensuring quality and accuracy of the generated content is paramount. While AI aids in creating content, it is susceptible to errors or inaccuracies. Educators must carefully review and verify AI-generated content to ensure accurate and reliable information for students, maintaining the integrity of the educational process.

Case 2: ChatGPT, Bing Chat, Bard, and Claude as Thinking Partners in Enhancing Chemistry Education

Background

A single case study using the content analysis methodology developed by Dos Santos (2023) aimed at identifying which generative AI application is more effective and efficient in learning chemistry through analysis of generative AI conversations which showed generative AI tools as "agents-to-think-with" that enhance and improve critical thinking skills, develop creative thought, and be a tool in personalized learning, by using the Socratic method in stimulating higher order thinking. The research points out the importance of designing precise prompts for the best responses from generative AI, emphasizing the training of educators to guarantee better outcomes for students.

The researcher took on a student role throughout the experiment and adopted student perspectives such as empathy in the research methodology. A series of four sessions replicated chemistry students' experiences in using the different generative AI tools. These sessions focused on students' primary challenges, particularly chemical reaction balancing. The process evolved into more in-depth discussions, with each AI response serving as a springboard for subsequent queries. Journals were logged with data from generative AI interaction and participant questions and answers, which were further reviewed for patterns and themes that appeared multiple times throughout the interaction, resulting in seven categories identified as:

- **Instructional Strategies:** Methodology in dispensing information
- **Engagement and Interactivity:** Prompts that triggered critical thinking, probing questions, eliciting responses, and promoting further exploration
- **Use of Analogy and Comparative Illustrations:** Simplifying and elucidating concepts through the use of figures of speech such as metaphors, parallels, and real-world examples
- **Reinforcement and Feedback:** Acknowledging, correcting, and reinforcing concepts from the user's input
- **Detail Depth and Content Recommendation:** Quality and depth of minutiae from the response, recommendations for further learning as well as content relevancy
- **Personalization and Personable Touch:** Responses that are tailor-made for specific requirements, the use of emoticons and empathetic responses for personalization

- **Meta-Discussion and Perspective Framing:** Examining implications of ideas beyond regular contexts; enabling the understanding of complex ideas and abstractions through comparison with real-world scenarios

Outcomes, Benefits, and Challenges Observed

The study concluded that ChatGPT performed at the optimal level with Bard and Claude following closely behind. All demonstrated highly satisfactory performance in contextual information and comprehension. Notably, generative AI-powered dialogues can bridge the gap between theoretical knowledge and practical application in chemistry education by letting students delve into explorations of philosophical questions, and in the process, obtaining information tailored to their own interests, diverting from traditional passive learning methods (Dunlop et al., 2020). The study highlighted various ways chemistry students can leverage generative AI to enhance their educational experiences, including posing complex chemistry problems and obtaining simplified but comprehensive breakdowns of concepts, especially in the areas of chemical reactions, chemical equilibrium, phase changes, gasses, stoichiometry, atoms and molecules, acids and bases, and covalent bonding. Despite its powerful metacognitive capacity, the study observed a key challenge: generative AI tools are stunted by their potential to produce hallucinated and inaccurate output.

Figure 1. Comparative analysis of ChatGPT, Bing Chat, Bard, and Claude

COMPARATIVE ANALYSIS OF CHATGPT, BING CHAT (COPILOT), BARD (GEMINI), AND CLAUDE

DOS SANTOS, 2023

CATEGORIES	CHATGPT	BING	BARD	CLAUDE
PERSONALIZATION & PERSONABLE TOUCH	VERY HIGH	FAIR	GOOD	HIGH
INSTRUCTIONAL STRATEGIES	VERY HIGH	GOOD	HIGH	GOOD
ENGAGEMENT & INTERACTIVITY	HIGH	FAIR	FAIR	GOOD
USE OF ANALOGY & COMPARATIVE ILLUSTRATIONS	HIGH	FAIR	GOOD	HIGH
DETAIL DEPTH & CONTENT RECOMMENDATION	HIGH	GOOD	HIGH	GOOD
REINFORCEMENT AND FEEDBACK	HIGH	FAIR	GOOD	GOOD
META-DISCUSSION& PERSPECTIVE FRAMING	GOOD	FAIR	HIGH	GOOD

(Excerpt from Dos Santos, 2023, p. 52)

Case 3: Generative AI in Support of Academic Research in a Graduate-Level Educational Technology Course

Background

This case study is designed for a graduate-level foundational educational technology course. Students are tasked with conducting a literature review on the application of AI in educational settings of their choice, such as elementary language arts classrooms, secondary mathematics classes, or college-level educational technology courses. The instructor will provide clear guidelines on best practices and potential pitfalls to avoid.

The course begins with an introduction and discussion about the benefits, challenges, and ethical concerns surrounding the use of generative AI in education. This activity fosters critical thinking and reflection, which are key elements of constructivist learning. Students then compare features of various AI-powered research tools, such as ResearchRabbit, Elicit, Scite, Connected Papers, Inciteful, Iris, and Litmaps. This comparison helps students understand the capabilities and limitations of different tools.

Next, students choose their top two AI research tools for their literature review assignment, justifying their choices based on their specific research needs. They post their selections and justifications in the online class discussion forum, promoting peer learning and collaborative knowledge construction. Detailed instructions on keyword searches (e.g., "benefits of AI in education," "challenges of AI in education") are provided to ensure students can effectively locate relevant literature. Using AI-powered research tools, students select five pertinent articles related to their topic. This process emphasizes active engagement and the integration of new information with prior knowledge, a core constructivist principle.

Students then learn about avoiding plagiarism when using tools like ChatGPT. They create headings for their literature review and compare them with AI-generated headings, allowing them to refine their work while maintaining academic integrity. Following this, students draft their literature reviews, incorporating insights from their selected articles and AI tools. This activity could be expanded to include developing an outline for a research proposal, providing a more comprehensive understanding of academic research processes.

Outcomes, Benefits, and Challenges Observed

The expected outcomes include students articulating their understanding of how AI can support learning after conducting their literature reviews and effectively locating relevant literature using AI-powered research tools. The benefits of this approach include enhanced research skills using advanced AI tools, improved critical thinking, and awareness of ethical considerations related to AI in education, as well as collaborative learning and peer feedback through online discussions.

However, challenges may arise, such as potential issues with plagiarism and the ethical use of AI-generated content and ensuring that students develop a deep understanding rather than relying solely on AI tools. By integrating generative AI with constructivist principles, this course aims to foster a deeper, more engaged learning experience for students, preparing them to utilize AI ethically and effectively in their future educational practices.

ETHICAL CONSIDERATIONS AND FUTURE RESEARCH

This section explores the ethical implications of using generative AI in educational settings and suggests potential future research directions, emphasizing the need for ongoing refinement and ethical considerations.

1. Ethical Considerations

The rise of generative AI technologies has raised several concerns. Biased outputs may stem from limited training data sets, while issues with plagiarism poses challenges to originality and academic integrity. Image-generating programs such as MidJourney also face potential copyright infringement for producing artwork resembling copyrighted material. There is a fear that AI tools' accessibility could normalize mediocrity, compromising quality for convenience. The ease of using these tools has led to concerns about academic cheating, with students relying on AI for assignments. Inherent biases in AI can perpetuate racial stereotypes and spread misinformation (Jenka, 2023). AI-generated content can also be inaccurate or misleading, sometimes fabricating information or providing incomplete details. There are also copyright issues, with debates on whether AI-produced content is new or derivative. Additionally, data privacy concerns and broader impacts such as job security fears and AI replacing human roles, highlight the need for careful regulation as AI technology evolves.

Ensuring Alignment with Constructivist Principles and Avoiding Overreliance on AI

In the context of education, teaching methods must align with constructivist principles and focus on analytical questioning methods that challenge students to exercise critical thinking through open-ended questions (Chen et al., 2023). Engage students by simulating \real-world problems, rather than focusing on tasks requiring memorization (Bobula, 2024). Innovative and diverse assessment formats, such as encouraging students' personal reflections (Gimpel et al., 2023), allow them to articulate their unique perspectives (Rudolph et al., 2023). Evaluating written work should emphasize the process of arriving at conclusions and thought processes, and understanding subject-matter approaches by reviewing drafts and final submissions, promoting originality and critical thinking over-reliance on AI-generated content (Smith & Francis, 2023).

Constructivist education philosophy emphasizes humanism (Herman, 1995), focusing on student empowerment, agency, dignity, and forming healthy relationships between learners and teachers (Grubaugh et al., 2023). Integrating AI into constructivist pedagogy requires upholding human-centered principles within the system's framework (Makridakis, 2017). Safeguards against dehumanizing output, data misuse, student data protection, and unethical applications of AI are essential, with designs compliant with Universal Design for Learning (UDL) principles (Grubaugh et al., 2023). To maintain a healthy human-AI relationship, incorporating student feedback is crucial in generative AI-student collaboration in educational environments (Roll et al., 2011), thus guaranteeing the promotion of healthy human-AI partnerships, positioning AI as a learning enhancement tool without replacing human involvement in the educational transaction (Grubaugh et al., 2023).

Addressing Potential Biases and Limitations of AI Models

Generative AI holds immense potential and power, but its misuse can have profound and lasting effects on education and society. Creating deep fakes or tampering with algorithms can lead to harmful outcomes such as offensive, discriminatory content, and toxicity (Zhou et al., 2023). It is ethically imperative to align training data by incorporating cultural sensitivity frameworks and through diverse datasets (Weidinger et al., 2021).

Deploying AI detectors and human oversight can curb plagiarism issues and ensure academic integrity (Cotton et al., 2023). Adhering to strict data privacy measures is essential to prevent leaks and maintain confidentiality (Fui-hoon Nah et al., 2023). Furthermore, democratizing AI access can bridge the digital divide, ensuring everyone equitable access to digital tools and opportunities (Bozkurt & Sharma, 2023).

Syllabi Policies and School Regulations

The absence of formal regulations governing generative AI in educational institutions presents a challenge, as Reed (2018) noted risks with unregulated use. Allen et al. (2024) emphasized the need for consensus-building to establish specific regulations tailored to each use case, preventing a potential system overload. Some institutions have started setting parameters for AI usage, often through syllabi policies –thanks to the crowdsourcing initiative of Lance Eaton (director of Digital Pedagogy at College Unbound, MA) (Syllabi Policies for AI Generative Tools - see reference list for full link) making these guidelines accessible online. Conducting a SWOT (Strengths, Weaknesses, Opportunities, Threats) analysis is recommended to develop guidelines ensuring that responses align with students' educational levels while upholding ethical standards (Allen et al., 2024).

Fostering hard and soft skills is imperative to prepare students for the increasing integration of generative AI in education and workplaces. Constant upskilling is essential to adjust, acclimate, and adapt to new and disruptive technologies that are becoming ubiquitous in today's society (Fui-hoon Nah et al., 2023).

2. Future Research

Suggestions for Potential Future Research Directions

Since its development, generative AI has advanced and significantly influenced various aspects of human life, yet the full extent of its potential benefits and risks remain untapped and unknown for the most part. In education, Alshahrani (2023) identified several areas warranting further research and exploration:

- **Long-Term Impact:** Longitudinal studies are needed to determine if generative AI's positive impacts are sustainable on student performance and retention
- **Learning Analytics:** Employing generative AI chatbots to understand learning performance patterns and to tailor instructional designs to meet student needs
- **Student Motivation:** Investigate student perceptions when using a generative AI chatbot, as well as attitudes, motivations, and self-efficacy
- **Ethical Considerations:** Thorough analysis to address potential biases and ethical issues to ensure appropriate AI responses for diverse students
- **Instructor Training:** Developing professional development programs designed for effective generative AI integration and skills training

- **Accessibility:** Consider specific student needs, diverse abilities, and backgrounds when integrating generative AI to ensure inclusivity
- **Comparative Studies:** Can shed light on best practices to compare different generative AI models, identifying effective approaches
- **Cross-Disciplinary Applications:** Further explorations in customizing generative AI chatbots for different contexts, educational levels, environments, and different subjects are needed

Future research directions should also explore how AI tools can enhance metacognitive skills and self-regulated learning. Developing frameworks for the responsible and ethical use of AI in educational settings is crucial. Additionally, investigating AI's impact on providing personalized scaffolding within students' Zone of Proximal Development (ZPD) presents a promising avenue for study. The role of AI in facilitating and enhancing collaborative learning experiences is also a significant research opportunity. Equally critical is investigating how AI tools can enhance students' intrinsic motivation in learning. Exploring the integration of AI in problem-based learning scenarios to enhance critical thinking skills offers another promising research direction. Researching AI's potential to create truly personalized learning experiences that adapt to individual student needs is crucial for maximizing educational outcomes, and developing and evaluating professional development programs for educators to effectively use AI in their teaching practices is essential.

The integration of AI in education offers numerous research opportunities that can profoundly impact teaching and learning. By exploring these areas, researchers can develop innovative strategies and tools that support effective, ethical, and personalized education for all students, effectively revolutionizing the educational landscape

CONCLUSION

The extensive literature review conducted in this study delves into the intersection of constructivist educational principles and generative AI, by examining the alignment and potential challenges between these two domains. We illuminate how generative AI can be effectively integrated into constructivist learning environments through research that underscores the use of generative AI to enhance active learning, social interaction, contextual learning, knowledge construction, reflective thinking, scaffolded support, and authentic assessments within educational settings. By focusing on these key constructivist themes, the study provides a comprehensive framework for educators seeking to leverage generative AI tools that align with constructivist methodologies.

Using generative AI with constructivist approaches is rich with promise for advancing education. These tools promote active, learner-centered experiences, capable of providing a customized learning environment and immediate feedback. These can also generate complex subject-related topics and assignments in a short amount of time. The study's findings emphasize AI's abilities to support higher-order cognitive skills such as problem-solving and metacognition. For example, generative AI tools like SRLbot and ChatGPT can be effectively integrated with constructivism principles, enabling learners to construct knowledge through real-world engagement and critical thinking practice, demonstrating how modern technology can enhance traditional learning theories by creating more dynamic and personalized educational experiences.

Generative AI tools have the potential to shape a transformative educational landscape in the future by helping develop self-regulated learning and critical thinking skills. These tools stimulate interactivity in discussions, student engagement, and ideating customized learning pathways. However, as these tools continue to evolve, examining ethical considerations is essential in ensuring responsible use. This investigation highlights crucial ethical considerations that must be addressed to ensure the responsible use of AI in education, maintaining that effective use of educational AI requires a clear framework and guidance from instructors, aligned with specific pedagogy goals for different use cases. The instructor's responsibilities shift from teaching to guiding. Addressing issues like data privacy and academic honesty is also of utmost importance, as research shows that generative AI can profoundly impact educational practices in different aspects.

The keywords guiding this study—constructivism, AI in education, constructivism and AI integration, and problem-based learning with AI—are instrumental in shaping the research focus and in ensuring that only relevant studies are included in the analysis.

Overall, this study contributes valuable insights and practical strategies for educators aiming to integrate generative AI into constructivist learning environments. It emphasizes the need for continued research to expand the body of knowledge on this topic, and for more comprehensive examples and use cases in various contexts to serve as references for educators. Through this ongoing exploration, the potential of generative AI to transform constructivist education can be fully realized, ultimately enhancing learning outcomes and fostering more dynamic, interactive, and personalized educational experiences.

REFERENCES

Alghamdy, R. Z. (2024). English teachers' practice of classroom discourse in light of zone of proximal development theory and scaffolding techniques. *Journal of Language Teaching and Researh*, 15(1), 46–54. DOI: 10.17507/jltr.1501.06

Ali, S. S. (2019). Problem based learning: A student-centered approach. *English Language Teaching*, 12(5), 73. Advance online publication. DOI: 10.5539/elt.v12n5p73

Allen, T., Villaflor-Wilson, R., Muljana, P., & Romero-Hall, E. (2024). AI-generated content: guidelines, higher-order thinking skills, and copyrights. *Education Technology Journal, 4*(1)1-5. https://journal.unesa.ac.id/index.php/etj

Alshahrani, A. (2023). The impact of ChatGPT on blended learning: Current trends and future research directions. *International Journal of Data and Network Science*, 7(4), 2029–2040. DOI: 10.5267/j.ijdns.2023.6.010

Baek, E., & Wilson, M. (2024). Boon or bane: An inquiry into the use of generative ai (artificial intelligence) and its implications in education. In J. Cohen & G. Solano (Eds.), *Proceedings of Society for Information Technology & Teacher Education International Conference* (pp. 1971-1976). Las Vegas, Nevada, United States: Association for the Advancement of Computing in Education (AACE). https://www.learntechlib.org/primary/p/224243/

Bello, C. (n.d.). *These AI tools could help boost your academic research.* Euronews. https://www.euronews.com/next/2024/01/20/best-ai-tools-academic-research-chatgpt-consensus-chatpdf-elicit-research-rabbit-scite

Bobula, M. (2024). Generative Artificial Intelligence (AI) in higher education: A comprehensive review of challenges, opportunities, and implications. *Journal of Learning Development in Higher Education*, 30(30). Advance online publication. DOI: 10.47408/jldhe.vi30.1137

Bonwell, C. C., & Eison, J. A. (1991). Active learning: creating excitement in the classroom. *1991 ASHE-ERIC Higher Education Reports, ERIC Clearinghouse on Higher Education.*https://eric.ed.gov/?id=ED336049

Bozkurt, A., & Sharma, R. C. (2023). Challenging the status quo and exploring the new boundaries in the age of algorithms: Reimagining the role of generative AI in distance education and online learning. *Asian Journal of Distance Education*, 18(1), 1–8. DOI: 10.5281/zenodo.7755273

Chatlabs as the best AI tool for medical students: use cases. ChatLabs - All the Best AI Models in One Place for Free. (n.d.). https://writingmate.ai/blog/chatlabs-as-the-best-ai-tool-for-medical-students-use-cases

Chen, H., Jiao, F., Li, X., Qin, C., Ravaut, M., Zhao, R., Xiong, C., & Joty, S. (2023). Chatgpt's one-year anniversary: Are open source large language models catching up? *arXiv preprint arXiv:2311.16989.*

Chien, C. C., Chan, H. Y., & Hou, H. T. (2024). Learning by playing with generative AI: Design and evaluation of a role-playing educational game with generative AI as scaffolding for instant feedback interaction. *Journal of Research on Technology in Education*, •••, 1–20. DOI: 10.1080/15391523.2024.2338085

Cotton, D. R. E., Cotton, P. A., & Shipway, J. R. (2023). Chatting and cheating: Ensuring academic integrity in the era of ChatGPT. *Innovations in Education and Teaching International*, 61(2), 228–239. DOI: 10.1080/14703297.2023.2190148

Dos Santos, R. P. D. (2023). Enhancing chemistry learning with ChatGPT, Bing Chat, Bard, and Claude as agents-to-think-with: a comparative case study. *arXiv preprint arXiv:2311.00709.*http://dx.doi.org/DOI: 10.2139/ssrn.4629567

Driscoll, M. (2018). Psychological Foundations of Instructional Design. In Reiser, R. A., & Dempsey, J. V. (Eds.), *Trends and issues in instructional design and technology* (4th ed., pp. 52–60). Pearson.

Duffy, T. M., & Cunningham, D. J. (1996). Constructivism: Implications for the design and delivery of instruction. In Jonassen, D. H. (Ed.), *Handbook of research for educational communications and technology* (pp. 170–198). Macmillan.

Duffy, T. M., & Jonassen, D. H. (2013). *Constructivism and the technology of instruction: A conversation*. Routledge, Taylor & Francis Group.

Dunlop, L., Hodgson, A., & Stubbs, J. E. (2020). Building capabilities in chemistry education: Happiness and discomfort through philosophical dialogue in chemistry. *Chemistry Education Research and Practice*, 21(1), 438–451. DOI: 10.1039/C9RP00141G

Dwivedi, Y. K., Kshetri, N., Hughes, L., Slade, E. L., Jeyaraj, A., Kar, A. K., Baabdullah, A. M., Koohang, A., Raghavan, V., Ahuja, M., Albanna, H., Albashrawi, M. A., Al-busaidi, A. S., Balakrishnan, J., Barlette, Y., Basu, S., Bose, I., Brooks, L., Buhalis, D., & Wright, R. (2023). Opinion paper: "So what if ChatGPT wrote it?" multidisciplinary perspectives on opportunities, challenges and implications of generative conversational AI for research, practice and policy. *International Journal of Information Management*, 71, 102642. DOI: 10.1016/j.ijinfomgt.2023.102642

Eaton, L. (N.d.). (2024). ms, Syllabi policies for generative AI tools. https://docs.google.com/document/d/1RMVwzjc1o0Mi8Blw_-JUTcXv02b2WRH86vw7mi16W3U/edit

Elsen-Rooney, M. (2023, January 3). NYC education department blocks ChatGPT on school devices, networks. https://www.chalkbeat.org/newyork/2023/1/3/23537987/nyc-schools-ban-chatgpt-writing-artificial-intelligence/ (Exintaris, B., Karunaratne, N., & Yuriev, E. (2023). Metacognition and critical thinking: Using ChatGPT-Generated responses as prompts for critique in a problem-solving workshop (SMARTCHEMPer). *Journal of Chemical Education, 100*(8), 2972–2980. https://doi.org/DOI: 10.1021/acs.jchemed.3c00481

Firaina, R., & Sulisworo, D. (2023). Exploring the usage of ChatGPT in higher education: Frequency and impact on productivity. *Bulletin Edukasi Indonesia*, 2(1), 39–46. DOI: 10.56741/bei.v2i01.310

Freeman, J. B., & Ambady, N. (2011). A dynamic interactive theory of personal constual. *Personnel Review*, 118(2), 247–279. DOI: 10.1037/a0022327 PMID: 21355661

Fui-Hoon Nah, F., Zheng, R., Cai, J., Siau, K., & Chen, L. (2023). Generative AI and ChatGPT: Applications, challenges, and AI-human collaboration. *Journal of Information Technology Case and Application Research*, 25(3), 277–304. DOI: 10.1080/15228053.2023.2233814

Gimpel, H., Hall, K., Decker, S., Eymann, T., Lammermann, L., Maedche, A., Roglinger, M., Ruiner, C., Schoch, M., Schoop, M., Urbach, N., & Vandirk, S. (2023). *Unlocking the power of generative AI models and systems such as GPT-4 and ChatGPT for higher education: a guide for students and lecturers*. Preprint., DOI: 10.12140/RG.2.2.20710.09287/2

Grubaugh, S., Levitt, G., & Deever, D. (2023). Harnessing AI to power constructivist learning: An evolution in educational methodologies. *Journal of Effective Teaching Methods*, 1(3), 81–83. DOI: 10.59652/jetm.v1i3.43

Guo, H., Yi, W., & Liu, K. (2024) Enhancing constructivist learning: the role of generative AI in personalised learning experiences. *Proceedings of the 26th International Conference on Enterprise Information Systems (ICEIS 2024), 1*, 767-770. https://doi.org/DOI: 10.5220/0012688700003690

Herman, W. E. (1995). Humanistic influences on a constructivist approach to teaching and learning. https://files.eric.ed.gov/fulltext/ED393814.pdf

Jarrahi, M. H. (2018). Artificial intelligence and the future of work: Human-AI symbiosis in organizational decision making. *Business Horizons, 61*(4), 577e586.

Jarrahi, M. H., Askay, D., Esraghi, A., & Smith, P. (2023). Artificial intelligence and knowledge management: A partnership between human and AI. *Business Horizons*, 66(1), 87–99. DOI: 10.1016/j.bushor.2022.03.002

Javaid, M., Haleem, A., Singh, R. P., Khan, S., & Khan, I. H. (2023). Unlocking the opportunities through ChatGPT Tool towards ameliorating the education system. *BenchCouncil Transactions on Benchmarks, Standards, and Evaluations*, 3(2), 100115. DOI: 10.1016/j.tbench.2023.100115

Jenka (2023). AI and the American Smile: How AI misrepresents culture through a facial expression. *Medium.com.*https://medium.com/@socialcreature/ai-and-the-american-smile-76d23a0fbfaf

Kasneci, E., Sessler, K., Kuchemann, S., Bannert, M., Dementieva, E., Fischer, F., Gasser, U., Groh, G., Gunnemann, S., Hullermeier, E., Krusche, S., Kutyniok, G., Michaeli, T., Nerdel, C., Pfeffer, J., Poquet, O., Sailer, M., Schmidt, A., Seidel, T., & Kasneci, G. (2023). ChatGPT for good? On opportunity and challenges of large language models for education. *Learning and Individual Differences*, 103, 102274. DOI: 10.1016/j.lindif.2023.102274

Kim, M., & Adlof, L. (2023). Adapting to the future: ChatGPT as a means for supporting constructivist learning environments. *TechTrends. 68,* 37e46. https://doi.org/DOI: 10.1007/s11528-023-00899-x

Lapuz, A. M. E., & Fulgencio, M. N. (2020). Improving the critical thinking skills of secondary students using problem-based learning. *International Journal of Academic Multidisciplinary Research (IJAMR), 4,*(1), 1-7. www.ijeais.org/ijamr. https://ssrn.com/abstract=3453211

Liang, J., Wang, L., Luo, J., Yan, Y., & Fan, C. (2023). The relationship between student interaction with generative artificial intelligence and learning achievement: Serial mediating roles of self-efficacy and cognitive engagement. *Frontiers in Psychology*, 14, 1285392. DOI: 10.3389/fpsyg.2023.1285392 PMID: 38187430

Liu, J., Ma, Y., Sun, X., Zhu, Z., & Xu, Y. (2022). A systematic review of higher-order thinking by visualizing its structure through HistCite and CiteSpace software. *The Asia-Pacific Education Researcher*, 31(6), 635–645. DOI: 10.1007/s40299-021-00614-5

Makridakis, S. (2017). The forthcoming artificial intelligence (AI) revolution: Its impact on society and firms. *Futures*, 90, 46–60. DOI: 10.1016/j.futures.2017.03.006

Marr, B. (2024, February 20). A short history of chatgpt: how we got to where we are today. *Forbes*.https://www.forbes.com/sites/bernardmarr/2023/05/19/a-short-history-of-chatgpt-how-we-got-to-where-we-are-today/

McGuire, A., Qureshi, W., & Saad, M. (2024). A constructivist model for leveraging GenAI tools for individualized, peer-simulated feedback on student writing. [IJTE]. *International Journal of Technology in Education*, 7(2), 326–352. DOI: 10.46328/ijte.639

Merrill, M. D. (1991). Constructivism and instructional design. *Educational Technology*, 31(5), 45–53.

Mollick, E. R., & Mollick, L. (2023). Using AI to implement effective teaching strategies in classrooms: five strategies, including prompts. *The Wharton School Research Paper, Available atSSRN:*https://ssrn.com/abstract=4391243 or http://dx.org/10.2139/ssrn.4391243 DOI: 10.2139/ssrn.4391243

Narayan, R., Rodriguez, C., Araujo, J., Shaqlaih, A., & Moss, G. (2013). Constructivism/Constructivist Learning Theory. In B. J. Irby, G. Brown, R. Lara-Alecio, & S. Jackson (Eds.), *The handbook of educational theories* (1st ed., pp.169-184). Information Age Publishing.

Ng, D. T. K., Tan, C. W., & Leung, J. K. L. (2024). Empowering student self-regulated learning and science education through ChatGPT: A pioneering pilot study. *British Journal of Educational Technology*, 55(4), 1328–1353. DOI: 10.1111/bjet.13454

O'brien, M. (2023, December 19). 2023: The year we played with Artificial Intelligence - and weren't sure what to do about it. *AP News*. https://apnews.com/article/ai-2023-artificial-intelligence-chatgpt-dangers-565ff5b817b5db0d4e74829ae3d68611

Paschen, U., Pitt, C., & Kietzmann, J. (2019). Artificial intelligence: building blocks and an innovation typology. *Business Horizons, 63*(2), 147e155.

Piaget, J. (1955). The construction of reality in the child. *Journal of Consulting Psychology*, •••, 19.

Rasul, T., Nair, S., Kalendra, D., Mulyadi, R., de Oliveira Santini, F., Ladeira, W. J., Sun, M., Day, I., Rather, R. A., & Heathcote, L. (2023). The role of ChatGPT in higher education: Benefits, challenges, and future research directions. *Journal of Applied Learning & Teaching*, 6(1), 41–56. DOI: 10.37074/jalt.2023.6.1.29

Reed, C. (2018). How should we regulate artificial intelligence? *Philosophical Transactions. Series A, Mathematical, Physical, and Engineering Sciences*, 376(2128), 20170360. Advance online publication. DOI: 10.1098/rsta.2017.0360 PMID: 30082306

Robertson, J., Ferreira, C., Botha, E., & Oosthuizen, K. (2024). Game changers: A generative AI prompt protocol to enhance human AI-knowledge co-construction. *Business Horizons*, 67(5), 499–510. Advance online publication. DOI: 10.1016/j.bushor.2024.04.008

Roll, I., Aleven, V., McLaren, B. M., & Koedinger, K. R. (2011). Improving students' help-seeking skills using metacognitive feedback in an intelligent tutoring system. *Learning and Instruction*, 21(2), 267–280. DOI: 10.1016/j.learninstruc.2010.07.004

Rosenblatt, K. (2023, May 18). New York City public schools remove ChatGPT ban. https://www.nbcnews.com/tech/chatgpt-ban-dropped-new-york-city-public-schools-rcna85089

Rudolph, J., Tan, S., & Tan, S. (2023). War of the chatbots: Bard, Bing Chat, ChatGPT, Ernie and beyond. The new AI gold rush and its impact in higher education. *Journal of Applied Learning & Teaching*, 6(1), 364–389. DOI: 10.37074/jalt.2023.6.1.23

Sazali, A. R. B., Khamarudin, F. B., & Abdul Alahdad, S. N. B. (2022). Maximizing the zone of proximal development benefits in group online learning. *International Journal of Academic Research in Business & Social Sciences*, 12(6), 1476–1496. DOI: 10.6007/IJARBSS/v12-i6/13861

Shanto, S. S., Ahmed, Z., & Jony, A. I. (2023). PAIGE: A generative AI-based framework for promoting assignment integrity in higher education. *STEM Education*, 3(4), 288–305. DOI: 10.3934/steme.2023018

Short, C. E., & Short, J. C. (2023). The artificially intelligent entrepreneur: ChatGPT, prompt engineering, and entrepreneurial rhetoric creation. *Journal of Business Venturing Insights*, 19, e00388. DOI: 10.1016/j.jbvi.2023.e00388

Siegel, J. (2023, September 14). 'Technology is not something we can hide from students': How NYC Public Schools invited AI into its classrooms. https://news.microsoft.com/source/features/digital-transformation/how-nyc-public-schools-invited-ai-into-its-classrooms

Smith, D. P., & Francis, N. J. (2023). Generative AI in assessment. https://network.febs.org/posts/generative-ai-in-assessment

Stojanov, A. (2023). Learning with ChatGPT 3.5 as a more knowledgeable other: An autoethnographic study. *International Journal of Educational Technology in Higher Education*, 20(1), 35. DOI: 10.1186/s41239-023-00404-7

Stretton, B., Kovoor, J., Arnold, M., & Bacchi, S. (2023). ChatGPT-Based Learning: Generative *Artificial Intelligence in Medical Education.Medical Science Educator*, 34(1), 215–217. Advance online publication. DOI: 10.1007/s40670-023-01934-5 PMID: 38510403

Strickland, E. (2023, July 12).https://spectrum.ieee.org/chatgpt-medical-exam Dr. CHATGPT will interface with you now. *IEEE Spectrum*.https://spectrum.ieee.org/chatgpt-medical-exam

Taber, K. (2011). Constructivism as educational theory: Contingency in learning, and optimally guided instruction. *Nova Science Publishers Inc.,* 39-61. https://science-education-research.com/KeithSTaber/Constructivism_files/Taber,%20K.%20S.%20%282011%29.%20Constructivism%20as%20educational%20theory.pdf

Tam, M. (2000). Constructivism, instructional design, and technology: Implications for transforming distance learning. *Journal of Educational Technology & Society*, 3(2), 50–60. https://www.jstor.org/stable/jeductechsoci.3.2.50

Vygotsky, L. (1978). *Mind in society*. Harvard University Press.

Wang, M. T., & Eccles, J. S. (2011). Adolescent behavior, emotional, and cognitive engagement trajectories in school and their differential relations to educational success. *Journal of Research on Adolescence*, 22(1), 31–29. DOI: 10.1111/j.1532-7795.2011.00753.x PMID: 22822296

Wang, W. (2023). The impact of ChatGPT on the interaction between teachers and students in primary and middle school English classes: Taking problems-based learning as an example. *Proceedings of the International Conference on Global Politics and Socio-Humanities*.https://doi.org/DOI: 10.54254/2753-7048/24/20230709

Weidinger, L., Mellor, J., Rauh, M., Griffin, C., Uesato, J., Huang, P. S., Cheng, M., Glaese, M., Balle, B., Kasirzadeh, A., Kenton, Z., Brown, S., Hawkins, W., Stepleton, T., Biles, C., Birhane, A., Haas, J., Rimmell, L., Hendricks, W., . . . Gabriel, I. (2021). Ethical and social risks of harm from language models. *arXiv preprint arXiv:2112.04359* (2021). https://doi.org//arXiv.2112.04359DOI: 10.48550

White, P. (2022). Problem solving in chemistry supported by metacognitive scaffolding: Teaching associates' perspectives and practices. *Chemistry Education Research and Practice*, 23(2), 436–451. DOI: 10.1039/D1RP00242B

Woods, R. (N.d.). (2023). Ms, Guide: Ramp up to AI. *The AI Exchange*.https://docs.google.com/document/d/1h9wWnRJ4zxNJah9J1l8CEgXgp3zNLy-JoSVhPWvCIAU/view

Wu, T., & Chang, M. (2023). Application of generative artificial intelligence to assessment and curriculum design for project-based learning. *2023 International Conference on Engineering and Emerging Technologies (ICEET),* Istanbul, Turkey, 2023, pp 1-6. https://doi.org/DOI: 10.1109/ICEET60227.2023.10525933

Yu, H., & Guo, Y. (2023). Generative artificial intelligence empowers educational reform: Current status, issues, and prospects. *Frontiers in Education*, 8, 1183162. Advance online publication. DOI: 10.3389/feduc.2023.1183162

Zhou, L., Rudin, C., Gombolay, M., Spohrer, J., Zhou, M., & Souren, P. (2023). From artificial intelligence (AI) to intelligence augmentation (IA): Design principles, potential risks, and emerging issues. *AIS Transactions on Human-Computer Interaction*, 15(1), 111–135. DOI: 10.17705/1thci.00185

Zhou, L., & Wei, L. (2024). Research on human-computer interactive interface in visualized information. *In 2010 IEEE 11th International Conference on Computer-Aided Industrial Design & Conceptual Design, 1*, 349-352.

Zhou, L., & Wei, Y. (2010). Research on human-computer interactive interface in visualized information. I*n 2010 IEEE 11th International Conference on Computer-Aided Industrial Design & Conceptual Design, 1,* 349–352. https://doi.org/DOI: 10.1109/CAIDCD.2010.5681337

Zhou, X., & Schofield, L. (2024). Using social learning theories to explore the role of generative artificial intelligence (AI) in collaborative learning. *Journal of Learning Development in Higher Education*, 30(30). Advance online publication. DOI: 10.47408/jldhe.vi30.1031

Zimmerman, B. J., & Schunk, D. H. (2011). Self-regulated learning and performance: an introduction and an overview. In Schunk, D. H., & Zimmerman, B. (Eds.), *Handbook of self-regulation of learning and performance* (pp. 15–26). Routledge.

Chapter 7
Personalized Language Learning With AI for Pedagogical and Andragogical Approaches

Goh Ying Yingsoon
https://orcid.org/0000-0002-6654-2887
Universiti Teknologi MARA, Malaysia

Nurul Ajleaa Abdul Rahman
Universiti Teknologi MARA, Malaysia

ABSTRACT

Language learning has traditionally relied on standardized pedagogical approaches for children and andragogical methods for adults. However, the emergence of Artificial Intelligence (AI) offers exciting possibilities for personalizing language education to cater to individual needs and learning styles across all ages. This chapter explores how AI can be leveraged to create effective personalized learning experiences within both pedagogical and andragogical frameworks. Furthermore, the integration of AI in language instruction has the potential to democratize access to quality education, ensuring that learners of diverse backgrounds can benefit from tailored learning paths that enhance retention and proficiency.

DOI: 10.4018/979-8-3693-6130-6.ch007

INTRODUCTION

AI can revolutionize language learning by personalizing instruction, providing adaptive assessments, and analyzing learning patterns to optimize curriculum design. This macro-level planning ensures that educational materials and methodologies are tailored to the needs of diverse student populations, fostering a more inclusive and effective learning environment. At a micro level, AI can offer individualized feedback, simulate conversational partners, and recommend personalized study plans, thereby supporting the specific requirements and learning styles of each student. This granular approach to planning caters to the unique needs of learners, promoting autonomy and self-directed learning, a core principle of andragogy. Both perspectives must be harmoniously integrated to leverage the full potential of AI in language education, ensuring that it enhances pedagogical practices while catering to the adult learner's particular needs and goals.

This chapter begins by outlining the current landscape of language education, highlighting the distinct approaches of pedagogy for children and andragogy for adults. It will then delve into the concept of personalized learning and its potential benefits for language acquisition. This chapter also delves into the integration of Artificial Intelligence (AI) in both pedagogical and andragogical language education, examining its potential to revolutionize teaching and learning processes. With a backdrop of evolving educational landscapes, the introduction highlights the necessity for innovative approaches to cater to diverse learning styles and age groups. The authors advocate for a strategic adoption of AI, emphasizing its role in enhancing educational outcomes and personalizing the language learning experience.

Pedagogy in language education refers to the method and practice of teaching languages, encompassing a range of techniques, strategies, and theoretical frameworks that educators employ to facilitate language acquisition. It involves the design of instructional materials, the creation of an engaging learning environment, and the implementation of activities that promote communication skills, linguistic knowledge, cultural awareness, and critical thinking, all tailored to meet the diverse needs and learning styles of students.

While andragogy in language education is an approach focused on teaching adults, characterized by its recognition of the unique needs, experiences, and motivations of adult learners. It emphasizes self-directed learning, problem-solving, and the practical application of knowledge, with the understanding that adult learners are often goal-oriented, bring a wealth of life experiences to the learning process and require a curriculum that is relevant to their personal and professional lives.

Personalized learning is recognized as important in language learning (Goh, 2010). This approach allows learners to progress at their own pace, focusing on their individual strengths and weaknesses, thereby enhancing the overall effectiveness of the learning process.

Personalized learning is an educational approach that focuses on creating a customized learning experience for each learner. It considers individual interests, needs, abilities, and learning preferences. In the context of language acquisition, personalized learning ensures that learners receive instruction that is relevant, engaging, and tailored to their specific goals and learning styles. (Goh, 2010).

The implementation of personalized learning in language acquisition offers several benefits, including enhanced learner engagement, improved learning outcomes, and the ability to cater to individual learning styles and paces, thereby creating a more effective and tailored educational experience. These include:

1. **Enhanced Motivation:** Personalized learning experiences inspire learners' interest and motivation, making them more willing to engage in the learning process.
2. **Improved Learning Outcomes:** By addressing individual needs and learning styles, personalized learning helps to enhance learners' language proficiency and academic performance.
3. **Increased Learner Autonomy:** Personalized learning encourages learners to take an active role in decision-making, self-assessment, and reflection, fostering their ability to learn independently.
4. **Flexibility and Adaptability:** Customized learning plans can be adjusted according to learners' progress and needs to accommodate a constantly evolving learning environment.
5. **Emphasis on Real-World Applications:** Personalized learning focuses on applying language knowledge to real-life situations, improving learners' practical language skills and communication abilities.

Seeing the benefits that personalized learning can offer, the role of AI in supporting both pedagogical and andragogical approaches is becoming increasingly significant. AI technologies can analyze learners' behaviors, preferences, and progress to dynamically adjust the content and delivery methods, thus ensuring that educational experiences are aligned with each student's unique needs. For pedagogical approaches, AI can assist educators in identifying and addressing knowledge gaps, while in andragogical contexts, it can empower adult learners by providing self-paced and self-directed learning opportunities that respect their autonomy and prior experience. This integration of AI not only enhances the effectiveness of teaching strategies but also promotes a more inclusive and adaptive learning environment.

The role of AI In offering personalized language learning for both pedagogical and andragogical approaches is thus significant. AI-powered language learning platforms can analyze learner data, such as their learning preferences, progress, and performance, to create tailored learning experiences. By understanding individual needs and learning styles, AI can deliver personalized content, exercises, and feedback, making the learning process more effective and engaging. Additionally, AI can provide adaptive learning paths that adjust to the learner's pace and proficiency level, ensuring that they receive appropriate challenges and support. This individualized approach not only enhances motivation and improves learning outcomes but also empowers learners to take ownership of their language-learning journey. AI-assisted language learning can be a valuable tool in bridging the gap between traditional teaching methods and personalized, learner-centered approaches, benefiting both children and adults in their language acquisition endeavors. (Goh, 2021).

However, to maximize the benefits of AI in language education, it is crucial to thoughtfully integrate pedagogical and andragogical approaches. Pedagogically, educators should focus on designing AI-enhanced activities that cater to diverse learning styles, provide personalized feedback, and foster student engagement, while andragogically, they should empower adult learners by encouraging self-direction, critical thinking, and the application of language skills in real-world contexts, thereby creating a blended learning environment that not only leverages AI's capabilities but also nurtures the unique needs and motivations of each learner. These are the problems that need to be handled.

In the next section, a related literature review on personalized Language Learning with AI for pedagogical and andragogical approaches is discussed. The synthesis of various case studies and theoretical frameworks will shed light on the potential benefits and challenges of integrating personalized AI-driven language learning into traditional educational settings.

LITERATURE REVIEW

This section will review existing research on the application of AI in language education. It will explore how AI technologies such as natural language processing, adaptive learning algorithms, and chatbots can be used to personalize learning content, activities, and feedback for individual learners.

The roles and research foci of artificial intelligence (AI) in language education have garnered significant attention in recent years, with numerous studies exploring the potential of AI technologies to enhance teaching and learning processes. An integrated bibliographic analysis and systematic review approach provides a comprehensive overview of the existing literature in this field. This approach allows researchers to identify key trends, methodologies, and findings, as well as to identify gaps in the current research (Liang, et al, 2023). By examining a wide range of studies, researchers can gain a deeper understanding of the various roles that AI can play in language education, such as personalized learning, language assessment, and language translation. Furthermore, they can explore different research fields, such as the effectiveness of AI-based language learning tools, the impact of AI on language teacher education, and the ethical considerations surrounding AI in language education. This integrated approach ultimately contributes to a more nuanced understanding of the potential benefits and challenges of incorporating AI technologies into language teaching and learning environments.

The integration of artificial intelligence (AI) in language education is revolutionizing the way language is taught and learned, offering a wide array of pedagogical and andragogical approaches. (Huang, et al, 2023). AI-powered tools and platforms can adapt to the individual needs and learning styles of students, fostering a more personalized and autonomous learning experience. For instance, intelligent tutoring systems can provide personalized feedback, recommend resources, and create a customized learning path for each learner, thus promoting self-directed and reflective learning. Moreover, AI-driven language learning apps can offer interactive and engaging activities, such as language games and virtual reality scenarios, that facilitate immersive and collaborative learning experiences. Additionally, AI can help language educators in analyzing large datasets to identify trends and patterns in language learning, thus informing evidence-based teaching practices and curriculum design. Overall, the application of AI in language education holds great potential in enhancing pedagogical approaches and fostering a more efficient, engaging, and student-centered learning environment.

The integration of AI technology in the development of an e-learning tool for engineering graduates aims to enhance their academic writing skills in English. (2020). By utilizing AI-powered writing assistance, the tool can provide personalized feedback, suggest improvements, and guide users through the writing process. This technology enables the creation of a customized learning experience, adapting to individual needs and preferences. Furthermore, AI can analyze user input, identify areas for improvement, and provide relevant resources, such as grammar rules, style guides, and writing tips. This innovative approach empowers engineering graduates to develop their academic writing skills efficiently and effectively, ultimately preparing them for success in their academic and professional endeavors.

The Integration of an autonomous learning system for Bengali characters using web-based intelligent handwriting recognition represents a significant advancement in AI for language education. (Khatun & Miwa, 2016). By leveraging AI technologies, such as machine learning and natural language processing, this system can effectively recognize and interpret Bengali handwriting, enabling a more personalized and interactive learning experience for students. This innovative approach not only enhances the accessibility of language education but also promotes the development of AI applications that cater to the diverse linguistic needs of diverse populations. By utilizing web-based platforms, this system can be easily accessed, making it an invaluable tool for language learners around the world.

iSTART-ALL is an innovative intelligent tutoring system designed to address the challenges faced by adults with low literacy skills in reading comprehension. (Johnson, et al, 2017). By leveraging advanced technologies, this program provides personalized instruction and support to help individuals overcome barriers to learning and improve their reading abilities. The system adapts to the individual's progress, offering tailored lessons and interventions based on their specific needs and learning styles. This adaptive approach ensures that learners receive the appropriate level of challenge and support, promoting effective learning and skill development. iSTART-ALL is a valuable resource for adults seeking to enhance their reading comprehension skills and improve their overall literacy proficiency.

The study conducted by Wijekumar et al. (2017) examined the effectiveness of a web-based text structure strategy instruction on seventh graders' content area reading comprehension. The research involved a sample of 487 seventh-grade students from low-income communities in the United States. The participants were randomly assigned to two groups, with one group receiving the web-based text structure strategy instruction and the other serving as a control group. The intervention group engaged in interactive lessons that focused on understanding the structure of texts, such as identifying main ideas, supporting details, and conclusions. On the other hand, the control group did not receive any specific intervention. The results revealed that the students who participated in the web-based text structure strategy instruction demonstrated significant improvements in their reading comprehension scores compared to the control group. These findings highlight the potential of web-based text structure strategy in enhancing the reading comprehension skills of seventh graders, particularly those from low-income backgrounds. The study underscores the importance of incorporating AI-driven interventions in learning environments to support students in developing effective reading strategies.

Pandarova et al. (2019) explored the applications of artificial intelligence in enhancing vocabulary and grammar learning. They emphasized the potential of AI tools to facilitate personalized and adaptive language instruction. These tools can analyze learner data to identify individual strengths and weaknesses, allowing for tailored exercise recommendations that target specific areas of improvement. Additionally, AI-powered language tutors can provide immediate feedback and guidance, helping learners correct errors and develop a deeper understanding of linguistic concepts. Furthermore, Pandarova et al. highlighted the utility of natural language processing techniques in creating intelligent vocabulary learning environments, such as context-sensitive dictionary applications and semantic analysis tools that assist in comprehending word meanings in different contexts. Overall, the study underscored the transformative role of AI in making language learning more effective, efficient, and accessible to learners of diverse abilities.

Ayedoun et al.'s (2019) study investigated the impact of incorporating communicative and affective strategies into an embodied conversational agent on second language learners' willingness to communicate. The research focused on 39 English as a Second Language (ESL) learners in France, who were randomly assigned to two groups. One group interacted with the embodied conversational agent, which was designed to integrate both communicative strategies, such as feedback and clarification, and affective strategies, like expressing empathy and encouragement. The other group engaged in conversations with a human partner. The results indicated that the learners who interacted with the embodied conversational agent exhibited greater improvements in their willingness to communicate compared to those who conversed with a human. The findings underscore the potential of AI-driven embodied conversational agents in facilitating second language learners' communication skills development, particularly when these agents are designed to incorporate both communicative and affective strategies. The study highlights the promise of AI applications in supporting language learners' speaking and listening abilities.

Table 1. Common applications of AI in language learning (Huang, et al, 2023)

Application	Key aspect	Researchers
1	AI applications in learning writing	Lin, et al, 2017 Khatun & Miwa, 2016
2	AI applications in learning reading	Johnson et al. (2017) Wijekumar et al. (2017)
3	AI applications in learning vocabulary and grammar	Pandarova et al. (2019)
4	AI applications in learning speaking and listening	Ayedoun et al. (2019)

Additionally, the theory for integrating AI into pedagogical and andragogical language education is based on the Social Constructivist Framework (Huang et al., 2024; Cronjé, 2024; Sankumpa et al., 2023). This framework posits that learning is a social process where knowledge is constructed through interactions with others and the environment. Language education is inherently social, with learners engaging in meaningful interactions to construct knowledge. AI can facilitate these interactions by providing personalized feedback, adaptive learning paths, and virtual language exchange opportunities, thereby enhancing the social aspect of language learning. AI can act as a scaffold, providing support to learners as they acquire language skills. This support can be in the form of intelligent tutoring systems, language practice platforms, and real-time language translation, which help learners bridge gaps in their knowledge and skills. According to Vygotsky, the ZPD is the difference between what a learner can do independently and what they can achieve with guidance and support. AI can identify a learner's ZPD and provide appropriate challenges and assistance, thus promoting optimal learning. AI can facilitate peer learning and collaboration by connecting learners with similar language proficiency levels and interests. Virtual language learning communities, powered by AI, can encourage learners to engage in discussions, projects, and other collaborative activities, fostering a supportive and interactive learning environment. By integrating AI within the Social Constructivist Framework, pedagogical and andragogical language education can be transformed to better meet the individual needs of learners, promote social interactions, and facilitate the acquisition of language skills in a culturally rich and engaging environment.

In sum, integration of AI in language education is theoretically supported by both pedagogical and andragogical approaches (Jeong-Bae Son et al., 2023; Liu, 2023; Liu, et al, 2023; Xi, 2023). Pedagogically, AI can tailor instruction to individual learners' needs, providing personalized feedback and adaptive learning paths that enhance motivation and engagement. Meanwhile, from an andragogical perspective, AI empowers adult learners by fostering autonomy, self-direction, and critical thinking, as it offers a flexible and self-paced learning environment that aligns with their unique learning styles and goals. Together, these approaches demonstrate how AI can effectively support language acquisition by addressing the diverse requirements of learners across different age groups and educational levels.

Pedagogical Considerations

Pedagogy refers to the methodologies and techniques used to educate children. In the context of language education, pedagogical approaches for children often focus on creating a fun, engaging, and interactive learning environment. These approaches incorporate various strategies such as games, songs, role-plays, and storytelling to facilitate language acquisition. The primary goal of pedagogy in language education is to inspire children's curiosity, motivate them to learn, and lay a solid foundation for their linguistic development.

A pedagogical approach to incorporating AI in language education involves integrating AI technologies into teaching and learning processes to enhance language acquisition. This approach leverages AI's capabilities in providing personalized learning experiences, automating language assessments, and facilitating language practice through interactive tools. In doing so, AI can adapt to learners' individual needs, provide instant feedback, and create a dynamic and engaging learning environment. Additionally, AI can analyze large amounts of data to identify patterns in learners' progress, enabling educators to make informed decisions about instruction and tailor their teaching methods to optimize language learning outcomes. By integrating AI into language education in a pedagogical manner, educators can harness its potential to support and enhance traditional teaching practices, ultimately empowering learners to develop their language skills more effectively.

The role of artificial intelligence (AI) in developing language learners' communication skills has become increasingly significant in recent years. Rusmiyanto et al. (2023) explore the potential of AI-based tools and platforms to facilitate language learning and enhance communicative abilities from pedagogical perspectives. By utilizing AI-driven language learning applications, learners can engage in interactive conversations with AI-generated characters, practice listening and speaking skills, and receive personalized feedback on their performance. Additionally, AI-powered language learning platforms can adapt to individual learners' needs and preferences, providing tailored instruction and practice activities that target specific areas for improvement. Furthermore, AI-generated language models can assist learners in generating responses, constructing sentences, and acquiring new vocabulary, thereby fostering autonomous language learning. Overall, the integration of AI in language learning pedagogical approaches holds immense promise in promoting effective communication skills among language learners.

Wang, et al. (2023) conducted a study that investigates the significance of pedagogical approaches in AI-supported language learning, focusing on human-AI interactions. Utilizing cluster analysis and epistemic network analysis, the researchers identified key factors that contribute to the effectiveness of AI-supported learning. The study highlights the importance of adaptive and personalized learning experiences, where AI systems tailor instruction to individual learners' needs and preferences. It also emphasizes the role of scaffolded learning, where AI provides guidance and support to learners as they progress through the learning journey. Additionally, the study reveals the value of social interaction and collaboration in AI-supported language learning, suggesting that incorporating human-AI partnerships can enhance learning outcomes. The findings underscore the necessity of integrating pedagogical approaches that leverage the strengths of AI technology, such as adaptability, personalization, and supportive scaffolding, to create engaging and effective learning environments for language learners.

Table 2 illustrates a pedagogical approach to incorporating AI in supporting character instruction for non-Chinese learners. In the first step, the instructor demonstrates how to write Chinese characters within an AI system, allowing learners to attempt the same task. The AI system features character recognition to help guide the learners' efforts. During the practice stage, the instructor's corrections, which are reflected in the AI system, enable learners to notice and learn from their mistakes. The AI system is equipped with a correction feature to provide immediate feedback on writing. In the self-correction stage, the instructor monitors the learners' progress as they receive instant feedback on their writing, again facilitated by the AI's character recognition system with a correction feature. In the peer learning stage, the instructor continues to monitor as learners engage in sharing their writing experiences, utilizing the AI system's correction feature to support their interactions. Finally, in the evaluation stage, the instructor presents the characters for learners to study and guides a post-lesson evaluation task. Upon completing this task, learners receive their evaluation results from the AI system, which grades their writing. This integration of AI into the teaching and learning process enhances the pedagogical approach by providing a comprehensive system that not only aids in character instruction but also fosters a supportive environment for non-Chinese learners to develop their Chinese character writing skills.

Table 2. Example of pedagogical consideration in using AI in supporting Chinese character instruction among non-Chinese learners

Step	Instructor's activities	Learners' activities	Technical support of AI
1 learning Chinese character stage	The instructor shows how to write in the AI system	Learners try	AI character recognition system
2 practice stage	Corrected by the instructor as reflected in the AI system	Noticed by the learners	AI character recognition system with correction feature
3 self-correction stage	Monitored by the instructor	Learners get immediate feedback on their writing	AI character recognition system with correction feature
4 peer learning stage	Monitored by the instructor	Learners exchange writing experiences with one another	AI character recognition system with correction feature
5 evaluation stage	Instructors show the characters which learners have to learn. At the end of the lesson, instructor gives instructions for learners to complete lesson-end evaluation task	Learners get evaluation results of their writing	AI character recognition system with grading feature

The key pedagogical considerations of AI in education involve monitoring, guidance, and the establishment of clear guidelines by leading organizations. Monitoring refers to the ability of AI systems to track and assess student progress, providing insights to educators who can then offer tailored support. Guidance is provided by AI in the form of personalized learning paths, adaptive assessments, and real-time feedback, which help students navigate their education effectively. Additionally, guidelines set by reputable educational institutions and governing bodies are crucial for ensuring that AI implementation aligns with educational standards and best practices. These guidelines help in creating a framework for the ethical use of AI, the protection of student data privacy, and the maintenance of quality in education. Clear leadership from organizations in the field of education ensures that AI is integrated thoughtfully and responsibly, with a focus on enhancing learning experiences and outcomes.

Andragogical Considerations

Andragogy, on the other hand, is the art and science of teaching adults. In language education, andragogical approaches emphasize self-directed learning, problem-solving, and real-world applications. Adult learners are often encouraged to take responsibility for their own learning, set personal goals, and engage in meaningful conversations and interactions. Andragogy recognizes the unique needs, experiences, and motivations of adult learners, tailoring the learning process to accommodate their diverse backgrounds and learning styles.

Andragogical considerations in using AI in language education focus on the unique needs and motivations of adult learners. Andragogy, as opposed to pedagogy, emphasizes the self-directed and experiential learning process of adults. When integrating AI into language learning for adults, it is crucial to prioritize learner autonomy, relevance, and collaboration. AI applications should enable adult learners to set their own learning goals, progress at their own pace, and have control over their learning materials and resources. Additionally, AI should facilitate the integration of real-life situations and practical applications of language skills to enhance relevance and engagement. Furthermore, AI can promote collaboration by providing platforms for adult learners to connect with peers, practice conversational skills, and engage in meaningful interactions. By addressing these andragogical considerations, AI can effectively support adult learners in their language education journey, fostering a personalized, relevant, and collaborative learning experience.

In their 2023 study, Lee and colleagues focus on the development of an AI-based English learning support system designed to enhance learner-generated context-based learning. The system is specifically tailored to facilitate and support learners in creating personalized contexts that are relevant to their individual needs and interests, thereby promoting more effective and engaging learning experiences. By integrating andragogical approaches, the system encourages self-directed learning and places learners in control of their learning paths. The learning path is carefully crafted to guide learners through a series of activities and exercises that are aligned with their specific learning goals, while also allowing for flexibility and adaptability to accommodate their unique learning styles and preferences. This approach not only promotes a deeper understanding of the English language, but also fosters essential skills such as critical thinking, problem-solving, and autonomy in learners. The learning path shown is closely related to self-regulated learning skills. (Tomaszewska, 2023).

Andragogical considerations in using AI in language education focus on the specific needs and characteristics of adult learners, which differ from the pedagogical approach tailored to children and young learners. Andragogy emphasizes self-directed learning, practical application, and the integration of real-life situations. When incorporating AI in language education for adults, it is essential to prioritize learner autonomy, allowing them to set personalized learning goals and progress at their own pace. AI should also provide relevant content that connects language learning to real-world contexts, making the learning experience more meaningful and engaging. Additionally, AI can facilitate collaboration and interaction among adult learners, fostering a sense of community and enabling them to practice conversational skills in a supported environment. By addressing these andragogical considerations, AI can effectively support adult learners in their language education journey, promoting self-directed, relevant, and collaborative learning experiences.

Table 3 outlines an example of how AI can be integrated into Chinese character learning for adult learners, focusing on andragogical principles. The first key aspect is self-directed learning, where the AI system provides access to pre-lesson self-learning materials, equipped with a Chinese characters recognition feature to guide learners in their independent study. The second aspect, practical application, allows learners to engage in their own practice and learning during the lesson, with the AI system aiding in tracing and monitoring their progress. The third aspect, integration of real-life situations, involves a self-assessment task following the lesson, enabling learners to review encountered characters and engage in self-learning, self-practice, and self-assessment. The AI system supports this process with an assessment feature, providing a comprehensive tool that fosters autonomy, practical application, and real-life integration, thereby enhancing the andragogical approach to Chinese characters learning.

Table 3. Example of andragogical consideration in using AI in supporting Chinese characters learning

Aspect	Key aspect	Notes	Key features of the AI system
1	Self-directed learning	Provide access for pre-lesson self learning	AI system with Chinese characters recognition feature
2	Practical application	During the lesson, allow learners to conduct their own practice and learning	The AI system in tracing and monitoring learners' own learning
3	integration of real-life situation	After the lesson, self-assessment task. Allow learners to check characters that they have encountered and able to do self-learning, self-practice and self-assessment.	AI system with assessment feature

In an andragogical approach to AI integration in education, the goal is to empower adult learners by minimizing instructor monitoring and interruptions. AI systems should be designed to allow learners to navigate through the learning process with as much autonomy as possible. This means that the AI should provide clear instructions, guidance, and feedback without the need for constant instructor oversight. Furthermore, the AI system should be capable of identifying when learners may require additional assistance or when they are struggling, and it should offer support or interventions at these moments. By doing so, the AI system can help to maintain a balance between self-directed learning and the necessary scaffolding that adult learners may need. This approach not only respects the adult learners' desire for independence but also maximizes the efficiency of the learning process, as it reduces the time spent on administrative tasks and allows instructors to focus on more meaningful interactions with their students.

Benefits of AI in Language Learning

AI offers opportunities for personalized language learning. However, it is also important to acknowledge the challenges of using AI in language education. Predicting the difficulty of exercise items for dynamic difficulty adaptation in adaptive language tutoring is essential for providing an effective and personalized learning experience. It shows the benefits and advantages in the use of AI in providing personalized learning experiences (Pandarova's et al., 2019). By accurately assessing the complexity of exercises, the tutoring system can adjust the difficulty level, accordingly, ensuring that students are challenged but not overwhelmed. This involves analyzing various factors such as the student's proficiency level, learning progress, and past performance. Machine learning algorithms can be employed to identify patterns and correlations between these factors, enabling the system to make informed decisions about the appropriate exercises to present. This approach enhances the adaptability of the tutoring system, promotes efficient learning, and supports students in achieving their language learning goals.

The benefits and advantages of AI technology in language education, as highlighted by Khatun and Miwa (2016), are numerous and significant. AI can revolutionize language learning by providing personalized and adaptive experiences that cater to the individual needs and learning styles of students. With its ability to analyze large amounts of data and identify patterns, AI can tailor learning materials and exercises to the specific strengths and weaknesses of each learner, thereby optimizing the learning process and improving outcomes. Additionally, AI-powered language learning platforms can offer immediate feedback and corrections, facilitating rapid improvement and ensuring that learners stay on track. Furthermore, AI can facilitate language learning by providing access to a wealth of resources and materials, including interactive exercises, language tutors, and cultural immersion experiences. By overcoming the limitations of traditional language learning methods, AI technology has the potential to make language education more engaging, effective, and accessible, empowering learners to achieve their language goals more efficiently.

Table 4. Advantages of using AI in language learning

Advantage	Key aspect	Researchers
1	Providing personalized learning experiences	Pandarova's et al. (2019)
2	Enabling immediate adjustment	Khatun and Miwa (2016)
3	Rich opportunities using AI in language learning	Mirzaei et al. (2018)

Challenges of Integrating AI into Language Learning

The reliability of AI technology is a significant challenge that has been highlighted by researchers such as Hwang, et al, in 2020. The issue arises from the fact that AI systems are not infallible and can produce errors or biases in their predictions or decisions. This is because AI systems are trained on large datasets, which may contain inaccuracies, and biases or be generated by algorithms that may not be perfect. As a result, AI systems may not always generalize well to new, unseen data, potentially leading to unreliable or inaccurate results. Furthermore, AI systems may also be vulnerable to adversarial attacks, where small, carefully crafted changes to the input data can lead to large changes in the output of the AI system.

This highlights the need for continued research and development to improve the reliability and robustness of AI technology.

The Integration of AI-powered technologies into foreign language education has become an increasingly important topic, as technology continues to advance at a rapid pace. (Pokrivcakova, 2019). However, this integration presents several challenges that must be addressed. One of the main challenges is the preparation of teachers for the application of these technologies in their teaching practices. Many teachers may not have the necessary knowledge or training in using AI tools, which can lead to a lack of confidence and hesitation in incorporating them into their lessons. Additionally, there may be concerns about the potential impact of AI on the quality of education and the role of teachers. It is important to provide professional development opportunities for teachers to learn how to effectively use AI tools and integrate them into their teaching practices in a way that complements their existing skills and knowledge. As teachers become more familiar and comfortable with AI-powered technologies, they can better understand their potential benefits and challenges and develop the skills necessary to effectively incorporate them into their lessons. This will help to ensure that AI-powered technologies can be successfully integrated into foreign language education and provide students with the benefits of personalized and adaptive learning experiences.

Goh, et al.'s (2023) study examines the impact of interface quality, system quality, and perceived usefulness on student satisfaction with an automated pronunciation scoring system. In today's digital age, AI-powered language education tools have become increasingly popular, aiming to provide personalized feedback and facilitate language learning. However, their effectiveness in improving user satisfaction remains a critical factor. The study highlights that a high-quality interface, which enhances user experience, plays a significant role in determining student satisfaction. A well-designed interface ensures ease of navigation and visually appealing features, making the learning process more enjoyable. Additionally, system quality, encompassing reliability, performance, and accuracy, is crucial in ensuring that the AI tool consistently provides accurate pronunciation feedback. When students perceive the system as useful, it fosters a sense of confidence in its ability to aid in their language learning journey. This perceived usefulness not only enhances their satisfaction but also encourages continued usage and engagement with the tool. Ultimately, this research underscores the importance of these three factors – interface quality, system quality, and perceived usefulness – in shaping student satisfaction with AI-powered language education tools, and by extension, their overall learning outcomes.

The Integration of artificial intelligence (AI) into language education has sparked a range of social issues, as highlighted in several studies. Luan et al. (2020) and Hwang et al. (2020) have pointed out that AI can exacerbate existing inequalities in the field of language learning. They argue that access to advanced AI technologies is often limited to wealthier institutions and countries, thereby widening the gap between privileged and underprivileged learners.

The integration of big data and artificial intelligence (AI) in education has the potential to revolutionize the way knowledge is imparted and learned, but this convergence also presents significant challenges that must be addressed. (Luan, et al, 2020). One of the primary challenges is the ethical use of student data, ensuring that privacy is protected, and that sensitive information is handled securely. Additionally, the vast volume and variety of educational data can lead to complexities in data analysis, requiring sophisticated algorithms and skilled data scientists to extract meaningful insights. Moreover, there is a risk of exacerbating inequalities if the implementation of AI and big data tools is not carefully managed, as it may benefit resource-rich institutions and students at the expense of those with fewer resources. Looking to the future, there is a need for continued research and development to refine AI algorithms to better understand and support the complexities of human learning, as well as to establish robust ethical frameworks and regulations to govern the use of educational data.

Furthermore, Zhang and Aslan (2021) and Yang (2021) have raised concerns about the potential for AI to perpetuate biases and discrimination in language education. They highlight that AI systems are only as fair and unbiased as the data they are trained on, and if this data contains biases, then the AI systems will also exhibit biased behavior. The integration of AI in language education has brought about significant social issues, primarily concerning the potential displacement of human educators, the ethical considerations of algorithmic bias, and the digital divide that may exacerbate educational inequalities. (Zhang and Aslan, 2021). While AI-powered language learning platforms offer personalized and adaptive learning experiences, there is a growing concern that these technologies could replace qualified language instructors, leading to a loss of the nuanced pedagogical approaches that human teachers provide. Moreover, the programming and datasets used by AI systems can inadvertently perpetuate biases, which may negatively impact students from diverse backgrounds. Ensuring equitable access to AI language education tools is also a pressing concern, as the digital divide can limit learning opportunities, potentially widening educational disparities. As research in AI for education continues to evolve, future directions should prioritize the development of unbiased algorithms, the integration of AI as a complementary tool to human educators, and the expansion of digital learning resources to underserved communities, aiming to strike a balance between the technological and human aspects of language education.

Precision education, an emerging trend in the field of education, presents a significant challenge for AI in this domain. (Yang, 2021). This approach tailors learning experiences to the individual needs of students, focusing on their unique strengths and weaknesses. To effectively support precision education, AI systems must go beyond traditional one-size-fits-all solutions and develop a deep understanding of each student's learning style, preferences, and requirements. This necessitates advanced data analysis techniques, personalized feedback mechanisms, and adaptable learning materials. As AI technology continues to evolve, it must address these challenges to provide an education system that can cater to the diverse needs of students, ultimately enhancing their learning experiences and outcomes.

Yang et al. (2021) also emphasize that AI can potentially undermine the development of critical thinking and problem-solving skills in learners, as it may overly rely on rote memorization and repetition. Human-centered artificial intelligence in education is transforming the way we perceive and address the invisible aspects of learning, such as emotional well-being, motivation, and personalized learning needs. By analyzing visible data, such as academic performance and interaction patterns, AI can identify underlying factors that may impact a student's learning journey. This enables educators to gain insights into the invisible aspects of their student's education, allowing them to provide tailored support and interventions. Through this approach, AI empowers educators to see the invisible and address the unique needs of each student, fostering a more inclusive and effective learning environment. Therefore, while AI has the potential to enhance language education, it is crucial to address these social issues to ensure equitable and unbiased access to quality language learning opportunities for all.

Table 5. Challenges using AI in language learning

Challenge	Key aspect	Researchers
1	Reliability of AI technology	Hwang et al, 2020
2	Acceptance by teachers and students	Pokrivcakova (2019) Goh et al (2023).
3	Social issues of AI in language education	Luan et al., 2020) Hwang et al. (2020) Zhang and Aslan (2021) Yang, 2021 Yang et al., 2021

In short, AI's natural language processing capabilities can sometimes struggle with understanding context and nuances in language learning, leading to misunderstandings and inaccuracies in instruction. Additionally, over-reliance on AI for language practice may hinder the development of genuine communication skills and cultural understanding.

CONCLUSION

The use of AI in language education has been a topic of debate, with some arguing that allowing students to use AI to generate output for learning is not a wise use of this technology. While AI can be a valuable tool in language learning, it is important to consider the potential drawbacks. Firstly, relying too heavily on AI for generating output may hinder students' ability to develop their own critical thinking and problem-solving skills. Language learning is not just about memorizing words and sentences, but also about understanding the culture and context behind the language. By using AI to generate output, students may miss out on the opportunity to engage with the language in a meaningful way and develop a deeper understanding of the language and culture. Secondly, AI-generated output may not always be accurate or appropriate, which could lead to confusion and misinformation. Students need to learn how to critically evaluate the information they receive and verify its accuracy before using it in their own communication. By allowing students to use AI to generate output for learning, we may inadvertently be encouraging them to rely too heavily on technology and undermine their own learning process. Instead, AI should be used as a tool to support and enhance traditional language learning methods, such as reading, writing, speaking, and listening. This can be done by using AI to provide personalized feedback, generate practice materials, or assist with language translation, but it is important to strike a balance and ensure that students are not over-relying on AI for their language learning needs.

The core tenet of the present chapter is that to realize the potential of AI in language education, the implementation of AI should be integrated with principles of pedagogical and andragogical approaches. Pedagogy, which focuses on teaching children, and andragogy, which focuses on adult learning, offer different strategies that can be combined to create a comprehensive language-learning experience. AI can enhance this integration by personalizing instruction to cater to individual learning styles and needs. For instance, AI-driven adaptive learning systems can assess students' strengths and weaknesses, providing tailored content and feedback to help them progress. Additionally, AI can offer adult learners self-paced modules and real-time translation assistance, promoting autonomy and self-directed learning. By leveraging the strengths of both pedagogical and andragogical approaches and incorporating AI, language educators can create an inclusive and effective learning environment that caters to students of all ages and learning preferences.

In sum, pedagogical approaches in AI-supported language education emphasize scaffolding learning, where AI systems provide structured guidance and support to assist learners in building their knowledge and skills. This approach ensures that learners receive the appropriate level of assistance tailored to their individual needs, enabling them to progress through the learning process effectively. On the other hand, andragogical approaches focus on self-regulated learning, where learners take responsibility for their own learning using AI tools. This approach empowers learners to identify their own goals, create personalized learning paths, and utilize AI resources to monitor their progress and adjust their strategies accordingly. In conclusion, both pedagogical and andragogical approaches are crucial in leveraging AI for language education, as they cater to different learning styles and preferences, ultimately enhancing the overall learning experience and promoting successful language acquisition.

REFERENCES

Ayedoun, E., Hayashi, Y., & Seta, K. (2019). Adding communicative and affective strategies to an embodied conversational agent to enhance second language learners' willingness to communicate. *International Journal of Artificial Intelligence in Education*, 29(1), 29–57. DOI: 10.1007/s40593-018-0171-6

Cronjé, J. C. (2024, March). A constructionist approach to learning with AI: An "old" solution to a "new" problem? In *Future of information and communication conference* (pp. 13–22). Springer Nature. DOI: 10.1007/978-3-031-53963-3_2

Goh, Y. S. (2021). Using AI technology to support speaking skill development for the teaching of Chinese as a foreign language. In *Multidisciplinary functions of blockchain technology in AI and IoT applications* (pp. 209–227). IGI Global.

Goh, Y. S., Yew, J. S., Chua, N. A., Saputra, J., Leng, N. K., & Cheong, W. H. (2023). *The effect of interface quality, system quality, and perceived usefulness of an automated pronunciation scoring system on student satisfaction.* https://www.semanticscholar.org/paper/The-effect-of-interface-quality%2C-system-quality%2C-of-Soon-Yew/ff3f97b32e86598374b053146ddc82237c88daca

Huang, X., Zou, D., Cheng, G., Chen, X., & Xie, H. (2023). Trends, research issues and applications of artificial intelligence in language education. *Journal of Educational Technology & Society*, 26(1), 112–131.

Huang, Z., Mao, Y., & Zhang, J. (2024). The Influence of Artificial Intelligence Technology on College Students' Learning Effectiveness from the Perspective of Constructivism—Taking ChatGPT as an Example. *Journal of Education. Humanities and Social Sciences*, 30, 40–46.

Hwang, G. J., Xie, H., Wah, B. W., & Gašević, D. (2020). Vision, challenges, roles and research issues of Artificial Intelligence in education. *Computers and Education: Artificial Intelligence*, 1, 100001. DOI: 10.1016/j.caeai.2020.100001

Jeong-Bae Son. Ružić, N. K., & Philpott, A. (2023). Artificial intelligence technologies and applications for language learning and teaching. *Journal of China Computer-Assisted Language Learning*. https://www.degruyter.com/document/doi/10.1515/jccall-2023-0015/html?lang=en

Johnson, A. M., Guerrero, T. A., Tighe, E. L., & McNamara, D. S. (2017). *iSTART-ALL: Confronting adult low literacy with intelligent tutoring for reading comprehension.* In *International Conference on Artificial Intelligence in Education* (pp. 125-136). Springer. https://doi.org/DOI: 10.1007/978-3-319-61425-0_11

Khatun, N., & Miwa, J. (2016). An autonomous learning system of Bengali characters using web-based intelligent handwriting recognition. *Journal of Education and Learning*, 5(3), 122–138. DOI: 10.5539/jel.v5n3p122

Lee, D., Kim, H. H., & Sung, S. H. (2023). Development research on an AI English learning support system to facilitate learner-generated-context-based learning. *Educational Technology Research and Development*, 71(2), 629–666. DOI: 10.1007/s11423-022-10172-2 PMID: 36533222

Liang, J. C., Hwang, G. J., Chen, M. R. A., & Darmawansah, D. (2023). Roles and research foci of artificial intelligence in language education: An integrated bibliographic analysis and systematic review approach. *Interactive Learning Environments*, 31(7), 4270–4296. DOI: 10.1080/10494820.2021.1958348

Lin, C. C., Liu, G. Z., & Wang, T. I. (2017). Development and usability test of an e-learning tool for engineering graduates to Develop academic writing in English: A Case study. *Journal of Educational Technology & Society*, 20(4), 148–161.

Liu, J., Li, S., Ren, C., Lyu, Y., Xu, T., Wang, Z., & Chen, W. (2023). AI enhancements for linguistic e-learning system. *Applied Sciences*. https://www.mdpi.com/2076-3417/13/19/10758

Liu, M. (2023). *Exploring the application of artificial intelligence in foreign language teaching: Challenges and future development*. SHS Web of Conferences. DOI: 10.1051/shsconf/202316803025

Luan, H., Geczy, P., Lai, H., Gobert, J., Yang, S. J., Ogata, H., Baltes, J., Guerra, R., Li, P., & Tsai, C. C. (2020). Challenges and future directions of big data and artificial intelligence in education. *Frontiers in Psychology*, 11, 580820. Advance online publication. DOI: 10.3389/fpsyg.2020.580820 PMID: 33192896

Mirzaei, M. S., Zhang, Q., van der Struijk, S., & Nishida, T. (2018). Language learning through conversation envisioning in virtual reality: A Sociocultural approach. In Taalas, P., Jalkanen, J., & Thouësny, S. (Eds.), *Future-proof cALL: Language learning as exploration and encounters-short papers from EUROCALL* (pp. 207–213)., DOI: 10.14705/rpnet.2018.26.838

Pandarova, I., Schmidt, T., Hartig, J., Boubekki, A., Jones, R. D., & Brefeld, U. (2019). Predicting the difficulty of exercise items for dynamic difficulty adaptation in adaptive language tutoring. *International Journal of Artificial Intelligence in Education*, 29(3), 342–367. DOI: 10.1007/s40593-019-00180-4

Pokrivcakova, S. (2019). Preparing teachers for the application of AI-powered technologies in foreign language education. *Journal of Language and Cultural Education*, 7(3), 135–153. DOI: 10.2478/jolace-2019-0025

Rusmiyanto, R., Huriati, N., Fitriani, N., Tyas, N. K., Rofi'i, A., & Sari, M. N. (2023). The role of artificial intelligence (AI) in developing English language learner's communication skills. *Journal of Education*, 6(1), 750–757.

Sankumpa, W., Kanjug, I., & Singma, S. (2023). Using constructivist integrated gamification and AI Assisted learning tool to enhance reading comprehension for fourth grade students. *IIAI Letters on Institutional Research, 3.*

Switzerland.Goh, Y. S. (2010, May). *Personalizing IQ Chinese reader in assisting struggling learners in the acquisition of reading skill among non-Chinese learners for the teaching of Chinese as a foreign language.* In *Global learn* (pp. 3522-3531). Association for the Advancement of Computing in Education (AACE).

Tomaszewska, R. (2023, December). *Andragogy Meets ChatGPT in Lifelong Learning: Exploring Opportunities and Challenges.* In *2023 IEEE International Conference on Data Mining Workshops (ICDMW)* (pp. 868-874). IEEE. DOI: 10.1109/ICDMW60847.2023.00117

Wang, X., Liu, Q., Pang, H., Tan, S. C., Lei, J., Wallace, M. P., & Li, L. (2023). What matters in AI-supported learning: A study of human-AI interactions in language learning using cluster analysis and epistemic network analysis. *Computers & Education*, 194, 104703. DOI: 10.1016/j.compedu.2022.104703

Wijekumar, K. K., Meyer, B. J., & Lei, P. (2017). Web-based text structure strategy instruction improves seventh graders' content area reading comprehension. *Journal of Educational Psychology*, 109(6), 741–760. DOI: 10.1037/edu0000168

Xi, X. (2023). Advancing language assessment with AI and ML–Leaning into AI is inevitable, but can theory keep up? *Language Assessment Quarterly*, 20(4-5), 357–376. DOI: 10.1080/15434303.2023.2291488

Yang, S. J. (2021). Guest editorial: Precision education new challenge for AI in education. *Journal of Educational Technology & Society*, 24(1), 105–108.

Yang, S. J., Ogata, H., Matsui, T., & Chen, N. S. (2021). Human-centered artificial intelligence in education: Seeing the invisible through the visible. *Computers and Education: Artificial Intelligence*, 2, 100008. DOI: 10.1016/j.caeai.2021.100008

Zhang, K., & Aslan, A. B. (2021). AI technologies for education: Recent research & future directions. *Computers and Education: Artificial Intelligence*, 100025, 100025. Advance online publication. DOI: 10.1016/j.caeai.2021.100025

Chapter 8
The Ethical Use of AI in Education

Becky Gail Sumbera
https://orcid.org/0000-0002-5855-1759
California State University, San Bernardino, USA

ABSTRACT

This chapter explores the ethical implications of integrating Artificial Intelligence (AI) into educational practices, focusing on the balance between technological advancement and moral responsibility. It examines the transformative potential of AI in personalized learning, administrative efficiency, and student engagement while addressing critical ethical concerns such as bias, transparency, privacy, and data security. The chapter also discusses the theoretical frameworks of Utilitarianism, Deontology, and Virtue Ethics as they apply to AI in education, providing a comprehensive guide for responsible AI deployment. Through case studies and analysis, the chapter offers insights into successful and problematic implementations of AI, emphasizing the need for robust ethical guidelines to ensure that AI enhances educational outcomes while safeguarding the rights and well-being of students.

INTRODUCTION

Overview of AI in Education

Artificial Intelligence (AI) in education has emerged as a transformative force over the past few decades, fundamentally altering traditional teaching and learning paradigms. AI encompasses a broad range of technologies, including machine learning, natural language processing, computer vision, and robotics, all of which have found diverse applications within educational contexts (Holmes et al., 2019).

DOI: 10.4018/979-8-3693-6130-6.ch008

The integration of AI into education can be traced back to the development of Intelligent Tutoring Systems (ITS) in the 1970s and 1980s, which aimed to provide personalized instruction by adapting to individual learner needs (Nkambou et al., 2018). Early AI focused on domains like mathematics and language learning, employing rule-based systems to guide students through instructional material. The 2000s witnessed significant advancements with the advent of more sophisticated machine learning algorithms and increased computational power. This period saw the rise of adaptive learning platforms capable of analyzing vast amounts of student data to tailor educational content dynamically (Zawacki-Richter et al., 2019). Such systems improved learning outcomes by identifying knowledge gaps and adjusting instructional strategies accordingly.

The global education sector has increasingly embraced AI technologies. According to a report by HolonIQ (2021), investment in AI-driven educational technologies reached unprecedented levels, with expectations of continued growth. Countries like China and the United States are leading in AI education initiatives, implementing nationwide programs to integrate AI into K-12 and higher education systems (Chen et al., 2020). The COVID-19 pandemic further accelerated AI adoption in education as institutions sought scalable solutions to facilitate remote learning. AI-powered platforms ensured the continuity of education by providing interactive and engaging learning experiences despite physical classroom closures (Dwivedi et al., 2020).

In recent years, AI's role in education has expanded exponentially, driven by the proliferation of big data and cloud computing technologies. Modern AI applications include programs like Magic School, an AI platform that provides tools and resources for educators and students. It has over sixty tools that assist teachers with developing lesson plans, designing assignments, generating materials, creating newsletters, drafting IEPs, and even assisting students in their learning. Personalized learning environments, such as platforms like Knewton and DreamBox, use AI to customize learning experiences based on real-time assessments of student performance and engagement (Li & Lalani, 2020). Other applications include automated assessment and feedback tools that can efficiently grade assignments and provide immediate, detailed feedback, freeing educators to focus on more complex teaching tasks (Singh et al., 2021). Additionally, intelligent virtual assistants, such as chatbots and virtual tutors, offer students on-demand support, enhancing accessibility and learning continuity outside traditional classroom settings (Ryu & Jeong, 2021). Predictive analytics is another critical application, with educational institutions employing AI to predict student outcomes, identify at-risk learners, and implement timely interventions to improve retention and success rates (Zhang & Aslan, 2021).

The integration of AI offers numerous benefits, including enhanced learning outcomes through personalized instruction that caters to diverse learning styles and paces, leading to improved comprehension and retention (Lu et al., 2018). AI also increases accessibility by supporting inclusive education through accommodations for students with disabilities, such as speech recognition for those with mobility impairments and text-to-speech for visually impaired learners (Okonkwo & Ade-Ibijola, 2021). Moreover, AI contributes to efficient administrative processes by assisting with written communication, automating routine tasks like scheduling and resource allocation, allowing educators to allocate more time to instructional planning, student engagement, and leading schools and districts (Papadakis et al., 2020).

Despite its advantages, the deployment of AI in education presents several challenges. Equity issues arise from disparities in access to technology, which can exacerbate educational inequalities, highlighting the need for equitable distribution of AI resources (Williamson & Eynon, 2020). Additionally, data privacy concerns are significant, as the collection and utilization of student data raise privacy and security issues that necessitate robust governance frameworks (Crawford & Calo, 2016). Ethical implications are also critical, as AI systems may inadvertently perpetuate biases present in their training data, leading to discriminatory outcomes and undermining fairness in education (Baker & Hawn, 2021).

The evolving landscape of AI in education presents both remarkable opportunities and profound ethical challenges. Understanding and addressing these issues is critical to harnessing AI's full potential to enhance educational experiences while safeguarding the rights and well-being of all stakeholders involved.

Importance of Ethics in AI

The integration of artificial intelligence (AI) in education has brought about transformative changes, reshaping how teaching and learning occur. AI's capabilities, such as personalized learning environments, automated assessments, and predictive analytics, offer unprecedented opportunities to enhance educational outcomes. However, alongside these benefits, the adoption of AI in education raises critical ethical concerns that must be addressed to ensure that these technologies are developed and deployed responsibly. Ethical considerations are essential in guiding the use of AI to prevent harm, promote fairness, and uphold the values of transparency and accountability in educational practices.

One of the primary ethical challenges associated with AI in education is the potential for bias and discrimination. AI systems, particularly those based on machine learning algorithms, are trained on large datasets that may contain inherent biases reflective of societal inequalities. When these biased datasets are used to develop AI models, there is a risk that the resulting systems will perpetuate or even exacerbate these biases, leading to unfair treatment of certain groups of students (Baker & Hawn, 2021). For example, an AI-driven admissions system might disadvantage applicants from underrepresented backgrounds if the training data does not adequately represent diversity. This underscores the necessity for ethical frameworks that prioritize fairness and actively work to identify and mitigate biases in AI systems used in education (Williamson & Eynon, 2020).

Transparency in AI systems is another crucial ethical consideration. AI technologies often operate as “black boxes,” where users do not easily understand the decision-making processes. This lack of transparency can lead to distrust among educators, students, and parents, especially when AI systems are used to make significant decisions, such as grading or student placement. It is imperative that AI systems in education are designed to be interpretable and explainable, allowing stakeholders to understand how decisions are made and ensuring that these decisions can be scrutinized and challenged when necessary (Singh et al., 2021). Transparency not only builds trust but also empowers users to hold AI systems accountable for their outcomes.

Accountability is closely linked to transparency and is a key ethical issue in the deployment of AI in education. As AI systems take on more roles traditionally held by educators, such as assessing student performance or predicting academic success, it becomes crucial to establish clear lines of accountability. This involves determining who is responsible when AI systems produce errors or unintended consequences and ensuring that there are mechanisms in place to address these issues promptly and fairly (Crawford & Calo, 2016). Without proper accountability, the use of AI in education could lead to a situation where no one is held responsible for decisions that negatively impact students, undermining trust in educational institutions and technologies.

Data privacy and security are also paramount ethical concerns in the context of AI in education. AI systems often require access to vast amounts of personal data, including sensitive information about students' academic performance, behavior, and even biometric data. Strict privacy protocols must govern the collection, storage, and analysis of this data to protect students' rights and prevent misuse or unauthorized access (Crawford & Calo, 2016). Additionally, there must be clear guidelines on data ownership, consent, and the right of students and parents to access and control their data. Failure to adequately protect student data not only poses ethical risks but also legal liabilities for educational institutions.

Moreover, the equitable distribution of AI resources is a critical ethical issue. The benefits of AI in education, such as personalized learning and automated support, are often more accessible to students in well-resourced institutions, exacerbating existing educational inequalities. To ensure that AI technologies do not widen the digital divide, there must be efforts to provide equitable access to these tools across all educational settings, including underfunded schools and marginalized communities (Okonkwo & Ade-Ibijola, 2021). This includes addressing infrastructure disparities, providing necessary training for educators, and developing AI tools that are adaptable to various contexts.

The rapid adoption of AI in education, accelerated by the COVID-19 pandemic, has highlighted both the potential and the ethical challenges of these technologies. The pandemic forced educational institutions to adopt AI-driven platforms to facilitate remote learning, which, while ensuring the continuity of education, also brought issues of accessibility, privacy, and equity to the forefront (Dwivedi et al., 2020). As AI continues to play a central role in education, it is imperative to establish a comprehensive ethical framework that addresses these challenges and guides the responsible use of AI.

By addressing the ethical challenges associated with AI in education and emphasizing the necessity for a robust framework that promotes fairness, transparency, and accountability, educators, policymakers, and technologists can work together to harness AI's potential to enhance educational experiences while safeguarding the rights and well-being of all stakeholders involved. Ethical AI in education is not just about preventing harm; it is about ensuring that AI technologies contribute positively to the educational mission, fostering an inclusive, equitable, and supportive learning environment for all students.

Integrating AI in education undoubtedly offers transformative benefits, yet it simultaneously introduces complex ethical challenges that demand careful consideration. To navigate these challenges and ensure that AI technologies are implemented in ways that are both responsible and equitable, it is essential to ground our understanding in robust ethical theories and principles. In the following section, we will explore three key theoretical frameworks that provide the ethical foundation for guiding the development and deployment of AI in educational settings. These frameworks will help illuminate the principles that should govern AI's role in shaping the future of education, ensuring that its benefits are realized while minimizing potential harms.

II. THEORETICAL FRAMEWORK

Ethical Theories and Principles

As we explore the ethical dimensions of artificial intelligence (AI) in education, we must ground our discussion in established ethical theories that provide a structured framework for evaluating the moral implications of AI technologies. Ethical theories serve as foundational pillars that guide our understanding of what is right and beneficial in various contexts, including the rapidly evolving field of AI in education. By examining these theories, we can better navigate the complex ethical landscape that AI presents, ensuring that deploying these technologies aligns with broader societal values and contributes positively to the educational experience.

The theoretical frameworks we will explore—Utilitarianism, Deontology, and Virtue Ethics—offer distinct perspectives on ethical decision-making and provide valuable insights into how AI can be responsibly integrated into educational settings. Each of these ethical theories emphasizes different aspects of morality and justice, from maximizing overall happiness to adhering to moral duties and fostering virtuous character. By applying these frameworks to the use of AI in education, we can develop a more nuanced understanding of the ethical challenges and opportunities accompanying these technologies. In the following sections, we will delve into each of these theories, exploring their relevance to AI in education and how they can inform the development of ethical AI practices that prioritize the well-being of all students.

Utilitarianism

Utilitarianism, as an ethical theory, is centered on the principle that actions are morally right if they result in the greatest overall happiness and well-being for the greatest number of people. This consequentialist approach emphasizes the outcomes of actions as the primary criterion for determining their morality (Mill, 1863). In the context of AI in education, utilitarianism provides a compelling framework for evaluating and guiding the development and deployment of AI technologies. It advocates for the implementation of AI systems that deliver the most significant benefits to the largest number of students, thereby enhancing the overall effectiveness of educational practices.

When applied to educational AI, utilitarianism encourages the prioritization of technologies that can significantly improve learning outcomes for the majority of students. For example, AI-driven personalized learning systems are designed to adapt to the individual needs of students, offering tailored educational experiences that can boost engagement, understanding, and academic achievement (Zhu et al., 2020). By maximizing the educational benefits for a large population of students, these AI systems align well with the utilitarian goal of increasing overall happiness and well-being within the educational context.

However, while utilitarianism advocates for the greatest good for the greatest number, it also presents a critical challenge when applied to educational AI: ensuring that the needs of marginalized or disadvantaged groups are not overlooked. The potential risk is that in striving to maximize benefits for the majority, the specific needs of vulnerable populations might be neglected, thereby exacerbating existing inequalities within the education system. To address this concern, it is essential that AI systems in education are designed with inclusivity in mind. This involves integrating features that cater to diverse learning needs and ensuring that these technologies are accessible to all students, regardless of their socioeconomic status, learning abilities, or other factors that may place them at a disadvantage (Williamson & Eynon, 2020).

Incorporating a utilitarian perspective into the ethical design and implementation of AI in education necessitates a careful balance between optimizing outcomes for the majority and safeguarding the rights and needs of the minority. It requires a commitment to developing AI systems that not only enhance the learning experiences of a wide array of students but also actively work to reduce disparities and promote equity in education. By doing so, utilitarianism can inform the creation of ethical AI practices that prioritize the well-being of all students, fostering an educational environment that is both effective and just.

Deontology

Deontological ethics, a framework rooted in the philosophy of Immanuel Kant, emphasizes the importance of adhering to moral duties, rules, and principles rather than focusing solely on the outcomes of actions. According to this ethical theory, actions are considered morally right if they align with established duties and respect the inherent rights and dignity of individuals, regardless of the consequences that might ensue (Kant, 2002). In the context of AI in education, deontological ethics provides a robust foundation for ensuring that the deployment of AI technologies is guided by unwavering ethical standards that prioritize the rights and well-being of students.

When applied to educational AI, deontological ethics would require that AI systems be designed and implemented in ways that fundamentally respect and protect the rights of students. This includes safeguarding student privacy, ensuring the security of personal data, and avoiding practices that could harm students' autonomy or well-being (Binns, 2018). The focus on duties and rights within this ethical framework demands that AI developers and educators prioritize the protection of students above all other considerations, ensuring that AI technologies do not compromise the dignity or rights of the individuals they are intended to serve.

A practical example of deontological ethics in action within educational AI is the development and use of AI-driven assessment tools. These tools must be designed to respect students' right to fair and just evaluation, a principle that is central to deontological thought. To adhere to this ethical standard, AI assessment systems should operate transparently, allowing students and educators to understand the decision-making processes behind the assessments. Moreover, these systems should provide mechanisms for students to contest or appeal decisions made by AI, ensuring that their rights to a fair assessment are upheld (Floridi & Cowls, 2019).

Additionally, deontological ethics would require that AI systems in education be designed with clear and stringent ethical guidelines that prevent any form of discrimination or bias. This approach ensures that all students are treated with equal fairness and respect, irrespective of their background, abilities, or any other distinguishing characteristics. By adhering to these ethical principles, educational institutions can foster an environment of trust and respect, where AI technologies are seen as tools that enhance, rather than undermine, the educational experience.

Ultimately, deontological ethics offers a crucial perspective on the development of AI in education, prioritizing adherence to moral principles and the protection of student rights. By focusing on duties and respecting the intrinsic dignity of all individuals, this ethical framework ensures that AI systems contribute positively to educational practices while safeguarding the fundamental rights and well-being of all students.

Virtue Ethics

Virtue ethics, a philosophical approach that centers on the character and virtues of the moral agent, offers a unique and valuable perspective on the ethical development and use of AI in education. Unlike deontological ethics, which focuses on adherence to rules and duties, or utilitarianism, which emphasizes the outcomes of actions, virtue ethics is concerned with cultivating moral virtues such as honesty, courage, compassion, and integrity. This approach to ethics is deeply rooted in the idea that moral excellence is achieved through the consistent practice of virtuous behavior, shaping not only actions but the character of individuals (Annas, 2011).

In the context of AI in education, virtue ethics advocates for the creation and use of AI systems that go beyond merely delivering educational content or automating tasks. It calls for the development of AI technologies that actively contribute to the moral and intellectual growth of students, fostering their development as virtuous individuals. This perspective encourages the design of AI systems that not only achieve practical educational outcomes but also inspire students to engage in critical thinking, creativity, and ethical decision-making. For instance, an AI-driven learning platform could be designed to present students with complex ethical dilemmas across various scenarios, challenging them to navigate these situations thoughtfully and develop a deeper understanding of moral principles (Williamson & Eynon, 2020).

Furthermore, virtue ethics places significant emphasis on the moral character of the developers and users of AI systems. This means that educators, developers, and policymakers involved in integrating AI into education must approach their work with a commitment to ethical principles and a dedication to promoting the well-being of students and society as a whole. The design and implementation of AI in education should not be driven solely by technological advancement or efficiency but by a sincere commitment to nurturing the virtues that contribute to human flourishing (Floridi & Cowls, 2019).

For example, developers creating AI systems for educational use should prioritize features that encourage honesty and transparency, such as clear communication about how AI-driven decisions are made. Similarly, educators using AI tools should do so in ways that promote courage and resilience among students by using AI to offer constructive feedback that challenges students to improve. Policymakers should ensure that AI regulations and guidelines reflect a commitment to compassion, ensuring that AI systems are inclusive and designed to support the diverse needs of all students.

Overall, virtue ethics provides a powerful framework for the ethical development and use of AI in education, emphasizing the importance of moral character and the cultivation of virtues in both the creators and users of AI technologies. By adopting a virtue ethics approach, educational AI systems can be designed to not only meet the practical needs of students but also to enhance their moral and intellectual development, contributing to the formation of individuals who are not only knowledgeable but also virtuous and ethical citizens.

III. ETHICAL ISSUES IN AI FOR EDUCATION

As the use of artificial intelligence (AI) in education continues to expand, it brings with it a range of ethical issues that must be carefully considered and addressed. AI systems in education, which often rely on vast amounts of data to function effectively, present both opportunities and challenges. On the one hand, the data collected can significantly enhance the personalization of learning experiences, enabling tailored educational pathways that meet the unique needs of each student. On the other hand, this data collection also raises substantial ethical concerns, particularly regarding privacy, data security, and the rights of students.

The ethical implications of AI in education extend beyond the mere technical aspects of data collection and storage; they touch upon fundamental issues of consent, autonomy, and the potential for misuse of sensitive information. As educational institutions increasingly incorporate AI technologies, they must navigate the delicate balance between leveraging data to improve educational outcomes and protecting the privacy and rights of their students. The following sections will delve into some of the most pressing ethical concerns related to AI in education, including privacy and data security, the practices surrounding data collection and storage, and the impact of these technologies on student privacy rights. By examining these issues, we can better understand the ethical landscape of AI in education and work towards developing responsible practices that prioritize the well-being and rights of all students.

Privacy and Data Security

Privacy and data security are critical concerns when it comes to the implementation of AI in education. As AI systems become increasingly integral to educational practices, the data they collect, process, and store grows exponentially. This data often includes highly sensitive information, such as student's academic records, behavioral patterns, health data, and even biometric information (Zawacki-Richter et al., 2019). The potential for this data to be misused, breached, or otherwise compromised poses significant risks not only to individual privacy but also to the integrity of educational institutions.

The ethical management of data is paramount, as any lapse in privacy and data security can have severe consequences for students. Data security breaches can lead to unauthorized access to personal information, potentially resulting in identity theft, stigmatization, or discrimination. Furthermore, the long-term implications of such breaches can affect students well into their futures, influencing everything from educational opportunities to employment prospects (Crawford & Calo, 2016). Therefore, it is crucial that educational institutions implement robust data security measures to protect against these risks and ensure that AI systems are designed with privacy considerations at their core.

To address these concerns, institutions must develop clear policies and practices for data collection and storage. Ethical data collection practices should prioritize data minimization, ensuring that only the information necessary for the AI system's functioning is collected. Additionally, institutions must establish secure data storage practices that protect student data from unauthorized access and breaches. These practices should be complemented by transparent policies that inform students and their guardians about what data is being collected, how it is being used, and who has access to it.

Data Collection and Storage Practices

AI systems in education often rely heavily on the collection and analysis of vast amounts of data to operate effectively and to provide personalized learning experiences tailored to individual students. This data typically includes a wide range of personal information, such as students' academic performance, behavioral patterns, and even sensitive biometric data like facial recognition or voice recordings (Zawacki-Richter et al., 2019). While the collection and utilization of such data can significantly enhance the educational experience by allowing for more customized and adaptive learning pathways, it simultaneously raises profound ethical concerns, particularly regarding privacy and data security.

One of the primary ethical challenges associated with data collection in educational AI systems is ensuring that the consent obtained from students and their guardians is genuinely informed. Informed consent is a cornerstone of ethical data collection practices, yet it can be particularly difficult to achieve in educational settings. Students, especially minors, may not fully comprehend the extent of the data being collected, how it will be used, or the potential risks associated with sharing their personal information. This challenge is further exacerbated in regions where digital literacy is low, making it even harder for students and their families to make truly informed decisions about data sharing (Regan & Jesse, 2019).

Moreover, the principle of data minimization—an ethical guideline emphasizing collecting only the data that is strictly necessary for the AI system to function—often conflicts with the practices observed in many educational settings. Many AI systems tend to collect more data than is required, either to improve system efficiency or for future undefined uses. This practice not only increases the risk of privacy breaches but also goes against the ethical principle of minimizing data collection to protect individuals' privacy (Slade & Prinsloo, 2018). As a result, educational institutions must carefully consider the amount and type of data they collect, ensuring that it aligns with ethical standards and genuinely contributes to the educational goals without compromising student privacy.

While data collection is essential for the effective functioning of AI systems in education, it must be approached with a strong ethical framework that prioritizes students' rights and autonomy. Ensuring informed consent and adhering to data minimization principles are critical steps in safeguarding privacy and maintaining trust when using AI in educational environments.

Student Privacy Rights and Concerns

The increasing integration of artificial intelligence (AI) in educational settings has brought student privacy rights to the forefront of ethical discussions. As AI technologies become more prevalent, students and their families are rightfully concerned about how personal data is collected, used, and shared by educational institutions and third-party vendors. These concerns are especially pressing given the potential for misuse of personal information, which could lead to unintended and potentially harmful consequences (Williamson & Eynon, 2020). Protecting student privacy is not just a technical issue but an ethical imperative that must be addressed to maintain trust in educational institutions and the technologies they deploy.

One of the primary privacy concerns associated with AI in education is the increased use of surveillance and monitoring technologies. AI-driven tools such as facial recognition, keystroke monitoring, and emotion detection are increasingly being employed to track student behavior and engagement in real time. While these technologies can provide valuable insights into student learning and behavior, they also raise significant concerns about the extent of surveillance and the potential for creating a culture of constant monitoring (Fawns et al., 2021). The pervasive use of such surveillance technologies can lead to an environment where students feel constantly watched, which may impact their behavior and overall learning experience. This raises important ethical questions about the balance between the benefits of AI monitoring tools and the rights of students to privacy and autonomy.

Another critical issue is the sharing of student data with third-party vendors. Many educational institutions partner with external companies to implement AI technologies, which often involves transferring student data to these entities. This practice raises concerns about how this data is used, who has access to it, and whether it is adequately protected against unauthorized use or breaches (Slade & Prinsloo, 2018). The involvement of third parties complicates the privacy landscape, as it introduces additional risks and uncertainties regarding the control and security of student data. Ensuring that stringent data protection agreements govern these partnerships is essential to safeguarding student privacy.

Additionally, the long-term storage of student data presents another significant privacy concern. AI systems generate vast amounts of data, and educational records, including AI-generated insights, can persist for many years. This long-term data retention can have far-reaching implications for students, potentially affecting their future opportunities in areas such as college admissions or job prospects (Crawford & Calo, 2016). For example, data from AI-driven disciplinary systems could be used to make judgments about a student's character or behavior long after the fact, raising ethical questions about fairness and the appropriate use of historical data. As such, it is crucial for educational institutions to carefully consider the duration for which student data is stored and the potential long-term impacts of retaining such information.

Overall, the ethical challenges related to student privacy in the context of AI in education are complex and multifaceted. Addressing these challenges requires a concerted effort to establish robust privacy protections, ensure transparency in data practices, and prioritize the rights and well-being of students. By doing so, educational institutions can foster an environment of trust and respect, where AI technologies are used responsibly to enhance learning without compromising the privacy and dignity of students.

IV. CASE STUDIES AND EXAMPLES

Successful Ethical AI Implementations

In exploring the practical applications of artificial intelligence (AI) in education, it is essential to examine real-world case studies that highlight both the successes and the ethical challenges of implementing AI technologies in K-12 and Higher Education settings. The following section presents a series of case studies that demonstrate how AI has been effectively integrated into educational environments to enhance learning outcomes and improve administrative processes. Each case study not only showcases the potential of AI to transform education but also emphasizes the importance of addressing ethical considerations to ensure that these technologies are used responsibly. Through these case studies, we gain insights into the opportunities and challenges of ethical AI implementation in education, providing valuable lessons for future applications of AI in schools.

K-12 Education Case Studies

Case Study 1: Personalized Learning with DreamBox in Elementary Schools

The first case study highlights the successful implementation of DreamBox Learning. This AI-driven adaptive learning platform has made significant strides in enhancing personalized learning in elementary schools across the United States. DreamBox Learning exemplifies how AI can be effectively used to cater to the individual learning needs of students, particularly in the area of mathematics, by creating personalized instructional pathways that adjust in real time based on each student's progress and understanding.

DreamBox's adaptive technology works by continuously analyzing student responses during math activities. The AI within the platform dynamically adjusts the difficulty and content of tasks to match the learner's current level of comprehension. This not only ensures that students are continually challenged at an appropriate level but also provides them with the support they need to grasp new concepts effectively. As a result, DreamBox can significantly improve learning outcomes by meeting students where they are in their learning journey and guiding them through a customized path that builds on their strengths and addresses their weaknesses (Watson, 2019).

A critical aspect of DreamBox's success is its commitment to equity and accessibility. The platform is designed to be inclusive, accommodating a diverse range of learning needs, including those of students with disabilities. Features such as visual aids, audio support, and various customizable settings allow DreamBox to serve students with different learning styles and abilities, ensuring that all learners have access to high-quality math instruction. This focus on inclusivity makes DreamBox a valuable tool in promoting educational equity, as it seeks to level the playing field for students who may face additional challenges in a traditional classroom setting (DreamBox Learning, 2020).

In addition to its instructional capabilities, DreamBox places a strong emphasis on data privacy, recognizing the importance of protecting student information in the digital age. The platform adheres to stringent data privacy protocols, collecting only the data necessary to personalize learning experiences while ensuring transparency about how this data is used. Measures such as data encryption and anonymization are employed to safeguard student information, reflecting DreamBox's commitment to ethical data practices. By prioritizing data privacy, DreamBox not only complies with legal requirements but also builds trust with educators, students, and parents, who can be confident that their information is handled responsibly (Watson, 2019).

Overall, the implementation of DreamBox Learning in elementary schools serves as a model for how AI can be harnessed to provide personalized, equitable, and secure educational experiences. By leveraging AI to tailor instruction to individual needs, DreamBox demonstrates the potential of technology to enhance learning outcomes while addressing the diverse needs of all students. This case study underscores the importance of combining technological innovation with ethical considerations, ensuring that the benefits of AI in education are accessible to all learners in a safe and supportive environment.

Case Study 2: AI-Driven Attendance Monitoring in K-12 Schools

A second case study example explores the implementation of AI-driven facial recognition systems for attendance monitoring in K-12 schools in China, highlighting both the technological advancements and the ethical challenges accompanying this approach. These systems represent a significant innovation in school administration, offering a highly efficient solution for automating attendance tracking and enhancing security within educational institutions. By using facial recognition technology, schools can automatically record student attendance and monitor their movements throughout the day, ensuring that attendance records are accurate and up-to-date and that unauthorized individuals do not gain access to school premises (Liang, 2020).

The deployment of such AI-driven systems brings several benefits to school management. It reduces the administrative burden on teachers, who traditionally had to manually track attendance, thereby allowing them to focus more on instructional tasks. Additionally, integrating facial recognition technology into school security protocols can enhance the safety of students by providing real-time monitoring and alerts in case of potential security breaches. This technological capability can be particularly valuable in large schools where managing and monitoring student attendance manually can be challenging and prone to errors.

However, using AI-driven facial recognition in schools also raises significant ethical concerns, particularly around issues of privacy and consent. One of the primary concerns is the extent to which these systems contribute to the surveillance of students. The constant monitoring enabled by facial recognition technology can lead to an environment where students feel they are perpetually being watched, which could have detrimental effects on their sense of autonomy and psychological well-being. Critics argue that such pervasive surveillance may infringe on students' right to privacy and could foster a culture of distrust within the school environment, where students feel less free to express themselves or engage in normal social interactions (Cai, 2020).

Moreover, implementing facial recognition systems brings to light the issue of informed consent. Questions have been raised about whether students and their parents are fully informed about using their biometric data and whether they have provided genuine consent for its collection and use. In many cases, the use of such technologies is mandated by school administrations, leaving little room for students and parents to opt-out, thereby raising concerns about the voluntary nature of consent (Zhang, 2020). Using biometric data, which is highly sensitive and personal, necessitates stringent consent protocols and clear communication about how the data will be used, stored, and protected.

While AI-driven facial recognition systems offer practical solutions for improving attendance monitoring and school security, their use in educational settings must be carefully balanced with ethical considerations. Protecting student privacy, ensuring informed consent, and mitigating the potential negative impacts of constant surveillance are critical factors that must be addressed to ensure that such technologies are implemented responsibly. This case study underscores the importance of developing ethical guidelines and policies that govern the use of AI in schools, ensuring that the benefits of technological advancements do not come at the expense of students' rights and well-being.

Higher Education Case Study

Case Study 3: AI-Driven Advising Systems at Georgia State University

Georgia State University's (GSU) implementation of the AI-driven advising system, PantherRetention, offers valuable insights into the potential for AI to impact higher education while also highlighting important ethical considerations positively. The PantherRetention system was introduced with the goal of improving student retention and graduation rates by using predictive analytics to identify students who are at risk of dropping out. The system then facilitates targeted interventions designed to support these students and keep them on track toward completing their degrees (Kessler, 2019).

One of the critical aspects of PantherRetention's success is its focus on fairness and bias prevention. Recognizing the potential for AI systems to inadvertently perpetuate existing inequalities, GSU took proactive steps to ensure that the algorithm used by PantherRetention does not disproportionately impact certain student groups, particularly low-income or minority students. This was achieved by incorporating a diverse data set in the development of the system and by conducting regular audits of the algorithm to identify and address any biases that may emerge. By taking these precautions, GSU aims to provide equitable support to all students, ensuring that the benefits of the AI system are accessible to everyone, regardless of their background (Kessler, 2019).

Another significant ethical consideration in the implementation of PantherRetention is transparency and accountability. GSU made it a priority to be transparent with both students and faculty about how the AI system works. This includes providing clear information on what data is used, how predictions are made, and the criteria for determining which students are identified as at risk. By demystifying the AI process and allowing for open communication, GSU has fostered an environment of trust and collaboration, where students and faculty feel informed and involved in using AI technology in the advising process (Jones & Watson, 2020).

The lessons from GSU's implementation of PantherRetention underscore the importance of addressing ethical considerations when integrating AI into educational practices. By focusing on fairness, bias prevention, and transparency, GSU has set a standard for how AI can be used responsibly to enhance student outcomes in higher education. This case study serves as a model for other institutions looking to adopt AI-driven systems, demonstrating that with careful planning and ethical oversight, AI can be a powerful tool for improving educational equity and supporting student success.

ETHICAL FAILURES AND LESSONS

K-12 Education Case Studies

Case Study 4: The Controversy of Predictive Analytics in UK Schools

The fourth case study delves into the ethical challenges and failures associated with implementing AI-driven predictive analytics systems in several UK schools in 2020. These systems were introduced to forecast student performance and behavior, thereby identifying students who might struggle academically or present disciplinary issues. While the intention behind these systems was to provide early interventions and support for at-risk students, the execution revealed significant ethical shortcomings that serve as important lessons for the future use of AI in education.

One of the most critical ethical failures of these predictive analytics systems was their tendency to produce inaccurate predictions. The models used by the AI systems often relied on flawed or biased data, leading to misclassifying students as "at-risk." This inaccuracy had serious consequences, particularly for students from minority backgrounds who were disproportionately flagged by the system. These students were subjected to unwarranted scrutiny and intervention, which not only stigmatized them but also potentially impacted their educational trajectories in negative ways (Jones & Miller, 2021). The bias embedded in the algorithms reflected broader societal prejudices, highlighting the danger of relying on AI systems that are not rigorously tested and validated for fairness and accuracy.

Another significant issue with implementing these predictive analytics systems was the lack of transparency. Students, parents, and even teachers were often kept in the dark about how the AI systems arrived at their predictions. This opacity made it difficult for those affected to understand why certain students were being flagged for intervention, undermining trust in the system. The absence of clear explanations or the ability to challenge the AI's decisions created a sense of helplessness and frustration among those targeted by the system (Smith, 2020). This lack of transparency is a fundamental ethical failure, as it violates the principles of accountability and informed consent, which are crucial in any educational context.

The controversy surrounding the use of predictive analytics in UK schools underscores the importance of approaching AI implementation in education with caution and a strong ethical framework. The lessons learned from this case study highlight the need for rigorous testing and validation of AI systems to ensure their accuracy and fairness, particularly when they are used to make decisions that can significantly impact students' lives. Moreover, transparency must be a key consideration in deploying such systems, with clear communication about how predictions are made and opportunities for students and parents to understand and contest decisions.

Ultimately, the ethical failures in this case study serve as a cautionary tale about the potential risks of integrating AI into educational practices without adequate safeguards. They emphasize the importance of developing and adhering to ethical guidelines that prioritize the rights, dignity, and well-being of all students, ensuring that AI enhances rather than undermines the educational experience.

Case Study 5: The UK Grading Algorithm Scandal

The UK government's use of an AI algorithm to assign grades during the COVID-19 pandemic provides a stark example of the ethical failures that can arise when AI is deployed in high-stakes educational contexts without sufficient oversight and consideration of fairness. In 2020, when traditional exams were canceled due to the pandemic, the government turned to an AI algorithm to standardize grades based on historical data from schools. This decision was intended to ensure consistency and fairness in the absence of formal exams, but it quickly became a source of national controversy due to its perceived inequities and flaws.

One of the most significant ethical failures of this AI grading system was its inherent bias and discriminatory impact on students from less affluent schools. The algorithm disproportionately downgraded the grades of students attending schools in disadvantaged areas, while students from more privileged backgrounds were more likely to receive favorable grades. This outcome highlighted a systemic bias embedded within the algorithm, reflecting and perpetuating existing inequalities within the education system (Jones, 2021). The use of historical data as a basis for grading, without considering the individual efforts and potential of each student, led to a situation where students were judged not on their merit but on the past performance of their school—a deeply flawed and unfair approach.

The backlash against the algorithm was swift and widespread, as students, parents, and educators protested what they saw as an unjust and discriminatory system. The public outcry was fueled by numerous examples of high-achieving students from underprivileged backgrounds receiving significantly lower grades than expected, thereby jeopardizing their chances of pursuing higher education and other opportunities. This case vividly illustrates the dangers of relying on AI systems that are not properly calibrated to account for equity and fairness, particularly when they are used to make decisions that have profound implications for students' futures.

Another critical ethical failure in this case was the lack of accountability regarding the design and implementation of the algorithm. When the issues with the grading system became apparent, there was widespread confusion and frustration about who was responsible for the decision to use the algorithm and how it was developed. The lack of transparency and clear lines of accountability not only exacerbated public distrust but also made it difficult to address and rectify the problems (Smith, 2020). This lack of accountability is a key lesson for deploying AI in education, underscoring the need for clear governance structures and transparent processes to ensure that AI systems are used responsibly and that those who design and implement these systems can be held accountable for their impact.

The controversy surrounding the AI grading algorithm in the UK serves as a powerful reminder of the ethical challenges and risks associated with using AI in education. It highlights the importance of carefully considering the potential biases and discriminatory effects of AI systems, particularly when they are used to make decisions that can significantly impact individuals' lives. Furthermore, it emphasizes the need for transparency, accountability, and rigorous oversight in the deployment of AI, ensuring that these technologies are used in ways that are fair, just, and aligned with the values of equity and inclusion.

Higher Education Case Study

Case Study 6: Automated Essay Scoring at the University of California

The case study of the University of California's (UC) experimentation with AI-driven automated essay-scoring tools highlights both the potential benefits and the significant ethical challenges of integrating AI into higher education. As the UC system sought to manage the large volumes of student essays that require grading, it turned to AI technologies capable of analyzing student writing for grammar, coherence, and content. These AI tools were designed to provide not only scores but also feedback to help students improve their writing skills (Wilson, 2020). However, the use of automated essay scoring systems has raised several critical ethical concerns that underscore the complexities of relying on AI for educational assessment.

One of the primary ethical issues with automated essay scoring is the potential for algorithmic bias. AI systems are trained on large datasets, and if these datasets contain biases, the AI is likely to replicate and even amplify those biases in its scoring. For instance, non-native English speakers or students who use non-standard writing styles may be unfairly penalized by the AI, as it may not accurately assess the nuances of their writing. This could result in lower scores for these students, not because of their actual writing abilities but due to the limitations and biases of the AI system (Perelman, 2020). Such outcomes are particularly concerning in a diverse educational environment like the UC system, where students come from a wide range of linguistic and cultural backgrounds. The risk of unfair grading due to algorithmic bias highlights the need for careful scrutiny and continuous refinement of AI tools to ensure that they provide equitable assessments for all students.

Another ethical consideration is the transparency and quality of the feedback provided by the AI. Unlike human graders, who can offer nuanced and context-sensitive feedback, AI systems may struggle to provide clear and constructive comments that students can easily understand and trust. The feedback generated by AI might lack the depth and personalization that students expect from their instructors, leading to confusion or dissatisfaction with the grading process (Wilson, 2020). This issue is particularly significant because feedback is a crucial component of the learning process, helping students identify their strengths and areas for improvement. If students cannot trust the feedback they receive or find it difficult to interpret, the effectiveness of the AI tool in supporting their educational development is compromised.

The lessons from the UC system's experience with automated essay scoring tools underscore the importance of addressing ethical concerns when deploying AI in educational contexts. Ensuring that AI systems are free from bias and capable of delivering meaningful, transparent feedback is essential to maintaining fairness and supporting student learning. This case study illustrates the challenges of balancing the efficiency gains offered by AI with the need to preserve the quality and equity of educational assessments. As AI continues to be integrated into higher education, institutions must remain vigilant in identifying and mitigating the ethical risks associated with these technologies, ensuring that they enhance rather than undermine the educational experience for all students.

V. GUIDELINES FOR ETHICAL AI USE IN EDUCATION

Developing Ethical AI Policies

As the integration of artificial intelligence (AI) into educational practices continues to grow, it becomes increasingly important to establish clear and robust guidelines to ensure that these technologies are used ethically and responsibly. The potential of AI to enhance learning, streamline administrative tasks, and support personalized education is immense, but it also brings with it significant ethical challenges that must be addressed. To navigate these challenges, educational institutions must develop comprehensive ethical policies that govern the use of AI, ensuring that its implementation aligns with fundamental ethical principles such as fairness, accountability, transparency, and respect for privacy (Whittlestone et al., 2019).

Institutional Policies and Frameworks

Developing and implementing ethical AI policies within educational institutions is a critical step towards ensuring that AI technologies are used responsibly and in alignment with the core values of education. These policies provide the foundational framework that guides the ethical use of AI at the organizational level, addressing key areas such as data privacy, bias, fairness, transparency, and accountability. By establishing clear and robust guidelines in these areas, institutions can safeguard student rights, promote equity, and ensure that AI technologies are deployed in ways that support and enhance their educational mission.

One of the primary components of an ethical AI policy is data privacy and security. Educational institutions must establish comprehensive policies that govern the collection, storage, and use of student data. These policies should be designed to comply with relevant laws and regulations, such as the General Data Protection Regulation (GDPR) in Europe or the Family Educational Rights and Privacy Act (FERPA) in the United States. By adhering to these regulations, institutions can protect student data from unauthorized access and misuse, ensuring that privacy is maintained throughout the AI deployment process (Slade & Prinsloo, 2018).

Another critical aspect of ethical AI policies is the commitment to bias detection and fairness. AI systems must be regularly audited to detect and mitigate any potential biases, particularly those that could disproportionately affect certain student groups. This involves using diverse training data, implementing bias detection algorithms, and ensuring that AI systems are tested across different demographic groups to confirm that they operate fairly and equitably. By addressing these issues proactively, institutions can help prevent the perpetuation of existing inequalities and ensure that all students benefit equally from AI technologies (Gebru et al., 2020).

Transparency and accountability are also essential components of an ethical AI policy. Institutions must ensure that AI systems are transparent in their decision-making processes, providing clear explanations of how decisions are made and what data is used. Additionally, accountability structures should be established to define who is responsible for AI systems' outcomes. This not only builds trust among students, parents, and educators but also ensures that there is a clear process for addressing any issues that arise from the use of AI in education (Diakopoulos, 2016).

By focusing on these key areas—data privacy and security, bias and fairness, and transparency and accountability—educational institutions can develop ethical AI policies that protect student rights and promote equity while also ensuring that AI technologies are used in ways that align with their broader educational goals. These policies serve as a vital tool in navigating the ethical complexities of AI in education, providing a clear framework for responsible and effective AI implementation.

National and International Guidelines

In addition to developing institutional policies, educational institutions must also align their AI practices with national and international ethical guidelines. These broader frameworks provide essential guidance that helps ensure the responsible and ethical use of AI across educational settings. By adhering to these guidelines, institutions can not only comply with legal requirements but also reflect the highest ethical standards in their AI initiatives. This alignment is crucial for maintaining public trust and for fostering an educational environment that prioritizes fairness, transparency, and respect for human rights.

One key international guideline is UNESCO's Recommendation on the Ethics of Artificial Intelligence, adopted in 2021. This recommendation offers a comprehensive global framework for the ethical use of AI, emphasizing critical principles such as human rights, inclusivity, and sustainability. By following UNESCO's guidelines, educational institutions can ensure that their AI practices are aligned with global efforts to promote ethical AI use, particularly in the context of protecting vulnerable populations and promoting equitable access to education (UNESCO, 2021).

Another important set of guidelines comes from the Organization for Economic Co-operation and Development (OECD), which established its Principles on AI in 2019. The OECD principles focus on promoting trust, transparency, and fairness in AI applications. These principles are particularly relevant for educational institutions as they provide a foundation for developing AI systems that are not only effective but also trustworthy and fair. By integrating the OECD's principles into their AI policies, institutions can create a transparent and accountable AI ecosystem that benefits all stakeholders, including students, educators, and administrators (OECD, 2019).

In addition to these international guidelines, many countries have developed their own national AI strategies, which often include specific ethical considerations for AI use in various sectors, including education. For instance, national strategies may outline ethical standards for data use, bias mitigation, and the transparency of AI systems. Educational institutions should ensure that their AI policies are consistent with these national strategies to promote consistency, accountability, and compliance with national regulations. By aligning with both national and international guidelines, educational institutions can navigate the complex ethical landscape of AI and contribute to the global effort to use AI technologies responsibly and ethically in education (Floridi & Cowls, 2019).

Overall, by adhering to national and international ethical guidelines, educational institutions can ensure that their AI practices are not only legally compliant but also ethically sound, promoting a fair, transparent, and inclusive educational environment for all.

Training and Awareness

Next, we will emphasize the importance of training and awareness for educators and administrators. To effectively implement ethical AI policies, it is crucial that those who are responsible for using and managing AI systems are well-informed about the ethical issues involved. Professional development programs, ethical decision-making training, and collaboration with AI experts are all key strategies for building the knowledge and skills needed to navigate the ethical complexities of AI in education. Through these efforts, educational institutions can foster a culture of ethical awareness and responsibility, ensuring that AI is used to enhance learning while upholding the values of fairness, transparency, and respect for all students.

Educating Educators and Administrators

Educating educators and administrators is the cornerstone of ensuring the ethical and responsible use of AI in education. As the primary users and managers of AI systems in schools and universities, educators and administrators must possess a deep understanding of both the technical functionalities and the ethical implications of these technologies. Their role is critical in shaping how AI is integrated into educational practices, influencing everything from curriculum design to student assessment and data management. Therefore, providing them with the necessary knowledge and tools to navigate the complexities of AI is not just beneficial—it is essential.

To empower educators and administrators, institutions must invest in comprehensive professional development programs that are specifically tailored to the unique challenges of AI in education. These programs should go beyond basic technical training, delving into the ethical considerations of using AI, such as data privacy, bias detection, and fairness in AI-driven decisions. By participating in these programs, educators and administrators can develop the skills needed to critically evaluate AI technologies, ensuring they are used to enhance learning outcomes while safeguarding students' rights and well-being (Jones & Watson, 2020).

Ethical decision-making is another crucial area where educators and administrators need robust training. AI in education often presents complex ethical dilemmas, such as balancing the benefits of personalized learning with the risks of data misuse. Through targeted training that includes case studies and real-world scenarios, educators and administrators can learn to navigate these dilemmas effectively, making informed decisions that reflect the values of fairness, transparency, and respect for all students (Whittlestone et al., 2019). This training is vital for preparing them to handle the ethical challenges that arise in the fast-evolving landscape of AI in education.

Moreover, fostering collaboration between educators, administrators, and AI experts is essential for integrating ethical considerations into the design and implementation of AI systems. By working together, these stakeholders can ensure that AI technologies are not only effective but also aligned with their institutions' ethical standards and educational goals. This interdisciplinary collaboration enriches the understanding of all parties involved, helping to create AI systems that are transparent, fair, and accountable (Greene et al., 2019).

Ultimately, educating educators and administrators empowers them to become ethical stewards of AI in education. Their ability to make informed, ethical decisions will directly impact how AI is used in classrooms and administrative settings, shaping the future of education in profound ways. By prioritizing their education and training, institutions can foster a culture of ethical awareness and responsibility, ensuring that AI enhances the educational experience while upholding the highest ethical standards.

VI. FUTURE DIRECTIONS AND CHALLENGES

Emerging Ethical Issues in AI

As artificial intelligence (AI) continues to evolve and become more deeply integrated into educational practices, it brings with it not only significant opportunities but also a host of emerging ethical challenges. In this section, we will explore the future directions of AI in education, focusing on the ethical issues that are likely to arise as these technologies develop. Addressing these challenges proactively is essential for ensuring that AI contributes positively to the educational experience while safeguarding the rights and well-being of all stakeholders.

AI and Data Sovereignty

AI and data sovereignty represent a critical emerging ethical issue as educational institutions increasingly integrate AI systems that process and store data in cloud environments. These cloud environments often operate across multiple countries, complicating the principle of data sovereignty, which holds that data is subject to the laws and governance structures of the nation where it is collected. The global nature of AI technologies challenges this principle by making it difficult to ensure that data remains within the legal jurisdiction where it was initially gathered.

As educational institutions adopt AI-driven systems to manage student data, instructional content, and administrative processes, the need to address data sovereignty becomes more urgent. When data is stored or processed in cloud servers located in different countries, it may be subject to foreign laws and regulations that differ significantly from those in the country where the data was collected. This can create legal and ethical dilemmas, particularly concerning data privacy and security. For instance, data that is protected under strict privacy laws in one country may be vulnerable to different treatment in another, potentially exposing sensitive student information to risks.

Moreover, compliance with local regulations becomes more complex when data crosses international borders. Educational institutions must navigate a web of varying legal requirements, which can include data protection laws, educational privacy standards, and international treaties. Failure to comply with these regulations can lead to significant legal consequences, including fines, penalties, and damage to the institution's reputation. It is, therefore, essential that institutions carefully consider where their data is stored and processed, ensuring that it is managed in accordance with the relevant legal and ethical standards (Sloan & Warner, 2018).

To address these challenges, educational institutions must implement robust data governance frameworks that prioritize data sovereignty. This involves not only understanding the legal implications of cross-border data flows but also taking proactive measures to ensure that data remains within appropriate legal jurisdictions. Additionally, institutions should work closely with cloud service providers to establish clear agreements on data management, including provisions for data localization, security measures, and compliance with local laws. By doing so, they can protect student data and uphold ethical standards in the increasingly globalized landscape of AI in education.

As AI continues to expand its role in education, the issue of data sovereignty will only become more pressing. Institutions must remain vigilant in their efforts to manage data responsibly, ensuring that they not only comply with the laws of their own country but also respect the legal frameworks of other nations involved in the data processing chain. This careful attention to data sovereignty is crucial for maintaining trust, protecting privacy, and ensuring the ethical use of AI technologies in education.

AI and Emotional and Behavioral Analytics

AI and emotional and behavioral analytics represent another significant emerging ethical issue in the context of education. Emotional AI technologies are designed to detect and respond to human emotions by analyzing various indicators such as facial expressions, voice patterns, and other behavioral cues. In educational settings, these technologies are increasingly being employed to monitor students' emotional states and engagement levels and even to predict potential mental health issues based on observed behavioral patterns (Zhang, 2020). While the application of emotional AI in education holds great promise for enhancing student well-being through personalized support, it also introduces a host of ethical concerns that must be carefully considered.

One of the primary ethical concerns with emotional AI is the issue of privacy. The collection and analysis of sensitive emotional and behavioral data can be deeply intrusive, raising questions about the extent to which students' personal information is being monitored and used. Unlike traditional educational data, which often focuses on academic performance, emotional and behavioral data delve into the personal and psychological aspects of a student's life. The potential for this data to be misused or misinterpreted—whether intentionally or unintentionally—poses significant risks to students' privacy and autonomy (Ahn & Jung, 2021).

Moreover, the use of emotional AI in educational settings brings up the critical issue of consent. Given the sensitive nature of the data being collected, it is essential that students and their guardians provide informed consent before any emotional or behavioral analytics are conducted. However, obtaining truly informed consent can be challenging, particularly in situations where students may not fully understand the implications of having their emotional states monitored. This is especially true for younger students or those with limited digital literacy, who may not be fully aware of the potential consequences of their data being analyzed in this way (Heath, 2022).

Another concern is the potential for the data collected by emotional AI systems to be misinterpreted. Human emotions and behaviors are complex and can be influenced by a wide range of factors that AI algorithms may not easily capture. For instance, a student who is feeling anxious or disengaged for reasons unrelated to school could be incorrectly flagged as at risk of mental health issues, leading to unnecessary or inappropriate interventions (Huang & Rust, 2022). Such misinterpretations can have serious implications for students, potentially affecting their educational experience and personal well-being.

Furthermore, integrating emotional AI into educational practices could inadvertently lead to a culture of constant surveillance, where students feel that they are always being watched and analyzed. This could create an environment of discomfort and distrust, which is counterproductive to the goal of fostering a supportive and nurturing educational experience (Lee, 2021). It is crucial to strike a balance between leveraging the benefits of emotional AI and maintaining a respectful and ethical approach to student monitoring.

In summary, while emotional AI technologies offer significant potential for improving student well-being by providing personalized support, they also raise critical ethical issues related to privacy, consent, and the risk of data misinterpretation. As these technologies become more prevalent in educational settings, it is essential for institutions to develop clear ethical guidelines and policies that address these concerns, ensuring that emotional AI is used in ways that are both beneficial and respectful of students' rights and dignity (Williamson & Eynon, 2020).

AI in Automated Decision-Making

AI in automated decision-making represents a critical and emerging ethical issue within educational contexts. As AI systems are increasingly employed to make decisions on a wide range of matters, including grading, admissions, and identifying students at risk of dropping out, the potential for these systems to reshape educational practices is profound. On one hand, AI can significantly enhance efficiency and accuracy, allowing institutions to process large volumes of data quickly and identify patterns that may not be immediately visible to human decision-makers. For instance, AI algorithms can swiftly analyze student performance data to provide real-time insights that support personalized learning or early intervention strategies (Luckin et al., 2020).

However, despite these benefits, the reliance on AI for automated decision-making in education also introduces substantial ethical risks, particularly when these decisions are high stakes. One of the primary concerns is the potential for bias in AI algorithms. If the data used to train these systems reflects existing inequalities or biases, the AI may inadvertently perpetuate these issues, leading to unfair outcomes for certain groups of students. For example, an AI system that is used for college admissions might unfairly disadvantage applicants from underrepresented backgrounds if the training data is biased towards profiles of previously successful candidates who do not represent the diversity of the applicant pool (Binns, 2020).

Another significant ethical issue is the lack of transparency in AI decision-making processes. Often referred to as the "black box" problem, this refers to the difficulty in understanding how AI systems arrive at certain decisions, especially when complex algorithms are involved. This lack of transparency can be problematic in educational settings, where students, parents, and educators need to trust the fairness and accuracy of the decisions being made. Without clear explanations of how decisions are reached, it becomes challenging to hold AI systems accountable or to contest decisions that may appear unjust (Ananny & Crawford, 2018).

Accountability is also a major concern with AI in automated decision-making. When algorithms, rather than humans, make decisions, it can be unclear who is responsible for the outcomes, especially if those outcomes negatively affect students. This lack of accountability can erode trust in the educational system and make it difficult to address grievances or rectify mistakes made by AI systems. Therefore, it is imperative that educational institutions establish robust ethical guidelines that clearly define the roles and responsibilities of both AI systems and human overseers in the decision-making process (Rahwan, 2020).

In conclusion, while AI in automated decision-making offers significant potential for improving educational outcomes, it also poses considerable ethical challenges. To address these challenges, educational institutions must develop and implement comprehensive ethical guidelines that govern the use of AI in decision-making. These guidelines should prioritize fairness, transparency, and accountability, ensuring that AI systems are used in ways that enhance education without compromising the rights and well-being of students (Whittlestone et al., 2019).

Preparing for Rapid Technological Advancements

In addition to addressing these emerging ethical issues, it is also essential to prepare for the rapid technological advancements in AI. This preparation involves adapting existing ethical frameworks to accommodate new AI technologies, such as advances in deep learning, natural language processing, and robotics. As these technologies evolve, so too must the guidelines that govern their use in education, ensuring they remain relevant and effective in addressing contemporary challenges (Floridi & Cowls, 2019).

Adapting Ethical Frameworks to New AI Technologies

As the pace of technological advancement in AI accelerates, it becomes increasingly important to continuously adapt and evolve ethical frameworks to address the new challenges and opportunities that arise. The rapid development of AI technologies, such as deep learning, natural language processing, and robotics, has brought about significant transformations in education. However, these advancements also introduce new ethical considerations that existing guidelines may not fully address. Therefore, to ensure that AI is used responsibly and effectively in educational contexts, it is essential to update and refine ethical frameworks in line with the latest developments in AI.

Adapting ethical frameworks to new AI technologies involves more than simply revising existing guidelines; it requires a proactive approach to anticipate and mitigate potential ethical issues that could emerge as AI continues to evolve. For example, the increasing sophistication of deep learning algorithms, which enable AI systems to make more complex and nuanced decisions, necessitates a re-examination of principles related to transparency and accountability. As AI systems become more autonomous and capable of making decisions with minimal human intervention, the ethical responsibility of these systems—and the institutions that deploy them—must be clearly defined (Floridi & Cowls, 2019).

Similarly, advances in natural language processing have enabled AI systems to engage in more human-like interactions, raising questions about the ethical implications of AI in communication and learning. As AI systems become more adept at understanding and responding to human language, there is a need to consider how these interactions might impact student learning, as well as issues related to trust, consent, and the potential for manipulation. Ethical frameworks must, therefore, be expanded to address these concerns, ensuring that AI-driven communication tools are used in ways that enhance learning without compromising ethical standards (Binns, 2020).

Robotics is another area where rapid advancements are challenging existing ethical frameworks. Integrating robotics into educational settings, whether through physical robots in the classroom or robotic process automation in administrative tasks, presents unique ethical challenges. These include concerns about the role of robots in replacing or augmenting human educators, the potential for dehumanization, and the implications of robots interacting with students in sensitive contexts. Ethical guidelines must be developed to ensure that the use of robotics in education respects the dignity and autonomy of students while also providing clear guidelines on the limitations and appropriate use of robotic technologies (Sharkey, 2021).

AI technologies continue to advance, it is imperative that ethical frameworks evolve in tandem to address the new challenges and opportunities these technologies present. This requires a commitment to ongoing ethical reflection and the development of guidelines that are both flexible and forward-looking. By adapting and adopting ethical frameworks to keep pace with technological advancements, educational institutions can ensure that AI is used in ways that are not only innovative and effective but also ethically sound and aligned with the values of education (Floridi & Cowls, 2019).

Preparing Educators and Students for AI-Driven Education

As AI becomes increasingly integrated into educational settings, the need to prepare both educators and students for AI-driven education is paramount. This preparation goes beyond mere technical training; it involves building a comprehensive AI literacy that encompasses an understanding of how AI works, its potential benefits, its risks, and the ethical considerations associated with its use. By fostering this deeper understanding, educational institutions can ensure that AI technologies are not only used effectively but also ethically, enhancing the overall learning experience while maintaining high ethical standards.

For educators, AI literacy is critical to their ability to integrate AI tools into their teaching practices in ways that are both innovative and responsible. Educators must understand the mechanics of AI systems, including how these technologies analyze data, make predictions, and adapt to different learning environments. This knowledge enables educators to harness the full potential of AI to personalize learning, improve student outcomes, and streamline administrative tasks. However, educators also need to be aware of the ethical implications of using AI, such as issues related to data privacy, bias, and the potential for AI to exacerbate existing inequalities (Holmes et al., 2021).

Moreover, preparing educators for AI-driven education involves equipping them with the skills to critically evaluate AI tools and make informed decisions about their use. This includes understanding the limitations of AI, recognizing when human judgment should override algorithmic recommendations, and ensuring that AI tools are aligned with the educational values of equity, inclusivity, and transparency. Professional development programs that focus on these aspects can empower educators to use AI in ways that are both pedagogically sound and ethically responsible (Williamson & Eynon, 2020).

For students, AI literacy is equally important. As future professionals and citizens, students need to be prepared to engage with AI technologies in various aspects of their lives. This preparation includes not only understanding how AI works but also being aware of the ethical issues that AI can raise, such as privacy concerns, algorithmic bias, and the implications of AI on employment and society at large. By developing a strong foundation in AI literacy, students can become more informed and critical users of AI technologies, capable of navigating the challenges and opportunities that AI presents (Zawacki-Richter et al., 2019).

Furthermore, fostering AI literacy among students can help to demystify AI, reduce fear and apprehension about the technology, and promote a more balanced perspective that recognizes both its potential benefits and risks. Educational institutions have a key role to play in this process by integrating AI literacy into the curriculum and providing opportunities for students to engage with AI technologies in hands-on, experiential learning environments. This approach can help students develop a nuanced understanding of AI, empowering them to use AI tools effectively and ethically in their academic and future professional lives (Holmes et al., 2021).

In conclusion, preparing educators and students for AI-driven education is essential for ensuring that AI technologies are used in ways that enhance learning while upholding the highest ethical standards. By building AI literacy and fostering a deeper understanding of the ethical implications of AI, educational institutions can create a learning environment that is both innovative and responsible, equipping educators and students alike to navigate the complexities of AI in education.

VII. CONCLUSION

Recap of Key Points

Summary of Ethical Challenges and Solutions

As we reach the conclusion of this chapter, it is essential to reflect on the significant ethical challenges that the integration of artificial intelligence (AI) in education presents. The rapid adoption of AI technologies within educational settings has brought about numerous benefits, such as personalized learning and increased efficiency in administrative tasks. However, these advancements are not without their ethical complexities. Throughout this chapter, we have delved into some of the most pressing ethical concerns, including issues related to data privacy, the risk of algorithmic bias, and the need for transparency in AI-driven decision-making processes. These challenges underscore the importance of ensuring that AI systems are designed and implemented with a strong ethical foundation, one that prioritizes fairness, accountability, and the safeguarding of individual rights.

Importance of Continuous Ethical Vigilance

To address these ethical challenges effectively, several solutions have been proposed. These include the development of comprehensive ethical frameworks, regular auditing of AI systems to detect and mitigate biases, ensuring transparency in AI processes, and adhering to national and international ethical guidelines. As AI technologies continue to evolve, educational institutions must remain vigilant, continuously updating their ethical practices to meet new challenges. By maintaining a commitment to ethical principles such as fairness, accountability, and transparency, educators can ensure that AI enhances educational outcomes without compromising the rights and well-being of students and educators alike. This conclusion emphasizes the necessity of ongoing ethical scrutiny and the importance of implementing solutions that keep pace with the ever-changing landscape of AI technology in education.

Call to Action

Encouraging Proactive Ethical Engagement

As we conclude our exploration of the ethical dimensions of AI in education, it is imperative to shift from understanding to action. The rapid integration of AI technologies into educational environments calls for proactive ethical engagement from all stakeholders—educators, developers, and policymakers alike. These groups must not only recognize the ethical challenges posed by AI but also take active steps to address them. This involves staying informed about the latest developments in AI, continuously reflecting on the ethical implications of these technologies, and advocating for policies and practices that protect the rights and well-being of students. By engaging with these issues early and consistently, stakeholders can help shape the future of AI in education in a way that aligns with our core values of fairness, accountability, and transparency.

Building a Culture of Ethical AI Use in Education

Beyond individual actions, there is a need to foster a broader culture that prioritizes ethical AI use in educational settings. This culture should be rooted in a shared commitment to upholding ethical standards and practices across all levels of AI integration. Educational institutions can play a crucial role in building this culture by embedding ethical considerations into their AI strategies, providing ongoing training and support for educators and administrators, and creating forums for open dialogue about the ethical use of AI. Moreover, by setting clear expectations and guidelines for ethical AI use, institutions can ensure that these technologies are implemented in ways that enhance educational outcomes while safeguarding the dignity and rights of all students. This collective effort to build a culture of ethical AI use is essential for ensuring that AI serves as a positive force in education, one that contributes to the development of a more just and equitable society.

REFERENCES

Annas, J. (2011). *Intelligent virtue*. Oxford University Press. DOI: 10.1093/acprof:oso/9780199228782.001.0001

Baker, T., & Hawn, O. (2021). Algorithmic fairness in education. *Educational Technology Research and Development*, 69(2), 423–442. DOI: 10.1007/s11423-021-09914-4

Binns, R. (2018). Fairness in machine learning: Lessons from political philosophy. *Proceedings of the 2018 Conference on Fairness, Accountability, and Transparency*, 149-159.

Cai, M. (2020). Privacy concerns with AI in schools. *Journal of Educational Technology*, 47(1), 23–35. DOI: 10.1177/0047239520934019

Chen, L., Xu, Z., & Li, Y. (2020). AI in education: Emerging trends and policy implications. *Journal of Learning Analytics*, 7(2), 23–42. DOI: 10.18608/jla.2020.7278

Crawford, K., & Calo, R. (2016). There is a blind spot in AI research. *Nature*, 538(7625), 311–313. DOI: 10.1038/538311a PMID: 27762391

Diakopoulos, N. (2016). Accountability in algorithmic decision making. *Communications of the ACM*, 59(2), 56–62. DOI: 10.1145/2844110

DreamBox Learning. (2020). DreamBox Learning privacy policy. https://www.dreambox.com/privacy-policy

Dwivedi, Y. K., Hughes, D. L., Ismagilova, E., Aarts, G., Coombs, C., Crick, T., & Raman, R. (2020). Artificial Intelligence (AI): Multidisciplinary perspectives on emerging challenges, opportunities, and agenda for research, practice and policy. *International Journal of Information Management*, 57, 101994. DOI: 10.1016/j.ijinfomgt.2019.08.002

Floridi, L., & Cowls, J. (2019). A unified framework of five principles for AI in society. *Harvard Data Science Review*, 1(1). Advance online publication. DOI: 10.1162/99608f92.8cd550d1

Gebru, T., Morgenstern, J., Vecchione, B., Vaughan, J. W., Wallach, H., Iii, H. D., & Crawford, K. (2020). Datasheets for datasets. *Communications of the ACM*, 64(12), 86–92. DOI: 10.1145/3458723

Greene, D., Hoffmann, A. L., & Stark, L. (2019). Better, nicer, clearer, fairer: A critical assessment of the movement for ethical artificial intelligence and machine learning. *Proceedings of the 52nd Hawaii International Conference on System Sciences*, 2122-2131. DOI: 10.24251/HICSS.2019.258

Holmes, W., Bialik, M., & Fadel, C. (2019). *Artificial Intelligence in Education: Promises and Implications for Teaching and Learning*. Center for Curriculum Redesign.

Jones, S., & Watson, A. (2020). Building trust in AI: The case of Georgia State University's PantherRetention system. *EDUCAUSE Review*, 55(4), 28–35. DOI: 10.17471/2409-3253-1336

Jones, T. M., & Miller, D. J. (2021). Predictive analytics in education: The ethics of identifying students at risk. *Journal of Educational Technology & Society*, 24(2), 112–123.

Kant, I. (2002). *Groundwork for the metaphysics of morals* (Abbott, T. K., Trans.). Yale University Press. (Original work published 1785)

Kessler, S. (2019). How Georgia State University used AI to help students stay in school. Fast Company. https://www.fastcompany.com/90271165/how-georgia-state-university-used-ai-to-help-students-stay-in-school

Li, C., & Lalani, F. (2020). The COVID-19 pandemic has changed education forever. World Economic Forum. https://www.weforum.org/agenda/2020/04/coronavirus-education-global-covid19-online-digital-learning

Liang, X. (2020). The use of AI in Chinese schools: Ethical concerns and policy implications. *Asian Journal of Educational Research*, 8(1), 34–45.

Lu, O. H. T., Huang, A. Y. Q., Huang, J. C. H., & Yang, S. J. H. (2018). Applying learning analytics for the early prediction of students' academic performance in blended learning. *Journal of Educational Technology & Society*, 21(2), 220–232.

Mill, J. S. (1863). *Utilitarianism*. Parker, Son, and Bourn.

Nkambou, R., Bourdeau, J., & Mizoguchi, R. (Eds.). (2018). *Advances in intelligent tutoring systems* (Vol. 308). Springer. DOI: 10.1007/978-3-319-91464-0

OECD. (2019). OECD principles on AI. OECD. https://www.oecd.org/going-digital/ai/principles/

Papadakis, S., Kalogiannakis, M., & Zaranis, N. (2020). Comparing tablets and computers for teaching mathematics to kindergarten children. In *Mobile learning applications in early childhood education* (pp. 24–44). IGI Global. DOI: 10.4018/978-1-7998-1486-3

Perelman, L. (2020). Automated essay scoring and the search for valid writing assessment. *Teachers College Record*, 122(4), 1–10.

Regan, P. M., & Jesse, J. (2019). Ethical challenges of edtech, big data, and personalized learning: Twenty-first century student sorting and tracking. *Ethics and Information Technology*, 21(3), 167–179. DOI: 10.1007/s10676-018-9492-2

Ryu, H., & Jeong, S. (2021). Intelligent virtual assistants and the future of work: A review and research agenda. *The Journal of Strategic Information Systems*, 30(2), 101625.

Singh, V., Thurman, A., & Holladay, C. (2021). Artificial intelligence in education: Applications and ethical considerations. *TechTrends*, 65(3), 298–305.

Slade, S., & Prinsloo, P. (2018). Learning analytics: Ethical issues and dilemmas. *The American Behavioral Scientist*, 57(10), 1510–1529. DOI: 10.1177/0002764213479366

Sloan, J., & Warner, J. (2018). Data sovereignty, law and policy: The global approach. *Journal of International Law*, 22(2), 110–134.

Smith, E. (2020). The UK grading algorithm scandal: Lessons learned. *Educational Review*, 73(1), 10–29.

UNESCO. (2021). Recommendation on the ethics of artificial intelligence. UNESCO. https://unesdoc.unesco.org/ark:/48223/pf0000377897

Watson, A. (2019). DreamBox Learning: Adaptive learning meets the classroom. *EDUCAUSE Review*, 54(6), 24–31.

Whittlestone, J., Nyrup, R., Alexandrova, A., & Dihal, K. (2019). Ethical and societal implications of algorithms, data, and artificial intelligence: A roadmap for research. Nuffield Foundation. https://www.nuffieldfoundation.org/project/ethical-and-societal-implications-of-data-and-ai-a-roadmap-for-research

Williamson, B., & Eynon, R. (2020). Historical threads, missing links, and future directions in AI in education. *Learning, Media and Technology*, 45(3), 223–235. DOI: 10.1080/17439884.2020.1798995

Wilson, M. (2020). Automated essay scoring in higher education: Ethical challenges and future directions. *Journal of Educational Technology Systems*, 48(2), 217–232.

Zawacki-Richter, O., Marín, V. I., Bond, M., & Gouverneur, F. (2019). Systematic review of research on artificial intelligence applications in higher education–where are the educators? *International Journal of Educational Technology in Higher Education*, 16(1), 39–56. DOI: 10.1186/s41239-019-0171-0

Zhang, L. (2020). Ethical implications of AI in K-12 education: A critical analysis of facial recognition systems in China. *Educational Review*, 72(4), 457–471. DOI: 10.1080/00131911.2020.1806789

Zhu, Y., Lee, W. S., & Ye, L. (2020). The role of AI in personalized learning and the ethics of education. *Journal of Educational Technology & Society*, 23(3), 98–111.

Zuboff, S. (2019). *The age of surveillance capitalism: The fight for a human future at the new frontier of power*. PublicAffairs.

Chapter 9 AI-Driven Innovations in Pedagogical and Andragogical Approaches: A Case Study Analysis

Andi Asrifan
https://orcid.org/0000-0002-9934-6129
Universitas Negeri Makassar, Indonesia

Zakila Mardatila Ersyad
https://orcid.org/0009-0008-6798-1938
Universitas Negeri Malang, Indonesia

Shafa Shafa
UIN Sultan Aji Muhammad Idris Samarinda, Indonesia

Sam Hermansyah
Universitas Muhammadiyah Sidenreng Rappang, Indonesia

Like Raskova Octaberliana
https://orcid.org/0009-0001-8829-5266
UIN Maulana Malik Ibrahim, Indonesia

Nur Alim Amri
Universitas Muhammadiyah Makassar, Indonesia

ABSTRACT

The chapter delves into the transformative potential of Artificial Intelligence (AI) in education, particularly through a qualitative case study at Deakin University. It explores how AI can enhance pedagogical and andragogical approaches by improving student learning outcomes and integrating seamlessly into educational frameworks. The anthology highlights various AI applications, such as intelligent tutoring systems and virtual reality in anatomy education, emphasizing the positive impact on teaching methods, assessments, and student support. Methodologically, the chapter employs rigorous research designs, including case studies, interviews, and document reviews, to showcase the innovative use of AI tools in education. It

DOI: 10.4018/979-8-3693-6130-6.ch009

also addresses potential biases and offers methodological suggestions for future research. The case study underscores the need for cautious yet optimistic adoption of AI in education, advocating for ongoing research to responsibly harness AI's capabilities while mitigating its limitations and biases.

INTRODUCTION

This is a qualitative case study on integrating artificial intelligent systems in a web-based learning environment. This case was done over 2 years on the Learning Management System (LMS) at Deakin University. During this case, the LMS was in development, and most of the data and intelligent systems will not be viewable to provide examples of the systems that were done. This is a fact, as the focus of this case would be the evident changes in the learning environment and whether AI can aid student learning. AI proponents believe that it can be used to enhance an individual's learning experience. This case will test to see if these beliefs are true. This will also show AI systems' difficulty and limitations in integrating into a complex system, such as learning, and what changes can be expected as technology advances.

Artificial intelligence (AI) is the field of computer science dedicated to solving cognitive problems commonly associated with human intelligence, such as learning, problem-solving, and pattern recognition (Kersting, 2020; Dohn et al., 2022; Halina, 2021; Chu et al., 2022). Education is an equally encompassing field. Educators must understand their students' cognitive processes to impart knowledge to them effectively. The need for an advanced individualized education becomes crucial with an ever-increasing population. A human alone cannot handle the complexities of providing advanced education for every individual (Trunk et al., 2020; Moshtari & Safarpour, 2024). This is where AI can greatly advance the field of education. This chapter aims to study the integration and application of AI in education and the learning process. This chapter will only cover the application of AI to learn what is to be learned and not the furthering of AI in educational software (teaching machines to teach). This chapter focuses on the application of AI in understanding and determining what content needs to be learned. It does not explore AI development for educational software designed to teach autonomously, such as systems that would enable machines to take on teaching roles.

Background of AI in Education

AI has already been around for more than 60 years. It started in 1967 when it was showcased in a film where a machine could answer any question (Jiang et al., 2022; Hassija et al., 2024). This film spurred much interest, and the idea of intelligent machines was planted in the minds of scientists. After that, in 1980, the first intelligent tutoring system was developed by researchers at Stanford University (Guo et al., 2021). From then on, many systems were developed and implemented in education. These systems were becoming increasingly sophisticated and could show the effectiveness of individualized tutoring compared to class-based teaching.

The implementation of AI systems in education has been becoming a critical issue in many developed countries and some developing countries where basic education needs have largely been met (Zhang & Aslan, 2021; Kabudi et al., 2021; Mhlanga, 2021). Rapid technological advancements and the move to IT-based learning systems make the traditional human educational experience difficult to maintain. To make these systems effective, a lot of development research is needed. The projects require collaboration between education experts and AI developers to integrate well-researched pedagogical practices into an intelligent tutoring system. This collaboration is a difficult, long-term, and expensive process, and system development often fails or produces results that were not expected. AI developers are attempting to resolve this problem by developing an AI system that can automatically learn and improve itself with time.

AI in education is defined as a process, a system, or a method of using AI to aid in delivering education and further learning (Zhai et al., 2021; Kabudi et al., 2021). This can be done using a computer; a teacher is not required. It can also be used with a teacher present to help with marking or in preparing and customizing resources for a particular student. The aim of AI in education is to provide methods of learning that are tailored to students' individual needs, pace of learning, style of learning, and so on, and also to free up teachers' time so that they can work on more creative aspects of teaching and let the AI system handle the more tedious administrative tasks (Bhutoria, 2022).

Purpose of the Case Study

Before designing intelligent tutoring systems, we must understand the educational processes to replicate and how technology may support them (Katz et al., 2021). 2021 (Schiff). Learn about teaching methods in a field and compare their efficacy. Knowledge underpins an intelligent tutoring system (Hemachandran et al., 2022). To develop effective educational AI, we must represent and utilize the best teaching approaches. Understanding how to design intelligent tutoring systems starts with studying AI in education and creating and implementing AI teaching systems. It is a realistic tool to evaluate instructional methods. Many OECD countries now teach programming and robotics, which incorporates AI (Paek & Kim, 2021). AI-based learning systems are growing in developed and developing nations (Sarker, 2022). Experts in AI in education must understand its consequences for educators and policymakers. This allows them to assess whether AI is suitable for their students' needs and work systems. Comparing and contrasting AI scenarios in education and analyzing them can help discover AI's strengths and flaws (Guan et al., 2020). This case study will examine an AI-based learning system and the debate among educators and policymakers over AI's use in education and its effects.

There is little literature on real-world classroom AI applications and teacher training initiatives. This research focuses on these topics, and the case study will inform policymakers, educators, and developers.

LITERATURE REVIEW

Previous AI-enhanced pedagogical and andragogical learning studies focused on intelligent tutoring systems. This research shows that education today needs AI. These studies suggest that understanding learning state and development improves learning. AI can shape education and learning (Markauskaite et al., 2022; Berendt, 2020). This planned learning helps students learn at the proper time and place. This is because pedagogical and pedagogical education research has demonstrated that adults and learners are more responsive to learning that directly benefits them or their goals. ITS can sequence material and quickly guide learners to the desired material (Haleem et al., 2022). ITS provides adaptable instruction, which is crucial for students nowadays. Learners need a combination of classroom and self-directed learning due to the many ways to get information. ITS makes "take-home" learning efficient by simulating a classroom (McKernon et al., 2024). All of these features demonstrate its ability to improve learning. Students need this, but instructors need it more. A more outcome-based education system will hold instructors more accountable for student performance (Kennedy & Birch, 2020). Studies have compared ITS learning efficiency to traditional instructional approaches. Nearly often, the ITS technique outperforms older methods.

This section discusses the theoretical basis of pedagogy and andragogy, the role of AI in education, and prior studies on AI in pedagogy—the intellectual foundations of pedagogy and andragogy shape education outcomes. Four of around two dozen recognized philosophical premises stand out as core (Desta & Gugssa, 2022; Hadžiomerović, 2023). These essential concepts constitute the foundation of pedagogy and andragogy and help educators plan and deliver education. These premises establish the basis for AI's role in educating and preparing students for a changing world. AI can be effective in employing the key premises of education since it can give systematic instruction and learning to prepare learners and improve their existing states.

Theoretical Foundations of Pedagogy and Andragogy

Traditional teaching methods often develop from pedagogical and pedagogical teaching theories. Pedagogical teaching is focused on how we construct learning and how we can teach in such a way as to facilitate learning more effectively (Cevikbas & Kaiser, 2020; Tuma, 2021; Munna & Kalam, 2021). It is teacher-centered, with the instructor telling the students what they need to know. Knowledge is viewed as subject-centered, and the main goal is to transfer this knowledge to the learner (Aslan, 2022; Hooper et al., 2020). It is often formal and structured, with the learning process being more important than the content. Learners are viewed as being very much dependent on the teacher. It is this method that AI is only now starting to replicate, with intelligent tutoring systems being the most typical example. These computer systems provide immediate and personalized feedback as students work through problems or concepts (Deeva et al., 2021; Hwang et al., 2020; Ouyang & Jiao, 2021; Bhutoria, 2022). This allows students to learn by doing, which constructivism tells us is the most effective way to learn. Andragogy, conversely, is teaching adults based on a humanistic concept of self-directed learning. Knowles (1984) proposed a model of andragogy that consists of four assumptions related to the motivation of learning as adults: 1) As a person matures, his or her self-concept moves from being a dependent personality to being a self-directed human being. 2) The adult has a deep-seated psychological need to be responsible for his or her decisions. 3) The adult must be seen and treated as capable of self-direction. 4) The readiness of an adult to learn is always closely related to the developmental tasks of his social role (Machynska & Boiko, 2020).

Role of AI in Education

A large body of literature has explored the potential applications of AI to learning, including its ability to provide individualized tutoring, its capacity to support the development of a deeper understanding of the student's cognitive processes, and to enhance instructional software (Kim et al., 2022; Bhutoria, 2022). AI is the "design of intelligent agents," where an intelligent agent is a system that perceives its environment and takes actions that maximize its chances of success (Hamal et al., 2021). Analyzing the environment and taking action to achieve a goal is an idea taken directly from theories of human learning. For example, the ACT-R cognitive architecture developed by John Anderson strongly resembles a production system, an intelligent agent. ACT-R is a theory about how human cognition is organized within the brain. It aims to understand how our information is represented and used to make decisions. It assumes a goal-oriented behavior where actions are taken in the environment to change the system's state closer to the desired goal.

Simulation-based learning environments for physics or algebra can take advantage of the enormous amount of research in cognitive science trying to understand how students learn concepts in these domains to build AI tutors that will scaffold the learning of a student, providing hints and feedback that is in line with the student's current understanding, similar to a more competent human tutor (Dai & Ke, 2022; Chernikova et al., 2020; Lin et al., 2022; Cowin et al., 2023). AI can achieve this by tracking what the student knows at each step in the tutoring session using a model tracing approach, which involves comparing the student's steps to a model of ideal problem-solving steps. This requires an intelligent tutor to make inferences about the student's knowledge. Research from a study of dropout students has shown that teachers often do not possess accurate knowledge of their students' understanding. AI tutors can overcome this by continually assessing the student's knowledge and understanding and adapting the tutoring to suit their current level (Minn, 2022; Katz et al., 2021; Zhai et al., 2021). This has improved academic outcomes for many students, from the learning disabled to the gifted. Finally, AI has the potential to automate the development of instructional software to free up human educators to work directly with students. This can be done using machine learning techniques to automate software creation based on instructional principles and knowledge of how students learn specific concepts.

Previous Studies on AI in Pedagogical and Andragogical Approaches

Over the years, AI applications have shown an interest in education (Chen et al., 2020; Zhai et al., 2021; Bates et al., 2020). These applications were designed to use human cognitive architecture to solve problems in a way similar to how a human would solve them. An early study at the Institute for Intelligent Systems at the University of Memphis tested the Instructo-Trace framework, which assists intelligent tutoring systems in making inferences about what a student needs to learn. The ITS is supposed to make inferences about a student's knowledge based on observable student behavior and other student data. The I-T system used a model of abductive diagnosis to make inferences about unspecified student knowledge (Pfister, 2022; Kimmel & Irran, 2022; Dean & Meir, 2021). The researchers in this study endeavored to provide a pragmatic method of integrating cognitive diagnosis into an existing ITS system. The researchers implemented part of the I-tutor mathematics word problem module to test a system that uses the Instructo-Trace model to provide cognitive diagnoses and tutorial strategies corresponding to the tutors' inferences. An intelligent tutor is only as good as the inferences it can make about a student, and the quality of the abductive diagnosis allows for sound inferences about student knowledge. This system will provide the foundation for future work in cognitive diagnosis for intelligent tutoring systems.

METHODOLOGY

The university and the involved companies obtained and granted Institutional Review Board (IRB) approval. The case study design was the most useful methodology for this research to a specific case of innovations; the targeted case was the development of AI in the DBS Bank. Several primary data collection methods were used to interview and acquire a deeper understanding of the scope of AI innovations and the individuals involved in the learning process. These methods include direct observation, interviews, and document reviews (Sahara, 2022; Chiarini & Kumar, 2021). All interviews were recorded and transcribed to ensure the data captured would be precise, and aspects of the interviews could be reviewed. Several secondary data analysis techniques were used to provide valuable input to the context and learning process for the case (Matarazzo et al., 2021; Bai et al., 2020; Dalkin et al., 2021). Publicly available information such as news chapter articles, internet sites, and interviews were analyzed to understand the case better. An internal organizational survey was administered to gather data on the current learning activities of employees. This research has successfully applied various methodologies to cover AI innovations comprehensively at DBS Bank in Singapore.

Case Study Design

The advantage of a case study is that it can deal with a large variety of evidence that is highly relevant to the phenomenon of study, such as documents, artifacts, interviews, and observation (Tomaszewski et al., 2020). In addition, case study methods provide a rationale for research grounded in the real world. It is often implemented because a theory is poorly understood and requires further explanation to rectify the gap between theory and practice. This is our intent, hoping to further the understanding of the relationship between artificial intelligence and traditional study methods. At a simple level, Goovers and van Thull theorize that a good case study is somehow the point of reconciliation between the research question and the theory (Welch et al., 2022; Magistretti et al., 2021). The research question then is: What effect will the innovation of machine learning and artificial intelligence have on traditional and non-traditional online study methods, student-teacher interaction activity, and communication, and is it a practical way to attempt to understand human learning processes?

The case study research provides a context within which we seek to understand the dynamic interactive phenomena regarding innovation in pedagogical and pedagogical approaches in a practical environment. The case is an attempt to understand a complex issue or object, and it can be an event, a person, a program, an activity, etc. Still, traditionally, it is a unique situation (Pan & Zhang, 2023; Allen et al., 2022).

Data Collection Methods

In this stage, the researcher must decide upon the method they intend to use to collect their data. This must be appropriate to the research question asked. Suppose the research question attempts to ascertain the effects of X on Y as a variable. In that case, this is the best way to show a cause-and-effect relationship between the variables. If the research question is attempting to generate a theory, understand a social process, or gain insight into a culture, perhaps a more suitable method of research would be to collect qualitative data. This can include methods such as ethnography, grounded theory, phenomenology, or case study. In this particular research chapter, the case study is the method used in an attempt to ascertain the best use of AI-driven technology to enhance learning in an adult student and to find out what the barriers and positive enablers are to implementing such change (Bhutoria, 2022; Helo & Hao, 2022). The plan was to use the case study method intrinsically to understand the nature of the case and what this technology might mean to learn (Bereczki & Kárpáti, 2021; Vinnervik, 2022; Oluyisola et al., 2022). This was assessed through an intensive study of the cases and then comparing the cases and differing periods.

Data Analysis Techniques

Leximancer has been used to achieve this successfully in various applications, including analyzing learning systems within a chemical engineering curriculum (Spina et al., 2021; Reyes et al., 2024). This research identified areas where student and teacher perspectives of learning outcomes differed, which may have led to confusion and mismatched expectations. A similar outcome is hoped for when Leximancer compares the culture and language of e-mentoring participants to traditional mentoring within the current study.

Leximancer will help researchers identify and compare concepts' implied meanings between different participant groups and their contexts with significantly less bias than a human analyst (MacCarthy & Shan, 2022; Robinson et al., 2022; Stoyanov & Kirschner, 2023). A semantic network map can be created for each document compiled by participants and compared to a network representing the combined data of all other participant groups or categories. This will allow visual identification of similarities and differences in understanding given concepts, identified by the proximity and connection of relevant concept clusters.

Leximancer will be utilized to gain a more comprehensive understanding of the language used by participants, compared to what would be achievable using more traditional methods in qualitative data analysis (Engstrom et al., 2022; Tunca et al., 2023). A study by Smith, Hey, and Stillman highlighted the ability of participants to imply meaning throughout discourse using a shared mental model (Heywood et al., 2022). This can lead to a situation where participants' meanings of words and phrases are taken for granted, with researchers believing they have a shared understanding of the topic at hand despite this not necessarily being the case.

All collected data will be analyzed using the artificial intelligence-based text analysis tool Leximancer. Leximancer is a software application that analyses text-based data to identify the relationship between words, concepts, and the context in which they are used (Goh & Wilk, 2022). The developers assert that the software has been designed to replicate the cognitive processes within the human mind, identifying and learning from patterns within the information. This is achieved by transforming the data into a semantic network of selected words and co-occurring concepts.

FINDINGS

The AI-driven reading experience occurred in a learning laboratory designed for research, teaching, and learning activities involving computer technologies (Bhutoria, 2022; Williamson & Eynon, 2024). This case study learning environment simultaneously compared two types of children's educational software: an educational computer game and the AI-driven reading experience. The learning laboratory participants were 19 children ranging from the ages of 7 to 11. Their task was to learn and comprehend three information units on the circulatory system. Data on the AI-driven reading experience was collected through participants' verbal protocols, think-aloud sessions, and immediate and delayed posttests. School marks were used as a means of data contrast for the children's comprehension of the circulatory system from the computer game. Data for comparing this case study was acquired from the children's game activities and post-game interviews, collected over approximately 10 sessions for each game unit.

The case study compares two reading experiences: one was conducted in 2015 at an elementary school in Alameda County, California, and the other was a study based on an AI-driven reading experience. By contrasting these two reading experiences, we aim to provide insight into the potential benefits of AI-driven learning environments on pedagogical learning theories and compare children's learning processes and knowledge transfer with current and traditional AI-driven pedagogical learning theories (Ebadi & Amini, 2022; Conati et al., 2021).

The case study analysis was conducted by gathering and comparing data from two studies on children's cognitive development with findings from an AI-based reading experience. The first three chapters have provided an extensive overview of the educational context, which has been used as a basis for this analysis. The data indicates that various social, emotional, and intellectual progression influences cognitive development in children. As educators strive to understand learning processes, progressions, and variations between individuals, the need for more effective teaching and learning practices intensifies (Weiss & Saklofske, 2020; Huisenga et al., 2021).

Overview of the Case Study Context

The case study was conducted at a professional development school in a large southeastern United States university. The school serves over 800 students in a small town in a rural county. Many of the town's residents have lived there all their lives, and some have lived there for several generations. A common perception is that many residents do not believe knowledge of the world outside their small community is important for themselves or their children (Koehrsen, 2021; Brooke & Clark, 2020). This belief has been perpetuated by the fact that most of the town's residents are employed in low-paying jobs in traditional industries and that very few of the town's students pursue post-secondary education. However, the school's faculty and staff are dedicated to providing students with a quality education that will prepare them to be productive citizens. The administrators of the school requested the case study in hopes that the data collected would provide them with insight into how they can use technology implemented in their school system as a means to promote positive change in the community and to develop students who are better prepared for life in the 21st century (González-Pérez & Ramírez-Montoya, 2022; Latha, 2020).

Implementation of AI-Driven Innovations

CMap tools provide the global community with concept map-building tools and knowledge modeling space with a WWW repository (Biswas & Wang, 2023). These tools use AI to intelligently search existing material and design new learning materials using models. It has been successfully implemented in engineering teaching and knowledge-based-aided design learning for mechanical equipment design and has been proven to enhance problem-solving skills. AI tutor systems are another right step in the direction of AI-driven education. AI tutors are intelligent tutoring systems that provide immediate and specific feedback to students' inputs as they work on practice problems (AlShaikh & Hewahi, 2021).

Such rich and diverse learning material can be developed using concept networks of AI. It is a multimedia construct of information and is cognitive, that is, organized information to provide meaningful access and that can be used for problem-solving and decision-making (Fang & Pan, 2024; Iku-Silan et al., 2023).

AI-driven innovations are typically implemented in higher education with a classified view of teaching, where faculties are supposed to feed the information to students, and students are to retain and reproduce the same during examinations (Dai et al., 2023). Healthier learning usually takes the backseat, and the teaching-learning process is set in a deteriorating direction. Even in professional science teaching, the concept of learning through data or experimentation remains far-fetched to a great extent due to the complexities and costs associated. AI-driven innovations are prospective in this scenario and add relevance to the innovative teaching-learning process. AI-driven tools can provide and conduct detailed analyses of students' learning problems and develop the required personalized study material.

Impact on Pedagogical Approaches

The analysis of transcripts, classroom observations, and focus group discussions revealed several changes in the teaching methods employed by the participant teachers. Some were direct results of the ILS tools; others were reactions to the more student-centered inquiry-based pedagogy that the teachers believed would effectively support the students' use of the ILS (Hmedna et al., 2023; Kapici & Akcay, 2023) (Shoaib et al., 2024) (Marosan et al., 2022). From the perspective of Pedagogical Content Knowledge, the most significant effect was the change from setting tasks to setting learning goals. This was most clear in the Simple Machines project, where a teacher might have previously set a task for the students to learn about levers by making one. The goal was to get the students to select an ILS activity at an appropriate level of challenge and learn about it. The lever activity was just one student-selected learning goal out of many for the unit. The teachers in the Tytherleigh Project also changed their views about effective ways to motivate learning of specific topics, shifting from believing that games were the best way to engage students in competition with each other to the view that competition between groups on ILS puzzles and activities was more effective and less detrimental to the less able students (Platt et al., 2024; Macfarlane, 2022). This led to changes in lesson planning and whole-class management. Several teachers also changed their approaches to assessment. The aim, in general, was to correlate this more closely with the ILS-based learning and design assessment tasks that were parallel to a related ILS activity in content but varied in mode and scaffolding. This should allow for a formative assessment of the learning process during the activity and a diagnostic assessment of strengths and difficulties in using the ILS.

Impact on Andragogical Approaches

It's impossible to compare, but teachers are relieved they can help students better. AI-driven systems simplify teaching and learning (Dai et al., 2023; Sarker, 2022; Kim, 2022). Adult learners own the growth experience. Hence, these occurrences are andragogy even though the system affects pedagogy more.

Students feel more experienced after these events. They believe the new system makes remote learning easier. Since they are already working, the system's convenience will help them balance employment and study (Tavakoli et al., 2022; Dogan, 2023). Their last attempt was to explain their project on the system. The system lets you build a virtual classroom with a message board. The result was mixed because the AI bot sometimes answered the topic differently. They like the experience overall. Besides that, pupils used the assignment feature. They can automate assignment submission and allocation here. AI software always improves automation, so this is another benefit. The algorithm still cannot distinguish between past and current courses, making assignment allocation ineffective (Luckin et al., 2022). It is a solid start, but further improvement can make assignment allocation smarter.

Part-time students used the system in their free time. They usually visit the announcement area for teaching staff updates. Since the announcement section is on the front page, they could immediately use the new system. Andragogy uses experience, and the new system made knowledge easier to access. To reiterate, andragogy is adult-focused learning (Sîrbu, 2020; Stanney et al., 2023). Most part-time IT students work in the sector. Consider them adult learners. Andragogy combines students' experience, self-motivation, and a problem-centered approach to emphasize process over material, unlike pedagogy, which is good for young pupils.

DISCUSSION

The Generation and Exploration System for Time-varying Effects (GEST) has been developed over the past 2 years to create an open platform for medical researchers to simulate time-varying treatments and compare different causal inference methods (Shahbaz et al., 2021) (Razmi et al., 2021). GEST has isolated a specific method or data-generating processes and investigated whether the RSI method provides unbiased estimates for the target estimation. The causally interpretable estimate or the risk difference comparing students who would know more basic science if given the active treatments vs. the same students with no access to the active treatment is estimated throughout their risk set (Radez et al., 2021). This method has been planned to be published step by step using simulations.

The discussion starts with explaining how this research has taken a direction and transformed the pedagogical methods by using artificial intelligence. The methods and the approach used to arrive at the findings have been explained in this research. The researchers first visualized a method, patented by Kaplan and Meier in 1958 for predicting and diagnosing survival data, called risk set identification (Martin-Hernandez et al., 2023; Ulloa et al., 2021). This method then utilized the potential outcome approach to counterfactuals to determine causal effects on time-varying treatments. An analogy for this approach relates to time-varying treatment effects in medical education using data from an adaptive e-learning platform designed to optimize basic science knowledge retention. This approach can potentially transform how medical educators estimate the efficacy of pedagogical methods for medical students (Zhao et al., 2020; Motte-Signoret et al., 2021). Due to its complexity, it is possible that researchers in medical education and other non-quantitative fields could misapply this approach. The researchers used an AI-based simulation to generate a sample dataset to:

1. Confirm whether investigators can correctly implement the RSI method.
2. Identify potential biases in estimating treatment effects.
3. Guide researchers seeking to apply time-varying causal methods.

Analysis of Findings

This section analyzes the case study findings using current AI research. The validity of data statements comes first. AI systems can analyze and understand data at numerous levels (Sarker, 2022). Complex systems can spot trends, make conclusions, and generate information, including 'why' and 'how' answers. The case study presented convincing evidence from many sources, yet the AI system could not explain student dropout (Tsai et al., 2020). The AI program was a basic correlation exercise that identified variables with a strong correlation to student retention and supplied an equation (Crawford et al., 2024; Li et al., 2022; Saks et al., 2022; Badali et al., 2022). Despite its predictive power, this does not explain. The more advanced AI programs mentioned above should be able to answer the 'why' and 'how' questions using a bigger knowledge base of similar studies and trial and error. Due to the complexity and duration of learning, an equation may not always accurately explain a causal link. A causal explanation from a more advanced system will help instructors understand and act on results (Pol et al., 2020). Ke et al. (2021) Greenhalgh and Manzano2022, Zhao et al. 2021, Callanan 2020. Most educators know that standard statistical analysis doesn't capture educational data's complexity and multi-level causes and relationships. The case study suggested that AI-driven analysis was more powerful than traditional statistical methods because it accounted for non-linearity, hierarchical structure, complicated variable relationships, and multivariate complexity. This is a big assertion, yet AI research lacks methods to execute these jobs.

Most AI learning simulations employ statistical models, including generalized linear models, discriminant analysis, logistic regression, and various types of ANOVA (Sarker, 2021; Travaini et al., 2022; Horváthová, 2021). The AI learns by adjusting model parameters based on input on its objective achievement (Karamitsos et al., 2020). It explores model space for the optimal model based on a criterion. Data-driven educators use stepwise regression to get a 'best fit' for their theories. Statistics lecturers should note that stepwise regression might overfit data and produce false conclusions. The case study identified a key knowledge acceptance issue using simple data mining and complex AI simulations.

Data mining and data-driven educators have defined hypotheses and searched the data for evidence against the null hypothesis to prove a theory or view. A high confidence level may lead to acceptance of the theory (Kurilovas, 2020; Teng et al., 2023) and Gamazo & Martínez-Abad, 2020). If not, they will lower the data set to uncover the analytical error and whether the 'causes' are effects. Their AI simulations identify phenomena and build models for successful intervention (Gibson et al., 2023; Boroujeni, 2024). In either scenario, educators often oversimplify learning and student behavior with little or no empirical data and create unhelpful ideas and solutions. Data-driven educators and AI simulations may tell educators about their findings for comparative efficacy (Guan et al., 2020; Dai & Ke, 2022). Current education theories and intervention effects are not well-articulated enough for extensive data analysis to put into global models.

Comparison with Existing Literature

The provided case study draws from two bodies of work that are, to some extent, preliminary. First, the chapter is mining the literature on how AI technologies are being integrated into education at various levels, and second, future research is concerned with the potential impacts of AI on human learning. As the first body of work, AI in education is currently a scattered field of research (Bozkurt et al., 2021; Paek & Kim, 2021; Davies et al., 2021). While there has been considerable work, much of it is only at the prototype stage. Findings are often published in venues on intelligent tutoring systems or educational software rather than in the broader education literature. Hence, the authors had difficulty locating potential subjects for the case study. This is compounded by the fact that the education community is often averse to taking up innovations perceived as too radical. So, while the authors managed to locate two high-quality projects, it is likely that there are similar projects still in their infancy and others that have been abandoned. Given the rapid turnover of educational software and practice, research dates from 2005.

In the late 1990s, there was considerable hype about intelligent tutoring systems, but there has been relatively little impact. More recently, enthusiasm has focused on constructivist microworlds, simulation-based learning environments, and the use of virtual agents (Guo et al., 2021; Wang et al., 2023; Frick, 2020; Azevedo et al., 2022). These technologies have yet to prove themselves as effective learning tools. Still, they are an active development area. They may hold more potential than intelligent tutoring because they embody the sought-after pedagogical characteristics—a recent book by the Military Special Interest Group of the Society for Learning Technology.

On the topic of learning environments for higher education in IT-intensive fields, there is a project waiting to happen to investigate how to use data mining methodologies to improve IT learning, customizing the sophistication level and style of teaching of different topics for individual learners based on an ongoing assessment of their metacognitive state and knowledge. This contrasts with the AToL project, with some definite parallels and interesting complementary possibilities on student modeling and may provide a good comparison case in the future (Andréfouët & Bionaz, 2021).

CONCLUSION

AI-integrated educational systems could alter pedagogy and andragogy by personalizing learning and changing educational processes. This chapter has investigated how AI-driven advancements like intelligent tutoring systems and virtual reality might improve learning outcomes and streamline instruction. AI has many benefits, but the deployment must be cautious to eliminate biases in AI systems to ensure equitable education for all students.

Educators, politicians, and researchers must work together to create ethical and educational AI technologies as we approach this technological progression. Research is ongoing to assess AI's effects, recommend improvements, and prioritize inclusive technology. Our ability to use AI to improve learning and defend justice and equity in education is the future of education.

This chapter encourages specialists to shape the future of AI in education. By working together, discussing AI's role in learning, and developing robust, ethical AI systems, we can make AI a force for good. Our task is difficult, but we can develop an innovative and inclusive educational environment that prepares future generations for an AI-enhanced world together.

REFERENCES

Allen, S. J., Rosch, D. M., & Riggio, R. E. (2022). Advancing leadership education and development: Integrating adult learning theory. [HTML]. *Journal of Management Education*, 46(2), 252–283. DOI: 10.1177/10525629211008645

AlShaikh, F., & Hewahi, N. (2021, September). Ai and machine learning techniques in the development of Intelligent Tutoring System: A review. *In 2021 International Conference on innovation and Intelligence for informatics, computing, and technologies* (3ICT) (pp. 403-410). IEEE. [HTML]DOI: 10.1109/3ICT53449.2021.9582029

Andréfouët, S. & Bionaz, O. (2021). Lessons from a global remote sensing mapping project. A review of the impact of the Millennium Coral Reef Mapping Project for science and management. *Science of the Total Environment.* sciencedirect.comDOI: 10.1016/j.scitotenv.2021.145987

Aslan, S. (2022). The Predictive Role of the Primary School Teachers' Educational Beliefs on Their Curriculum Design Orientation Preferences. *International Journal of Psychology and Educational Studies, 9*(3), 765-781. https://dx.doi.org/ ed.govDOI: 10.52380/ijpes.2022.9.3.776

Azevedo, R., Bouchet, F., Duffy, M., Harley, J., Taub, M., Trevors, G., ... & Cerezo, R. (2022). Lessons learned and future directions of MetaTutor: Leveraging multichannel data to scaffold self-regulated learning with an intelligent tutoring system. *Frontiers in Psychology, 13*, 813632. https://doi.org/ frontiersin.orgDOI: 10.3389/fpsyg.2022.813632

Badali, M., Hatami, J., Banihashem, S. K., Rahimi, E., Noroozi, O., & Eslami, Z. (2022). The role of motivation in MOOCs' retention rates: a systematic literature review. *Research and Practice in Technology Enhanced Learning, 17*(1), 5. https://doi.org/ springer.comDOI: 10.1186/s41039-022-00181-3

Bai, C., Dallasega, P., Orzes, G., & Sarkis, J. (2020). Industry 4.0 technologies assessment: A sustainability perspective. *International journal of production economics, 229*, 107776. https://doi.org/ sciencedirect.comDOI: 10.1016/j.ijpe.2020.107776

Bates, T., Cobo, C., Mariño, O., & Wheeler, S. (2020). Can artificial intelligence transform higher education?. *International Journal of Educational Technology in Higher Education, 17*, 1-12. https://doi.org/ springer.comDOI: 10.1186/s41239-020-00218-x

Bereczki, E. O. & Kárpáti, A. (2021). Technology-enhanced creativity: A multiple case study of digital technology-integration expert teachers' beliefs and practices. *Thinking Skills and Creativity*. https://doi.org/ sciencedirect.comDOI: 10.1016/j.tsc.2021.100791

Berendt, B., Littlejohn, A., & Blakemore, M. (2020). AI in education: Learner choice and fundamental rights. *Learning, Media and Technology*, 45(3), 312–324. ucl.ac.uk. DOI: 10.1080/17439884.2020.1786399

Bhutoria, A. (2022). Personalized education and artificial intelligence in the United States, China, and India: A systematic review using a human-in-the-loop model. *Computers and Education: Artificial Intelligence*. https://doi.org/ sciencedirect.comDOI: 10.1016/j.caeai.2022.100068

Biswas, A. & Wang, H. C. (2023). Autonomous vehicles enabled by the integration of IoT, edge intelligence, 5G, and blockchain. *Sensors*. https://doi.org/ mdpi.comDOI: 10.3390/s23041963

Boroujeni, S. P. H., Razi, A., Khoshdel, S., Afghah, F., Coen, J. L., O'Neill, L., Fule, P., Watts, A., Kokolakis, N.-M. T., & Vamvoudakis, K. G. (2024). A comprehensive survey of research towards ai-enabled unmanned aerial systems in pre-, active-, and post-wildfire management. [HTML]. *Information Fusion*, 108, 102369. DOI: 10.1016/j.inffus.2024.102369

Bozkurt, A., Karadeniz, A., Baneres, D., Guerrero-Roldán, A. E., & Rodríguez, M. E. (2021). Artificial intelligence and reflections from educational landscape: A review of AI Studies in half a century. *Sustainability, 13*(2), 800. https://doi.org/ mdpi.comDOI: 10.3390/su13020800

Brooke, J. & Clark, M. (2020). Older people's early experience of household isolation and social distancing during COVID-19. *Journal of Clinical Nursing*. https://doi.org/ wiley.comDOI: 10.1111/jocn.15485

Callanan, M. A., Legare, C. H., Sobel, D. M., Jaeger, G. J., Letourneau, S., McHugh, S. R., Willard, A., Brinkman, A., Finiasz, Z., Rubio, E., Barnett, A., Gose, R., Martin, J. L., Meisner, R., & Watson, J. (2020). Exploration, explanation, and parent–child interaction in museums. [nih.gov]. *Monographs of the Society for Research in Child Development*, 85(1), 7–137. DOI: 10.1111/mono.12412 PMID: 32175600

Cevikbas, M. & Kaiser, G. (2020). Flipped classroom as a reform-oriented approach to teaching mathematics. *Zdm*. https://doi.org/ springer.comDOI: 10.1007/s11858-020-01191-5

Chen, X., Xie, H., Zou, D., & Hwang, G. J. (2020). Application and theory gaps during the rise of artificial intelligence in education. *Computers and Education: Artificial Intelligence, 1*, 100002. https://doi.org/ sciencedirect.comDOI: 10.1016/j.caeai.2020.100002

Chernikova, O., Heitzmann, N., Stadler, M., Holzberger, D., Seidel, T., & Fischer, F. (2020). Simulation-based learning in higher education: A meta-analysis. *Review of Educational Research, 90*(4), 499-541. https://doi.org/ sagepub.comDOI: 10.3102/0034654320933544

Chiarini, A., & Kumar, M. (2021). Lean Six Sigma and Industry 4.0 integration for Operational Excellence: evidence from Italian manufacturing companies. *Production planning & control.* cardiff.ac.uk

Chu, S. T., Hwang, G. J., & Tu, Y. F. (2022). Artificial intelligence-based robots in education: A systematic review of selected SSCI publications. *Computers and education: Artificial intelligence, 3*, 100091. https://doi.org/ sciencedirect.comDOI: 10.1016/j.caeai.2022.100091

Conati, C., Barral, O., Putnam, V., & Rieger, L. (2021). Toward personalized XAI: A case study in intelligent tutoring systems. [PDF]. *Artificial Intelligence*, 298, 103503. DOI: 10.1016/j.artint.2021.103503

Cowin, J., Oberer, B., Lipuma, J., Leon, C., & Erkollar, A. (2023, September). Accelerating Higher Education Transformation: Simulation-Based Training and AI Coaching for Educators-in-Training. In International Conference on Interactive Collaborative Learning (pp. 532-541). *Cham: Springer Nature Switzerland.* https://doi.org/ [HTML]DOI: 10.1007/978-3-031-51979-6_55

Crawford, J., Allen, K. A., Pani, B., & Cowling, M. (2024). When artificial intelligence substitutes humans in higher education: the cost of loneliness, student success, and retention. *Studies in Higher Education*, 1-15. https://doi.org/ tandfonline.comDOI: 10.1080/03075079.2024.2326956

Dai, C. P. & Ke, F. (2022). Educational applications of artificial intelligence in simulation-based learning: A systematic mapping review. *Computers and Education: Artificial Intelligence*. https://doi.org/ sciencedirect.comDOI: 10.1016/j.caeai.2022.100087

Dai, Y., Liu, A., & Lim, C. P. (2023). Reconceptualizing ChatGPT and generative AI as a student-driven innovation in higher education. *Procedia CIRP*. https://doi.org/ sciencedirect.comDOI: 10.1016/j.procir.2023.05.002

Dalkin, S., Forster, N., Hodgson, P., Lhussier, M., & Carr, S. M. (2021). Using computer assisted qualitative data analysis software (CAQDAS; NVivo) to assist in the complex process of realist theory generation, refinement and testing. *International Journal of Social Research Methodology, 24*(1), 123-134. https://doi.org/ tandfonline.comDOI: 10.1080/13645579.2020.1803528

Davies, H. C., Eynon, R., & Salveson, C. (2021). The mobilisation of AI in education: A Bourdieusean field analysis. *Sociology*. https://doi.org/ sagepub.comDOI: 10.1177/0038038520967888

Dean, C., & Meir, K. (2021). Model-based diagnosis with uncertain observations. [HTML]. *International Journal of Intelligent Systems*, 36(7), 3259–3292. Advance online publication. DOI: 10.1002/int.22416

Deeva, G., Bogdanova, D., Serral, E., Snoeck, M., & De Weerdt, J. (2021). A review of automated feedback systems for learners: Classification framework, challenges and opportunities. [kuleuven.be]. *Computers & Education*, 162, 104094. DOI: 10.1016/j.compedu.2020.104094

Desta, S. Z. & Gugssa, M. A. (2022). The implementation of andragogy in the adult education program in Ethiopia. *Education research international*. https://doi.org/ hindawi.comDOI: 10.1155/2022/2028248

Dogan, M. E., Goru Dogan, T., & Bozkurt, A. (2023). The use of artificial intelligence (AI) in online learning and distance education processes: A systematic review of empirical studies. *Applied Sciences*. https://doi.org/ mdpi.comDOI: 10.3390/ app13053056

Dohn, N. B., Kafai, Y., Mørch, A., & Ragni, M. (2022). Survey: Artificial Intelligence, computational thinking and learning. *KI-Künstliche Intelligenz*. https://doi .org/ google.comDOI: 10.1007/s13218-021-00751-5

Ebadi, S., & Amini, A. (2022). Examining the roles of social presence and human-likeness on Iranian EFL learners' motivation using artificial intelligence technology: A case of CSIEC chatbot. [HTML]. *Interactive Learning Environments*. Advance online publication. DOI: 10.1080/10494820.2022.2096638

Engstrom, T., Strong, J., Sullivan, C., & Pole, J. D. (2022). A Comparison of Leximancer semi-automated content analysis to manual content analysis: a healthcare exemplar using emotive Transcripts of COVID-19 Hospital staff interactive webcasts. *International Journal of Qualitative Methods, 21*, 16094069221118993. https://doi .org/ sagepub.comDOI: 10.1177/16094069221118993

Fang, R., & Pan, L. (2024). Refocusing on the start and end of tourists' decision-making: *Measuring thresholds and information loop limits.* [HTML]. *Tourism Management*, 104, 104918. Advance online publication. DOI: 10.1016/j.tourman.2024.104918

Frick, T. W. (2020). Education systems and technology in 1990, 2020, and beyond. TechTrends. https://doi.org/ springer.comDOI: 10.1007/s11528-020-00527-y

Gamazo, A. & Martínez-Abad, F. (2020). An exploration of factors linked to academic performance in PISA 2018 through data mining techniques. *Frontiers in Psychology*. https://doi.org/ frontiersin.orgDOI: 10.3389/fpsyg.2020.575167

Gibson, D., Kovanovic, V., Ifenthaler, D., Dexter, S., & Feng, S. (2023). Learning theories for artificial intelligence promoting learning processes. *British Journal of Educational Technology, 54*(5), 1125-1146. https://doi.org/ wiley.comDOI: 10.1111/bjet.13341

Goh, E., & Wilk, V. (2022). Showcasing Leximancer in tourism and hospitality research: A review of Leximancer-based research published in tourism and hospitality journals during 2014–2020. [HTML]. *Tourism Recreation Research*. Advance online publication. DOI: 10.1080/02508281.2022.2129284

González-Pérez, L. I. & Ramírez-Montoya, M. S. (2022). Components of Education 4.0 in 21st century skills frameworks: Systematic review. *Sustainability*. https://doi.org/ mdpi.comDOI: 10.3390/su14031493

Greenhalgh, J., & Manzano, A. (2022). Understanding 'context'in realist evaluation and synthesis. *International Journal of Social Research Methodology, 25*(5), 583-595. https://doi.org/ tandfonline.comDOI: 10.1080/13645579.2021.1918484

Guan, C., Mou, J., & Jiang, Z. (2020). Artificial intelligence innovation in education: A twenty-year data-driven historical analysis. *International Journal of Innovation Studies*. https://doi.org/ sciencedirect.comDOI: 10.1016/j.ijis.2020.09.001

Guo, L., Wang, D., Gu, F., Li, Y., Wang, Y., & Zhou, R. (2021). Evolution and trends in intelligent tutoring systems research: a multidisciplinary and scientometric view. *Asia Pacific Education Review, 22*(3), 441-461. https://doi.org/ springer.comDOI: 10.1007/s12564-021-09697-7

Hadžiomerović, A. I. (2023). Questioning Assumptions About Developing an Andragogy Study Program in Bosnia and Herzegovina. *Andragoška spoznanja*. uni-lj.si
Haleem, A., Javaid, M., Qadri, M. A., & Suman, R. (2022). Understanding the role of digital technologies in education: A review. *Sustainable Operations and Computers, 3*, 275-285. https://doi.org/ sciencedirect.comDOI: 10.1016/j.susoc.2022.05.004

Halina, M. (2021). Insightful artificial intelligence. *Mind & Language*. https://doi.org/ wiley.comDOI: 10.1111/mila.12321

Hamal, O., Faddouli, E., & Harouni, M. H. A. (2021). Design and Implementation of the Multi-Agent System in Education. *World Journal on Educational Technology: Current Issues, 13*(4), 775-793. https://doi.org/ed.govDOI: 10.18844/wjet.v13i4.6264

Hassija, V., Chamola, V., Mahapatra, A., Singal, A., Goel, D., Huang, K., ... & Hussain, A. (2024). Interpreting black-box models: a review on explainable artificial intelligence. *Cognitive Computation, 16*(1), 45-74. https://doi.org/ springer.comDOI: 10.1007/s12559-023-10179-8

Helo, P. & Hao, Y. (2022). Artificial intelligence in operations management and supply chain management: An exploratory case study. *Production Planning & Control*. https://doi.org/ tandfonline.comDOI: 10.1080/09537287.2021.1882690

Hemachandran, K., Verma, P., Pareek, P., Arora, N., Kumar, K. V. R., Ahanger, T. A., ... & Ratna, R. (2022). Artificial intelligence: a universal virtual tool to augment tutoring in higher education. *Computational Intelligence and Neuroscience, 2022*. https://doi.org/ hindawi.comDOI: 10.1155/2022/1410448

Heywood, L., Conti, J., & Hay, P. (2022). Chapter 1: a systematic synthesis of narrative therapy treatment components for the treatment of eating disorders. *Journal of Eating Disorders*. https://doi.org/ springer.comDOI: 10.1186/s40337-022-00635-5

Hmedna, B., Bakki, A., Mezouary, A. E., & Baz, O. (2023). Unlocking teachers' potential: MOOCLS, a visualization tool for enhancing MOOC teaching. *Smart Learning Environments*. https://doi.org/ springer.comDOI: 10.1186/s40561-023-00277-3

Hooper, B., Molineux, M., & Wood, W. (2020). The subject-centered integrative learning model: A new model for teaching occupational therapy's distinct value. *Journal of Occupational Therapy Education, 4*(2), 1. https://doi.org/ eku.eduDOI: 10.26681/jote.2020.040201

Horváthová, J., Mokrišová, M., & Petruška, I. (2021). Selected methods of predicting financial health of companies: neural networks versus discriminant analysis. *Information*. https://doi.org/ mdpi.comDOI: 10.3390/info12120505

Huisenga, D., La Bastide-Van Gemert, S., Van Bergen, A., Sweeney, J., & Hadders-Algra, M. (2021). Developmental outcomes after early surgery for complex congenital heart disease: A systematic review and meta-analysis. *Developmental Medicine & Child Neurology, 63*(1), 29-46. https://doi.org/ wiley.comDOI: 10.1111/dmcn.14512

Hwang, G. J., Xie, H., Wah, B. W., & Gašević, D. (2020). Vision, challenges, roles and research issues of Artificial Intelligence in Education. *Computers and Education: Artificial Intelligence, 1*, 100001. https://doi.org/ sciencedirect.comDOI: 10.1016/j.caeai.2020.100001

Iku-Silan, A., Hwang, G. J., & Chen, C. H. (2023). Decision-guided chatbots and cognitive styles in interdisciplinary learning. [HTML]. *Computers & Education*, 201, 104812. Advance online publication. DOI: 10.1016/j.compedu.2023.104812

Jiang, Y., Li, X., Luo, H., Yin, S., & Kaynak, O. (2022). Quo vadis artificial intelligence?. *Discover Artificial Intelligence*. https://doi.org/ springer.comDOI: 10.1007/s44163-022-00022-8

Kabudi, T., Pappas, I., & Olsen, D. H. (2021). AI-enabled adaptive learning systems: A systematic mapping of the literature. *Computers and Education: Artificial Intelligence, 2*, 100017. https://doi.org/ sciencedirect.comDOI: 10.1016/j.caeai.2021.100017

Kapici, H. O., & Akcay, H. (2023). Improving student teachers' TPACK self-efficacy through lesson planning practice in the virtual platform. [HTML]. *Educational Studies*, 49(1), 76–98. Advance online publication. DOI: 10.1080/03055698.2020.1835610

Karamitsos, I., Albarhami, S., & Apostolopoulos, C. (2020). Applying DevOps practices of continuous automation for machine learning. *Information*. https://doi.org/ mdpi.comDOI: 10.3390/info11070363

Katz, S., Albacete, P., Chounta, I. A., Jordan, P., McLaren, B. M., & Zapata-Rivera, D. (2021). Linking dialogue with student modelling to create an adaptive tutoring system for conceptual physics. *International journal of artificial intelligence in education, 31*(3), 397-445. https://doi.org/ springer.comDOI: 10.1007/s40593-020-00226-y

Ke, L., Sadler, T. D., Zangori, L., & Friedrichsen, P. J. (2021). Developing and using multiple models to promote scientific literacy in the context of socio-scientific issues. *Science & Education*. https://doi.org/ springer.comDOI: 10.1007/s11191-021-00206-1

Kennedy, M., & Birch, P. (2020). Reflecting on outcome-based education for human services programs in higher education: A policing degree case study. [HTML]. *Journal of Criminological Research, Policy and Practice*, 6(2), 111–122. DOI: 10.1108/JCRPP-12-2019-0071

Kersting, K. (2020). Rethinking computer science through AI. *KI-Künstliche Intelligenz*. https://doi.org/ springer.comDOI: 10.1007/s13218-020-00692-5

Kim, J., Lee, H., & Cho, Y. H. (2022). Learning design to support student-AI collaboration: Perspectives of leading teachers for AI in education. *Education and Information Technologies*. https://doi.org/ springer.comDOI: 10.1007/s10639-021-10831-6

Kim, J. H., Kim, M., Kwak, D. W., & Lee, S. (2022). Home-tutoring services assisted with technology: Investigating the role of artificial intelligence using a randomized field experiment. *Journal of Marketing Research, 59*(1), 79-96. https://doi.org/ sagepub.comDOI: 10.1177/00222437211050351

Kimmel, M. & Irran, C. (2022). Decision-making in Shiatsu bodywork: Complementariness of embodied coupling and conceptual inference. *Phenomenology and the Cognitive Sciences*. https://doi.org/ springer.comDOI: 10.1007/s11097-020-09718-7

Koehrsen, J. (2021). Muslims and climate change: How Islam, Muslim organizations, and religious leaders influence climate change perceptions and mitigation activities. *Wiley Interdisciplinary Reviews: Climate Change*. https://doi.org/ wiley.comDOI: 10.1002/wcc.702

Kurilovas, E. (2020). On data-driven decision-making for quality education. [HTML]. *Computers in Human Behavior*, 107, 105774. Advance online publication. DOI: 10.1016/j.chb.2018.11.003

Latha, S. (2020). Vuca in engineering education: Enhancement of faculty competency for capacity building. *Procedia Computer Science*. https://doi.org/ sciencedirect.comDOI: 10.1016/j.procs.2020.05.106

Li, X., Jiang, M. Y. C., Jong, M. S. Y., Zhang, X., & Chai, C. S. (2022). Understanding medical students' perceptions of and behavioral intentions toward learning artificial intelligence: A survey study. *International Journal of Environmental Research and Public Health, 19*(14), *8733*. https://doi.org/ mdpi.comDOI: 10.3390/ijerph19148733

Lin, P. C., Hou, H. T., & Chang, K. E. (2022). … of a collaborative problem solving environment that integrates a scaffolding mind tool and simulation-based learning: An analysis of learners' performance and their…. [HTML]. *Interactive Learning Environments*, 30(7), 1273–1290. Advance online publication. DOI: 10.1080/10494820.2020.1719163

Luckin, R., Cukurova, M., Kent, C., & du Boulay, B. (2022). Empowering educators to be AI-ready. *Computers and Education: Artificial Intelligence, 3*, 100076. https://doi.org/ sciencedirect.comDOI: 10.1016/j.caeai.2022.100076

MacCarthy, M. & Shan, H. (2022). Machine infelicity in a poignant visitor setting: Comparing human and AI's ability to analyze discourse. *Current Issues in Tourism*. https://doi.org/ tandfonline.comDOI: 10.1080/13683500.2021.1915252

Macfarlane, B. (2022). A voyage around the ideological islands of higher education research. *Higher education research & development*. https://doi.org/ tandfonline.comDOI: 10.1080/07294360.2021.2002275

Machynska, N., & Boiko, H. (2020). Andragogy–The science of adult education: Theoretical aspects. *Journal of Innovation in Psychology* [ub.ro]. *Education and Didactics*, 24(1), 25–34.

Magistretti, S., Ardito, L., & Messeni Petruzzelli, A. (2021). Framing the microfoundations of design thinking as a dynamic capability for innovation: Reconciling theory and practice. *Journal of Product Innovation Management, 38*(6), 645-667. https://doi.org/ wiley.comDOI: 10.1111/jpim.12586

Markauskaite, L., Marrone, R., Poquet, O., Knight, S., Martinez-Maldonado, R., Howard, S., ... & Siemens, G. (2022). Rethinking the entwinement between artificial intelligence and human learning: What capabilities do learners need for a world with AI?. *Computers and Education: Artificial Intelligence, 3*, 100056. https://doi.org/ sciencedirect.comDOI: 10.1016/j.caeai.2022.100056

Marosan, Z., Savic, N., Klasnja-Milicevic, A., Ivanovic, M., & Vesin, B. (2022). Students' perceptions of ils as a learning-style-identification tool in e-learning environments. *Sustainability, 14*(8), 4426. https://doi.org/ mdpi.comDOI: 10.3390/su14084426

Martin-Hernandez, R., Espeso-Gil, S., Domingo, C., Latorre, P., Hervas, S., Hernandez Mora, J. R., & Kotelnikova, E. (2023). Machine learning combining multi-omics data and network algorithms identifies adrenocortical carcinoma prognostic biomarkers. *Frontiers in Molecular Biosciences, 10*, 1258902. https://doi.org/ frontiersin.orgDOI: 10.3389/fmolb.2023.1258902

Matarazzo, M., Penco, L., Profumo, G., & Quaglia, R. (2021). Digital transformation and customer value creation in Made in Italy SMEs: A dynamic capabilities perspective. [HTML]. *Journal of Business Research*, 123, 642–656. DOI: 10.1016/j.jbusres.2020.10.033

McKernon, S. L., Adderton, E. A., & Dawson, L. J. (2024). Using Technology-Supported Approaches for the Development of Technical Skills Outside of the Classroom. *Education Sciences*. https://doi.org/ mdpi.comDOI: 10.3390/educsci14030329

Mhlanga, D. (2021). Artificial intelligence in the industry 4.0, and its impact on poverty, innovation, infrastructure development, and the sustainable development goals: Lessons …. *Sustainability*. https://doi.org/ mdpi.comDOI: 10.3390/su13115788

Minn, S. (2022). AI-assisted knowledge assessment techniques for adaptive learning environments. *Computers and Education: Artificial Intelligence*. https://doi.org/ sciencedirect.comDOI: 10.1016/j.caeai.2022.100050

Moshtari, M. & Safarpour, A. (2024). Challenges and strategies for the internationalization of higher education in low-income East African countries. *Higher Education*. https://doi.org/ springer.comDOI: 10.1007/s10734-023-00994-1

Motte-Signoret, E., Labbé, A., Benoist, G., Linglart, A., Gajdos, V., & Lapillonne, A. (2021). Perception of medical education by learners and teachers during the COVID-19 pandemic: a cross-sectional survey of online teaching. *Medical education online, 26*(1), 1919042. https://doi.org/ tandfonline.comDOI: 10.1080/10872981.2021.1919042

Munna, A. S., & Kalam, M. A. (2021). Teaching and learning process to enhance teaching effectiveness: A literature review. [IJHI]. *International Journal of Humanities and Innovation*, 4(1), 1–4. DOI: 10.33750/ijhi.v4i1.102

Oluyisola, O. E., Bhalla, S., Sgarbossa, F., & Strandhagen, J. O. (2022). Designing and developing smart production planning and control systems in the industry 4.0 era: a methodology and case study. *Journal of Intelligent Manufacturing, 33*(1), 311-332. https://doi.org/ springer.comDOI: 10.1007/s10845-021-01808-w

Ouyang, F. & Jiao, P. (2021). Artificial intelligence in education: The three paradigms. *Computers and Education: Artificial Intelligence*. https://doi.org/ sciencedirect.comDOI: 10.1016/j.caeai.2021.100020

Paek, S. & Kim, N. (2021). Analysis of worldwide research trends on the impact of artificial intelligence in education. *Sustainability*. https://doi.org/ mdpi.comDOI: 10.3390/su13147941

Pan, Y., & Zhang, L. (2023). Integrating BIM and AI for smart construction management: Current status and future directions. [HTML]. *Archives of Computational Methods in Engineering*, 30(2), 1081–1110. Advance online publication. DOI: 10.1007/s11831-022-09830-8

Pfister, R. (2022). Towards a theory of abduction based on conditionals. *Synthese*. https://doi.org/ springer.comDOI: 10.1007/s11229-022-03581-6

Platt, I. A., Hochard, K. D., Tytherleigh, M., Kannangara, C., Carson, J., McFaul, C., & North, C. (2024). The Hummingbird Project year 2: decreasing distress and fostering flourishing in a pragmatic pre–post study. *Frontiers in Psychology, 15*, 1257446. https://doi.org/ frontiersin.orgDOI: 10.3389/fpsyg.2024.1257446

Pol, R., Balagué, N., Ric, A., Torrents, C., Kiely, J., & Hristovski, R. (2020). Training or synergizing? Complex systems principles change the understanding of sport processes. *Sports Medicine-Open, 6*, 1-13. https://doi.org/ springer.comDOI: 10.1186/s40798-020-00256-9

Radez, J., Reardon, T., Creswell, C., Lawrence, P. J., Evdoka-Burton, G., & Waite, P. (2021). Why do children and adolescents (not) seek and access professional help for their mental health problems? A systematic review of quantitative and qualitative studies. *European child & adolescent psychiatry, 30*(2), 183-211. https://doi.org/ springer.comDOI: 10.1007/s00787-019-01469-4

Razmi, S. F., Moghadam, M. H., & Behname, M. (2021). Time-varying effects of monetary policy on Iranian renewable energy generation. [HTML]. *Renewable Energy*, 177, 1161–1169. Advance online publication. DOI: 10.1016/j.renene.2021.06.020

Reyes, C. T., Thompson, C. D., Lawrie, G. A., & Kyne, S. H. (2024). Insights into a Community of Inquiry that emerged during academics' emergency remote university teaching of chemistry in response to concern for students. *Research in Science & Technological Education*, 1-27. https://doi.org/ tandfonline.comDOI: 10.1080/02635143.2023.2202387

Robinson, K., McKenna, B., & Rooney, D. (2022). The relationship of risk to rules, values, virtues, and moral complexity: What we can learn from the moral struggles of military leaders. *Journal of Business Ethics*. https://doi.org/ springer.comDOI: 10.1007/s10551-021-04874-5

Sahara, S. (2022, February). Analysis of factors causing delay in unloading imported goods. In Conference on Broad Exposure to Science and Technology 2021 (BEST 2021) (pp. 345-351). *Atlantis Press*. atlantis-press.com DOI: 10.2991/aer.k.220131.051

Saks, K., Hunt, P., Leijen, Ä., & Lepp, L. (2022). To stay or not to stay: An empirical model for predicting teacher persistence. *British Journal of Educational Studies, 70*(6), 693-717. https://doi.org/ tandfonline.comDOI: 10.1080/00071005.2021.2004995

Sarker, I. H. (2021). Machine learning: Algorithms, real-world applications and research directions. *SN computer science*. https://doi.org/ springer.comDOI: 10.1007/s42979-021-00592-x

Sarker, I. H. (2022). AI-based modeling: techniques, applications and research issues towards automation, intelligent and smart systems. *SN Computer Science*. https://doi.org/ springer.comDOI: 10.1007/s42979-022-01043-x

Schiff, D. (2021). Out of the laboratory and into the classroom: the future of artificial intelligence in education. *AI & society*. https://doi.org/ springer.comDOI: 10.1007/s00146-020-01033-8

Shahbaz, M., Destek, M. A., Dong, K., & Jiao, Z. (2021). Time-varying impact of financial development on carbon emissions in G-7 countries: Evidence from the long history. *Technological Forecasting and Social Change, 171*, 120966. uni-muenchen.de Shoaib, L. A., Safii, S. H., Idris, N., Hussin, R., & Sazali, M. A. H. (2024). Utilizing decision tree machine model to map dental students' preferred learning styles with suitable instructional strategies. *BMC Medical Education, 24*(1), 58. https://doi.org/ springer.comDOI: 10.1186/s12909-023-05022-5

Sîrbu, A. (2020). Basic andragogy-oriented strategies and communication in online education. *InInternational Conference Knowledge-based Organization* (Vol. 26, No. 2, pp. 350-356). https://doi.org/ sciendo.comDOI: 10.2478/kbo-2020-0103

Spina, D., Vindigni, G., Pecorino, B., Pappalardo, G., D'Amico, M., & Chinnici, G. (2021). Identifying themes and patterns on management of horticultural innovations with an automated text analysis. *Agronomy, 11*(6), 1103. https://doi.org/ mdpi.comDOI: 10.3390/agronomy11061103

Stanney, K. M., Skinner, A., & Hughes, C. (2023). Exercisable learning-theory and evidence-based andragogy for training effectiveness using XR (ELEVATE-XR): Elevating the ROI of immersive technologies. *International Journal of Human–Computer Interaction, 39*(11), 2177-2198. https://doi.org/ tandfonline.comDOI: 10.1080/10447318.2023.2188529

Stoyanov, S., & Kirschner, P. A. (2023). Text analytics for uncovering untapped ideas at the intersection of learning design and learning analytics: Critical interpretative synthesis. *Journal of Computer Assisted Learning, 39*(3), 899-920. https://doi.org/ wiley.comDOI: 10.1016/j.aei.2021.101508

Tavakoli, M., Faraji, A., Vrolijk, J., Molavi, M., Mol, S. T., & Kismihók, G. (2022). An AI-based open recommender system for personalized labor market driven education. *Advanced Engineering Informatics, 52*, 101508. https://doi.org/ sciencedirect.comDOI: 10.1016/j.aei.2021.101508

Teng, Y., Zhang, J., & Sun, T. (2023). Data-driven decision-making model based on artificial intelligence in higher education system of colleges and universities. [HTML]. *Expert Systems: International Journal of Knowledge Engineering and Neural Networks*, 40(4), e12820. Advance online publication. DOI: 10.1111/exsy.12820

Tomaszewski, L. E., Zarestky, J., & Gonzalez, E. (2020). Planning qualitative research: Design and decision making for new researchers. *International journal of qualitative methods, 19*, 1609406920967174. https://doi.org/ sagepub.comDOI: 10.1177/1609406920967174

Travaini, G. V., Pacchioni, F., Bellumore, S., Bosia, M., & De Micco, F. (2022). Machine learning and criminal justice: A systematic review of advanced methodology for recidivism risk prediction. *International journal of environmental research and public health, 19*(17), 10594. https://doi.org/ mdpi.comDOI: 10.3390/ijerph191710594

Trunk, A., Birkel, H., & Hartmann, E. (2020). On the current state of combining human and artificial intelligence for strategic organizational decision making. *Business Research*. https://doi.org/ springer.comDOI: 10.1007/s40685-020-00133-x

Tsai, S. C., Chen, C. H., Shiao, Y. T., Ciou, J. S., & Wu, T. N. (2020). Precision education with statistical learning and deep learning: a case study in Taiwan. *International Journal of Educational Technology in Higher Education, 17*, 1-13. https://doi.org/ springer.comDOI: 10.1186/s41239-020-00186-2

Tuma, F. (2021). The use of educational technology for interactive teaching in lectures. *Annals of Medicine and Surgery*. https://doi.org/ sciencedirect.comDOI: 10.1016/j.amsu.2021.01.051

Tunca, S., Sezen, B., & Wilk, V. (2023). An exploratory content and sentiment analysis of the guardian metaverse articles using leximancer and natural language processing. *Journal of Big Data*. https://doi.org/ springer.comDOI: 10.1186/s40537-023-00773-w

Ulloa Cerna, A. E., Jing, L., Good, C. W., vanMaanen, D. P., Raghunath, S., Suever, J. D., Nevius, C. D., Wehner, G. J., Hartzel, D. N., Leader, J. B., Alsaid, A., Patel, A. A., Kirchner, H. L., Pfeifer, J. M., Carry, B. J., Pattichis, M. S., Haggerty, C. M., & Fornwalt, B. K. (2021). Deep-learning-assisted analysis of echocardiographic videos improves predictions of all-cause mortality. [HTML]. *Nature Biomedical Engineering*, 5(6), 546–554. DOI: 10.1038/s41551-020-00667-9 PMID: 33558735

Vinnervik, P. (2022). Implementing programming in school mathematics and technology: teachers' intrinsic and extrinsic challenges. *International journal of technology and design education, 32*(1), 213-242. https://doi.org/ springer.comDOI: 10.1007/s10798-020-09602-0

Wang, H., Tlili, A., Huang, R., Cai, Z., Li, M., Cheng, Z., ... & Fei, C. (2023). Examining the applications of intelligent tutoring systems in real educational contexts: A systematic literature review from the social experiment perspective. *Education and information technologies, 28*(7), 9113-9148. https://doi.org/ springer.comDOI: 10.1007/s10639-022-11555-x

Weiss, L. G., & Saklofske, D. H. (2020). Mediators of IQ test score differences across racial and ethnic groups: The case for environmental and social justice. [HTML]. *Personality and Individual Differences*, 161, 109962. Advance online publication. DOI: 10.1016/j.paid.2020.109962

Welch, C., Paavilainen-Mäntymäki, E., Piekkari, R., & Plakoyiannaki, E. (2022). Reconciling theory and context: How the case study can set a new agenda for international business research. [HTML]. *Journal of International Business Studies*, 53(1), 4–26. DOI: 10.1057/s41267-021-00484-5

Williamson, B. & Eynon, R. (). Historical threads, missing links, and future directions in AI in education. *Learning*. https://doi.org/ tandfonline.comDOI: 10.1080/17439884.2020.1798995

Zhai, X., Chu, X., Chai, C. S., Jong, M. S. Y., Istenic, A., Spector, M., ... & Li, Y. (2021). A Review of Artificial Intelligence (AI) in Education from 2010 to 2020. *Complexity*, 1-18. https://doi.org/ hindawi.comDOI: 10.1155/2021/8812542

Zhang, K. & Aslan, A. B. (2021). AI technologies for education: Recent research & future directions. *Computers and Education: Artificial Intelligence*. https://doi.org/ sciencedirect.comDOI: 10.1016/j.caeai.2021.100025

Zhao, J., Xu, X., Jiang, H., & Ding, Y. (2020). The effectiveness of virtual reality-based technology on anatomy teaching: a meta-analysis of randomized controlled studies. *BMC medical education*. https://doi.org/ springer.comDOI: 10.1186/s12909-020-1994-z

Chapter 10
AI in Education: Reflections and Future Directions for Pedagogical and Andragogical Integration

Greg Kaiser
Azusa Pacific University, USA

Sue Kaiser
California State University, San Bernardino, USA

ABSTRACT

This chapter serves as a culmination of our exploration into the integration of artificial intelligence (AI) in both pedagogical and andragogical education. It synthesizes the comprehensive analysis presented throughout the book on how AI is reshaping teaching and learning for children and adults. The chapter underscores the transformative potential of AI in creating personalized, engaging, and effective educational environments while addressing the critical challenges of data privacy, algorithmic bias, and the digital divide. Through a review of key findings, ethical considerations, and practical implications, the chapter provides a forward-looking perspective on the future of AI in education. It emphasizes the need for a collaborative effort among educators, technologists, and policymakers to harness AI's potential effectively, supported by case studies that illustrate successful implementations. The insights offered aim to inspire and guide educators, researchers, and decision-makers as they navigate the evolving landscape of AI in education.

DOI: 10.4018/979-8-3693-6130-6.ch010

INTRODUCTION

As we conclude our exploration of integrating artificial intelligence (AI) into pedagogical and andragogical education, it is essential to reflect on the journey we have undertaken. This book has comprehensively analyzed the multifaceted ways AI is transforming teaching and learning for children and adults. The synthesis of these insights not only underscores the potential of AI, but also highlights the challenges and considerations that educators must address to harness this potential effectively.

Throughout this book, we have delved into various dimensions of AI in education, exploring its implications for teaching methods, learning processes, and educational outcomes. We have examined how AI technologies can be leveraged to create more personalized, engaging, and effective learning environments. By integrating AI into educational practices, we can better meet the needs of diverse learners, provide real-time feedback, and foster a more inclusive and equitable educational landscape.

We have discussed the ethical and practical considerations that come with the adoption of AI in education. Ensuring data privacy, addressing algorithmic biases, and bridging the digital divide are crucial aspects that educators and policymakers must tackle. The successful integration of AI into education requires a collaborative effort from all stakeholders, including teachers, administrators, technologists, and policymakers. We have also examined a variety of case studies and success stories that highlight the transformative potential of AI in education, offering concrete examples of how these technologies can be implemented effectively.

This chapter examines the key findings and provides a forward-looking perspective on the future of AI in education. We will reflect on the evolution of AI technologies, their impacts on pedagogical and andragogical practices, and the ethical and practical challenges that must be addressed. By synthesizing these insights, we hope to offer a comprehensive conclusion that will inform and inspire educators, policymakers, and researchers in their work to integrate AI into education.

THE EVOLUTION OF AI IN EDUCATION

The integration of AI into education is not a new phenomenon, but its rapid evolution and increasing sophistication have made it a central topic in contemporary educational discourse. From early implementations of adaptive learning systems to the sophisticated AI-driven personalized learning environments we see today, the trajectory of AI in education has been marked by continuous innovation and improvement (Luckin et al., 2016).

AI's initial foray into education involved simple automation tasks and rudimentary adaptive learning systems. These early systems, although limited, laid the groundwork for more advanced applications. Over time, AI technologies have evolved to include complex algorithms capable of deep learning, natural language processing, and real-time data analysis, significantly enhancing their educational utility (Holmes et al., 2019).

One of the earliest examples of AI in education was the development of intelligent tutoring systems (ITS). These systems used rule-based algorithms to provide personalized instruction and feedback to students. Early ITS, such as SCHOLAR and PLATO, demonstrated the potential of AI to support individualized learning. However, these systems were constrained by their dependence on pre-programmed rules and lacked the capacity to adapt to each learner's specific needs (Wenger, 1987). For instance, SCHOLAR, developed in the 1960s, was an early ITS that provided geography instruction by responding to student queries using a large knowledge base of facts. As AI technologies advanced, so did the capabilities of educational applications. Machine learning and data mining techniques has enabled more advanced analysis of student data. Adaptive learning platforms, such as Knewton and DreamBox, emerged, leveraging AI to tailor instructional content to each student's specific needs and preferences. These platforms analyze extensive datasets to detect patterns and trends, allowing them to make real-time adjustments to the learning experience. (Pane et al., 2015). For example, Knewton's adaptive learning platform uses predictive analytics to recommend personalized learning paths, improving student outcomes in various subjects.

The development of natural language processing (NLP) technologies further expanded the possibilities for AI in education. NLP enables AI systems to understand and generate human language, providing more interactive and intuitive educational tools. For example, AI-powered chatbots can answer student queries instantly, simulate conversations, and offer personalized guidance. AI-powered content creation tools can produce personalized learning materials, such as quizzes, summaries, and flashcards, thereby enhancing the efficiency and effectiveness of teaching and learning. (Chen et al., 2020). An example is the AI-driven platform Cognii, which uses NLP to provide real-time feedback on students' written responses, promoting deeper understanding and critical thinking skills.

AI has progressed to encompass more advanced applications, including predictive analytics and machine learning. Predictive analytics can forecast student outcomes and identify at-risk students who may need additional support. This proactive approach enables educators to intervene early and provide targeted assistance, potentially improving student retention and success rates. Machine learning algorithms, conversely, can continuously learn from new data, enhancing their accuracy and effectiveness over time. This capability allows AI systems to evolve alongside educational needs and trends, ensuring they remain relevant and impactful (Aguilar, 2018).

Another significant development in AI's evolution in education is the integration of AI with other emerging technologies, such as virtual reality (VR) and augmented reality (AR). These technologies, when combined with AI, can create immersive learning environments that offer experiential learning opportunities. For instance, VR can transport students to historical events or scientific phenomena, allowing them to interact with content in ways that traditional instructional methods cannot match. AI can enhance these experiences by personalizing the content and providing real-time feedback, making the learning process more engaging and effective (Freina & Ott, 2015).

The future of AI in education is poised to bring even more innovative solutions. Developments in AI technologies, such as deep learning and neural networks, are anticipated to enhance the capabilities of educational applications further. These technologies can improve the accuracy of predictive models, enable more sophisticated data analysis, and support the development of advanced educational tools that can address complex learning needs. As AI continues to evolve, it will undoubtedly play an increasingly important role in shaping the future of education (Russell & Norvig, 2016).

Recent advancements in AI, such as the development of transformer models like GPT-4, have shown the potential to create more sophisticated educational tools. These models can generate human-like text, answer complex questions, and assist with language translation, providing new avenues for educational content creation and personalized learning experiences. For instance, AI-driven writing assistants can aid students in enhancing their writing skills by offering real-time feedback on grammar, style, and coherence, while language translation tools can support multilingual education by making content accessible in various languages (Brown et al., 2020).

Integrating AI in education also opens up new possibilities for lifelong learning and professional development. With AI-powered platforms, learners can access personalized learning resources, receive targeted recommendations, and engage in self-paced learning activities. This is particularly valuable in today's rapidly changing job market, where individuals must continuously update their skills and knowledge to stay competitive. By leveraging AI, educational institutions and employers can provide tailored learning opportunities that meet each learner's specific needs and goals, fostering a culture of continuous learning and adaptability (Baker & Inventado, 2014).

Pedagogical Impacts

In the realm of pedagogy, AI has demonstrated significant potential in enhancing student engagement, personalization, and outcomes. AI-powered tools can provide real-time feedback, adapt learning pathways based on individual student performance, and identify areas where students may need additional support. These capabilities enable a more personalized and responsive educational experience, fostering deeper engagement and understanding (Hwang et al., 2020).

One of the key benefits of AI in pedagogy is its ability to provide personalized learning experiences. Conventional teaching methods often employ a one-size-fits-all approach, which may not address individual students' diverse needs and learning styles. AI-powered adaptive learning platforms, such as ALEKS and Smart Sparrow, use algorithms to analyze student performance data and customize the content and pace of instruction accordingly. This tailored approach permits students to learn at their own pace, reinforcing concepts they find challenging and progressing quicker through material they easily grasp. (Pane et al., 2015).

AI can enhance student engagement by providing interactive and immersive learning experiences. Virtual reality (VR) and augmented reality (AR) technologies, powered by AI, can create realistic simulations and environments that make learning more engaging and enjoyable. For example, students can explore historical sites, conduct virtual science experiments, or practice language skills through immersive simulations. These experiences make learning more fun and encourage participation and deeper learning of the subject matter (Bacca et al., 2014). For instance, the use of VR in a history class can allow students to virtually visit ancient civilizations, making the subject matter more tangible and memorable.

AI-powered tools also provide timely and actionable feedback to students. In traditional classroom settings, feedback is often delayed due to the workload of teachers and the time required to grade assignments. AI-driven assessment tools, such as Gradescope and Turnitin, can automate the grading process, providing instant feedback on assignments, quizzes, and exams. AI-powered tools also provide timely and actionable feedback to students. (Gehringer, 2017). This immediate feedback loop not only enhances the learning process but also alleviates the administrative burden on teachers, enabling them to devote more time to personalized instruction and student support.

AI can facilitate differentiated instruction, a pedagogical approach that involves tailoring teaching methods and resources to meet the diverse needs of students. For example, AI-powered platforms like DreamBox Learning use adaptive algorithms to adjust the difficulty of tasks based on a student's performance in real-time. This adaptability ensures that each student is appropriately challenged, promoting growth and preventing frustration or boredom. Studies have shown that such adaptive learning technologies can significantly improve student achievement and engagement, particularly in mathematics and reading (Kulik & Fletcher, 2016).

Another significant impact of AI in pedagogy is the enhancement of collaborative learning. AI-driven tools can enhance group work by pairing students according to their skills and learning styles, promoting diverse and effective collaboration. Tools like Piazza and Slack, augmented with AI, can manage discussions, answer frequently asked questions, and provide resources, thus enhancing the collaborative learning experience. This fosters a sense of community and improves critical thinking and communication skills among students (Rosé et al., 2015).

However, the integration of AI in pedagogical settings also raises critical issues related to data privacy, equity, and the role of human teachers. Ensuring that AI tools are used ethically and inclusively is paramount. Teachers must remain central to the educational process, with AI serving as a supportive tool rather than a replacement (Williamson, 2017). Concerns about data privacy emerge from the extensive collection and analysis of student information by AI systems. It is vital to implement strong data protection measures and ensure that students' personal information is managed securely and transparently. (West, 2019).

Equity is another significant concern in the integration of AI in education. While AI has the potential to close educational gaps and offer personalized learning opportunities, it can also worsen existing inequalities if not implemented thoughtfully. AI-powered tools and resources access may be limited for students from disadvantaged backgrounds, widening the digital divide. To ensure equitable access, policymakers and educators must work together to provide the necessary infrastructure, training, and support for all students (Selwyn, 2019). For instance, initiatives such as providing free or subsidized internet access and devices to underserved communities can help bridge this gap.

The role of human teachers remains crucial in the AI-integrated classroom. While AI can offer personalized and efficient support, the importance of human interaction, empathy, and mentorship cannot be understated. Teachers bring a unique human element to education, fostering relationships, understanding individual student needs, and providing emotional and social support that AI cannot replicate. The integration of AI should enhance the teacher's role, allowing them to focus on these critical aspects rather than replace them (Darling-Hammond, 2020).

For successful implementation of AI, teachers must acquire the knowledge and skills to seamlessly integrate AI tools into their educational practices. This includes how to appropriately interpret data provided by AI systems, adapting teaching strategies based on AI-generated insights, and addressing ethical and privacy concerns. Continuous professional development programs provide the opportunity for teachers stay current with the latest advancements in AI technology and pedagogical best practices, ensuring they can apply AI to enhance their teaching and support their students (Holmes et al., 2019).

Andragogical Impacts

AI can support the principles of andragogy, which emphasize self-directed learning, experiential learning, and the application of knowledge to real-world contexts. Adult learners typically bring a wealth of prior knowledge and experience to their learning, and AI can help leverage this background to create more relevant and meaningful learning experiences. For example, AI-powered learning management systems (LMS) can analyze learners' profiles, including their work history, skills, and learning preferences, to recommend personalized learning paths and resources (Knowles et al., 2020). An example is the AI-driven platform LinkedIn Learning, which suggests courses based on users' professional backgrounds and career aspirations.

AI-driven platforms can offer flexible learning opportunities that accommodate the demanding schedules of adult learners. Online learning platforms, such as Coursera, edX, and Udacity, offer various courses and programs that learners can access anytime, anywhere. These platforms use AI to personalize the learning experience, recommend courses based on learners' interests and goals, and provide real-time feedback and support. This flexibility allows adult learners to pursue educational goals without compromising their work or personal responsibilities (Kumar et al., 2019). AI can also facilitate lifelong learning by providing continuous and adaptive learning opportunities. In today's rapidly changing world, the need for upskilling and reskilling has become increasingly important.

AI-powered platforms can assist adult learners in staying updated with the latest industry developments, acquiring new skills, and advancing their careers. For example, AI-driven recommendation engines can suggest relevant courses, articles, and resources based on learners' career goals and interests, enabling them to continuously expand their knowledge and skills (Chen et al., 2020). AI can support andragogical principles by fostering self-directed learning and critical thinking. AI-driven tools, including intelligent tutoring systems and virtual mentors, can offer personalized guidance and support, helping learners set goals, plan their learning journeys, and monitor their progress. These tools can also encourage learners to engage in reflective practice, critical thinking, and problem-solving, essential skills for lifelong learning and professional development (Gikandi et al., 2011). For instance, the AI-powered platform Replika offers a virtual mentor that helps users practice self-reflection and develop emotional intelligence.

In corporate training environments, AI-driven platforms are being used to deliver personalized and scalable training programs. IBM's Watson, for instance, is utilized to create customized learning paths for employees, providing them with tailored content that aligns with their career development goals. This has significantly improved employee engagement and skill acquisition (Marr, 2018). Such applications highlight the potential of AI to support continuous professional development and ensure that adult learners can keep pace with industry advancements.

However, similar to pedagogical contexts, there are challenges to address in the integration of AI in andragogical education. Providing access to AI tools is accessible for all adult learners, regardless of their technological proficiency, is essential. Many adult learners may have limited experience with digital technologies, and providing adequate training and support is vital to ensure effective use of AI-powered tools. It is important to ensure that AI tools support rather than hinder the development of critical thinking and self-directed learning skills. AI should be used as a supportive tool that enhances learners' autonomy and critical thinking, rather than as a substitute for these essential skills (Williamson, 2017).

There is a need for continuous assessment and improvement of AI-driven educational tools to ensure they meet the evolving needs of adult learners. Regular feedback from users can help developers refine these tools, making them more effective and user-friendly. Collaborative efforts between educators, technologists, and learners are essential to create AI solutions that truly enhance the learning experience (Holmes et al., 2019).

The integration of AI in andragogical education must consider the diverse backgrounds and experiences of adult learners. AI tools should be designed to be culturally responsive and inclusive, recognizing the unique challenges faced by learners from different socio-economic, cultural, and professional backgrounds. This requires a concerted effort from developers and educators to ensure that AI systems are not only technically proficient but also socially aware and sensitive to the needs of all learners (Brookfield, 2013).

The use of AI in andragogical education can support the development of essential soft skills, such as communication, collaboration, and emotional intelligence. AI-powered simulations and virtual reality environments can create realistic scenarios where learners can practice these skills in a safe and controlled setting. For example, AI-driven virtual reality training programs in the healthcare industry allow medical professionals to practice patient interactions, improving their communication and empathy skills. Such applications demonstrate AI's potential to enhance technical skills and interpersonal competencies that are crucial for success in various professional contexts (Zary et al., 2019).

Case Studies and Success Stories

Throughout this book, we have examined a variety of case studies that highlighted the transformative impact of AI in education. These examples demonstrate how AI can enhance learning experiences, improve educational outcomes, and support educators in their teaching practices. From AI-powered tutoring systems to intelligent content creation tools, the possibilities are vast and varied.

One notable case study involved the use of an AI-driven platform in a K-12 setting, where the technology was used to personalize learning paths for students. The results showed significant improvements in student engagement and academic performance, highlighting the potential of AI to revolutionize traditional educational models (Pane et al., 2015). In a middle school in California, the implementation of an AI-powered adaptive learning platform resulted in a 20% increase in math scores and a 15% increase in reading comprehension scores over a single academic year. Teachers reported that the platform helped identify students' learning gaps and provided targeted interventions, significantly enhancing the overall learning experience (Pane et al., 2015).

In higher education, another case study focused on an AI system designed to assist with grading and providing feedback on assignments. The system not only reduced the workload for instructors but also provided timely and detailed feedback to students, enhancing their learning experience (Breslow et al., 2013). At a university in the United Kingdom, the implementation of an AI-driven grading system for essay assignments led to a 30% reduction in grading time for instructors and improved the quality of feedback provided to students. Students reported higher satisfaction with the feedback received, as it was more detailed, specific, and actionable, helping them improve their writing skills (Breslow et al., 2013).

AI-powered tools can support language learning and cultural exchange programs. For example, Duolingo, an AI-driven language learning platform, has successfully helped millions of users worldwide learn new languages through personalized and gamified learning experiences. The platform uses AI algorithms to adapt to the difficulty and content of lessons based on users' progress, ensuring a tailored learning experience that keeps learners engaged and motivated (Settles et al., 2018). Duolingo's success story demonstrates how AI can make language learning more accessible and enjoyable, breaking down language barriers and fostering cross-cultural understanding (Settles et al., 2018).

Another success story comes from the corporate training sector, where AI-powered platforms enhance employee training and development programs. For instance, IBM's Watson AI developed personalized learning experiences for employees, providing customized training modules, career recommendations, and real-time support. Implementing Watson AI in IBM's training programs resulted in a 50% increase in employee engagement and a 30% improvement in skill acquisition and retention. This case study highlights the potential of AI to support continuous learning and professional development in the workplace (Marr, 2018).

In addition to these examples, AI has also been used to support special education. Tools like the AI-powered app KidSense use speech recognition technology to help children with speech and language difficulties improve their communication skills. By providing real-time feedback and personalized exercises, KidSense has helped many children make significant progress in their speech development. This application of AI demonstrates its potential to provide targeted support to students with special needs, improving their educational outcomes and overall quality of life (Golonka et al., 2014).

AI has been instrumental in facilitating remote learning, particularly during the COVID-19 pandemic. AI-driven platforms like Google Classroom and Microsoft Teams have enabled schools to transition to online learning seamlessly. These platforms use AI to manage administrative tasks, facilitate communication, and provide personalized learning resources, ensuring that students can continue their education despite disruptions. The success of these platforms during the pandemic underscores the importance of AI in supporting flexible and resilient educational systems (Huang et al., 2020).

AI-powered platforms like Khan Academy have played a crucial role in democratizing education by providing free access to high-quality educational content worldwide. During the COVID-19 pandemic, Khan Academy saw a significant increase in users, with millions of students and teachers relying on the platform for remote learning. The platform uses AI to personalize learning paths, provide instant feedback, and offer resources tailored to individual student needs. This widespread adoption and impact highlight the potential of AI to make education more accessible and equitable on a global scale (Khan, 2020).

AI has been used to develop innovative assessment tools that provide more holistic evaluations of student performance. Platforms like Gradescope use AI to assist in grading complex assignments, such as essays and coding projects. These tools can identify patterns, provide detailed feedback, and ensure consistency and fairness in grading. By automating repetitive tasks, AI frees up educators' time, allowing them to focus on more meaningful interactions with students and support their learning more effectively (Piech et al., 2015).

Impact on Policy Development

The integration of AI into education has profound implications for policy development at local, national, and international levels. Policymakers must consider the regulatory frameworks, ethical guidelines, and strategic plans necessary to support the effective and responsible use of AI in education. The following subsections discuss key areas where AI impacts policy development and the steps needed to address these issues.

Data Privacy and Security Policies

One of the most critical policy areas impacted by AI in education is data privacy and security. AI systems rely on large datasets, often containing sensitive personal information about students, teachers, and educational institutions. Policymakers must develop robust data privacy and security regulations to protect this information from misuse and breaches. These policies should define clear guidelines for data collection, storage, processing, and sharing practices. (West, 2019). The General Data Protection Regulation (GDPR) in the European Union sets stringent standards for data protection and privacy. Educational institutions using AI must ensure compliance with such regulations to safeguard the personal information of their students and staff. Policymakers should also promote transparency by requiring institutions to inform stakeholders about data usage practices and secure informed consent for data collection and processing (Regan & Jesse, 2019).

Policies must address the ethical use of data in AI systems. This includes ensuring that data is used to promote educational goals and not for commercial exploitation. The Family Educational Rights and Privacy Act (FERPA) in the United States provides guidelines on the use and protection of student data, emphasizing the need for consent and transparency. Policymakers can look to such regulations as models for developing comprehensive data privacy policies that protect students' rights while allowing for the innovative use of AI in education (Schneider, 2020).

Access and Equity

AI has the potential to both bridge and widen educational disparities, depending on how it is implemented. Policymakers must develop strategies to ensure equitable access to AI-powered educational tools and resources, particularly for students from disadvantaged backgrounds. This may involve investing in infrastructure, such as high-speed internet and digital devices, and providing financial support to schools and communities in need (Selwyn, 2019).

Policies should promote digital literacy and competency among students and educators. It is essential to offer training and professional development opportunities to ensure that all stakeholders have the skills and knowledge needed to effectively utilize AI technologies. Policymakers should also encourage the development of AI tools that are accessible and user-friendly for individuals with varying levels of technological proficiency (Holmes et al., 2019). Initiatives like the Digital India campaign aim to enhance digital infrastructure and literacy across the country, ensuring that students in rural and underserved areas have access to digital learning resources. Such policies can serve as models for other countries looking to bridge the digital divide and ensure that AI technologies benefit all students, regardless of their socio-economic background (Pradhan & Dash, 2017).

Policies should address the affordability of AI-powered educational tools and resources. This may involve partnerships between governments, educational institutions, and technology companies to provide subsidized or free access to AI tools for schools and students in need. Policymakers can promote a more equitable educational environment by ensuring that financial constraints do not restrict access to AI technologies, where all students have the opportunity to benefit from personalized and engaging learning experiences (Selwyn, 2019)

Teacher Training and Professional Development

Substantial investment in teacher training and professional development is essential for successfully integrating AI in education. Policymakers should endorse initiatives that equip educators with the skills and knowledge to successfully incorporate AI tools into their teaching practices. This may involve funding for training programs, workshops, and online courses that focus on AI literacy and its applications in education (Popenici & Kerr, 2017).

Policies should also encourage the incorporation of AI-related content into teacher education programs. By embedding AI literacy into the curriculum, future educators can be better prepared to leverage AI technologies in their classrooms. Ongoing professional development training should be provided to ensure educators remain current with the latest advancements and best practices in AI integration. (Luckin et al., 2016). The Future of Learning Fund in the UK provides grants to schools and educational institutions for the professional development of teachers in AI and digital technologies. These initiatives can act as examples for other countries aiming to enhance the digital skills of their educators and ensure that they can effectively integrate AI into their teaching practices (BESA, 2019).

Teacher training programs should focus on developing critical thinking and ethical decision-making skills in the context of AI. Educators must recognize the potential biases and ethical implications of AI technologies and be equipped to address these issues in their classrooms. Encouraging a culture of ethical awareness and responsibility, teacher training programs can ensure that educators are prepared to use AI tools in ways that promote fairness, equity, and student well-being (Holmes et al., 2019).

Research and Innovation

Promoting research and innovation in AI for education is essential for driving progress and addressing the challenges associated with its integration. Policymakers should support funding for research initiatives that explore the development and impact of AI technologies in educational settings. Collaborative partnerships between educational institutions, technology companies, and research organizations can foster innovation and ensure that AI solutions are evidence-based and effective (Holmes et al., 2019).

Policies should also encourage the dissemination of research findings and best practices to inform policy development and educational practice. By creating platforms for knowledge exchange and collaboration, policymakers can help build a robust evidence base that supports the responsible and effective use of AI in education (Chen et al., 2020). The US National Science Foundation (NSF) funds research projects that explore the integration of AI in education, supporting studies on the effectiveness of AI-driven learning tools and the development of ethical guidelines for AI use. Such initiatives not only advance the understanding of AI's impact on education but also provide valuable insights for policymakers and educators seeking to implement AI technologies in their institutions (National Science Foundation, 2018).

Innovation hubs and incubators can play a crucial role in fostering the development of new AI technologies for education. These hubs can bring together researchers, educators, and technology developers to collaborate on innovative solutions that address the specific needs and challenges of educational settings. By supporting these collaborative environments, policymakers can help drive the creation of cutting-edge AI tools that enhance teaching and learning (Luckin et al., 2016).

International Collaboration

The global nature of AI development and its applications in education necessitates international collaboration and cooperation. Policymakers should collaborate internationally to establish shared standards and guidelines for the ethical and responsible implementation of AI in education. International organizations, such as UNESCO and the OECD, can be instrumental in fostering dialogue and coordination among countries. (UNESCO, 2019).

Collaborative efforts can ensure that AI technologies are developed and implemented in ways that advance global educational goals, including equity, inclusion, and quality education for all. By sharing resources, knowledge, and best practices, countries can collectively address the challenges and opportunities associated with AI in education (OECD, 2019). The AI for Education initiative by UNESCO aims to promote the ethical use of AI in education and foster international collaboration on

AI-related research and policy development. The initiative brings together experts from various countries to share insights, develop guidelines, and support the implementation of AI technologies in educational systems worldwide. Such collaborative efforts can help ensure that AI technologies align with global educational objectives and promote equity and inclusion. (UNESCO, 2019).

The Future of AI in Education

Looking ahead, the future of AI in education is both exciting and challenging. Developments in AI technologies, including natural language processing, machine learning, and cognitive computing, will continue to create new opportunities for personalized and adaptive learning. However, the effective integration of AI into education will rely on our ability to tackle the associated challenges and ensure that these technologies are employed in ways that are ethical, inclusive, and aligned with educational objectives. (Chen et al., 2020).

Natural language processing (NLP) is one of the most promising areas of AI in education. NLP enables AI systems to understand, interpret, and generate human language, facilitating more interactive and intuitive learning experiences. For example, AI-powered chatbots can answer student queries instantly, simulate conversations, and offer personalized guidance. These chatbots can be used to support language learning, provide tutoring in various subjects, and assist with administrative tasks. As NLP technologies advance, more sophisticated and human-like interactions between students and AI systems will occur, thereby enhancing the overall learning experience. (Chen et al., 2020).

Machine learning, a branch of AI that analyzes large data sets and make predictions or decisions, holds substantial potential in the educational sector. Machine learning can analyze student performance data, identify learning patterns, and predict future outcomes. For example, predictive analytics can identify students at risk and provide timely interventions to support their learning. Machine learning can be employed to develop adaptive learning platforms that continuously adjusts the pacing of instruction based on individual student performance, providing a truly personalized learning experience (Luckin et al., 2016).

Cognitive computing, which involves simulating human thought processes in AI systems, offers exciting possibilities for enhancing critical thinking and problem-solving skills. Cognitive computing systems can analyze vast amounts of data, generate insights, and provide recommendations to support decision-making. In education, cognitive computing can be used to develop intelligent tutoring systems that provide personalized guidance and feedback, fostering deeper understanding and critical thinking. For example, an AI-powered tutoring system can guide students through complex problem-solving tasks, encouraging critical thinking and apply their knowledge in new ways (Holmes et al., 2019).

However, successfully integrating these advanced AI technologies in education requires careful consideration of ethical, practical, and pedagogical issues. Ensuring data privacy, addressing algorithmic bias, and bridging the digital divide remain critical challenges that must be addressed. It is essential to provide adequate training and support to educators and students to ensure they can effectively use AI-powered tools. Policymakers and educational leaders must work together to develop guidelines and policies that promote the ethical and inclusive use of AI in education (Selwyn, 2019).

The future of AI in education also hinges on developing a culture of innovation and collaboration. Educational institutions, technology companies, researchers, and policymakers must work together to explore new possibilities, share best practices, and address common challenges. Collaborative initiatives, such as research partnerships, pilot programs, and professional development networks, can help accelerate the adoption and integration of AI in education. By nurturing a collaborative and innovative mindset, the potential of AI to revolutionize teaching and learning can be fully leveraged. (Holmes et al., 2019).

One promising area for future research is the development of AI systems understands and adapts to the emotional and social needs of learners. Affective computing, a field of study that explores the development of systems that can recognize and respond to human emotions, has the potential to create more empathetic and supportive educational environments. For example, AI systems could use facial recognition and voice analysis to detect when a student is frustrated or confused and provide appropriate support and encouragement. This could enhance the overall learning experience and improve student outcomes (Picard, 1997).

The future of AI in education may involve the integration of AI with other emerging technologies, such as blockchain and the Internet of Things (IoT). Blockchain technology can provide secure and transparent record-keeping for educational credentials and achievements, while IoT devices can create smart learning environments that adapt to the needs of students in real-time. These technologies, when combined with AI, have the potential to create more efficient, secure, and personalized educational systems (Grech & Camilleri, 2017).

The future of AI in education could see the rise of AI-driven virtual classrooms that provide immersive and interactive learning experiences. These virtual classrooms can recreate real-world settings and scenarios, enabling students to participate in hands-on learning activities and collaborate with peers globally. simulated environment, offering a safe and cost-effective alternative to traditional lab setups. Such innovations can revolutionize the way we approach education, making learning more accessible, engaging, and effective (Freina & Ott, 2015).

The future of AI in education may involve the development of AI systems that can support personalized learning plans for students with special needs. By evaluating individual learning profiles and tailoring instructional strategies accordingly, AI can facilitate the creation of more inclusive learning environments that address the diverse needs of all students. AI-powered assistive technologies, such as speech recognition and text-to-speech tools, can provide personalized support to students with disabilities, enhancing their learning experiences and promoting their academic success (Holmes et al., 2019).

CONCLUSION AND FINAL THOUGHTS

In conclusion, the integration of AI into pedagogical and andragogical education offers tremendous potential to enhance and transform teaching and learning. By harnessing AI's capabilities, educators can develop effective learning experiences for students of all ages. However, realizing AI's potential requires careful consideration of ethical, practical, and pedagogical issues. As AI continues to evolve, it is essential to understand its educational potential, promoting a collaborative and informed approach to its integration. By doing so, we can ensure that AI serves as an increasingly powerful tool to support and enhance education, empowering learners and educators alike.

Thank you for joining us on this journey. We hope that this book has provided valuable insights and inspired new ideas for integrating AI into pedagogical and andragogical education. The future of education is bright, and with thoughtful and responsible integration of AI, we can create a more equitable, effective, and engaging educational landscape for all.

REFERENCES

Aguilar, S. J. (2018). Learning analytics: At the nexus of big data, digital innovation, and social justice in education. *TechTrends*, 62(1), 37–45. DOI: 10.1007/s11528-017-0226-9

Bacca, J., Baldiris, S., Fabregat, R., & Graf, S., & Kinshuk. (2014). Augmented reality trends in education: A systematic review of research and applications. *Journal of Educational Technology & Society*, 17(4), 133–149.

Binns, R. (2018). Fairness in machine learning: Lessons from political philosophy. In *Proceedings of the 2018 Conference on Fairness, Accountability, and Transparency* (pp. 149-159).

Breslow, L., Pritchard, D. E., DeBoer, J., Stump, G. S., Ho, A. D., & Seaton, D. T. (2013). Studying learning in the worldwide classroom: Research into edX's first MOOC. *Research & Practice in Assessment*, 8, 13–25.

Chen, X., Zou, D., Cheng, G., & Xie, H. (2020). Detecting and addressing students' problematic learning behaviors in MOOCs: A neural network-based approach. *Computers in Human Behavior*, 104, 106159.

Floridi, L., Cowls, J., Beltrametti, M., Chatila, R., Chazerand, P., Dignum, V., Luetge, C., Madelin, R., Pagallo, U., Rossi, F., Schafer, B., Valcke, P., & Vayena, E. (2018). AI4People—An ethical framework for a good AI society: Opportunities, risks, principles, and recommendations. *Minds and Machines*, 28(4), 689–707. DOI: 10.1007/s11023-018-9482-5 PMID: 30930541

Freina, L., & Ott, M. (2015). A literature review on immersive virtual reality in education: State of the art and perspectives. In *The International Scientific Conference eLearning and Software for Education* (pp. 133-141). DOI: 10.12753/2066-026X-15-020

Gikandi, J. W., Morrow, D., & Davis, N. E. (2011). Online formative assessment in higher education: A review of the literature. *Computers & Education*, 57(4), 2333–2351. DOI: 10.1016/j.compedu.2011.06.004

Golonka, E. M., Bowles, A. R., Frank, V. M., Richardson, D. L., & Freynik, S. (2014). Technologies for foreign language learning: A review of technology types and their effectiveness. *Computer Assisted Language Learning*, 27(1), 70–105. DOI: 10.1080/09588221.2012.700315

Grech, A., & Camilleri, A. F. (2017). *Blockchain in education*. Publications Office of the European Union.

Holmes, W., Bialik, M., & Fadel, C. (2019). *Artificial intelligence in education: Promises and implications for teaching and learning*. Center for Curriculum Redesign.

Huang, R. H., Liu, D. J., Tlili, A., Yang, J. F., & Wang, H. H. (2020). *Handbook on facilitating flexible learning during educational disruption: The Chinese experience in maintaining undisrupted learning in COVID-19 outbreak*. Smart Learning Institute of Beijing Normal University.

Hwang, G. J., Xie, H., Wah, B. W., & Gasevic, D. (2020). Vision, challenges, roles, and research issues of artificial intelligence in education. *Computers & Education: Artificial Intelligence*, 1, 100001.

Knowles, M. S., Holton, E. F.III, & Swanson, R. A. (2020). *The adult learner: The definitive classic in adult education and human resource development* (9th ed.). Routledge. DOI: 10.4324/9780429299612

Kulik, J. A., & Fletcher, J. D. (2016). Effectiveness of intelligent tutoring systems: A meta-analytic review. *Review of Educational Research*, 86(1), 42–78. DOI: 10.3102/0034654315581420

Luckin, R., Holmes, W., Griffiths, M., & Forcier, L. B. (2016). *Intelligence unleashed: An argument for AI in education*. Pearson Education.

Marr, B. (2018). How IBM is using AI, IoT, and blockchain to transform the food industry. *Forbes*.

OECD. (2019). *AI in education: Challenges and opportunities for sustainable development*. OECD Publishing.

Pane, J. F., Steiner, E. D., Baird, M. D., & Hamilton, L. S. (2015). *Continued progress: Promising evidence on personalized learning*. RAND Corporation. DOI: 10.7249/RR1365

Picard, R. W. (1997). *Affective computing*. MIT Press. DOI: 10.7551/mitpress/1140.001.0001

Popenici, S. A., & Kerr, S. (2017). Exploring the impact of artificial intelligence on teaching and learning in higher education. *Research and Practice in Technology Enhanced Learning*, 12(1), 22. DOI: 10.1186/s41039-017-0062-8 PMID: 30595727

Regan, P. M., & Jesse, J. (2019). Ethical challenges of edtech, big data and personalized learning: Twenty-first century student sorting and tracking. *Ethics and Information Technology*, 21(3), 167–179. DOI: 10.1007/s10676-018-9492-2

Rosé, C. P., Wang, Y. C., Cui, Y., Arguello, J., Stegmann, K., Weinberger, A., & Fischer, F. (2015). Analyzing collaborative learning processes automatically: Exploiting the advances of computational linguistics in computer-supported collaborative learning. *International Journal of Computer-Supported Collaborative Learning*, 3(3), 237–271. DOI: 10.1007/s11412-007-9034-0

Russell, S. J., & Norvig, P. (2021). *Artificial intelligence: A modern approach* (4th ed.). Pearson.

Selwyn, N. (2019). Should robots replace teachers? AI and the future of education. *British Journal of Educational Technology*, 50(6), 1263–1272.

Settles, B., Brust, C., Gustafson, E., Hagiwara, M., & Madnani, N. (2018). Second language acquisition modeling. In *Proceedings of the Thirteenth Workshop on Innovative Use of NLP for Building Educational Applications* (pp. 56-65). DOI: 10.18653/v1/W18-0506

UNESCO. (2019). *Artificial intelligence in education: Challenges and opportunities for sustainable development*. UNESCO Publishing.

Wenger, E. (1987). *Artificial intelligence and tutoring systems: Computational and cognitive approaches to the communication of knowledge*. Morgan Kaufmann Publishers.

West, S. M. (2019). Data capitalism: Redefining the logics of surveillance and privacy. *Business & Society*, 58(1), 20–41. DOI: 10.1177/0007650317718185

Williamson, B. (2017). Decoding ClassDojo: Psycho-policy, social-emotional learning and persuasive educational technologies. *Learning, Media and Technology*, 42(4), 440–453. DOI: 10.1080/17439884.2017.1278020

Compilation of References

AbuSahyon, A. S. E., Alzyoud, A., Alshorman, O., & Al-Absi, B. (2023). AI-driven technology and thatbots as tools for enhancing English language learning in the context of second language acquisition: A review study. *International Journal of Membrane Science and Technology*, 10(1), 1209–1223. DOI: 10.15379/ijmst.v10i1.2829

Adams, C., Pente, P., Lemermeyer, G., & Rockwell, G. (2023). Ethical principles for artificial intelligence in K-12 education. *Computers and Education: Artificial Intelligence*, 4, 100131.

Afini Normadhi, N. B., Shuib, L., Md Nasir, H. N., Bimba, A., Idris, N., & Balakrishnan, V. (2019). Identification of personal traits in adaptive learning environment: Systematic literature review. *Computers & Education*, 130, 168–190. https://doi.org/10.1016/j.compedu.2018.11.005

Aguilar, S. J. (2018). Learning analytics: At the nexus of big data, digital innovation, and social justice in education. *TechTrends*, 62(1), 37–45. DOI: 10.1007/s11528-017-0226-9

Akatsuka, Y. (2019). Awareness of critical thinking attitudes and English speaking skills: The effects of questions involving higher-order thinking. *Journal of Pan-Pacific Association of Applied Linguistics*, 23(2), 59–84. DOI: 10.25256/PAAL.23.2.4

Akbulut, Y., & Cardak, C. S. (2012). Adaptive educational hypermedia accommodating learning styles: A content analysis of publications from 2000 to 2011. *Computers & Education*, 58(2), 835–842. https://doi.org/10.1016/j.compedu.2011.10.008

Akgun, S., & Greenhow, C. (2022). Artificial intelligence in education: Addressing ethical challenges in K-12 settings. *AI and Ethics*, 2(3), 431–440. https://doi.org/10.1007/s43681-021-00096-7

Alghamdy, R. Z. (2024). English teachers' practice of classroom discourse in light of zone of proximal development theory and scaffolding techniques. *Journal of Language Teaching and Researh*, 15(1), 46–54. DOI: 10.17507/jltr.1501.06

Ali, S. S. (2019). Problem based learning: A student-centered approach. *English Language Teaching*, 12(5), 73. Advance online publication. DOI: 10.5539/elt.v12n5p73

Allen, T., Villaflor-Wilson, R., Muljana, P., & Romero-Hall, E. (2024). AI-generated content: guidelines, higher-order thinking skills, and copyrights. *Education Technology Journal, 4*(1)1-5. https://journal.unesa.ac.id/index.php/etj

Allen, S. J., Rosch, D. M., & Riggio, R. E. (2022). Advancing leadership education and development: Integrating adult learning theory. [HTML]. *Journal of Management Education*, 46(2), 252–283. DOI: 10.1177/10525629211008645

Almaraz-Menéndez, F., Maz-Machado, A., López-Esteban, C., & Almaraz-López, C. (Eds.). (2022). *Strategy, policy, practice, and governance for AI in higher education institutions.* IGI Global.

Alshahrani, A. (2023). The impact of ChatGPT on blended learning: Current trends and future research directions. *International Journal of Data and Network Science*, 7(4), 2029–2040. DOI: 10.5267/j.ijdns.2023.6.010

AlShaikh, F., & Hewahi, N. (2021, September). Ai and machine learning techniques in the development of Intelligent Tutoring System: A review. *In 2021 International Conference on innovation and Intelligence for informatics, computing, and technologies* (3ICT) (pp. 403-410). IEEE. [HTML]DOI: 10.1109/3ICT53449.2021.9582029

Andréfouët, S. & Bionaz, O. (2021). Lessons from a global remote sensing mapping project. A review of the impact of the Millennium Coral Reef Mapping Project for science and management. *Science of the Total Environment.* sciencedirect.comDOI: 10.1016/j.scitotenv.2021.145987

Annas, J. (2011). *Intelligent virtue*. Oxford University Press. DOI: 10.1093/acprof:oso/9780199228782.001.0001

Aslan, S. (2022). The Predictive Role of the Primary School Teachers' Educational Beliefs on Their Curriculum Design Orientation Preferences. *International Journal of Psychology and Educational Studies, 9*(3), 765-781. https://dx.doi.org/ed.govDOI: 10.52380/ijpes.2022.9.3.776

Ayedoun, E., Hayashi, Y., & Seta, K. (2019). Adding communicative and affective strategies to an embodied conversational agent to enhance second language learners' willingness to communicate. *International Journal of Artificial Intelligence in Education*, 29(1), 29–57. DOI: 10.1007/s40593-018-0171-6

Ayeni, O. O., Al Hamad, N. M., Chisom, O. N., Osawaru, B., & Adewusi, O. E. (2024). AI in education: A review of personalized learning and educational technology. *GSC Advanced Research and Reviews*, 18(2), 261–271. https://doi.org/10.30574/gscarr.2024.18.2.0062

Azevedo, R., Bouchet, F., Duffy, M., Harley, J., Taub, M., Trevors, G., ... & Cerezo, R. (2022). Lessons learned and future directions of MetaTutor: Leveraging multichannel data to scaffold self-regulated learning with an intelligent tutoring system. *Frontiers in Psychology, 13*, 813632. https://doi.org/ frontiersin.orgDOI: 10.3389/fpsyg.2022.813632

Bacca, J., Baldiris, S., Fabregat, R., & Graf, S., & Kinshuk. (2014). Augmented reality trends in education: A systematic review of research and applications. *Journal of Educational Technology & Society*, 17(4), 133–149.

Badali, M., Hatami, J., Banihashem, S. K., Rahimi, E., Noroozi, O., & Eslami, Z. (2022). The role of motivation in MOOCs' retention rates: a systematic literature review. *Research and Practice in Technology Enhanced Learning, 17*(1), 5. https://doi.org/ springer.comDOI: 10.1186/s41039-022-00181-3

Baek, E., & Wilson, M. (2024). Boon or bane: An inquiry into the use of generative ai (artificial intelligence) and its implications in education. In J. Cohen & G. Solano (Eds.), *Proceedings of Society for Information Technology & Teacher Education International Conference* (pp. 1971-1976). Las Vegas, Nevada, United States: Association for the Advancement of Computing in Education (AACE). https://www.learntechlib.org/primary/p/224243/

Bahroun, Z., Anane, C., Ahmed, V., & Zacca, A. (2023). Transforming education: A comprehensive review of generative artificial intelligence in educational settings through bibliometric and content analysis. *Sustainability*, 15(17), 12983. https://doi.org/10.3390/su151712983

Bai, C., Dallasega, P., Orzes, G., & Sarkis, J. (2020). Industry 4.0 technologies assessment: A sustainability perspective. *International journal of production economics, 229*, 107776. https://doi.org/ sciencedirect.comDOI: 10.1016/j.ijpe.2020.107776

Baker, R. S., & Hawn, A. (2021). Algorithmic bias in education. *Journal of Educational Data Mining*, 13(2), 1–22.

Baker, T., & Hawn, O. (2021). Algorithmic fairness in education. *Educational Technology Research and Development*, 69(2), 423–442. DOI: 10.1007/s11423-021-09914-4

Bates, T., Cobo, C., Mariño, O., & Wheeler, S. (2020). Can artificial intelligence transform higher education?. *International Journal of Educational Technology in Higher Education, 17*, 1-12. https://doi.org/ springer.comDOI: 10.1186/s41239-020-00218-x

Bello, C. (n.d.). *These AI tools could help boost your academic research.* Euronews. https://www.euronews.com/next/2024/01/20/best-ai-tools-academic-research-chatgpt-consensus-chatpdf-elicit-research-rabbit-scite

Bereczki, E. O. & Kárpáti, A. (2021). Technology-enhanced creativity: A multiple case study of digital technology-integration expert teachers' beliefs and practices. *Thinking Skills and Creativity*. https://doi.org/ sciencedirect.comDOI: 10.1016/j.tsc.2021.100791

Berendt, B., Littlejohn, A., & Blakemore, M. (2020). AI in education: Learner choice and fundamental rights. *Learning, Media and Technology*, 45(3), 312–324. ucl.ac.uk. DOI: 10.1080/17439884.2020.1786399

Bernacki, M. L., Greene, M. J., & Lobczowski, N. G. (2021). A systematic review of research on personalized learning: Personalized by whom, to what, how, and for what Purpose(s)? *Educational Psychology Review*, 33(4), 1675–1715. https://doi.org/10.1007/s10648-021-09615-8

Bhutoria, A. (2022). Personalized education and artificial intelligence in the United States, China, and India: A systematic review using a human-in-the-loop model. *Computers and Education: Artificial Intelligence*. https://doi.org/ sciencedirect.comDOI: 10.1016/j.caeai.2022.100068

Binns, R. (2018). Fairness in machine learning: Lessons from political philosophy. In *Proceedings of the 2018 Conference on Fairness, Accountability, and Transparency* (pp. 149–159).

Biswas, A. & Wang, H. C. (2023). Autonomous vehicles enabled by the integration of IoT, edge intelligence, 5G, and blockchain. *Sensors*. https://doi.org/ mdpi.comDOI: 10.3390/s23041963

Bloom, B. S. (1984). The 2 sigma problem: The search for methods of group instruction as effective as one-to-one tutoring. *Educational Researcher*, 13(6), 4. https://doi.org/10.2307/1175554

Bobula, M. (2024). Generative Artificial Intelligence (AI) in higher education: A comprehensive review of challenges, opportunities, and implications. *Journal of Learning Development in Higher Education*, 30(30). Advance online publication. DOI: 10.47408/jldhe.vi30.1137

Bonwell, C. C., & Eison, J. A. (1991). Active learning: creating excitement in the classroom. *1991 ASHE-ERIC Higher Education Reports, ERIC Clearinghouse on Higher Education.*https://eric.ed.gov/?id=ED336049

Boroujeni, S. P. H., Razi, A., Khoshdel, S., Afghah, F., Coen, J. L., O'Neill, L., Fule, P., Watts, A., Kokolakis, N.-M. T., & Vamvoudakis, K. G. (2024). A comprehensive survey of research towards ai-enabled unmanned aerial systems in pre-, active-, and post-wildfire management. [HTML]. *Information Fusion*, 108, 102369. DOI: 10.1016/j.inffus.2024.102369

Bowers, A. J., Bang, A., Pan, Y., & Graves, K. E. (2019). Education Leadership Data Analytics (ELDA): A White Paper Report on the 2018 ELDA Summit. *Online Submission*.

Bozkurt, A., Karadeniz, A., Baneres, D., Guerrero-Roldán, A. E., & Rodríguez, M. E. (2021). Artificial intelligence and reflections from educational landscape: A review of AI Studies in half a century. *Sustainability, 13*(2), 800. https://doi.org/ mdpi.comDOI: 10.3390/su13020800

Bozkurt, A., & Sharma, R. C. (2023). Challenging the status quo and exploring the new boundaries in the age of algorithms: Reimagining the role of generative AI in distance education and online learning. *Asian Journal of Distance Education*, 18(1), 1–8. DOI: 10.5281/zenodo.7755273

Breslow, L., Pritchard, D. E., DeBoer, J., Stump, G. S., Ho, A. D., & Seaton, D. T. (2013). Studying learning in the worldwide classroom: Research into edX's first MOOC. *Research & Practice in Assessment*, 8, 13–25.

Brooke, J. & Clark, M. (2020). Older people's early experience of household isolation and social distancing during COVID-19. *Journal of Clinical Nursing*. https:// doi.org/ wiley.comDOI: 10.1111/jocn.15485

Brookfield, S. D. (2005). *The power of critical theory*. Jossey-Bass.

Brown, H. D. (2007). *Principles of language learning and teaching: A course in second language acquisition* (5th ed.). Pearson.

Bruce, B. C., & Casey, L. (2012). The practice of inquiry: A pedagogical 'Sweet spot' for digital literacy? *Computers in the Schools*, 29(1-2), 191–206. DOI: 10.1080/07380569.2012.657994

Bulathwela, S., Perez-Ortiz, M., Holloway, C., & Shawe-Taylor, J. (2021). Could AI democratize education? *Socio-Technical Imaginaries of an EdTech Revolution.*

Cai, M. (2020). Privacy concerns with AI in schools. *Journal of Educational Technology*, 47(1), 23–35. DOI: 10.1177/0047239520934019

California Department of Education. (2024). Artificial intelligence in California schools. California Department of Education. https://www.cde.ca.gov/ci/pl/aiincalifornia.asp

California Department of Education. (n.d.). Learning With AI, Learning About AI - Professional Learning (CA Dept of Education). Retrieved from https://www.cde.ca.gov/ci/pl/aiincalifornia.asp

Callanan, M. A., Legare, C. H., Sobel, D. M., Jaeger, G. J., Letourneau, S., McHugh, S. R., Willard, A., Brinkman, A., Finiasz, Z., Rubio, E., Barnett, A., Gose, R., Martin, J. L., Meisner, R., & Watson, J. (2020). Exploration, explanation, and parent–child interaction in museums. [nih.gov]. *Monographs of the Society for Research in Child Development*, 85(1), 7–137. DOI: 10.1111/mono.12412 PMID: 32175600

Cardona, M. A., Rodríguez, R. J., & Ishmael, K. (2023). Artificial intelligence and the future of teaching and learning: Insights and recommendations. U.S. Department of Education, Office of Educational Technology. https://tech.ed.gov/files/2023/05/ai-future-of-teaching-and-learning-report.pdf

Cassidy, S. (2012). Exploring individual differences as determining factors in student academic achievement in higher education. *Studies in Higher Education*, 37(7), 793–810. https://doi.org/10.1080/03075079.2010.545948

Celik, I. (2023). Towards Intelligent-TPACK: An empirical study on teachers' professional knowledge to ethically integrate artificial intelligence (AI)-based tools into education. *Computers in Human Behavior*, p. *138*, 107468.

Cevikbas, M. & Kaiser, G. (2020). Flipped classroom as a reform-oriented approach to teaching mathematics. *Zdm*. https://doi.org/ springer.comDOI: 10.1007/s11858-020-01191-5

Chan, C. K. Y. (2023). A comprehensive AI policy education framework for university teaching and learning. *International Journal of Educational Technology in Higher Education*, 20(1), 38.

Charles, F. (2023). AI-powered personalized mobile education for New Zealand students. [IJSECS]. *International Journal Software Engineering and Computer Science*, 3(1), 33–39.

Chatlabs as the best AI tool for medical students: use cases. ChatLabs - All the Best AI Models in One Place for Free. (n.d.). https://writingmate.ai/blog/chatlabs-as-the-best-ai-tool-for-medical-students-use-cases

Chen, H., Jiao, F., Li, X., Qin, C., Ravaut, M., Zhao, R., Xiong, C., & Joty, S. (2023). Chatgpt's one-year anniversary: Are open source large language models catching up? *arXiv preprint arXiv:2311.16989.*

Chen, X., Xie, H., Zou, D., & Hwang, G. J. (2020). Application and theory gaps during the rise of artificial intelligence in education. *Computers and Education: Artificial Intelligence, 1*, 100002. https://doi.org/ sciencedirect.comDOI: 10.1016/j.caeai.2020.100002

Chen, L. (2010). Web-based learning programs: Use by learners with various cognitive styles. *Computers & Education*, 54(4), 1028–1035. https://doi.org/10.1016/j.compedu.2009.10.008

Chen, L., Chen, P., & Lin, Z. (2020). Artificial intelligence in education: A review. *IEEE Access : Practical Innovations, Open Solutions*, 8, 75264–75278.

Chen, L., Xu, Z., & Li, Y. (2020). AI in education: Emerging trends and policy implications. *Journal of Learning Analytics*, 7(2), 23–42. DOI: 10.18608/jla.2020.7278

Chen, X., Zou, D., Cheng, G., & Xie, H. (2020). Detecting and addressing students' problematic learning behaviors in MOOCs: A neural network-based approach. *Computers in Human Behavior*, 104, 106159.

Chernikova, O., Heitzmann, N., Stadler, M., Holzberger, D., Seidel, T., & Fischer, F. (2020). Simulation-based learning in higher education: A meta-analysis. *Review of Educational Research, 90*(4), 499-541. https://doi.org/ sagepub.comDOI: 10.3102/0034654320933544

Chiarini, A., & Kumar, M. (2021). Lean Six Sigma and Industry 4.0 integration for Operational Excellence: evidence from Italian manufacturing companies. *Production planning & control.* cardiff.ac.uk

Chien, C. C., Chan, H. Y., & Hou, H. T. (2024). Learning by playing with generative AI: Design and evaluation of a role-playing educational game with generative AI as scaffolding for instant feedback interaction. *Journal of Research on Technology in Education*, •••, 1–20. DOI: 10.1080/15391523.2024.2338085

Childress, S., & Benson, S. (2014). Personalized learning for every student every day. *Phi Delta Kappan*, 95(8), 33–38. https://doi.org/10.1177/003172171409500808

Chiu, T. K., Moorhouse, B. L., Chai, C. S., & Ismailov, M. (2023). Teacher support and student motivation to learn with artificial intelligence (AI) based chatbot. *Interactive Learning Environments*, 1–17. https://doi.org/10.1080/10494820.2023.2172044

Chu, S. T., Hwang, G. J., & Tu, Y. F. (2022). Artificial intelligence-based robots in education: A systematic review of selected SSCI publications. *Computers and education: Artificial intelligence, 3*, 100091. https://doi.org/ sciencedirect.comDOI: 10.1016/j.caeai.2022.100091

Chun, D., Kern, R., & Smith, B. (2016). Technology in language use, language teaching, and language learning. *Modern Language Journal*, 100(S1), 64–80. https://doi.org/10.1111/modl.12302

Conati, C., Barral, O., Putnam, V., & Rieger, L. (2021). Toward personalized XAI: A case study in intelligent tutoring systems. [PDF]. *Artificial Intelligence*, 298, 103503. DOI: 10.1016/j.artint.2021.103503

Cook-Sather, A., & Matthews, K. (2023). Practising student voice in university teaching and learning: Three anchoring principles. *Journal of University Teaching & Learning Practice*, 20(6), 1–13. DOI: 10.53761/1.20.6.2

Cotton, D. R. E., Cotton, P. A., & Shipway, J. R. (2023). Chatting and cheating: Ensuring academic integrity in the era of ChatGPT. *Innovations in Education and Teaching International*, 61(2), 228–239. DOI: 10.1080/14703297.2023.2190148

Cowin, J., Oberer, B., Lipuma, J., Leon, C., & Erkollar, A. (2023, September). Accelerating Higher Education Transformation: Simulation-Based Training and AI Coaching for Educators-in-Training. In International Conference on Interactive Collaborative Learning (pp. 532-541). *Cham: Springer Nature Switzerland*. https://doi.org/ [HTML]DOI: 10.1007/978-3-031-51979-6_55

Cranton, P. (2006). *Understanding and promoting transformative learning: A guide for educators of adults*. Jossey-Bass.

Cranton, P., & Hoggan, C. (2012). We are evaluating transformative learning. In Taylor, E. W., & Cranton, P. (Eds.), *Handbook of transformative learning: Theory, research, and practice*. Jossey-Bass.

Crawford, J., Allen, K. A., Pani, B., & Cowling, M. (2024). When artificial intelligence substitutes humans in higher education: the cost of loneliness, student success, and retention. *Studies in Higher Education*, 1-15. https://doi.org/ tandfonline.comDOI: 10.1080/03075079.2024.2326956

Crawford, K., & Calo, R. (2016). There is a blind spot in AI research. *Nature*, 538(7625), 311–313. DOI: 10.1038/538311a PMID: 27762391

Creely, E., & Blannin, J. (2023). The implications of generative AI for creative composition in higher education and initial teacher education. In Cochrane, T., Narayan, V., Brown, C., MacCallum, K., Bone, E., Deneen, C., & Vanderburg, R. (Eds.), *ASCILITE publications* (pp. 357–361)., DOI: 10.14742/apubs.2023.618

Cronjé, J. C. (2024, March). A constructionist approach to learning with AI: An "old" solution to a "new" problem? In *Future of information and communication conference* (pp. 13–22). Springer Nature. DOI: 10.1007/978-3-031-53963-3_2

Dai, C. P. & Ke, F. (2022). Educational applications of artificial intelligence in simulation-based learning: A systematic mapping review. *Computers and Education: Artificial Intelligence*. https://doi.org/ sciencedirect.comDOI: 10.1016/j.caeai.2022.100087

Dai, Y., Liu, A., & Lim, C. P. (2023). Reconceptualizing ChatGPT and generative AI as a student-driven innovation in higher education. *Procedia CIRP*. https://doi.org/ sciencedirect.comDOI: 10.1016/j.procir.2023.05.002

Dalkin, S., Forster, N., Hodgson, P., Lhussier, M., & Carr, S. M. (2021). Using computer assisted qualitative data analysis software (CAQDAS; NVivo) to assist in the complex process of realist theory generation, refinement and testing. *International Journal of Social Research Methodology, 24*(1), 123-134. https://doi.org/ tandfonline.comDOI: 10.1080/13645579.2020.1803528

Daud, N. M., & Husin, Z. (2004). Developing critical thinking skills in computer-aided extended reading classes. *British Journal of Educational Technology*, 35(4), 477–487. DOI: 10.1111/j.0007-1013.2004.00405.x

Davies, H. C., Eynon, R., & Salveson, C. (2021). The mobilisation of AI in education: A Bourdieusean field analysis. *Sociology*. https://doi.org/ sagepub.comDOI: 10.1177/0038038520967888

Dean, C., & Meir, K. (2021). Model-based diagnosis with uncertain observations. [HTML]. *International Journal of Intelligent Systems*, 36(7), 3259–3292. Advance online publication. DOI: 10.1002/int.22416

Deeva, G., Bogdanova, D., Serral, E., Snoeck, M., & De Weerdt, J. (2021). A review of automated feedback systems for learners: Classification framework, challenges and opportunities. [kuleuven.be]. *Computers & Education*, 162, 104094. DOI: 10.1016/j.compedu.2020.104094

Desta, S. Z. & Gugssa, M. A. (2022). The implementation of andragogy in the adult education program in Ethiopia. *Education research international*. https://doi.org/ hindawi.comDOI: 10.1155/2022/2028248

DeWaelsche, S. A. (2015). Critical thinking, questioning and student engagement in Korean university English courses. *Linguistics and Education*, 32, 131–147. DOI: 10.1016/j.linged.2015.10.003

Dewey, J. (1938). *Education and experience*. Collier Books.

Diakopoulos, N. (2016). Accountability in algorithmic decision making. *Communications of the ACM*, 59(2), 56–62. DOI: 10.1145/2844110

Dignum, V. (2021). The role and challenges of education for responsible AI. *London Review of Education*, 19(1), 1–11. DOI: 10.14324/LRE.19.1.01

Ding, X. (2016). The effect of WeChat-assisted problem-based learning on the critical thinking disposition of EFL learners. [iJET]. *International Journal of Emerging Technologies in Learning*, 11(12), 23–29. DOI: 10.3991/ijet.v11i12.5927

Dizon, G., Tang, D., & Yamamoto, Y. (2022). A case study of using Alexa for out-of-class, self-directed Japanese language learning. *Computers and Education: Artificial Intelligence*, 3, 100088. https://doi.org/10.1016/j.caeai.2022.100088

Dogan, M. E., Goru Dogan, T., & Bozkurt, A. (2023). The use of artificial intelligence (AI) in online learning and distance education processes: A systematic review of empirical studies. *Applied Sciences*. https://doi.org/ mdpi.comDOI: 10.3390/app13053056

Dohn, N. B., Kafai, Y., Mørch, A., & Ragni, M. (2022). Survey: Artificial Intelligence, computational thinking and learning. *KI-Künstliche Intelligenz*. https://doi.org/ google.comDOI: 10.1007/s13218-021-00751-5

Dos Santos, R. P. D. (2023). Enhancing chemistry learning with ChatGPT, Bing Chat, Bard, and Claude as agents-to-think-with: a comparative case study. *arXiv preprint arXiv:2311.00709.*http://dx.doi.org/DOI: 10.2139/ssrn.4629567

Drachsler, H., & Greller, W. (2016). Privacy and analytics — It's a DELICATE issue. A Checklist for trusted learning analytics. Proceedings of the 6th International Conference on Learning Analytics and Knowledge (LAK '16), 25–29 April 2016, Edinburgh, UK (pp. 89–98). New York, NY: ACM. https://doi.org/10.1145/2883851.2883893

DreamBox Learning. (2020). DreamBox Learning privacy policy. https://www.dreambox.com/privacy-policy

Driscoll, M. (2018). Psychological Foundations of Instructional Design. In Reiser, R. A., & Dempsey, J. V. (Eds.), *Trends and issues in instructional design and technology* (4th ed., pp. 52–60). Pearson.

Duffy, T. M., & Jonassen, D. H. (2013). *Constructivism and the technology of instruction: A conversation*. Routledge, Taylor & Francis Group.

Duffy, T. M., & Cunningham, D. J. (1996). Constructivism: Implications for the design and delivery of instruction. In Jonassen, D. H. (Ed.), *Handbook of research for educational communications and technology* (pp. 170–198). Macmillan.

Dunlop, L., Hodgson, A., & Stubbs, J. E. (2020). Building capabilities in chemistry education: Happiness and discomfort through philosophical dialogue in chemistry. *Chemistry Education Research and Practice*, 21(1), 438–451. DOI: 10.1039/C9RP00141G

Du, X., & Zhang, L. (2022). Investigating EFL learners' perceptions of critical thinking learning affordances: Voices from Chinese university English majors. *SAGE Open*, 12(2), 1–12. DOI: 10.1177/21582440221094584

Dwivedi, Y. K., Hughes, D. L., Ismagilova, E., Aarts, G., Coombs, C., Crick, T., & Raman, R. (2020). Artificial Intelligence (AI): Multidisciplinary perspectives on emerging challenges, opportunities, and agenda for research, practice and policy. *International Journal of Information Management*, 57, 101994. DOI: 10.1016/j.ijinfomgt.2019.08.002

Dwivedi, Y. K., Kshetri, N., Hughes, L., Slade, E. L., Jeyaraj, A., Kar, A. K., Baabdullah, A. M., Koohang, A., Raghavan, V., Ahuja, M., Albanna, H., Albashrawi, M. A., Al-busaidi, A. S., Balakrishnan, J., Barlette, Y., Basu, S., Bose, I., Brooks, L., Buhalis, D., & Wright, R. (2023). Opinion paper: "So what if ChatGPT wrote it?" multidisciplinary perspectives on opportunities, challenges and implications of generative conversational AI for research, practice and policy. *International Journal of Information Management*, 71, 102642. DOI: 10.1016/j.ijinfomgt.2023.102642

Eaton, L. (N.d.). (2024). ms, Syllabi policies for generative AI tools. https://docs.google.com/document/d/1RMVwzjc1o0Mi8Blw_-JUTcXv02b2WRH86vw7mi16W3U/edit

Ebadi, S., & Amini, A. (2022). Examining the roles of social presence and human-likeness on Iranian EFL learners' motivation using artificial intelligence technology: A case of CSIEC chatbot. [HTML]. *Interactive Learning Environments*. Advance online publication. DOI: 10.1080/10494820.2022.2096638

Egitim, S. (2017). The role of autonomy in critical thinking. *Global Japanese Review, 9*(1), 155-164. http://hdl.handle.net/10291/20647

Egitim, S. (2022a). Do Japanese students lack critical thinking? Addressing the misconception. *Power and Education*, 14(3), 304–309. DOI: 10.1177/17577438221107203

Egitim, S. (2022b). Voices on language teacher stereotypes: Critical cultural competence building as a pedagogical strategy. *Journal of Language, Identity, and Education*, •••, 1–15. DOI: 10.1080/15348458.2022.2070847

Elhussein, G., Hasselaar, E., Lutsyshyn, O., Milberg, T., & Zahidi, S. (2024, April). Shaping the future of learning: the role of AI in Education 4.0. World Economic Forum

Elias, J. L., & Merriam, S. B. (2004). *Philosophical foundations of adult education* (3rded.). Krieger Publishing Company.

Elias, J. L., & Merriam, S. B. (1995). *Philosophical foundations of adult education*. Krieger Publishing Company.

Elsen-Rooney, M. (2023, January 3). NYC education department blocks ChatGPT on school devices, networks. https://www.chalkbeat.org/newyork/2023/1/3/23537987/nyc-schools-ban-chatgpt-writing-artificial-intelligence/ (Exintaris, B., Karunaratne, N., & Yuriev, E. (2023). Metacognition and critical thinking: Using ChatGPT-Generated responses as prompts for critique in a problem-solving workshop (SMARTCHEMPer). *Journal of Chemical Education, 100*(8), 2972–2980. https://doi.org/DOI: 10.1021/acs.jchemed.3c00481

Engstrom, T., Strong, J., Sullivan, C., & Pole, J. D. (2022). A Comparison of Leximancer semi-automated content analysis to manual content analysis: a healthcare exemplar using emotive Transcripts of COVID-19 Hospital staff interactive webcasts. *International Journal of Qualitative Methods, 21*, 16094069221118993. https://doi.org/ sagepub.comDOI: 10.1177/16094069221118993

Every Student Succeeds Act, Pub. L. No. 114-95 (2015), https://www.govinfo.gov/app/details/PLAW-114publ95

Fang, R., & Pan, L. (2024). Refocusing on the start and end of tourists' decision-*making: Measuring thresholds and information loop limits.* [HTML]. *Tourism Management*, 104, 104918. Advance online publication. DOI: 10.1016/j.tourman.2024.104918

Firaina, R., & Sulisworo, D. (2023). Exploring the usage of ChatGPT in higher education: Frequency and impact on productivity. *Bulletin Edukasi Indonesia*, 2(1), 39–46. DOI: 10.56741/bei.v2i01.310

Floridi, L., & Cowls, J. (2019). A unified framework of five principles for AI in society. *Harvard Data Science Review*, 1(1). Advance online publication. DOI: 10.1162/99608f92.8cd550d1

Floridi, L., Cowls, J., Beltrametti, M., Chatila, R., Chazerand, P., Dignum, V., Luetge, C., Madelin, R., Pagallo, U., Rossi, F., Schafer, B., Valcke, P., & Vayena, E. (2018). AI4People—An ethical framework for a good AI society: Opportunities, risks, principles, and recommendations. *Minds and Machines*, 28(4), 689–707. DOI: 10.1007/s11023-018-9482-5 PMID: 30930541

Freeman, J. B., & Ambady, N. (2011). A dynamic interactive theory of personal constual. *Personnel Review*, 118(2), 247–279. DOI: 10.1037/a0022327 PMID: 21355661

Freina, L., & Ott, M. (2015). A literature review on immersive virtual reality in education: State of the art and perspectives. In *The International Scientific Conference eLearning and Software for Education* (pp. 133-141). DOI: 10.12753/2066-026X-15-020

Freire, P. (1970). *Pedagogy of the oppressed.* Seabury Press.

Frick, T. W. (2020). Education systems and technology in 1990, 2020, and beyond. TechTrends. https://doi.org/ springer.comDOI: 10.1007/s11528-020-00527-y

Fui-Hoon Nah, F., Zheng, R., Cai, J., Siau, K., & Chen, L. (2023). Generative AI and ChatGPT: Applications, challenges, and AI-human collaboration. *Journal of Information Technology Case and Application Research*, 25(3), 277–304. DOI: 10.1080/15228053.2023.2233814

Gamazo, A. & Martínez-Abad, F. (2020). An exploration of factors linked to academic performance in PISA 2018 through data mining techniques. *Frontiers in Psychology*. https://doi.org/ frontiersin.orgDOI: 10.3389/fpsyg.2020.575167

Gebru, T., Morgenstern, J., Vecchione, B., Vaughan, J. W., Wallach, H., Iii, H. D., & Crawford, K. (2020). Datasheets for datasets. *Communications of the ACM*, 64(12), 86–92. DOI: 10.1145/3458723

Georgia State University, Office of Institutional Research. (2017). GPS Advising. https://success.gsu.edu/initiatives/gps-advising/

Gibson, D., Kovanovic, V., Ifenthaler, D., Dexter, S., & Feng, S. (2023). Learning theories for artificial intelligence promoting learning processes. *British Journal of Educational Technology, 54*(5), 1125-1146. https://doi.org/ wiley.comDOI: 10.1111/bjet.13341

Gikandi, J. W., Morrow, D., & Davis, N. E. (2011). Online formative assessment in higher education: A review of the literature. *Computers & Education*, 57(4), 2333–2351. DOI: 10.1016/j.compedu.2011.06.004

Gimpel, H., Hall, K., Decker, S., Eymann, T., Lammermann, L., Maedche, A., Roglinger, M., Ruiner, C., Schoch, M., Schoop, M., Urbach, N., & Vandirk, S. (2023). *Unlocking the power of generative AI models and systems such as GPT-4 and ChatGPT for higher education: a guide for students and lecturers*. Preprint., DOI: 10.12140/RG.2.2.20710.09287/2

Godwin-Jones, R. (2019). In a World of SMART Technology, Why Learn Another Language? *Journal of Educational Technology & Society*, 22(2), 4–13. https://www.jstor.org/stable/26819613

Goh, Y. S., Yew, J. S., Chua, N. A., Saputra, J., Leng, N. K., & Cheong, W. H. (2023). *The effect of interface quality, system quality, and perceived usefulness of an automated pronunciation scoring system on student satisfaction*. https://www.semanticscholar.org/paper/The-effect-of-interface-quality%2C-system-quality%2C-of-Soon-Yew/ff3f97b32e86598374b053146ddc82237c88daca

Goh, E., & Wilk, V. (2022). Showcasing Leximancer in tourism and hospitality research: A review of Leximancer-based research published in tourism and hospitality journals during 2014–2020. [HTML]. *Tourism Recreation Research*. Advance online publication. DOI: 10.1080/02508281.2022.2129284

Goh, Y. S. (2021). Using AI technology to support speaking skill development for the teaching of Chinese as a foreign language. In *Multidisciplinary functions of blockchain technology in AI and IoT applications* (pp. 209–227). IGI Global.

Golonka, E. M., Bowles, A. R., Frank, V. M., Richardson, D. L., & Freynik, S. (2014). Technologies for foreign language learning: A review of technology types and their effectiveness. *Computer Assisted Language Learning*, 27(1), 70–105. DOI: 10.1080/09588221.2012.700315

González-Pérez, L. I. & Ramírez-Montoya, M. S. (2022). Components of Education 4.0 in 21st century skills frameworks: Systematic review. *Sustainability*. https://doi.org/ mdpi.comDOI: 10.3390/su14031493

Grech, A., & Camilleri, A. F. (2017). *Blockchain in education*. Publications Office of the European Union.

Greene, D., Hoffmann, A. L., & Stark, L. (2019). Better, nicer, clearer, fairer: A critical assessment of the movement for ethical artificial intelligence and machine learning. *Proceedings of the 52nd Hawaii International Conference on System Sciences*, 2122-2131. DOI: 10.24251/HICSS.2019.258

Greenhalgh, J., & Manzano, A. (2022). Understanding 'context'in realist evaluation and synthesis. *International Journal of Social Research Methodology, 25*(5), 583-595. https://doi.org/ tandfonline.comDOI: 10.1080/13645579.2021.1918484

Griffin, T. D., Wiley, J., & Salas, C. R. (2013). Supporting effective self-regulated learning: The critical role of monitoring. *International Handbook of Metacognition and Learning Technologies*, 19-34. https://doi.org/10.1007/978-1-4419-5546-3_2

Grubaugh, S., Levitt, G., & Deever, D. (2023). Harnessing AI to power constructivist learning: An evolution in educational methodologies. *Journal of Effective Teaching Methods*, 1(3), 81–83. DOI: 10.59652/jetm.v1i3.43

Guan, C., Mou, J., & Jiang, Z. (2020). Artificial intelligence innovation in education: A twenty-year data-driven historical analysis. *International Journal of Innovation Studies*. https://doi.org/ sciencedirect.comDOI: 10.1016/j.ijis.2020.09.001

Gudivada, V. N. (2017). Cognitive Analytics Driven Personalized Learning. *Educational Technology*, 57(1), 23–31. http://www.jstor.org/stable/44430537

Gunawardena, M., Bishop, P., & Aviruppola, K. (2024). Personalized learning: The simple, the complicated, the complex and the chaotic. *Teaching and Teacher Education*, 139, 104429. https://doi.org/10.1016/j.tate.2023.104429

Guo, L., Wang, D., Gu, F., Li, Y., Wang, Y., & Zhou, R. (2021). Evolution and trends in intelligent tutoring systems research: a multidisciplinary and scientometric view. *Asia Pacific Education Review, 22*(3), 441-461. https://doi.org/ springer.comDOI: 10.1007/s12564-021-09697-7

Guo, H., Yi, W., & Liu, K. (2024) Enhancing constructivist learning: the role of generative AI in personalised learning experiences. *Proceedings of the 26th International Conference on Enterprise Information Systems (ICEIS 2024), 1*, 767-770. https://doi.org/DOI: 10.5220/0012688700003690

Habermas, J. (1971). *Knowledge and human interests*. Beacon Press.

Hadžiomerović, A. I. (2023). Questioning Assumptions About Developing an Andragogy Study Program in Bosnia and Herzegovina. *Andragoška spoznanja*. uni-lj.si
Haleem, A., Javaid, M., Qadri, M. A., & Suman, R. (2022). Understanding the role of digital technologies in education: A review. *Sustainable Operations and Computers, 3*, 275-285. https://doi.org/ sciencedirect.comDOI: 10.1016/j.susoc.2022.05.004

Halina, M. (2021). Insightful artificial intelligence. *Mind & Language*. https://doi.org/ wiley.comDOI: 10.1111/mila.12321

Hamal, O., Faddouli, E., & Harouni, M. H. A. (2021). Design and Implementation of the Multi-Agent System in Education. *World Journal on Educational Technology: Current Issues, 13*(4), 775-793. https://doi.org/ed.govDOI: 10.18844/wjet.v13i4.6264

Harris, J., Mishra, P., & Koehler, M. (2009). Teachers' technological pedagogical content knowledge and learning activity types. *Journal of Research on Technology in Education*, 41(4), 393–416. https://doi.org/10.1080/15391523.2009.10782536

Hartse, J. H., & Morphett, T. (2024, March 26). Writing is a technology that restructures thought - and in an AI age, universities need to teach it more. *The Conversation*. https://theconversation.com/writing-is-a-technology-that-restructures-thought-and-in-an-ai-age-universities-need-to-teach-it-more-219482

Hassija, V., Chamola, V., Mahapatra, A., Singal, A., Goel, D., Huang, K., ... & Hussain, A. (2024). Interpreting black-box models: a review on explainable artificial intelligence. *Cognitive Computation, 16*(1), 45-74. https://doi.org/ springer.comDOI: 10.1007/s12559-023-10179-8

Heflin, H., Shewmaker, J., & Nguyen, J. (2017). Impact of mobile technology on student attitudes, engagement, and learning. *Computers & Education*, 107, 91–99. https://doi.org/10.1016/j.compedu.2017.01.006

Helo, P. & Hao, Y. (2022). Artificial intelligence in operations management and supply chain management: An exploratory case study. *Production Planning & Control*. https://doi.org/ tandfonline.comDOI: 10.1080/09537287.2021.1882690

Hemachandran, K., Verma, P., Pareek, P., Arora, N., Kumar, K. V. R., Ahanger, T. A., ... & Ratna, R. (2022). Artificial intelligence: a universal virtual tool to augment tutoring in higher education. *Computational Intelligence and Neuroscience, 2022*. https://doi.org/ hindawi.comDOI: 10.1155/2022/1410448

Herman, W. E. (1995). Humanistic influences on a constructivist approach to teaching and learning. https://files.eric.ed.gov/fulltext/ED393814.pdf

Heywood, L., Conti, J., & Hay, P. (2022). Chapter 1: a systematic synthesis of narrative therapy treatment components for the treatment of eating disorders. *Journal of Eating Disorders*. https://doi.org/ springer.comDOI: 10.1186/s40337-022-00635-5

Hmedna, B., Bakki, A., Mezouary, A. E., & Baz, O. (2023). Unlocking teachers' potential: MOOCLS, a visualization tool for enhancing MOOC teaching. *Smart Learning Environments*. https://doi.org/ springer.comDOI: 10.1186/s40561-023-00277-3

Holian, J. (1971). Alienation and social awareness among college students. *The Sociological Quarterly*, 13(1), 114–125. DOI: 10.1111/j.1533-8525.1971.tb01835.x

Holmes, W., Bialik, M., & Fadel, C. (2019). *Artificial intelligence in education: Promises and implications for teaching and learning*. Center for Curriculum Redesign.

Holmes, W., Bialik, M., & Fadel, C. (2019). *Artificial Intelligence in Education: Promises and Implications for Teaching and Learning*. Center for Curriculum Redesign.

Holstein, K., McLaren, B. M., & Aleven, V. (2019). Co-designing a real-time classroom orchestration tool to support teacher–AI complementarity. *Journal of Learning Analytics*, 6(2), 27–52. DOI: 10.18608/jla.2019.62.3

Hooper, B., Molineux, M., & Wood, W. (2020). The subject-centered integrative learning model: A new model for teaching occupational therapy's distinct value. *Journal of Occupational Therapy Education, 4*(2), 1. https://doi.org/ eku.eduDOI: 10.26681/jote.2020.040201

Hopfenbeck, T. N., Zhang, Z., Sun, S. Z., Robertson, P., & McGrane, J. A. (2023). Challenges and opportunities for classroom-based formative assessment and AI: A perspective article. *Frontiers in Education*, 8, 1–9. DOI: 10.3389/feduc.2023.1270700

Horváthová, J., Mokrišová, M., & Petruška, I. (2021). Selected methods of predicting financial health of companies: neural networks versus discriminant analysis. *Information*. https://doi.org/ mdpi.comDOI: 10.3390/info12120505

Howard, S. K., Swist, T., Gasevic, D., Bartimote, K., Knight, S., Gulson, K., & Selwyn, N. (2022). Educational data journeys: Where are we going, what are we taking and making for AI? *Computers and Education: Artificial Intelligence*, (p. 3), 100073.

Huang, A. Y., Lu, O. H., Huang, J. C., Yin, C. J., & Yang, S. J. (2020). Predicting students' academic performance by using educational big data and learning analytics: Evaluation of classification methods and learning logs. *Interactive Learning Environments*, 28(2), 206–230.

Huang, R. H., Liu, D. J., Tlili, A., Yang, J. F., & Wang, H. H. (2020). *Handbook on facilitating flexible learning during educational disruption: The Chinese experience in maintaining undisrupted learning in COVID-19 outbreak*. Smart Learning Institute of Beijing Normal University.

Huang, X., Zou, D., Cheng, G., Chen, X., & Xie, H. (2023). Trends, research issues and applications of artificial intelligence in language education. *Journal of Educational Technology & Society*, 26(1), 112–131.

Huang, Z., Mao, Y., & Zhang, J. (2024). The Influence of Artificial Intelligence Technology on College Students' Learning Effectiveness from the Perspective of Constructivism—Taking ChatGPT as an Example. *Journal of Education. Humanities and Social Sciences*, 30, 40–46.

Hughes, G. (2011). Towards a personal best: A case for introducing ipsative assessment in higher education. *Studies in Higher Education*, 36(3), 353–367. DOI: 10.1080/03075079.2010.486859

Huisenga, D., La Bastide-Van Gemert, S., Van Bergen, A., Sweeney, J., & Hadders-Algra, M. (2021). Developmental outcomes after early surgery for complex congenital heart disease: A systematic review and meta-analysis. *Developmental Medicine & Child Neurology, 63*(1), 29-46. https://doi.org/ wiley.comDOI: 10.1111/dmcn.14512

Hutson, J., Plate, D., & Berry, K. (2024). Embracing AI in English composition: Insights and innovations in hybrid pedagogical practices. *International Journal of Changes in Education*, 19–31. DOI: 10.47852/bonviewIJCE42022290

Hwang, G. J., Xie, H., Wah, B. W., & Gašević, D. (2020). Vision, challenges, roles and research issues of Artificial Intelligence in education. *Computers and Education: Artificial Intelligence*, 1, 100001. DOI: 10.1016/j.caeai.2020.100001

Hwang, G. J., Xie, H., Wah, B. W., & Gasevic, D. (2020). Vision, challenges, roles, and research issues of artificial intelligence in education. *Computers & Education: Artificial Intelligence*, 1, 100001.

Idowu, J. A., Koshiyama, A. S., & Treleaven, P. (2024). Investigating Algorithmic Bias in Student Progress Monitoring. *Computers and Education: Artificial Intelligence*, 100267. Kshetri, N. (2013). Privacy and security issues in cloud computing: The role of institutions and institutional evolution. *Telecommunications Policy*, 37(4-5), 372–386.

Iku-Silan, A., Hwang, G. J., & Chen, C. H. (2023). Decision-guided chatbots and cognitive styles in interdisciplinary learning. [HTML]. *Computers & Education*, 201, 104812. Advance online publication. DOI: 10.1016/j.compedu.2023.104812

Jarrahi, M. H. (2018). Artificial intelligence and the future of work: Human-AI symbiosis in organizational decision making. *Business Horizons, 61*(4), 577e586.

Jarrahi, M. H., Askay, D., Esraghi, A., & Smith, P. (2023). Artificial intelligence and knowledge management: A partnership between human and AI. *Business Horizons*, 66(1), 87–99. DOI: 10.1016/j.bushor.2022.03.002

Javaid, M., Haleem, A., Singh, R. P., Khan, S., & Khan, I. H. (2023). Unlocking the opportunities through ChatGPT Tool towards ameliorating the education system. *BenchCouncil Transactions on Benchmarks, Standards, and Evaluations*, 3(2), 100115. DOI: 10.1016/j.tbench.2023.100115

Jenka (2023). AI and the American Smile: How AI misrepresents culture through a facial expression. *Medium.com.*https://medium.com/@socialcreature/ai-and-the-american-smile-76d23a0fbfaf

Jeong-Bae Son. Ružić, N. K., & Philpott, A. (2023). Artificial intelligence technologies and applications for language learning and teaching. *Journal of China Computer-Assisted Language Learning*. https://www.degruyter.com/document/doi/10.1515/jccall-2023-0015/html?lang=en

Jiang, Y., Li, X., Luo, H., Yin, S., & Kaynak, O. (2022). Quo vadis artificial intelligence?. *Discover Artificial Intelligence*. https://doi.org/ springer.comDOI: 10.1007/s44163-022-00022-8

Jin, S., Im, K., Yoo, M., Roll, I., & Seo, K. (2023). Supporting students' self-regulated learning in online learning using artificial intelligence applications. *International Journal of Educational Technology in Higher Education*, 20(1). https://doi.org/10.1186/s41239-023-00406-5

Johnson, A. M., Guerrero, T. A., Tighe, E. L., & McNamara, D. S. (2017). *iSTART-ALL: Confronting adult low literacy with intelligent tutoring for reading comprehension.* In *International Conference on Artificial Intelligence in Education* (pp. 125-136). Springer. https://doi.org/DOI: 10.1007/978-3-319-61425-0_11

Jones, S., & Watson, A. (2020). Building trust in AI: The case of Georgia State University's PantherRetention system. *EDUCAUSE Review*, 55(4), 28–35. DOI: 10.17471/2409-3253-1336

Jones, T. M., & Miller, D. J. (2021). Predictive analytics in education: The ethics of identifying students at risk. *Journal of Educational Technology & Society*, 24(2), 112–123.

Kabudi, T., Pappas, I., & Olsen, D. H. (2021). AI-enabled adaptive learning systems: A systematic mapping of the literature. *Computers and Education: Artificial Intelligence, 2*, 100017. https://doi.org/ sciencedirect.comDOI: 10.1016/j.caeai.2021.100017

Kabudi, T., Pappas, I., & Olsen, D. H. (2021). AI-enabled adaptive learning systems: A systematic mapping of the literature. *Computers and Education: Artificial Intelligence, 2.*

Kant, I. (2002). *Groundwork for the metaphysics of morals* (Abbott, T. K., Trans.). Yale University Press. (Original work published 1785)

Kapici, H. O., & Akcay, H. (2023). Improving student teachers' TPACK self-efficacy through lesson planning practice in the virtual platform. [HTML]. *Educational Studies*, 49(1), 76–98. Advance online publication. DOI: 10.1080/03055698.2020.1835610

Karamitsos, I., Albarhami, S., & Apostolopoulos, C. (2020). Applying DevOps practices of continuous automation for machine learning. *Information*. https://doi.org/ mdpi.comDOI: 10.3390/info11070363

Kasneci, E., Sessler, K., Kuchemann, S., Bannert, M., Dementieva, E., Fischer, F., Gasser, U., Groh, G., Gunnemann, S., Hullermeier, E., Krusche, S., Kutyniok, G., Michaeli, T., Nerdel, C., Pfeffer, J., Poquet, O., Sailer, M., Schmidt, A., Seidel, T., & Kasneci, G. (2023). ChatGPT for good? On opportunity and challenges of large language models for education. *Learning and Individual Differences*, 103, 102274. DOI: 10.1016/j.lindif.2023.102274

Kaswan, K. S., Dhatterwal, J. S., & Ojha, R. P. (2024). AI in personalized learning. In *Advances in Technological Innovations in Higher Education* (pp. 103–117). CRC Press.

Katz, S., Albacete, P., Chounta, I. A., Jordan, P., McLaren, B. M., & Zapata-Rivera, D. (2021). Linking dialogue with student modelling to create an adaptive tutoring system for conceptual physics. *International journal of artificial intelligence in education, 31*(3), 397-445. https://doi.org/ springer.comDOI: 10.1007/s40593-020-00226-y

Ke, L., Sadler, T. D., Zangori, L., & Friedrichsen, P. J. (2021). Developing and using multiple models to promote scientific literacy in the context of socio-scientific issues. *Science & Education*. https://doi.org/ springer.comDOI: 10.1007/s11191-021-00206-1

Kennedy, M., & Birch, P. (2020). Reflecting on outcome-based education for human services programs in higher education: A policing degree case study. [HTML]. *Journal of Criminological Research, Policy and Practice*, 6(2), 111–122. DOI: 10.1108/JCRPP-12-2019-0071

Kentucky Department of Education. (2024). Artificial Intelligence Guidance Brief. www.education.ky.gov/districts/tech/Documents/AI%20Guidance%20Brief.pdf

Kerr, K. (2020). Ethical Considerations When Using Artificial Intelligence-Based Assistive Technologies in Education. In B. Brown, V. Roberts, M. Jacobsen, C. Hurrell, K. Kerr, H. van Streun, N. J. Neutzling, J. Lowry, S. Zarkovic, J. Ansorger, T. Marles, E. Lockyer, & D. Parthenis (Eds.), *Ethical use of technology in digital learning environments: Graduate student perspectives – Simple book publishing*. Library Publishing for Open Textbooks. https://pressbooks.openeducationalberta.ca/educationaltechnologyethics/

Kersting, K. (2020). Rethinking computer science through AI. *KI-Künstliche Intelligenz*. https://doi.org/ springer.comDOI: 10.1007/s13218-020-00692-5

Kessler, S. (2019). How Georgia State University used AI to help students stay in school. Fast Company. https://www.fastcompany.com/90271165/how-georgia-state-university-used-ai-to-help-students-stay-in-school

Khan, S. (2023). The Ethical Imperative: Addressing Bias and Discrimination in AI-Driven Education. *Social Sciences Spectrum*, 2(1), 89–96.

Khatun, N., & Miwa, J. (2016). An autonomous learning system of Bengali characters using web-based intelligent handwriting recognition. *Journal of Education and Learning*, 5(3), 122–138. DOI: 10.5539/jel.v5n3p122

Kidd, J. R. (1973). *How adults learn* (revised). Association Press.

Kim, J. H., Kim, M., Kwak, D. W., & Lee, S. (2022). Home-tutoring services assisted with technology: Investigating the role of artificial intelligence using a randomized field experiment. *Journal of Marketing Research, 59*(1), 79-96. https://doi.org/ sagepub.comDOI: 10.1177/00222437211050351

Kim, J., Lee, H., & Cho, Y. H. (2022). Learning design to support student-AI collaboration: Perspectives of leading teachers for AI in education. *Education and Information Technologies*. https://doi.org/ springer.comDOI: 10.1007/s10639-021-10831-6

Kim, M., & Adlof, L. (2023). Adapting to the future: ChatGPT as a means for supporting constructivist learning environments. *TechTrends. 68,* 37e46. https://doi.org/DOI: 10.1007/s11528-023-00899-x

Kimmel, M. & Irran, C. (2022). Decision-making in Shiatsu bodywork: Complementariness of embodied coupling and conceptual inference. *Phenomenology and the Cognitive Sciences*. https://doi.org/ springer.comDOI: 10.1007/s11097-020-09718-7

Kim, N. J., & Kim, M. K. (2022). Teacher's perceptions of using an artificial intelligence-based educational tool for scientific writing. *Frontiers in Education*, 7, 7. DOI: 10.3389/feduc.2022.755914

Kim, S. (2013). Confucianism and acceptable inequalities. *Philosophy and Social Criticism*, 39(10), 983–1004. DOI: 10.1177/0191453713507015

Kinney, L. B. (1953). *The measure of a good teacher*. Teachers Association.

Klimova, B., Pikhart, M., & Kacetl, J. (2023). Ethical issues of the use of AI-driven mobile apps for education. *Frontiers in Public Health*, 10. https://doi.org/10.3389/fpubh.2022.1118116

Knowles, M. S., Holton, E., & Swanson, A. (2011). *The adult learner: The definitive classic in adult education and human resource development* (7th ed.). Taylor & Francis.

Knowles, M. S. (1975). *Self-directed learning*. Association Press.

Knowles, M. S. (1980). *The modern practice of adult education: From pedagogy to andragogy*. Association Press.

Knowles, M. S., Holton, E., & Swanson, A. (1998). *The adult learner: The definitive classic in adult education and human resource development*. Gulf Publishing Company.

Koehrsen, J. (2021). Muslims and climate change: How Islam, Muslim organizations, and religious leaders influence climate change perceptions and mitigation activities. *Wiley Interdisciplinary Reviews: Climate Change*. https://doi.org/ wiley.comDOI: 10.1002/wcc.702

Kulik, J. A., & Fletcher, J. D. (2016). Effectiveness of intelligent tutoring systems: A meta-analytic review. *Review of Educational Research*, 86(1), 42–78. DOI: 10.3102/0034654315581420

Kurilovas, E. (2020). On data-driven decision-making for quality education. [HTML]. *Computers in Human Behavior*, 107, 105774. Advance online publication. DOI: 10.1016/j.chb.2018.11.003

Lapuz, A. M. E., & Fulgencio, M. N. (2020). Improving the critical thinking skills of secondary students using problem-based learning. *International Journal of Academic Multidisciplinary Research (IJAMR), 4,*(1), 1-7. www.ijeais.org/ijamr. https://ssrn.com/abstract=3453211

Latha, S. (2020). Vuca in engineering education: Enhancement of faculty competency for capacity building. *Procedia Computer Science*. https://doi.org/ sciencedirect.comDOI: 10.1016/j.procs.2020.05.106

Lee, D., Kim, H. H., & Sung, S. H. (2023). Development research on an AI English learning support system to facilitate learner-generated-context-based learning. *Educational Technology Research and Development*, 71(2), 629–666. DOI: 10.1007/s11423-022-10172-2 PMID: 36533222

Lee, J., & Park, O. (2008). Adaptive instructional systems. In Spector, J. M., Merrill, M. D., Merriënboer, J. v., & Driscoll, M. P. (Eds.), *Handbook of research on educational communications and technology* (3rd ed., pp. 469–484). Taylor Francis.

Lee, S. J., & Kwon, K. (2024). A systematic review of AI education in K-12 classrooms from 2018 to 2023: Topics, strategies, and learning outcomes. *Computers and Education: Artificial Intelligence*, 6, 100211. https://doi.org/10.1016/j.caeai.2024.100211

Leung, K.-H. (2019). *The picture of artificial intelligence and the secularization of thought.* Political Theology. DOI: 10.1080/1462317X.2019.1605725

Lewis, A., & Stoyanovich, J. (2022). Teaching responsible data science: Charting new pedagogical territory. *International Journal of Artificial Intelligence in Education*, 32(3), 783–807. DOI: 10.1007/s40593-021-00241-7 PMID: 33880114

Li, C., & Lalani, F. (2020). The COVID-19 pandemic has changed education forever. World Economic Forum. https://www.weforum.org/agenda/2020/04/coronavirus-education-global-covid19-online-digital-learning

Li, X., Jiang, M. Y. C., Jong, M. S. Y., Zhang, X., & Chai, C. S. (2022). Understanding medical students' perceptions of and behavioral intentions toward learning artificial intelligence: A survey study. *International Journal of Environmental Research and Public Health, 19*(14), *8733*. https://doi.org/ mdpi.comDOI: 10.3390/ijerph19148733

Liang, J. C., Hwang, G. J., Chen, M. R. A., & Darmawansah, D. (2023). Roles and research foci of artificial intelligence in language education: An integrated bibliographic analysis and systematic review approach. *Interactive Learning Environments*, 31(7), 4270–4296. DOI: 10.1080/10494820.2021.1958348

Liang, J., Wang, L., Luo, J., Yan, Y., & Fan, C. (2023). The relationship between student interaction with generative artificial intelligence and learning achievement: Serial mediating roles of self-efficacy and cognitive engagement. *Frontiers in Psychology*, 14, 1285392. DOI: 10.3389/fpsyg.2023.1285392 PMID: 38187430

Liang, X. (2020). The use of AI in Chinese schools: Ethical concerns and policy implications. *Asian Journal of Educational Research*, 8(1), 34–45.

Li, J., & Hayhoe, R. (2012). Confucianism and higher education. In Banks, J. A. (Ed.), *SAGE encyclopedia of diversity in education* (Vol. 1, pp. 443–446). Sage.

Li, J., Peng, Y., & Su, J. (2023). Analysis of the impact of artificial intelligence on college students and countermeasures based on the perspective of comprehensive development. The *Frontiers of Society. Science, and Technology*, 5(9), 24–33.

Lin, C. C., Liu, G. Z., & Wang, T. I. (2017). Development and usability test of an e-learning tool for engineering graduates to Develop academic writing in English: A Case study. *Journal of Educational Technology & Society*, 20(4), 148–161.

Lindeman, E. C. (1926). *The meaning of adult education*. Research Center for Continuing Professional and Higher Education.

Lin, L., & Reinders, H. (2019). Students' and teachers' readiness for autonomy: Beliefs and practices in developing autonomy in the Chinese context. *Asia Pacific Education Review*, 20(1), 69–89. DOI: 10.1007/s12564-018-9564-3

Lin, M. P., & Chang, D. (2023). CHAT-ACTS: A pedagogical framework for personalized chatbot to enhance active learning and self-regulated learning. *Computers and Education: Artificial Intelligence*, 5, 100167. https://doi.org/10.1016/j.caeai.2023.100167

Lin, P. C., Hou, H. T., & Chang, K. E. (2022). … of a collaborative problem solving environment that integrates a scaffolding mind tool and simulation-based learning: An analysis of learners' performance and their…. [HTML]. *Interactive Learning Environments*, 30(7), 1273–1290. Advance online publication. DOI: 10.1080/10494820.2020.1719163

Liu, J., Li, S., Ren, C., Lyu, Y., Xu, T., Wang, Z., & Chen, W. (2023). AI enhancements for linguistic e-learning system. *Applied Sciences*. https://www.mdpi.com/2076-3417/13/19/10758

Liu, M. (2023). *Exploring the application of artificial intelligence in foreign language teaching: Challenges and future development*. SHS Web of Conferences. DOI: 10.1051/shsconf/202316803025

Liu, J., Ma, Y., Sun, X., Zhu, Z., & Xu, Y. (2022). A systematic review of higher-order thinking by visualizing its structure through HistCite and CiteSpace software. *The Asia-Pacific Education Researcher*, 31(6), 635–645. DOI: 10.1007/s40299-021-00614-5

Loewenberg Ball, D., Thames, M. H., & Phelps, G. (2008). Content knowledge for teaching. *Journal of Teacher Education*, 59(5), 389–407. https://doi.org/10.1177/0022487108324554

Luan, H., Geczy, P., Lai, H., Gobert, J., Yang, S. J., Ogata, H., Baltes, J., Guerra, R., Li, P., & Tsai, C. C. (2020). Challenges and future directions of big data and artificial intelligence in education. *Frontiers in Psychology*, 11, 580820. Advance online publication. DOI: 10.3389/fpsyg.2020.580820 PMID: 33192896

Luckin, R., Cukurova, M., Kent, C., & du Boulay, B. (2022). Empowering educators to be AI-ready. *Computers and Education: Artificial Intelligence, 3*, 100076. https://doi.org/ sciencedirect.comDOI: 10.1016/j.caeai.2022.100076

Luckin, R., & Cukurova, M. (2019). Designing educational technologies in the age of AI: A learning sciences-driven approach. *British Journal of Educational Technology*, 50(6), 2824–2838.

Luckin, R., Holmes, W., Griffiths, M., & Forcier, L. B. (2016). *Intelligence unleashed: An argument for AI in education*. Pearson Education.

Lu, O. H. T., Huang, A. Y. Q., Huang, J. C. H., & Yang, S. J. H. (2018). Applying learning analytics for the early prediction of students' academic performance in blended learning. *Journal of Educational Technology & Society*, 21(2), 220–232.

MacCarthy, M. & Shan, H. (2022). Machine infelicity in a poignant visitor setting: Comparing human and AI's ability to analyze discourse. *Current Issues in Tourism*. https://doi.org/ tandfonline.comDOI: 10.1080/13683500.2021.1915252

Macfarlane, B. (2022). A voyage around the ideological islands of higher education research. *Higher education research & development*. https://doi.org/ tandfonline.comDOI: 10.1080/07294360.2021.2002275

Machynska, N., & Boiko, H. (2020). Andragogy–The science of adult education: Theoretical aspects. *Journal of Innovation in Psychology* [ub.ro]. *Education and Didactics*, 24(1), 25–34.

Magistretti, S., Ardito, L., & Messeni Petruzzelli, A. (2021). Framing the microfoundations of design thinking as a dynamic capability for innovation: Reconciling theory and practice. *Journal of Product Innovation Management, 38*(6), 645-667. https://doi.org/ wiley.comDOI: 10.1111/jpim.12586

Mahoney, J. M., & Quick, B. G. (2000). Personality correlates of alienation in a university sample. *Psychological Reports*, 87(3_suppl), 1094–1100. DOI: 10.2466/pr0.2000.87.3f.1094 PMID: 11272749

Makridakis, S. (2017). The forthcoming artificial intelligence (AI) revolution: Its impact on society and firms. *Futures*, 90, 46–60. DOI: 10.1016/j.futures.2017.03.006

Manalo, E., Kusumi, T., Koyasu, M., Michita, Y., & Tanaka, Y. (2013). To what extent do culture-related factors influence university students' critical thinking use? *Thinking Skills and Creativity*, 10, 121–132. DOI: 10.1016/j.tsc.2013.08.003

Marginson, S. (2011). Higher education in East Asia and Singapore: Rise of the Confucian model. *Higher Education*, 61(5), 587–611. DOI: 10.1007/s10734-010-9384-9

Markauskaite, L., Marrone, R., Poquet, O., Knight, S., Martinez-Maldonado, R., Howard, S., ... & Siemens, G. (2022). Rethinking the entwinement between artificial intelligence and human learning: What capabilities do learners need for a world with AI?. *Computers and Education: Artificial Intelligence, 3*, 100056. https://doi.org/ sciencedirect.comDOI: 10.1016/j.caeai.2022.100056

Marosan, Z., Savic, N., Klasnja-Milicevic, A., Ivanovic, M., & Vesin, B. (2022). Students' perceptions of ils as a learning-style-identification tool in e-learning environments. *Sustainability, 14*(8), 4426. https://doi.org/ mdpi.comDOI: 10.3390/su14084426

Marr, B. (2024, February 20). A short history of chatgpt: how we got to where we are today. *Forbes*.https://www.forbes.com/sites/bernardmarr/2023/05/19/a-short-history-of-chatgpt-how-we-got-to-where-we-are-today/

Marr, B. (2018). How IBM is using AI, IoT, and blockchain to transform the food industry. *Forbes*.

Martin-Hernandez, R., Espeso-Gil, S., Domingo, C., Latorre, P., Hervas, S., Hernandez Mora, J. R., & Kotelnikova, E. (2023). Machine learning combining multi-omics data and network algorithms identifies adrenocortical carcinoma prognostic biomarkers. *Frontiers in Molecular Biosciences, 10*, 1258902. https://doi.org/ frontiersin.orgDOI: 10.3389/fmolb.2023.1258902

Maslow, A. H. (1970). *Motivation and personality* (2nd ed.). Harper Collins.

Matarazzo, M., Penco, L., Profumo, G., & Quaglia, R. (2021). Digital transformation and customer value creation in Made in Italy SMEs: A dynamic capabilities perspective. [HTML]. *Journal of Business Research*, 123, 642–656. DOI: 10.1016/j.jbusres.2020.10.033

Mathur, S. R., Gehrke, R., & Kim, S. H. (2012). Impact of a teacher mentorship program on mentors' and Mentees' perceptions of classroom practices and the mentoring experience. *Assessment for Effective Intervention*, 38(3), 154–162. https://doi.org/10.1177/1534508412457873

Ma, Y., McCabe, D. L., & Liu, R. (2013). Students' academic cheating in Chinese universities: Prevalence, influencing factors, and proposed action. *Journal of Academic Ethics*, 11(3), 169–184. DOI: 10.1007/s10805-013-9186-7

McGuire, A., Qureshi, W., & Saad, M. (2024). A constructivist model for leveraging GenAI tools for individualized, peer-simulated feedback on student writing. [IJTE]. *International Journal of Technology in Education*, 7(2), 326–352. DOI: 10.46328/ijte.639

McGuire, J. M. (2007). Why has the critical thinking movement not come to Korea? *Asia Pacific Education Review*, 8(2), 224–232. DOI: 10.1007/BF03029258

McKernon, S. L., Adderton, E. A., & Dawson, L. J. (2024). Using Technology-Supported Approaches for the Development of Technical Skills Outside of the Classroom. *Education Sciences*. https://doi.org/ mdpi.comDOI: 10.3390/educsci14030329

McKinley, J. (2013). Displaying critical thinking in EFL academic writing: A discussion of Japanese to English contrastive rhetoric. *RELC Journal*, 44(2), 195–208. DOI: 10.1177/0033688213488386

Memarian, B., & Doleck, T. (2023). Fairness, Accountability, Transparency, and Ethics (FATE) in Artificial Intelligence (AI), and higher education: A systematic review. *Computers and Education: Artificial Intelligence*, 100152.

Merriam, S. B., & Brockett, R. G. (1997). *The profession and practice of adult education: An introduction*. Jossey-Bass.

Merrill, M. D. (1991). Constructivism and instructional design. *Educational Technology*, 31(5), 45–53.

Mezirow, J. (1975). *Education for perspective transformation: Women's reentry programs in community colleges*. Center for Adult Education, Teachers College, Columbia University.

Mezirow, J. (1991). *Transformative dimension of adult learning*. Jossey-Bass.

Mezirow, J. (2000). Learning to think like an adult. In Mezirow, J. (Eds.), *Learning as transformation: Critical perspectives on a theory in progress* (pp. 3–31). Jossey-Bass.

Mhlanga, D. (2021). Artificial intelligence in the industry 4.0, and its impact on poverty, innovation, infrastructure development, and the sustainable development goals: Lessons …. *Sustainability*. https://doi.org/ mdpi.comDOI: 10.3390/su13115788

Mickunas, A., & Pilotta, J. (2023). *A critical understanding of artificial intelligence: A phenomenological foundation*. Bentham Books. DOI: 10.2174/97898151234011230101

Miller, F. A., Katz, J. H., & Gans, R. (2018). The OD imperative to add inclusion to the algorithms of artificial intelligence. *OD Practitioner*, 5(1), 6–12.

Mill, J. S. (1863). *Utilitarianism*. Parker, Son, and Bourn.

Minn, S. (2022). AI-assisted knowledge assessment techniques for adaptive learning environments. *Computers and Education: Artificial Intelligence*. https://doi.org/ sciencedirect.comDOI: 10.1016/j.caeai.2022.100050

Mirzaei, M. S., Zhang, Q., van der Struijk, S., & Nishida, T. (2018). Language learning through conversation envisioning in virtual reality: A Sociocultural approach. In Taalas, P., Jalkanen, J., & Thouësny, S. (Eds.), *Future-proof cALL: Language learning as exploration and encounters-short papers from EUROCALL* (pp. 207–213)., DOI: 10.14705/rpnet.2018.26.838

Mishra, C., Ha, S. J., Parker, L. C., & Clase, L., K. (2019). Describing teacher conceptions of technology in authentic science inquiry using technological pedagogical content knowledge as a lens. *Biochemistry and Molecular Biology Education*, 47(4), 380–387. https://doi.org/10.1002/bmb.21242

Mishra, P., & Koehler, M. J. (2006). Technological pedagogical content knowledge: A framework for teacher knowledge. *Teachers College Record*, 108(6), 1017–1054. DOI: 10.1111/j.1467-9620.2006.00684.x

Mohammed, A. S. (2023). Examining the implementation of artificial intelligence in early childhood education settings in Ghana: Educators' attitudes and perceptions towards its long-term viability. *American Journal of Education and Technology*, 2(4), 36–49. DOI: 10.54536/ajet.v2i4.2201

Molenaar, I. (2022). The concept of hybrid human-AI regulation: Exemplifying how to support young learners' self-regulated learning. *Computers and Education: Artificial Intelligence*, 3, 100070. https://doi.org/10.1016/j.caeai.2022.100070

Mollick, E. R., & Mollick, L. (2023). Using AI to implement effective teaching strategies in classrooms: five strategies, including prompts. *The Wharton School Research Paper, Available atSSRN:*https://ssrn.com/abstract=4391243 or http://dx .org/10.2139/ssrn.4391243 DOI: 10.2139/ssrn.4391243

Montebello, M. (2021). Personalized Learning Environments. *International Symposium on Educational Technology (ISET)* (pp. 134-138).

Moshtari, M. & Safarpour, A. (2024). Challenges and strategies for the internationalization of higher education in low-income East African countries. *Higher Education*. https://doi.org/ springer.comDOI: 10.1007/s10734-023-00994-1

Motte-Signoret, E., Labbé, A., Benoist, G., Linglart, A., Gajdos, V., & Lapillonne, A. (2021). Perception of medical education by learners and teachers during the COVID-19 pandemic: a cross-sectional survey of online teaching. *Medical education online, 26*(1), 1919042. https://doi.org/ tandfonline.comDOI: 10.1080/10872981.2021.1919042

Moustaghfir, S., & Brigui, H. (2023). Exploring Moroccan English teacher's perception towards the use of interactive tools in teaching English as a foreign language on the development of critical thinking skills in young students. *International Journal of Linguistics, Literature, and Translation*, 6(8), 236–249. DOI: 10.32996/ ijllt.2023.6.8.24

Munna, A. S., & Kalam, M. A. (2021). Teaching and learning process to enhance teaching effectiveness: A literature review. [IJHI]. *International Journal of Humanities and Innovation*, 4(1), 1–4. DOI: 10.33750/ijhi.v4i1.102

Nagar, N. (2024). Importance of artificial intelligence in education. [IJSREM]. *International Journal of Scientific Research in Engineering and Management*, 8(4).

Narayan, R., Rodriguez, C., Araujo, J., Shaqlaih, A., & Moss, G. (2013). Constructivism/Constructivist Learning Theory. In B. J. Irby, G. Brown, R. Lara-Alecio, & S. Jackson (Eds.), *The handbook of educational theories* (1st ed., pp.169-184). Information Age Publishing.

National Institute for Student Success. (n.d.). *Elevating Student Success at a Scale*. https://niss.gsu.edu/

Ng, D. T. K., Tan, C. W., & Leung, J. K. L. (2024). Empowering student self-regulated learning and science education through ChatGPT: A pioneering pilot study. *British Journal of Educational Technology*, 55(4), 1328–1353. DOI: 10.1111/bjet.13454

Nguyen, A., Ngo, H. N., Hong, Y., Dang, B., & Nguyen, B. P. T. (2023). Ethical principles for artificial intelligence in education. *Education and Information Technologies*, 28(4), 4221–4241.

Nicolaides, A., & Marsick, V. (2016). Understanding adult learning in the midst of complex social "liquid modernity.". *New Directions for Adult and Continuing Education*, 149(Spring), 9–20. DOI: 10.1002/ace.20172

Niederhauser, J. S. (2012). Motivating learners at South Korean universities. *English Teaching Forum, 50*(3), 28-31. https://files.eric.ed.gov/fulltext/EJ997526.pdf

Nkambou, R., Bourdeau, J., & Mizoguchi, R. (Eds.). (2018). *Advances in intelligent tutoring systems* (Vol. 308). Springer. DOI: 10.1007/978-3-319-91464-0

O'brien, M. (2023, December 19). 2023: The year we played with Artificial Intelligence - and weren't sure what to do about it. *AP News*. https://apnews.com/article/ai-2023-artificial-intelligence-chatgpt-dangers-565ff5b817b5db0d4e74829ae3d68611

OECD. (2019). *AI in education: Challenges and opportunities for sustainable development*. OECD Publishing.

OECD. (2019). OECD principles on AI. OECD. https://www.oecd.org/going-digital/ai/principles/

Oluyisola, O. E., Bhalla, S., Sgarbossa, F., & Strandhagen, J. O. (2022). Designing and developing smart production planning and control systems in the industry 4.0 era: a methodology and case study. *Journal of Intelligent Manufacturing, 33*(1), 311-332. https://doi.org/ springer.comDOI: 10.1007/s10845-021-01808-w

Ouyang, F. & Jiao, P. (2021). Artificial intelligence in education: The three paradigms. *Computers and Education: Artificial Intelligence*. https://doi.org/ sciencedirect.comDOI: 10.1016/j.caeai.2021.100020

Owan, V. J., Abang, K. B., Idika, D. O., Etta, E. O., & Bassey, B. A. (2023). Exploring the potential of artificial intelligence tools in educational measurement and assessment. *Eurasia Journal of Mathematics, Science and Technology Education*, 19(8), em2307.

Ozturgut, O., null, , null, , & null, . (2011). Learning by example: Standardized testing in the cases of China, Korea, Japan, and Taiwan. *Academic Leadership: The Online Journal*, 9(3), 1–10. DOI: 10.58809/DPYD4742

Paek, S. & Kim, N. (2021). Analysis of worldwide research trends on the impact of artificial intelligence in education. *Sustainability*. https://doi.org/ mdpi.comDOI: 10.3390/su13147941

Pandarova, I., Schmidt, T., Hartig, J., Boubekki, A., Jones, R. D., & Brefeld, U. (2019). Predicting the difficulty of exercise items for dynamic difficulty adaptation in adaptive language tutoring. *International Journal of Artificial Intelligence in Education*, 29(3), 342–367. DOI: 10.1007/s40593-019-00180-4

Pane, J. F., Steiner, E. D., Baird, M. D., & Hamilton, L. S. (2015). *Continued progress: Promising evidence on personalized learning*. RAND Corporation. DOI: 10.7249/RR1365

Pan, Y., & Zhang, L. (2023). Integrating BIM and AI for smart construction management: Current status and future directions. [HTML]. *Archives of Computational Methods in Engineering*, 30(2), 1081–1110. Advance online publication. DOI: 10.1007/s11831-022-09830-8

Papadakis, S., Kalogiannakis, M., & Zaranis, N. (2020). Comparing tablets and computers for teaching mathematics to kindergarten children. In *Mobile learning applications in early childhood education* (pp. 24–44). IGI Global. DOI: 10.4018/978-1-7998-1486-3

Papadima, G. (2021, July). Is there a split between adult educator's educational philosophy in learning and teaching process? *International Journal of Instruction*, 14(3), 583–596. DOI: 10.29333/iji.2021.14334a

Park, M., & Chesla, C. (2007). Revisiting Confucianism as a conceptual framework for Asian family study. *Journal of Family Nursing*, 13(3), 293–311. DOI: 10.1177/1074840707304400 PMID: 17641110

Parycek, P., Schmid, V., & Novak, A. S. (2023). Artificial Intelligence (AI) and automation in administrative procedures: Potentials, limitations, and framework conditions. *Journal of the Knowledge Economy*, 1–26.

Paschen, U., Pitt, C., & Kietzmann, J. (2019). Artificial intelligence: building blocks and an innovation typology. *Business Horizons, 63*(2), 147e155.

Perelman, L. (2020). Automated essay scoring and the search for valid writing assessment. *Teachers College Record*, 122(4), 1–10.

Personalized learning. (2024, April 22). Ohio Department of Education and Workforce. https://education.ohio.gov/Topics/Teaching/Personalized-Learning

Pfister, R. (2022). Towards a theory of abduction based on conditionals. *Synthese*. https://doi.org/ springer.comDOI: 10.1007/s11229-022-03581-6

Pham, T. N., Lin, M., Trinh, V. Q., & Bui, L. T. P. (2020). Electronic peer feedback, EFL academic writing and reflective thinking: Evidence from a Confucian context. *SAGE Open*, 10(1), 1–20. DOI: 10.1177/2158244020914554

Piaget, J. (1955). The construction of reality in the child. *Journal of Consulting Psychology*, •••, 19.

Picard, R. W. (1997). *Affective computing*. MIT Press. DOI: 10.7551/mitpress/1140.001.0001

Platt, I. A., Hochard, K. D., Tytherleigh, M., Kannangara, C., Carson, J., McFaul, C., & North, C. (2024). The Hummingbird Project year 2: decreasing distress and fostering flourishing in a pragmatic pre–post study. *Frontiers in Psychology, 15*, 1257446. https://doi.org/ frontiersin.orgDOI: 10.3389/fpsyg.2024.1257446

Pokrivcakova, S. (2019). Preparing teachers for the application of AI-powered technologies in foreign language education. *Journal of Language and Cultural Education*, 7(3), 135–153. DOI: 10.2478/jolace-2019-0025

Pol, R., Balagué, N., Ric, A., Torrents, C., Kiely, J., & Hristovski, R. (2020). Training or synergizing? Complex systems principles change the understanding of sport processes. *Sports Medicine-Open, 6*, 1-13. https://doi.org/ springer.comDOI: 10.1186/s40798-020-00256-9

Popenici, S. A., & Kerr, S. (2017). Exploring the impact of artificial intelligence on teaching and learning in higher education. *Research and Practice in Technology Enhanced Learning*, 12(1), 22. DOI: 10.1186/s41039-017-0062-8 PMID: 30595727

Pratama, M. P., Sampelolo, R., & Lura, H. (2023). Revolutionizing education: harnessing the power of artificial intelligence for personalized learning. *Klasikal: Journal of Education. Language Teaching and Science*, 5(2), 350–357.

Radez, J., Reardon, T., Creswell, C., Lawrence, P. J., Evdoka-Burton, G., & Waite, P. (2021). Why do children and adolescents (not) seek and access professional help for their mental health problems? A systematic review of quantitative and qualitative studies. *European child & adolescent psychiatry, 30*(2), 183-211. https://doi.org/ springer.comDOI: 10.1007/s00787-019-01469-4

Rasul, T., Nair, S., Kalendra, D., Mulyadi, R., de Oliveira Santini, F., Ladeira, W. J., Sun, M., Day, I., Rather, R. A., & Heathcote, L. (2023). The role of ChatGPT in higher education: Benefits, challenges, and future research directions. *Journal of Applied Learning & Teaching*, 6(1), 41–56. DOI: 10.37074/jalt.2023.6.1.29

Razmi, S. F., Moghadam, M. H., & Behname, M. (2021). Time-varying effects of monetary policy on Iranian renewable energy generation. [HTML]. *Renewable Energy*, 177, 1161–1169. Advance online publication. DOI: 10.1016/j.renene.2021.06.020

Reed, C. (2018). How should we regulate artificial intelligence? *Philosophical Transactions. Series A, Mathematical, Physical, and Engineering Sciences*, 376(2128), 20170360. Advance online publication. DOI: 10.1098/rsta.2017.0360 PMID: 30082306

Regan, P. M., & Jesse, J. (2019). Ethical challenges of edtech, big data, and personalized learning: Twenty-first century student sorting and tracking. *Ethics and Information Technology*, 21(3), 167–179. DOI: 10.1007/s10676-018-9492-2

Reiss, M. J. (2021). The use of AI in education: Practicalities and ethical considerations. *London Review of Education*, 19(1). https://doi.org/10.14324/lre.19.1.05

Renandya, W. A., Ivone, F. M., & Hidayati, M. (2023). Harnessing the power of technology in ELT. *Journal of Studies in the English Language*, 18(2), 143–160. https://so04.tci-thaijo.org/index.php/jsel/article/view/268591

Reyes, C. T., Thompson, C. D., Lawrie, G. A., & Kyne, S. H. (2024). Insights into a Community of Inquiry that emerged during academics' emergency remote university teaching of chemistry in response to concern for students. *Research in Science & Technological Education*, 1-27. https://doi.org/ tandfonline.comDOI: 10.1080/02635143.2023.2202387

Robertson, J., Ferreira, C., Botha, E., & Oosthuizen, K. (2024). Game changers: A generative AI prompt protocol to enhance human AI-knowledge co-construction. *Business Horizons*, 67(5), 499–510. Advance online publication. DOI: 10.1016/j.bushor.2024.04.008

Robinson, K., McKenna, B., & Rooney, D. (2022). The relationship of risk to rules, values, virtues, and moral complexity: What we can learn from the moral struggles of military leaders. *Journal of Business Ethics*. https://doi.org/ springer.comDOI: 10.1007/s10551-021-04874-5

Rogers, C. R. (1969). *Freedom to learn*. Merrill.

Roll, I., Aleven, V., McLaren, B. M., & Koedinger, K. R. (2011). Improving students' help-seeking skills using metacognitive feedback in an intelligent tutoring system. *Learning and Instruction*, 21(2), 267–280. DOI: 10.1016/j.learninstruc.2010.07.004

Rosé, C. P., McLaughlin, E. A., Liu, R., & Koedinger, K. R. (2019). Explanatory learner models: Why machine learning (alone) is not the answer. *British Journal of Educational Technology*, 50(6), 2943–2958. DOI: 10.1111/bjet.12858

Rosé, C. P., Wang, Y. C., Cui, Y., Arguello, J., Stegmann, K., Weinberger, A., & Fischer, F. (2015). Analyzing collaborative learning processes automatically: Exploiting the advances of computational linguistics in computer-supported collaborative learning. *International Journal of Computer-Supported Collaborative Learning*, 3(3), 237–271. DOI: 10.1007/s11412-007-9034-0

Rosenblatt, K. (2023, May 18). New York City public schools remove ChatGPT ban. https://www.nbcnews.com/tech/chatgpt-ban-dropped-new-york-city-public-schools-rcna85089

Rudolph, J., Tan, S., & Tan, S. (2023). War of the chatbots: Bard, Bing Chat, ChatGPT, Ernie and beyond. The new AI gold rush and its impact in higher education. *Journal of Applied Learning & Teaching*, 6(1), 364–389. DOI: 10.37074/jalt.2023.6.1.23

Rusmiyanto, R., Huriati, N., Fitriani, N., Tyas, N. K., Rofi'i, A., & Sari, M. N. (2023). The role of artificial intelligence (AI) in developing English language learner's communication skills. *Journal of Education*, 6(1), 750–757.

Russell, S. J., & Norvig, P. (2021). *Artificial intelligence: A modern approach* (4th ed.). Pearson.

Ryu, H., & Jeong, S. (2021). Intelligent virtual assistants and the future of work: A review and research agenda. *The Journal of Strategic Information Systems*, 30(2), 101625.

Saaida, M. B. (2023). AI-Driven transformations in higher education: Opportunities and challenges. *International Journal of Educational Research and Studies*, 5(1), 29–36.

Sahara, S. (2022, February). Analysis of factors causing delay in unloading imported goods. In Conference on Broad Exposure to Science and Technology 2021 (BEST 2021) (pp. 345-351). *Atlantis Press*. atlantis-press.com DOI: 10.2991/aer.k.220131.051

Saks, K., Hunt, P., Leijen, Ä., & Lepp, L. (2022). To stay or not to stay: An empirical model for predicting teacher persistence. *British Journal of Educational Studies, 70*(6), 693-717. https://doi.org/ tandfonline.comDOI: 10.1080/00071005.2021.2004995

Saltman, K. J. (2020). Artificial intelligence and the technological turn of public education privatization: In defence of democratic education. *London Review of Education*, 18(2). Advance online publication. DOI: 10.14324/LRE.18.2.04

Sankumpa, W., Kanjug, I., & Singma, S. (2023). Using constructivist integrated gamification and AI Assisted learning tool to enhance reading comprehension for fourth grade students. *IIAI Letters on Institutional Research, 3.*

Sanusi, I. T., Olaleye, S. A., Agbo, F. J., & Chiu, T. K. (2022). The role of learners' competencies in artificial intelligence education. *Computers and Education: Artificial Intelligence*, 3, 100098. https://doi.org/10.1016/j.caeai.2022.100098

Sarker, I. H. (2021). Machine learning: Algorithms, real-world applications and research directions. *SN computer science*. https://doi.org/ springer.comDOI: 10.1007/s42979-021-00592-x

Sarker, I. H. (2022). AI-based modeling: techniques, applications and research issues towards automation, intelligent and smart systems. *SN Computer Science*. https://doi.org/ springer.comDOI: 10.1007/s42979-022-01043-x

Sazali, A. R. B., Khamarudin, F. B., & Abdul Alahdad, S. N. B. (2022). Maximizing the zone of proximal development benefits in group online learning. *International Journal of Academic Research in Business & Social Sciences*, 12(6), 1476–1496. DOI: 10.6007/IJARBSS/v12-i6/13861

Schenck, A. (2023). Investigating the influence of classroom leadership preferences on the use of technology: A survey of Korean university learners. *Journal of Higher Education Policy and Leadership Studies*, 4(3), 118–130. DOI: 10.61186/johepal.4.3.118

Schenck, A. (2024a). ChatGPT is powerful, but does it have power distance? A study of culturally imbued discourse in AI-generated essays. [IJAET]. *International Journal of Adult Education and Technology*, 15(1), 1–17. DOI: 10.4018/IJAET.338219

Schenck, A. (2024b). Examining relationships between classroom leadership styles and Confucian values: A study of Korean EFL learner preferences. *The Asia-Pacific Education Researcher*, 33(3), 659–670. DOI: 10.1007/s40299-023-00762-w

Schenck, A. (2024c). Examining relationships between technology and critical thinking: A Study of South Korean EFL Learners. *Education Sciences*, 14(6), 1–14. DOI: 10.3390/educsci14060652

Schiff, D. (2021). Out of the laboratory and into the classroom: the future of artificial intelligence in education. *AI & society*. https://doi.org/ springer.comDOI: 10.1007/s00146-020-01033-8

Schiff, D. (2022). Education for AI, not AI for education: The role of education and ethics in national AI policy strategies. *International Journal of Artificial Intelligence in Education*, 32(3), 527–563.

Schmid, R., & Petko, D. (2019). Does the use of educational technology in personalized learning environments correlate with self-reported digital skills and beliefs of secondary-school students? *Computers & Education*, 136, 75–86. https://doi.org/10.1016/j.compedu.2019.03.006

Selman, G. (1989). The enemies of adult education. *Canadian Journal of University Continuing Education*, 15, 68–81.

Selwyn, N. (2019). Should robots replace teachers? AI and the future of education. *British Journal of Educational Technology*, 50(6), 1263–1272.

Seo, K., Yoo, M., Dodson, S., & Jin, S. H. (2024). Augmented teachers: K–12 teachers' needs for artificial intelligence's complementary role in personalized learning. *Journal of Research on Technology in Education*, 1–18. DOI: 10.1080/15391523.2024.2330525

Settles, B., Brust, C., Gustafson, E., Hagiwara, M., & Madnani, N. (2018). Second language acquisition modeling. In *Proceedings of the Thirteenth Workshop on Innovative Use of NLP for Building Educational Applications* (pp. 56-65). DOI: 10.18653/v1/W18-0506

Shahbaz, M., Destek, M. A., Dong, K., & Jiao, Z. (2021). Time-varying impact of financial development on carbon emissions in G-7 countries: Evidence from the long history. *Technological Forecasting and Social Change, 171*, 120966. uni-muenchen. de Shoaib, L. A., Safii, S. H., Idris, N., Hussin, R., & Sazali, M. A. H. (2024). Utilizing decision tree machine model to map dental students' preferred learning styles with suitable instructional strategies. *BMC Medical Education, 24*(1), 58. https://doi.org/ springer.comDOI: 10.1186/s12909-023-05022-5

Shanto, S. S., Ahmed, Z., & Jony, A. I. (2023). PAIGE: A generative AI-based framework for promoting assignment integrity in higher education. *STEM Education*, 3(4), 288–305. DOI: 10.3934/steme.2023018

Sharadgah, T. A., & Sa'di, R. A. (2022). A systematic review of research on the use of artificial intelligence in English language teaching and learning (2015-2021): What are the current effects? *Journal of Information Technology Education*, 21, 337–377. DOI: 10.28945/4999

Shemshack, A., & Spector, J. M. (2020). A systematic literature review of personalized learning terms. *Smart Learning Environments, 7*(1). https://doi.org/10.1186/s40561-020-00140-9

Shin, S., & Koh, M. S. (2005). Korean education in cultural context. *Essays in Education*, 14(1), 1–10. https://openriver.winona.edu/eie/vol14/iss1/10

Short, C. E., & Short, J. C. (2023). The artificially intelligent entrepreneur: ChatGPT, prompt engineering, and entrepreneurial rhetoric creation. *Journal of Business Venturing Insights*, 19, e00388. DOI: 10.1016/j.jbvi.2023.e00388

Shulman, L. S. (1986). Those who understand: Knowledge growth in teaching. *Educational Researcher*, 15(2), 4. https://doi.org/10.2307/1175860

Siegel, J. (2023, September 14). 'Technology is not something we can hide from students': How NYC Public Schools invited AI into its classrooms. https://news.microsoft.com/source/features/digital-transformation/how-nyc-public-schools-invited-ai-into-its-classrooms

Singh, V., Thurman, A., & Holladay, C. (2021). Artificial intelligence in education: Applications and ethical considerations. *TechTrends*, 65(3), 298–305.

Sîrbu, A. (2020). Basic andragogy-oriented strategies and communication in online education. *InInternational Conference Knowledge-based Organization* (Vol. 26, No. 2, pp. 350-356). https://doi.org/ sciendo.comDOI: 10.2478/kbo-2020-0103

Skinner, B. F. (1974). *About behaviorism.* Knopf.

Slade, S., & Prinsloo, P. (2018). Learning analytics: Ethical issues and dilemmas. *The American Behavioral Scientist*, 57(10), 1510–1529. DOI: 10.1177/0002764213479366

Sloan, J., & Warner, J. (2018). Data sovereignty, law and policy: The global approach. *Journal of International Law*, 22(2), 110–134.

Smith, D. P., & Francis, N. J. (2023). Generative AI in assessment. https://network .febs.org/posts/generative-ai-in-assessment

Smith, E. (2020). The UK grading algorithm scandal: Lessons learned. *Educational Review*, 73(1), 10–29.

Snell, R. S., Wu, C. X., & Lei, H. W. (2022). Junzi virtues: A Confucian foundation for harmony within organizations. *Asian Journal of Business Ethics*, 11(1), 183–226. DOI: 10.1007/s13520-022-00146-1

Soccorsi, L. (2013). Instilling a personal teaching philosophy in preservice teachers: Vitally important but not always easy to achieve. *Journal of Student Engagement: Education Matters*, 3(1), 21–28.

Spina, D., Vindigni, G., Pecorino, B., Pappalardo, G., D'Amico, M., & Chinnici, G. (2021). Identifying themes and patterns on management of horticultural innovations with an automated text analysis. *Agronomy, 11*(6), 1103. https://doi.org/ mdpi. comDOI: 10.3390/agronomy11061103

Stanney, K. M., Skinner, A., & Hughes, C. (2023). Exercisable learning-theory and evidence-based andragogy for training effectiveness using XR (ELEVATE-XR): Elevating the ROI of immersive technologies. *International Journal of Human–Computer Interaction, 39*(11), 2177-2198. https://doi.org/ tandfonline.comDOI: 10.1080/10447318.2023.2188529

Stojanov, A. (2023). Learning with ChatGPT 3.5 as a more knowledgeable other: An autoethnographic study. *International Journal of Educational Technology in Higher Education*, 20(1), 35. DOI: 10.1186/s41239-023-00404-7

Stoyanov, S., & Kirschner, P. A. (2023). Text analytics for uncovering untapped ideas at the intersection of learning design and learning analytics: Critical interpretative synthesis. *Journal of Computer Assisted Learning, 39*(3), 899-920. https://doi.org/ wiley.comDOI: 10.1016/j.aei.2021.101508

Stretton, B., Kovoor, J., Arnold, M., & Bacchi, S. (2023). ChatGPT-Based Learning: Generative *Artificial Intelligence in Medical Education.Medical Science Educator*, 34(1), 215–217. Advance online publication. DOI: 10.1007/s40670-023-01934-5 PMID: 38510403

Strickland, E. (2023, July 12).https://spectrum.ieee.org/chatgpt-medical-exam Dr. CHATGPT will interface with you now. *IEEE Spectrum*.https://spectrum.ieee.org/chatgpt-medical-exam

Susanto, S., Andrianingsih, A., Sutawan, K., Marwintaria, V. A., & Astika, R. (2023). Transformation of learner learning: Improving reasoning skills through artificial intelligence (AI). [JoERI]. *Journal of Education, Religious, and Instructions*, 1(2), 37–46. DOI: 10.60046/joeri.v1i2.74

Switzerland.Goh, Y. S. (2010, May). *Personalizing IQ Chinese reader in assisting struggling learners in the acquisition of reading skill among non-Chinese learners for the teaching of Chinese as a foreign language*. In *Global learn* (pp. 3522-3531). Association for the Advancement of Computing in Education (AACE).

Sysoyev, P. V. (2023). Artificial intelligence in education: Awareness, readiness and practice of using artificial intelligence technologies in professional activities by university faculty. *Vysshee Obrazovanie v Rossii = Higher Education in Russia, 32*(10), 9–33. DOI: 10.31992/0869-3617-2023-32-10-9-33

Taber, K. (2011). Constructivism as educational theory: Contingency in learning, and optimally guided instruction. *Nova Science Publishers Inc.,* 39-61. https://science-education-research.com/KeithSTaber/Constructivism_files/Taber,%20K.%20S.%20%282011%29.%20Constructivism%20as%20educational%20theory.pdf

Tam, M. (2000). Constructivism, instructional design, and technology: Implications for transforming distance learning. *Journal of Educational Technology & Society*, 3(2), 50–60. https://www.jstor.org/stable/jeductechsoci.3.2.50

Tan, C. (2017). Confucianism and education. In Noblit, G. (Ed.), *Oxford research encyclopedia of education* (pp. 1–18). Oxford University Press. DOI: 10.1093/acrefore/9780190264093.013.226

Teng, Y., Zhang, J., & Sun, T. (2023). Data-driven decision-making model based on artificial intelligence in higher education system of colleges and universities. [HTML]. *Expert Systems: International Journal of Knowledge Engineering and Neural Networks*, 40(4), e12820. Advance online publication. DOI: 10.1111/exsy.12820

The Institute for Ethical AI in Education. (2020). Interim report: towards a shared vision of ethical AI in Education. https://www.buckingham.ac.uk/wp-content/uploads/2021/03/The-Institute-for-Ethical-AI-in-Education-The-Ethical-Framework-for-AI-in-Education.pdf

Thorndike, E. L., Bregman, E. O., Tilton, J. W., & Woodyard, E. (1928). *Adult learning*. Macmillan.

Tisdell, E. J., & Taylor, E. W. (2000). Adult education philosophy informs practice. *Adult Learning*, 11(2), 6–10. DOI: 10.1177/104515959901100203

Tomaszewska, R. (2023, December). *Andragogy Meets ChatGPT in Lifelong Learning: Exploring Opportunities and Challenges*. In *2023 IEEE International Conference on Data Mining Workshops (ICDMW)* (pp. 868-874). IEEE. DOI: 10.1109/ICDMW60847.2023.00117

Tomaszewski, L. E., Zarestky, J., & Gonzalez, E. (2020). Planning qualitative research: Design and decision making for new researchers. *International journal of qualitative methods, 19*, 1609406920967174. https://doi.org/ sagepub.comDOI: 10.1177/1609406920967174

Top, E., Baser, D., Akkus, R., Akayoglu, S., & Gurer, M. D. (2021). Secondary school teachers' preferences in the process of individual technology mentoring. *Computers & Education*, 160, 104030. https://doi.org/10.1016/j.compedu.2020.104030

Torrisi-Steele, G., & Carim, G.Jr. (2019). An adult-learner approach to the learning design of safety management system training in aviation. *International Journal of Adult Vocational Education and Technology*, 10(3), 39–53. DOI: 10.4018/IJAVET.2019070103

Travaini, G. V., Pacchioni, F., Bellumore, S., Bosia, M., & De Micco, F. (2022). Machine learning and criminal justice: A systematic review of advanced methodology for recidivism risk prediction. *International journal of environmental research and public health, 19*(17), 10594. https://doi.org/ mdpi.comDOI: 10.3390/ijerph191710594

Trunk, A., Birkel, H., & Hartmann, E. (2020). On the current state of combining human and artificial intelligence for strategic organizational decision making. *Business Research*. https://doi.org/ springer.comDOI: 10.1007/s40685-020-00133-x

Tsai, S. C., Chen, C. H., Shiao, Y. T., Ciou, J. S., & Wu, T. N. (2020). Precision education with statistical learning and deep learning: a case study in Taiwan. *International Journal of Educational Technology in Higher Education, 17*, 1-13. https://doi.org/ springer.comDOI: 10.1186/s41239-020-00186-2

Tseng, J. C., Chu, H., Hwang, G., & Tsai, C. (2008). Development of an adaptive learning system with two sources of personalization information. *Computers & Education*, 51(2), 776–786. https://doi.org/10.1016/j.compedu.2007.08.002

Tsui, A. P. Y., & Ngo, H. Y. (2016). Social-motivational factors affecting business students' cheating behavior in Hong Kong and China. *Journal of Education for Business*, 91(7), 365–373. DOI: 10.1080/08832323.2016.1231108

Tuma, F. (2021). The use of educational technology for interactive teaching in lectures. *Annals of Medicine and Surgery*. https://doi.org/ sciencedirect.comDOI: 10.1016/j.amsu.2021.01.051

Tunca, S., Sezen, B., & Wilk, V. (2023). An exploratory content and sentiment analysis of the guardian metaverse articles using leximancer and natural language processing. *Journal of Big Data*. https://doi.org/ springer.comDOI: 10.1186/s40537-023-00773-w

U. S. Department U.S. Department of Education. (2016). *Future ready learning: Reimagining the role of technology in education*. Createspace Independent Publishing Platform.

U.S. Department of Education. (2021). *Family Educational Rights and Privacy Act (FERPA)*. https://www2.ed.gov/policy/gen/guid/fpco/ferpa/index.html

Ulloa Cerna, A. E., Jing, L., Good, C. W., vanMaanen, D. P., Raghunath, S., Suever, J. D., Nevius, C. D., Wehner, G. J., Hartzel, D. N., Leader, J. B., Alsaid, A., Patel, A. A., Kirchner, H. L., Pfeifer, J. M., Carry, B. J., Pattichis, M. S., Haggerty, C. M., & Fornwalt, B. K. (2021). Deep-learning-assisted analysis of echocardiographic videos improves predictions of all-cause mortality. [HTML]. *Nature Biomedical Engineering*, 5(6), 546–554. DOI: 10.1038/s41551-020-00667-9 PMID: 33558735

UNESCO. (2019). *Artificial intelligence in education: Challenges and opportunities for sustainable development*. UNESCO Publishing.

UNESCO. (2021). Recommendation on the ethics of artificial intelligence. UNESCO. https://unesdoc.unesco.org/ark:/48223/pf0000377897

Ungerer, L., & Slade, S. (2022). Ethical considerations of artificial intelligence in learning analytics in distance education contexts. In *Learning analytics in open and distributed learning: Potential and challenges* (pp. 105–120). Springer Nature Singapore.

UNICEF. (2013). Accessible Digital Textbooks: Creating Digital Tools to Enable Inclusive Education, Jamaica. https://www.unicef.org/innocenti/media/2641/file/UNICEF-Accessible-Digital-Textbooks-Jamaica-2023.pdf

UNICEF. (n.d.). Accessible digital textbooks for learners with and without disabilities. https://www.unicef.org/reports/accessible-digital-textbooks-all

United Nations, Department of Economic and Social Affairs, Disability. (2006). *Conventions on the Rights of Persons with Disabilities (CRPD)*, Article 24. https://www.un.org/development/desa/disabilities/convention-on-the-rights-of-persons-%20%20%20with-%20%20disabilities/article-24-education.html#:~:text=States%20Parties%20shall%20ensure%20that%20persons%20with%20disabilities%20are%20able,an%20equal%20basis%20with%20others

United States Agency for International Development. (2023). Testing and Scaling an Artificial Intelligence-Based Functional Literacy Program. https://divportal.usaid.gov/s/project/a0g3d000000cbEmAAI/testing-and-scaling-an-artificial-intelligence-based-functional-literacy-program

Vinnervik, P. (2022). Implementing programming in school mathematics and technology: teachers' intrinsic and extrinsic challenges. *International journal of technology and design education, 32*(1), 213-242. https://doi.org/ springer.comDOI: 10.1007/s10798-020-09602-0

Vygotsky, L. (1978). *Mind in society*. Harvard University Press.

Walter, Y. (2024). Embracing the future of artificial intelligence in the classroom: The relevance of AI literacy, prompt engineering, and critical thinking in modern education. *International Journal of Educational Technology in Higher Education*, 21(15), 1–29. DOI: 10.1186/s41239-024-00448-3

Wang, H., Tlili, A., Huang, R., Cai, Z., Li, M., Cheng, Z., ... & Fei, C. (2023). Examining the applications of intelligent tutoring systems in real educational contexts: A systematic literature review from the social experiment perspective. *Education and information technologies, 28*(7), 9113-9148. https://doi.org/ springer.comDOI: 10.1007/s10639-022-11555-x

Wang, J. (2001). Contexts of mentoring and opportunities for learning to teach: A comparative study of mentoring practice. *Teaching and Teacher Education*, 17(1), 51–73. https://doi.org/10.1016/s0742-051x(00)00038-x

Wang, M. T., & Eccles, J. S. (2011). Adolescent behavior, emotional, and cognitive engagement trajectories in school and their differential relations to educational success. *Journal of Research on Adolescence*, 22(1), 31–29. DOI: 10.1111/j.1532-7795.2011.00753.x PMID: 22822296

Wang, S., Christensen, C., Cui, W., Tong, R., Yarnall, L., Shear, L., & Feng, M. (2020). When adaptive learning is effective learning: Comparison of an adaptive learning system to teacher-led instruction. *Interactive Learning Environments*, 31(2), 793–803. https://doi.org/10.1080/10494820.2020.1808794

Wang, V. (2003). *Principles of adult education.* Pearson.

Wang, V., & Torrisi-Steele, G. (2015). Confucian and Western teaching and learning. [IJAVET]. *International Journal of Adult Vocational Education and Technology*, 6(1), 52–64. DOI: 10.4018/ijavet.2015010104

Wang, W. (2023). The impact of ChatGPT on the interaction between teachers and students in primary and middle school English classes: Taking problems-based learning as an example. *Proceedings of the International Conference on Global Politics and Socio-Humanities.* https://doi.org/DOI: 10.54254/2753-7048/24/20230709

Wang, X., Liu, Q., Pang, H., Tan, S. C., Lei, J., Wallace, M. P., & Li, L. (2023). What matters in AI-supported learning: A study of human-AI interactions in language learning using cluster analysis and epistemic network analysis. *Computers & Education*, 194, 104703. DOI: 10.1016/j.compedu.2022.104703

Watson, A. (2019). DreamBox Learning: Adaptive learning meets the classroom. *EDUCAUSE Review*, 54(6), 24–31.

Weidinger, L., Mellor, J., Rauh, M., Griffin, C., Uesato, J., Huang, P. S., Cheng, M., Glaese, M., Balle, B., Kasirzadeh, A., Kenton, Z., Brown, S., Hawkins, W., Stepleton, T., Biles, C., Birhane, A., Haas, J., Rimmell, L., Hendricks, W., . . . Gabriel, I. (2021). Ethical and social risks of harm from language models. *arXiv preprint arXiv:2112.04359* (2021). https://doi.org//arXiv.2112.04359DOI: 10.48550

Weiss, L. G., & Saklofske, D. H. (2020). Mediators of IQ test score differences across racial and ethnic groups: The case for environmental and social justice. [HTML]. *Personality and Individual Differences*, 161, 109962. Advance online publication. DOI: 10.1016/j.paid.2020.109962

Wei, Z. (2019). *Constructivism and teachers in Chinese culture: Enriching Confucianism with constructivism.* Springer., DOI: 10.1007/978-981-13-2691-2

Welch, C., Paavilainen-Mäntymäki, E., Piekkari, R., & Plakoyiannaki, E. (2022). Reconciling theory and context: How the case study can set a new agenda for international business research. [HTML]. *Journal of International Business Studies*, 53(1), 4–26. DOI: 10.1057/s41267-021-00484-5

Wenger, E. (1987). *Artificial intelligence and tutoring systems: Computational and cognitive approaches to the communication of knowledge*. Morgan Kaufmann Publishers.

West, S. M. (2019). Data capitalism: Redefining the logics of surveillance and privacy. *Business & Society*, 58(1), 20–41. DOI: 10.1177/0007650317718185

White, G. (2020). Adaptive learning technology relationship with student learning outcomes. *Journal of Information Technology Education*, 19, 113–130. https://doi.org/10.28945/4526

White, P. (2022). Problem solving in chemistry supported by metacognitive scaffolding: Teaching associates' perspectives and practices. *Chemistry Education Research and Practice*, 23(2), 436–451. DOI: 10.1039/D1RP00242B

Whittlestone, J., Nyrup, R., Alexandrova, A., & Dihal, K. (2019). Ethical and societal implications of algorithms, data, and artificial intelligence: A roadmap for research. Nuffield Foundation. https://www.nuffieldfoundation.org/project/ethical-and-societal-implications-of-data-and-ai-a-roadmap-for-research

Wijekumar, K. K., Meyer, B. J., & Lei, P. (2017). Web-based text structure strategy instruction improves seventh graders' content area reading comprehension. *Journal of Educational Psychology*, 109(6), 741–760. DOI: 10.1037/edu0000168

Williamson, B. (2017). Decoding ClassDojo: Psycho-policy, social-emotional learning and persuasive educational technologies. *Learning, Media and Technology*, 42(4), 440–453. DOI: 10.1080/17439884.2017.1278020

Williamson, B., & Eynon, R. (2020). Historical threads, missing links, and future directions in AI in education. *Learning, Media and Technology*, 45(3), 223–235. DOI: 10.1080/17439884.2020.1798995

Willis, M., Duckworth, P., Coulter, A., Meyer, E. T., & Osborne, M. (2020). Qualitative and quantitative approach to assess the potential for automating administrative tasks in general practice. *BMJ Open*, 10(6), e032412.

Wilson, M. (2020). Automated essay scoring in higher education: Ethical challenges and future directions. *Journal of Educational Technology Systems*, 48(2), 217–232.

Wong, R. S. Y., Ming, L. C., & Ali, R. A. R. (2023). The intersection of ChatGPT, clinical medicine, and medical education. In *JMIR Medical Education* (Vol. 9, Issue 1). DOI: 10.2196/47274

Woods, R. (N.d.). (2023). Ms, Guide: Ramp up to AI. *The AI Exchange*.https://docs.google.com/document/d/1h9wWnRJ4zxNJah9J1l8CEgXgp3zNLy-JoSVhPWvCIAU/view

Wu, S., & Yang, K. (2022). The effectiveness of teacher support for students' learning of artificial intelligence popular science activities. *Frontiers in Psychology*, •••, 13.https://doi.org/10.3389/fpsyg.2022.868623

Wu, T., & Chang, M. (2023). Application of generative artificial intelligence to assessment and curriculum design for project-based learning. *2023 International Conference on Engineering and Emerging Technologies (ICEET),* Istanbul, Turkey, 2023, pp 1-6. https://doi.org/DOI: 10.1109/ICEET60227.2023.10525933

Xi, X. (2023). Advancing language assessment with AI and ML–Leaning into AI is inevitable, but can theory keep up? *Language Assessment Quarterly*, 20(4-5), 357–376. DOI: 10.1080/15434303.2023.2291488

Xu, G., Chen, Y., & Xu, L. (Eds.). (2018). *Understanding Chinese culture: Philosophy, religion, science and technology*. Palgrave Macmillan. DOI: 10.1007/978-981-10-8162-0

Xu, W. (2024). The correction strategy of artificial intelligence embedding into the negative social mentality of the marginal group of college students in the new era. *Journal of Electrical Systems*, 20(2). https://journal.esrgroups.org/jes/article/view/1222

Yang, S. J. (2021). Guest editorial: Precision education new challenge for AI in education. *Journal of Educational Technology & Society*, 24(1), 105–108.

Yang, S. J., Ogata, H., Matsui, T., & Chen, N. S. (2021). Human-centered artificial intelligence in education: Seeing the invisible through the visible. *Computers and Education: Artificial Intelligence*, 2, 100008. DOI: 10.1016/j.caeai.2021.100008

Yang, Y. T. C., Gamble, J. H., Hung, Y. W., & Lin, T. Y. (2014). An online adaptive learning environment for critical-thinking-infused English literacy instruction. *British Journal of Educational Technology*, 45(4), 723–747. DOI: 10.1111/bjet.12080

Yang, Y. T. C., & Wu, W. C. I. (2012). Digital storytelling for enhancing student academic achievement, critical thinking, and learning motivation: A year-long experimental study. *Computers & Education*, 59(2), 339–352. DOI: 10.1016/j.compedu.2011.12.012

Yu, H., & Guo, Y. (2023). Generative artificial intelligence empowers educational reform: Current status, issues, and prospects. *Frontiers in Education*, 8, 1183162. Advance online publication. DOI: 10.3389/feduc.2023.1183162

Zadorina, O., Kurskaya, V., Sobolyeva, S., Grekova, L., & Vasylyuk-Zaitseva, S. (2024). The role of artificial intelligence in the creation of future education: Possibilities and challenges. *Futurity Education*, 4(2), 163–185.

Zawacki-Richter, O., Marín, V. I., Bond, M., & Gouverneur, F. (2019). Systematic review of research on artificial intelligence applications in higher education–where are the educators? *International Journal of Educational Technology in Higher Education*, 16(39), 1–27. DOI: 10.1186/s41239-019-0171-0

Zhai, X., Chu, X., Chai, C. S., Jong, M. S. Y., Istenic, A., Spector, M., ... & Li, Y. (2021). A Review of Artificial Intelligence (AI) in Education from 2010 to 2020. *Complexity*, 1-18. https://doi.org/ hindawi.comDOI: 10.1155/2021/8812542

Zhang, K. & Aslan, A. B. (2021). AI technologies for education: Recent research & future directions. *Computers and Education: Artificial Intelligence*. https://doi .org/ sciencedirect.comDOI: 10.1016/j.caeai.2021.100025

Zhang, K., & Aslan, A. B. (2021). AI technologies for education: Recent research & future directions. *Computers and Education: Artificial Intelligence*, 2, 100025. https://doi.org/10.1016/j.caeai.2021.100025

Zhang, L. (2020). Ethical implications of AI in K-12 education: A critical analysis of facial recognition systems in China. *Educational Review*, 72(4), 457–471. DOI: 10.1080/00131911.2020.1806789

Zhang, L., Basham, J. D., & Yang, S. (2020). Understanding the implementation of Personalized learning: A research synthesis. *Educational Research Review*, 31, 100339. DOI: 10.1016/j.edurev.2020.100339

Zhang, M. (2022). A survey of English majors' attitudes towards critical thinking. *Athens Journal of Humanities & Arts*, 9(1), 27–48. DOI: 10.30958/ajha.8-1-2

Zhang, Y., & Yin, H. (2019). Collaborative cheating among Chinese college students: The effects of peer influence and individualism-collectivism orientations. *Assessment & Evaluation in Higher Education*, 45(1), 54–69. DOI: 10.1080/02602938.2019.1608504

Zhao, J., Xu, X., Jiang, H., & Ding, Y. (2020). The effectiveness of virtual reality-based technology on anatomy teaching: a meta-analysis of randomized controlled studies. *BMC medical education*. https://doi.org/ springer.comDOI: 10.1186/s12909-020-1994-z

Zhou, L., & Wei, L. (2024). Research on human-computer interactive interface in visualized information. *In 2010 IEEE 11th International Conference on Computer-Aided Industrial Design & Conceptual Design, 1*, 349-352.

Zhou, L., & Wei, Y. (2010). Research on human-computer interactive interface in visualized information. I*n 2010 IEEE 11th International Conference on Computer-Aided Industrial Design & Conceptual Design, 1,* 349–352. https://doi.org/DOI: 10.1109/CAIDCD.2010.5681337

Zhou, L., Rudin, C., Gombolay, M., Spohrer, J., Zhou, M., & Souren, P. (2023). From artificial intelligence (AI) to intelligence augmentation (IA): Design principles, potential risks, and emerging issues. *AIS Transactions on Human-Computer Interaction*, 15(1), 111–135. DOI: 10.17705/1thci.00185

Zhou, X., & Schofield, L. (2024). Using social learning theories to explore the role of generative artificial intelligence (AI) in collaborative learning. *Journal of Learning Development in Higher Education*, 30(30). Advance online publication. DOI: 10.47408/jldhe.vi30.1031

Zhou, Y. (2022). Beliefs and practice evaluation based on artificial intelligence models under the IP environment. *Journal of Environmental and Public Health*, 2022(1), 1415142. DOI: 10.1155/2022/1415142 PMID: 36203503

Zhu, Y., Lee, W. S., & Ye, L. (2020). The role of AI in personalized learning and the ethics of education. *Journal of Educational Technology & Society*, 23(3), 98–111.

Zimmerman, B. J., & Schunk, D. H. (2011). Self-regulated learning and performance: an introduction and an overview. In Schunk, D. H., & Zimmerman, B. (Eds.), *Handbook of self-regulation of learning and performance* (pp. 15–26). Routledge.

Zuboff, S. (2019). *The age of surveillance capitalism: The fight for a human future at the new frontier of power*. PublicAffairs.

About the Contributors

Viktor Wang, professor in the Department of Educational Leadership & Technology, at California State University, San Bernardino, USA, is a pioneering figure in the field of Education. With a prolific output of over 240 refereed publications, Dr. Wang has not only advanced scholarly discourse but has also nurtured the academic growth of his peers and students. His leadership has fostered the research endeavors of numerous colleagues, resulting in the contribution of over 200 articles to his journals and 1500 chapters to his books by colleagues and doctoral students alike. Dr. Wang's journals and books, featuring contributions from leading scholars worldwide, are esteemed resources cataloged by prestigious institutions like the John M. Pfau Library and other renowned university libraries across the globe. Recognized for his exceptional leadership, Dr. Wang was honored with the 2016 Presidential Award for Exceptional and Innovative Leadership by the American Association for Adult and Continuing Education, in addition to multiple institutional accolades such as the Distinguished Faculty & Scholarly Achievement Award. With a legacy of mentoring and guiding more than 70 dissertation candidates, Dr. Wang continues to shape the future of education through his unwavering commitment to excellence and innovation.

* * *

Nurul Ajleaa binti Abdul Rahman is a Head Centre of Studies at the Academy of Language Studies, Universiti Teknologi MARA (Terengganu). She received the Ph.D degree in TESL from Universiti Kebangsaan Malaysia (UKM), in 2017. She has more than 15 years of teaching experience. She is currently teaching several English language proficiency courses. Her interests are ESL Writing Skills, ESL Oral Communication Skills, Education, Social Sciences and Innovative Teaching and Learning.

Nur Alim Amri was born on the 17th day of Ramadan in 1987 in Menge, Belawa District, Wajo. An avid coffee enthusiast, he completed his undergraduate studies at Alauddin State Islamic University Makassar in 2010 and his master's degree in 2012. Nur Alim has been active in early childhood education since 2012, founding the TK Insan Cita kindergarten in Masamba and teaching at various institutions, including the State University of Makassar, STKIP Hasanuddin, and the Open University UPBJJ Makassar. In 2015, he became a permanent foundation lecturer at Muhammadiyah University of Makassar in the Early Childhood Teacher Education Study Program. Since 2019, Nur Alim has been an assessor for BAN PAUD and PNF South Sulawesi and is actively involved in research and community service, with his work accessible on Google Scholar. He is also registered as a facilitator for the 2nd batch of the Driving School under the scope of the Big Teacher Driving Center of South Sulawesi. This extended biography captures the educational background, career achievements, and current roles of Dr. Hajerah, Dr. Syamsuardi, and Nur Alim Amri, highlighting their significant contributions to early childhood education in Indonesia.

Andi Asrifan, S.Pd, M.Pd, a distinguished figure in the realm of education, particularly in English Language Education, has made significant contributions through his extensive research, teaching, and leadership roles. As the Head of the Institute for Cooperation and International Affairs at Universitas Muhammadiyah Sidenreng Rappang, Dr. Asrifan's academic journey is marked by a rich tapestry of achievements, including a Doctor of Education in English Language Education. His work spans various facets of education, language, and technology, reflecting the diverse topics covered in his publications and research endeavors. These include, but are not limited to, the impact of the COVID-19 pandemic on educational practices, methodologies in English as a Foreign Language (EFL) classrooms, and the integration of technology in teaching and learning processes. Dr. Asrifan's commitment to advancing educational standards and practices is further evidenced by his active participation in international conferences, webinars, and workshops across countries like India, the Philippines, and Pakistan. These events, organized by various institutions and associations, underscore his role as a global educator and thought leader. His dedication to professional development is also highlighted through his involvement in numerous courses and certifications in personal branding, public speaking, and literacy teaching. Moreover, Dr. Asrifan's leadership extends beyond academia into organizational and educational development, where he has served in various capacities, including as an external examiner for Ph.D. dissertations and a reviewer for scientific journals. His accolades, memberships in professional organizations, and roles as an ambassador for international associations speak volumes of his influence and commitment to fostering educational excellence and sustainable development goals globally.

Eun-Ok Baek serves as the Professor and Program Coordinator for the Instructional Design and Technology program within the Department of Educational Leadership and Technology at California State University, San Bernardino. Her research is centered on the transformative potential of technology to enhance educational outcomes. She has a particular emphasis on the integration of generative AI into educational settings, the creation of online and mobile learning communities, the promotion of culturally relevant STEM education, and the exploration of socio-cultural factors influencing technology adoption.

Praveen Dubey is an assistant professor of education and director of clinical experiences and partnerships at Montana State University Northern. His research interest focuses in the areas of Multicultural Education, Diversity, Equity, & Inclusivity, Leadership and Change, Technology in Education (Digital Equity & AI), STEM education, Immigrant Education, Comparative and International Education, Teacher Quality, and Teacher Choice for diverse classrooms. In his research, he uses the statistical tools of Structural Education Modelling (SEM), Mediation & Moderation, and R programming to address the issues that intersect in improving the learning experiences of diverse student population, immigrant/refugee students, and minority students. He has presented research papers at several national research conferences such as AERA, UCIE, AEFP, SREE, etc. and is currently working on different projects and grants.

Linda Ellington, after working in IBM for 23 years, Linda is a Professor of Business at Southern New Hampshire University, where she has taught since 2010. She conducted her doctoral research at the University of Oxford and the University of Warwick, United Kingdom. Her research focus is on the intersection of leadership and organizational change, uncovering strategies that explore how effective leaders navigate complex challenges to make impactful strategic choices. Dr. Ellington has published extensively in top-tier journals, scholarly books, and is a member of several university doctoral dissertations, such as at the University of Johannesburg, South Africa. Beyond academia, she has published eight children's books in the genre of bullying and taking care of the planet. She collaborates with community leaders to read stories to local children, fostering a love of literacy and inspiring the next generation of readers. She lives with her two coolest four-legged friends, Max and Riley.

Zakila Mardatila Ersyad, a dedicated 20-year-old from Malang, Indonesia, is currently pursuing a degree in English Language Education at Universitas Negeri

Malang. Fluent in Javanese, Indonesian, and English, Zakila's proficiency in English is further enhanced by her two-year experience living in Australia. With a strong passion for teaching, she has accumulated substantial experience, particularly with young learners and elementary school students. Zakila's digital skills are well-honed, with expertise in Office applications such as Canva, PowerPoint, Excel, and Word. Her administrative abilities include data entry, filing, and business correspondence, particularly in coordinating with conference presenters. Additionally, she has experience as an event organizer, public speaker, announcer, and presenter at international conferences, all conducted in English. Her active involvement in various competitions, including singing and English speech contests, highlights her versatile talents. Zakila has also served as an English Master of Ceremony and participated in community service by teaching English at an orphanage. Her teaching internship abroad in Chiang Rai, Thailand, further showcases her commitment to education. Zakila's dedication to continuous learning and her diverse skill set underscore her ability to make a positive impact in her field.

Sam Hermansyah, born on June 12, 1982, in Rappang, is a distinguished academic in the field of English education. He began his educational journey at SD 4 Maroangin, completing it in 1996, followed by SMPN 1 Maiwa in 1998, and Private SMAN 1 Maiwa, where he graduated in 2001. Pursuing higher education, Dr. Hermansyah earned his undergraduate degree in English Education from STAIN Parepare in 2007. He then obtained his Magister degree in English Education from the University of Muhammadiyah Parepare in 2012. His academic pursuits culminated in a Doctoral degree in English Language Studies from Hasanuddin University in 2021. Currently, Dr. Hermansyah is a lecturer in the English Education Program at Muhammadiyah University Sidenreng Rappang. He is also an author, having written the book "English for Tourism Industry," contributing significantly to the field of English education and tourism.

Greg Kaiser, PhD, is a distinguished Professor of Education at Azusa Pacific University, where he has dedicated 29 years to advancing the field of educational leadership. Earning his doctorate from Claremont Graduate University, Dr. Kaiser is recognized for his expertise in systems and school leadership, as well as his deep understanding of organizational structures in schools and the translation of theory into practice. An innovative and creative educator, Dr. Kaiser is known for being at the cutting edge of educational strategies, continually pushing the boundaries of traditional teaching and leadership methodologies to inspire and equip the next generation of educational leaders.

Sue Kaiser, EdD, is a respected faculty member at California State University, San Bernardino, with a doctorate in Educational Administration from the University of Southern California. With over 40 years of experience in education, Dr. Kaiser has held numerous leadership roles, including teacher, administrator, and consultant. Her expertise lies in leadership development, organizational change, and educational equity, making her a sought-after authority in the field. Dr. Kaiser is deeply committed to mentoring future educational leaders, contributing significantly to both the academic and practical aspects of educational leadership through her teaching, research, and extensive consulting work.

Chang Liu is an art educator and artist with a passion for enhancing the learning experience. As an international graduate student at CSUSB's MA in Instructional Design and Technology program, she is dedicated to developing innovative and accessible teaching materials. Her work engages the intersection of education and technology, where she explores new methods to enrich education through digital tools and platforms.

Dayna Lynn Mitchell is an Assistant Professor of Educational Leadership at California State Polytechnic University, Pomona. With a 35-year career in PK-12 education, Dr. Mitchell has held various roles, including Teacher, Assistant Principal, Principal, Director of Curriculum, Instruction, and Assessment, and Assistant Superintendent of Educational Services. Her research centers on educational equity, eliminating opportunity gaps, and improving student engagement and social-emotional and academic learning outcomes.

Like Raskova Octaberliana, M.Ed, stands out as a distinguished educational figure, particularly in English language teaching. With an impressive educational background that includes a Master's degree from Monash University, Australia, and a Doctorate from the State University of Malang, Indonesia, she brings a wealth of knowledge and expertise to her profession. Prof. Like Raskova Octaberliana is recognized for her academic achievements and dynamic involvement in various capacities, such as a speaker, trainer, and keynote speaker at national and international platforms. Her contributions extend to numerous conferences, workshops, and seminars, where she shares her insights on English language teaching, education, and motivation training. Her professional journey is marked by a strong foundation in English linguistics, literature, and language teaching methodologies, complemented by her publications in several esteemed journals. Prof. Like Raskova Octaberliana's dedication to the field is further evidenced by her active participation in international conferences and research projects and her commitment to teaching English. As a member of various professional organizations, she has enriched her experience by working across different educational institutions, fostering an environment of learning and growth. Moreover, Prof. Like Raskova Octaberliana's expertise is not limited to language teaching; she is also highly skilled in public speaking, human resource development, and personality character building. Her motivational training sessions are particularly noteworthy, as she has earned numerous awards and scholarships. This recognition is a testament to her impactful contributions to education and her ability to inspire and cultivate the minds of learners and educators alike. Prof. Dr. Like Raskova Octaberliana, M.Ed, embodies the essence of a dedicated educator and mentor whose work continues to influence English language teaching and beyond.

Andrew Schenck is currently an assistant professor of English at Fort Hays State University. He has taught English for over 20 years, gaining valuable experience in countries which include the United States, South Korea, and China. Through additional study, he has earned an Ed.D. in Educational Leadership with a specialization in English and a Ph.D. in English Language and Literature. With this research as a foundation, he continues to complete studies which explore education in Confucian contexts.

Shafa, an accomplished academic with a robust educational background, earned his S1 from IAIN/UIN Alauddin Makassar in 2004, S2 from Universitas Negeri Makassar in 2007, and S3 from the same institution in 2021. Currently serving as a lecturer at the Faculty of Tarbiyah and Teacher Training at UIN Sultan Aji Muhammad Idris Samarinda, Dr. Shafa has held numerous academic positions, including Assistant Lecturer at IAIN Alauddin Makassar, Lecturer at STITEK Bontang, and Coordinator of English at STAIN Samarinda. His professional experience extends to roles such as secretary at LP2M STAIN Samarinda and Vice Dean at UINSI. Actively engaged in various organizations in Samarinda, Dr. Shafa has also contributed significantly to academic conferences and workshops, both as a participant and presenter. His publications cover a range of topics from linguistic theory to multicultural education, highlighting his diverse research interests and commitment to advancing educational practices.

Becky Sumbera is the Assistant Dean and Associate Professor for the College of Education at CSU, San Bernardino. She has taught courses in educational leadership, pedagogy and andragogy, educational equity, advocacy, and strategic/structural reform in the Credential programs (Teacher & Administration preliminary credential programs), Master's, and Doctorate Programs. She has also been a K-12 Educator in the Inland Empire as a County, District, Site Administrator, and Teacher. She spent 12 years at the county level focused on school reform as data Team Lead,

Professional Learning Communities trainer, Technology Implementation trainer, and grant implementation coordinator with Riverside and San Bernardino County school districts. Her statewide leadership includes serving as the 2019-2021 President of the California Association of Professors of Education Administration (CAPEA). She holds an Ed.D. in Educational Leadership, Administration, and Policy from Pepperdine University, a Master's in Education, a Clear Administration Credential, a Clear Teaching Credential, and three bachelor's degrees in Political Science, Sociology, and Physical Education. Her research focuses on educational reform and how to restructure the academic environment to support social-cognitive structural, cultural, and leadership change that contributes to re-engaging our most vulnerable youth (emotionally, behaviorally, and cognitively).

Romina "Mina" Wilson is a graduate of CSUSB's MA in Instructional Design and Technology program, recognized as the Outstanding Graduate Student of the Year by the Watson College of Education in Spring 2024. As a Student Ambassador for the IDT program, she showcased leadership and commitment to academic community engagement. With an undergraduate degree in Broadcast Communication and Management from the University of the Philippines in the Visayas, Mina brings a unique perspective from her diverse career background. Her research explores the intersection and applications of generative AI technology and education. Currently, she is the interim Program Assistant for CSUSB's Verizon Innovative Learning program.

Seema Yadav has academic qualifications of M. Sc. (Chemistry), M Ed (RIE), UGC-NET, and PhD in Education. Presently she is working as an Assistant Professor, in the Department of Education at The Bhopal School of Education, Bhopal. She has almost 18 years of teaching experience. Her area of specialization is educational psychology, environmental education, and curriculum development. She has published articles in UGC-CARE Journals and Scopus index books.

Goh Yingsoon is a senior lecturer and he currently teaches Mandarin as the third language to non-native learners in MARA University of Technology, Malaysia. He is a member of the International Society for Chinese Language Teaching. He has experiences in teaching Mandarin at primary, secondary and tertiary level for more than 25 years. He has been actively presenting papers in national and international conferences. His research interests are on the use of educational technology in Mandarin teaching and learning, web-based instruction, translation, and etc. Updated resume: click here (dropbox). Google Scholar record. researchgate, academia.edu, cnki, scopus (Author ID: 25925392000), book publication, http://www.researcherid

.com/rid/U-7238-2017, https://orcid.org/0000-0002-6654-2887, http://myrid.gov.my/2014-1221-3221.

Index

A

B

C

D

E

F

G

I

L

M

P

R

S

T

www.ingramcontent.com/pod-product-compliance
Lightning Source LLC
LaVergne TN
LVHW081338300926
849161LV00008B/2006

* 9 7 9 8 3 6 9 3 6 1 3 0 6 *